French-English
English-French
Dictionary

LUCEM LIBRIS
DISSEMINAMUS

GEDDES&
GROSSET

Published by Geddes & Grosset, an imprint of
Children's Leisure Products Limited

© 1998 Children's Leisure Products Limited
David Dale House, New Lanark ML11 9DJ, Scotland

First published 1998
Reprinted 1999 (twice)

ISBN 1 85534 360 6

Printed and bound in the UK

	Abbreviations	**Abréviations**
abrev	abbreviation	abréviation
adj	adjective	adjectif
adv	adverb	adverbe
art	article	articule
auto	automobile	automobile
aux	auxiliary	auxiliaire
bot	botany	botanique
chem, chim	chemistry	chimie
col	colloquial term	expression familière
com	commerce	commerce
compd	compound	compound
comput	computers	informatique
conj	conjunction	conjonction
culin	culinary term	vocabulaire culinaire
excl	exclamation	exclamation
f	feminine noun	substantif fémenin
fam	colloquial term	expression familière
fig	figurative	figuré
geol	geology	géologie
gr	grammar	grammaire
imp	impersonal	impersonnel
inform	computers	informatique
interj	interjection	interjection
invar	invariable	invariable
irr	irregular	irrégulier
jur	law term	jurisprudence
law	law term	jurisprudence
ling	linguistics	linguistique
m	masculine noun	substantif masculin
mar	marine term	vocabulaire marin
mat, math	mathematics	matémathiques
med	medicine	médicine

mil	military term	vocabulaire militaire
mus	music	musique
n	noun	substantif
orn	ornithology	ornithologie
pej	pejorative	péjoratif
pl	plural	pluriel
pn	pronoun	pronom
poet	poetical term	vocabulaire poétique
pol	political term	vocabulaire politque
pp	past participle	participe passé
prep	preposition	préposition
rad	radio	radio
rail	railway	chemin de fer
sl	slang	argot
teat	theatre	théâtre
tec	technology	technologie
TV	television	télévision
vi	intransitive verb	verbe intransitif
vr	reflexive verb	verbe réfléchi
vt	transitive verb	verbe transitif
zool	zoology	zoologie

French-English Dictionary

A

à *prép* (in)to; at; on; by, per:—**aller ~ l'école** to go to school.

abaisser *vt* to lower.

abandon *m* abandonment, desertion.

abandonner *vt to* abandon, leave.

abattement *m* despondency; exhaustion.

abattoir *m* abattoir, slaughterhouse.

abattu *adj* despondent; exhausted.

abbaye *f* abbey.

abcès *m* abscess.

abdomen *m* abdomen.

abeille *f* bee.

aberration *f* aberration.

abîmer *vt* spoil, damage.

abolir *vt* to abolish.

abolition *f* abolition.

abondamment *adv* abundantly.

abondance *f* abundance.

abondant *adj* abundant, plentiful.

abonder *vi* to be abundant *ou* plentiful.

abonné *m*, **-ée** *f*:—*adj* subscriber.

abonnement *m* subscription.

abonner s'~ *vr* to subscribe, take out a subscription (*à* to).

abord *m*:—**d'~** first (of all).

aborder *vt* to approach.

aboutir *vi* to succeed.

aboutissement *m* outcome; success.

abréger *vt* to shorten; abridge.

abréviation *f* abbreviation.

abri *m* shelter.

abriter *vt* **to shelter:**—**s'~** *vr* **to shelter.**

abrupt *adj* abrupt:—**~ement** *adv* abruptly.

absence *f* absence.

absent *adj* absent.

absenter (s') *vr* to leave, go out.

absolu *adj* absolute:—**~ment** *adv* absolutely:—*m* absolute.

absorbant *adj* absorbent.

absorber *vt to* absorb.

absorption *f* absorption.

abstinence *f* abstinence.

abstrait *adj* abstract.

absurde *adj* absurd:—**~ment** *adv* absurdly.

absurdité *f* absurdity.

abus *m* abuse.

abuser *vt* **~ de** to exploit; abuse.

académie *f* academy.

accélérateur *m* accelerator.

accélération *f* acceleration.

accélérer *vi* to speed up, accelerate.

accent *m* accent.

accentuer *vt* to accentuate.

acceptable *adj* acceptable.

accepter *vt* to accept.

accès *m* access.

accessible *adj* accessible.

accident *m* accident.

accidentel *adj* accidental:—**~le-ment** *adv* accidentally.

accommodant *adj* accommodating.

accommoder *vt* to prepare; adapt.

accompagner *vt* to accompany.

accomplir *vt* to do, accomplish.

accomplissement *m* accomplishment.

accord *m* agreement:—**d'~!** okay!, all right!:—**être d'~** to agree.

accorder *vt* to give:—**s'~** *vr* to agree.

accoucher *vi* to give birth.

accrocher *vt* to hang up (*à* on).

accroissement *m* increase.

accroître *vt* to increase.

accueil *m* welcome, reception.

accueillir *vt* to welcome.

accumuler *vt* to accumulate.

accusation *f* accusation.

accusé *m*, **-ée** *f* accused, defendant.

accuser *vt* to accuse.

achat *m* purchase.

acheter *vt* to buy.

acheteur *m* **-euse** *f* buyer.

achèvement *m* completion.

achever *vt* to finish; complete.

acide *adj* acidic:—*m* acid.

acier *m* steel.

acoustique *adj* acoustic:—*f* acoustics.

acquérir *vt* to buy, purchase.

acrobate *mf* acrobat.

acte *m* act; deed.

acteur *m* **actrice** *f* actor.

actif *adj* active.

action *f* act, action; share.

activement *adv* actively.

activer *vt* to speed up.

activité *f* activity.

actualité *f*:—**l'~** current events.

actuel *adj* current, present:—**~lement** *adv* currently.

adaptable *adj* adaptable.

adaptation *f* adaptation.

adapter *vt* to adapt (*à* to):—**s'~** *vr* to adapt (*à* to).

addition *f* addition; bill.

adéquat *adj* suitable, appropriate.

adhérer *vi* to adhere, stick.

adhésif *adj* adhesive.

adjectif *m* adjective.

admettre *vt* to admit; accept; assume.

administrer *vt* to run; administer.

admirable *adj* admirable:**-ment** *adv* admirably, brilliantly.

admiration *f* admiration.

admirer *vt* to admire.

adolescence *f* adolescence.

adolescent *m*, **-e** *f* adolescent.

adopter *vt* to adopt.

adorer *vt* to adore, worship.

adrénaline *f* adrenalin.

adresse *f* address; skill.

adresser *vt* to address; send.

adroit *adj* deft, skilful:—**~ement** *adv* deftly, skilfully.

adulte *mf* adult, grown-up:—*adj* adult, full-grown.

adversité *f* adversity.

aérodrome *m* aerodrome, airfield.

aéroport *m* airport.

affable *adj* affable.

affaiblir *vt* to weaken:—**s'~** *vr* to weaken, grow weaker.

affaire *f* matter.

affamé *adj* starving.

affamer *vt* to starve.

affection *f* affection.

affectueusement *adv* affectionately.

affectueux *adj* affectionate.

affermir *vt* to strengthen.

affiche *f* poster.

affiner *vt* to refine.

affirmatif *adj* affirmative.

affirmation *f* assertion.

affirmer *vt* to assert.

affluent *m* tributary.

affoler *vt* to throw into a panic:—**s'~** *vr* to get into a panic.

affréter *vt* to charter.

affreux *adj* horrible; awful.

afin *prép*:—**~ de** (in order) to:—**~ que** in order that.

africain *adj, mf* African.

Afrique *f* Africa.

âge *m* age:—**quel ~ as-tu?** how old are you?

âgé *adj* old:—**~ de 10 ans** 10 years old.

agence *f* agency; branch; offices.

agenda *m* diary.

agenouiller (s') *vr* to kneel (down).

agent *m* agent; policeman.

agglomération *f* town, urban area.

aggraver *vt* to make worse; increase.

agile *adj* agile, nimble:—**~ment** *adv* nimbly.

agilité *f* agility.

agir *vi* to act.

agitation *f* agitation.

agiter *vt* to shake; wave:—**s'~** *vr* to move about; fidget.

agneau *m* lamb.

agrandir *vt* to make bigger; to widen; to expand.

agrandissement *m* enlargement.

agréable *adj* agreeable, pleasant.

agressif *adj* aggressive.

agression *f* attack.

agriculteur *m* farmer.

agriculture *f* agriculture, farming.

ahuri *adj* stunned; stupefied.

aide *f* help; aid;

aider *vt* to help.

aigle *m* eagle.

aigre *adj* sour, bitter:—**~ment** *adv* sourly.

aigu *adj* (*f* **aiguë**) shrill; acute.

aiguille *f* needle.

ail *m* garlic.

ailleurs *adv* elsewhere:—**partout ~** everywhere else:—**nulle part ~** nowhere else:—**d'~** moreover; by the way.

aimable *adj* kind:—**~ment** *adv* kindly.

aimant *m* magnet.

aimer *vt* to love.

aîné *m*, **aînée** *f* eldest child:—*adj* elder; eldest.

ainsi *adv* so, thus.

air *m* air:—**avoir l'~ content** to look happy.

aire *f* area.

aisé *adj* easy; well-off:—**~ment** *adv* easily.

ajouter *vt* to add.

ajuster *vt* to adjust.

alarme *f* alarm.

alarmer *vt* to alarm:—**s'~** *vr* to get alarmed (*de* at, about).

album *m* album.

alcool *m* alcohol.

alentours *mpl* surroundings, neighbourhood.

alerte *adj* alert; agile:—*f* alarm, alert.

alerter *vt* to alert; notify; warn.

algue *f* seaweed.

aligner *vt* to align, line up.

aliment *m* food.

alimenter *vt* to feed:—**s'~** *vr* to eat.

alinéa *m* paragraph.

allée *f* avenue; path.

alléger *vt* to make lighter; alleviate.

aller *vi* to go:—**comment allez-vous?** how are you?:—**allons-y** let's go:—**s'en aller** to go away, leave:—*m* single ticket.

allergie *f* allergy.

alliance *f* alliance; marriage; wedding ring.

allô *excl* hello!

allocation *f* allocation; allowance.

allouer *vt* to allocate.

allumer *vt* to light; turn *ou* switch on.

allumette *f* match.

allure *f* speed; look.

alors *adv* then:—**~ que** while; whereas.

alphabet *m* alphabet.

alpiniste *mf* mountaineer.

altérer *vt* to change, alter.

alternatif *adj* alternate.

alternative *f* alternative.

altitude *f* altitude, height.

amabilité *f* kindness.

amaigrir *vt* to make thin.

amant *m* lover.

amas *m* pile, heap.

amasser *vt* to amass, pile up.

amateur *m* amateur; connaisseur.

ambassade *f* embassy.

ambassadeur *m*, **-drice** *f* ambassa-dor.

ambiance *f* atmosphere.

ambigu *adj*, *f* **ambiguë** ambiguous.

ambitieux *adj* ambitious.

ambition *f* ambition.

ambulance *f* ambulance.

âme *f* soul.

amélioration *f* improvement.

améliorer *vt* to improve:—**s'~** *vr* to improve.

aménagement *m* fitting out; adjustment;development.

aménager *vt* to fit out; adjust; develop.

amener *vt* to bring.

amer *adj* bitter.

Américain *m*, **-e** *f* American.

américain *adj* American.

Amérique *f* America.

ameublement *m* furniture.

ami *m*, **-ie** *f* friend.

amical *adj* friendly:—**~ement** *adv* in a friendly manner.

amitié *f* friendship.

amnistie *f* amnesty.

amoindrir *vt* to weaken; reduce.

amorcer *vt* to bait; begin.

amortir *vt* to soften; deaden.

amour *m* love.

amoureux *adj* in love (*de* with).

amovible *adj* detachable.

amphibie *adj* amphibious.

ample *adj* roomy; wide.

ampleur *f* fullness; range.

amplifier *vt* to increase; amplify.

amusant *adj* amusing.

amuser *vt* to amuse.

an *m* year:—**avoir vingt ~s** to be 20 (years old).

analogie *f* analogy.

analphabète *adj* illiterate.

analyse *f* analysis; test.

analyser *vt* to analyse.

analyste *mf* analyst; psychoanalyst.

ananas *m* pineapple.

anarchie *f* anarchy.

anatomie *f* anatomy.

ancestral *adj* ancestral.

ancêtre *m* ancestor.

ancien *adj* old; former:—**~nement** *adv* formerly.

ancre *f* anchor.

âne *m* ass, donkey.

anecdote *f* anecdote.

anesthésie *f* anaesthetic; anaesthesia.

ange *m* angel.

Anglais *m*, **-e** *f* Englishman; English-woman.

anglais *adj* English:—*m (ling)* English.

angle *m* angle; corner.

Angleterre *f* England.

anglophone *adj* English-speaking:—*mf* English speaker.

angoisse *f* anguish.

animal *m* animal.

animation *f* animation.

animé *adj* busy; lively.

animosité *f* animosity.

anneau *m* ring.

année *f* year:—**les ~s soixante** the Sixties.

annexe *f* annexe:—*adj* subsidiary.

annexer *vt* to annex; append.

anniversaire *m* birthday:—**joyeux ~!** happy birthday!

annonce *f* advertisement; announce-ment.

annoncer *vt* to announce *(à to)*.

annuaire *m* telephone directory, phone book.

annuel *adj* annual:—**~lement** *adv* annually.

annuler *vt* to cancel; nullify.

anomalie *f* anomaly.

anonyme*adj* anonymous; imper-sonal:—**~ment** *adv* anonymously.

anorexique *adj*, *mf* anorexic.

anormal *adj* abnormal:—**~ement** *adv* abnormally.

antagonisme *m* antagonism.

antenne *f (rad, tv)* aerial; *(zool)* feeler.

antérieur *adj* earlier, previous.

anthologie *f* anthology.

anticancéreux *adj* cancer.

anticipation *f* anticipation.

anticonceptionnel *adj* contraceptive.

anticyclone *m* anticyclone.

antidote *m* antidote.

antigel *m* antifreeze.

antipathie *f* antipathy.

antipathique *adj* unpleasant.

antique *adj* ancient.

antiquité *f* antiquity; antique.

antirouille *adj invar* rustproof.

antisocial *adj* antisocial.

antithèse *f* antithesis.

antonyme *m* antonym.

anxiété *f* anxiety.

anxieux *adj* anxious.

août *m* August.

apaisant *adj* soothing.

apaiser *vt* to calm (down); relieve.

apathie *f* apathy.

apathique *adj* apathetic.

apercevoir *vt* to see; catch a glimpse of.

apéritif *m* aperitif.

apeuré *adj* frightened.

aphone *adj* voiceless, hoarse.

aphrodisiaque *adj, m* aphrodisiac.

apitoyer *vt* to move to pity:—**s'~** *vr* to feel pity *(sur* for*)*.

aplanir *vt* to level (out); smooth away.

aplati *adj* flat.

apolitique *adj* apolitical; non-political.

apologie *f* apology.

apostrophe *f* apostrophe.

apparaître *vi* to appear.

appareil *m* device; appliance; (tele)-phone;—**~photo** camera.

apparence *f* appearance.

apparent *adj* apparent.

appartement *m* flat, apartment.

appartenir *vi:*—**~ à** to belong to.

appauvrir *vt* to impoverish:—**s'~** *vr* to grow poorer.

appel *m* call; appeal.

appeler *vt* to call:—**s'~** *vr* **je m'appelle Léon** my name is Leon.

appellation *f* appellation; name.

appétissant *adj* appetising.

appétit *m* appetite *(de* for*)*.

applaudir *vt vi* to applaud.

application *f* application; use.

appliquer *vt* to apply:—**s'~** *vr* to apply oneself.

apporter *vt* to bring.

appréciation *f* estimation, assessment

apprécier *vt* to assess; appreciate.

appréhender *vt* to apprehend; to dread.

appréhension *f* apprehension.

apprendre *vt* to learn:—**~ à lire** to learn to read:—**~ à lire à un enfant** to teach a child to read.

apprenti *m*, **-ie** *f* apprentice.

apprentissage *m* apprenticeship.

approbation *f* approval.

approche *f* approach.

approcher *vt* to move near; approach:—**s'~** *vr* to approach.

approuver *vt* to approve of.

approvisionner *vt* to supply:—**s'~** *vr* to stock up *(de, en* with*)*.

approximatif *adj* approximate.

appui *m* support.

appuyer *vt* to support *vi* to press:—*vr* **s'~ sur** to lean on.

âpre *adj* bitter:—**~ment** *adv* bitter-ly.

après *prép* after:—**après tout** after all:—**d'~ elle** according to her.

après-midi *m/f invar* afternoon.

apte *adj* capable *(à* of*)*.

aptitude *f* aptitude:—ability.

aquatique *adj* aquatic.

araignée *f* spider.

arbitraire *adj* arbitrary:—**~ment** *adv* arbitrarily.

arbitre *m* arbiter; referee.

arbitrer *vt* to arbitrate; referee.

arbre *m* tree.

arc *m* bow; arc; arch.

arc-en-ciel *m*, *pl* **arcs-en-ciel** rainbow.

arche *f* arche.

archéologie *f* archaeology.

archipel *m* archipelago.

architecte *mf* architect.

architecture *f* architecture.

archiver *vt* to file, archive.

archives *fpl* archives, records.

ardu *adj* difficult.

argent *m* silver; money.

argument *m* argument.

argumenter *vi* to argue *(sur* about*)*.

aride *adj* arid.

aristocrate *mf* aristocrat.

aristocratie *f* aristocracy.

arithmétique *f* arithmetic:—*adj* arithmetical.

arme *f* arm, weapon.

armée *f* army.

armer *vt* to arm:—**s'~** *vr* to arm oneself.

armoire *f* cupboard; wardrobe.

aromatique *adj* aromatic.

arôme *m* aroma; flavour.

arqué *adj* curved, arched.

arracher *vt* to pull (out); to tear off.

arrangement *m* arrangement.

arranger *vt* to arrange:—**s'~** *vr* to come to an arrangement.

arrêt *m* stopping; stop (button).

arrêter *vt* to stop:—**s'~** *vr* to stop.

arrière *m invar* back:—**en ~** back(wards):

—à l'~ at the back:—*adj invar* back, rear.

arrière-plan *m* background.

arrivant *m*, **-e** *f* newcomer.

arrivée *f* arrival, coming.

arriver *vi* to arrive, come.

arrogant *adj* arrogant.

arrondir *vt* to make round; to round off.

arrondissement *m* district.

arsenal *m* arsenal.

art *m* art.

artère *f* artery; road.

article *m* article.

articuler *vt* to articulate.

artificiel *adj* artificial:—**~lement** *adv* artificially.

artisan *m* artisan, craftsman.

artisanat *m* craft industry.

artiste *mf* artist.

artistique *adj* artistic:—**~ment** *adv* artistically.

ascenseur *m* lift, elevator.

ascension *f* ascent.

asiatique *adj* Asian.

asile *m* refuge; asylum.

aspect *m* appearance, look.

asphyxier *vt* to asphyxiate, suffocate.

aspirateur *m* vacuum cleaner.

aspirine *f* aspirin.

assaillant *m* assailant.

assaillir *vt* to assail.

assainir *vt* to clean up; to purify.

assaisonner *vt* to season.

assassin *m* murderer; assassin.

assassiner *vt* to assassinate.

assaut *m* assault, attack.

assemblage *m* assembly; assembling.

assemblée *f* meeting.

assembler *vt* to assemble:—**s'~** *vr* to assemble.

asseoir (s') *vr* to sit down.

assertion *f* assertion.

asservissement *m* enslavement; slavery.

assez *adv* enough; quite, rather:— avoir ~ d'argent to have enough money:—**~ bien** quite well.

assidu *adj* assiduous; regular.

assiette *f* plate.

assigner *vt* to assign.

assimiler *vt* to assimilate.

assis *adj* seated, sitting (down).

assistant(e) *m(f)* assistant.

assister *vt* to attend; to assist.

association *f* association.

associé(e) *m(f)* associate, partner.

assombrir *vt* to darken:—**s'~** to darken.

assommer *vt* to stun.

assortir *vt* to match:—**s'~** *vr* to go well together.

assoupir (s') *vr* to doze off.

assourdir *vt* to deafen; to muffle.

assourdissant *adj* deafening.

assouvir *vt* to satisfy.

assumer *vt* to assume.

assurance *f* (self-)assurance; assurance; insurance (policy).

assuré *m*, **-e** *f* assured:—*adj* assured.

assurer *vt* to assure:—**s'~** *vr* to insure oneself.

asthme *m* asthma.

astre *m* star.

astreignant *adj* demanding.

astreindre *vt* to force, compel.

astrologie *f* astrology.

astrologue *m* astrologer.

astronaute *m* astronaut.

astronome *m* astronomer.

astronomie *f* astronomy.

astuce *f* shrewdness; (clever) trick; pun.

astucieux *adj* astute.

atelier *m* workshop; studio.

athée *mf* atheist:—*adj* atheistic.

athlète *mf* athlete.

athlétisme *m* athletics.

atlas *m* atlas.

atmosphère *f* atmosphere.

atome *m* atom.

atomique *adj* atomic.

atout *m* trump; advantage, asset.

atroce *adj* atrocious; dreadful.

atrocité *f* atrocity.

attaché *m*, **-e** *f* attaché; assistant.

attacher *vt* to tie together; tie up; fasten; attach (*à* to).

attaque *f* attack.

attaquer *vt* to attack; tackle.

attarder (s') *vr* to linger.

atteindre *vt* to reach; affect; contact.

atteinte *f* attack (*à* on):—**hors d'~** beyond *ou* out of reach.

attendre *vt* to wait:—**s'~** *vr* :—**s'~ à qch** to expect something.

attendrir *vt* to fill with pity:—**s'~** *vr* to be moved (*sur* by).

attendrissant *adj* touching, moving.

attendu *adj* expected; long-awaited.

attentat *m* attack (*contre* on); murder attempt.

attente *f* wait; expectation.

attention *f* attention; care.

attentionné *adj* considerate, thoughtful (*pour* towards).

atténuer *vt* to alleviate; ease.

atterrir *vi* to land, touch down.

atterrissage *m* landing, touch down.

attester *vt* to testify to.

attirant *adj* attractive.

attirer *vt* to attract.

attitude *f* attitude; bearing.

attrait *m* attraction, appeal.

attraper *vt* to catch.

attribuer *vt* to attribute; award.

attribut *m* attribute.

attribution *f* attribution.

attrister *vt* to sadden.

au = à le.

aube *f* dawn, daybreak.

auberge *f* inn:—**~ de jeunesse** youth hostel.

aucun *adj* no; not any; any:—**~ement** *adv* in no way:—*pron* none; not any; any (one):—**~ d'entre eux** none of them.

audacieux *adj* audacious, bold; daring.

audience *f* audience; hearing.

auditeur *m*, **-trice** *f* listener; auditor.

auditoire *m* audience.

augmentation *f* increase, rise (*de* in); increasing (*de* of).

augmenter *vt* to increase, raise.

aujourd'hui *adv* today.

auparavant *adv* before, previously; before, first.

auprès *prép* ~ **de** next to; compared (with).

auquel = à lequel.

aurore *f* dawn, first light.

aussi *adv* too, also; so:—**nous ~** us too:—**une ~ belle journée** such a beautiful day.

aussitôt *adv* immediately:—**~ dit, ~ fait** no sooner said than done:—**~ que** as soon as.

autant *adv* as much; as many; so much; such; so many; such a lot of; the same:—**~ que je sache** as far as I know:—**~ que possible** as much as possible.

autel *m* altar.

auteur *m* author.

authentique *adj* authentic:—**~ment** *adv* authentically.

auto-école f driving school.

auto-stop m hitchhiking:—**faire de l'~** to hitchhike.

auto-stoppeur m, **-euse** f hitchhiker.

autobiographie f autobiography.

autocar m coach.

autodéfense f self-defence.

autodidacte mf self-taught.

automatique adj automatic:—**~ment** adv automatically.

automne m autumn.

automobile f motor car.

automobiliste mf motorist.

autonome adj autonomous.

autopsie f autopsy, post-mortem (examination).

autorisation f authorisation, permission; permit.

autoriser vt to authorise, give permission for.

autorité f authority.

autoroute f motorway.

autour prép ~ **de** (a)round:—adv (a)round.

autre adj other:—**~ chose** something else ou different:—**~ part** somewhere else:—**d'~ part** on the other hand:— pn another.

autrefois adv in the past, in days gone by.

autrement adv differently; otherwise:—**je n'ai pas pu faire ~** I couldn't do differently ou otherwise.

aux = **à les**.

auxiliaire adj auxiliary:—m auxiliary:—mf assistant.

avalanche f avalanche.

avaler vt to swallow.

avance f advance; lead:—**arriver en ~** to arrive early:—**payer d'~** to pay in advance.

avancer vt to move forward:—**s'~** vr to advance, move forward:—vi move forward, advance; make progress.

avant prép before:—**~ peu** shortly:—**~ tout** above all:—adv before:—**en ~** in front, ahead:—m front; bow; forward.

avant-bras m invar forearm.

avant-hier adv the day before yesterday.

avantage m advantage.

avantageux adj profitable, worthwhile; attractive; flattering.

avarie f damage.

avec prép with; to.

avenir m future.

aventure f adventure; venture; experience.

avenue f avenue.

avérer (s') vr to turn out, prove to be.

aversion f aversion.

avertir vt to warn; inform.

avertissement m warning.

aveugle adj blind:—mf blind person.

aveuglement m blindness.

aveugler vt to blind.

aviation f flying; aviation.

avide adj greedy; eager.

avion m (air)plane, aircraft.

avis m opinion.

avisé adj wise, sensible.

aviser vt to advise:—**s'~** vr **s'aviser de** to realise suddenly.

avoir vt to have:—**il y a** there is/are:—**il y a deux mois** two months ago:—**qu'as-tu?** what's the matter?:—m resources; credit.

avortement m abortion.

avoué m solicitor.

avril m April.

axe m axis; axle; main road.

B

babiole f trinket, trifle.

bac m ferry.

badge m badge.

bagage m luggage.

bagarre f fight, brawl.

bagatelle f trinket; trifling sum.

bague f ring.

baguette f stick; loaf of French bread.

baie f (geog) bay.

baigner vt vi to bathe:—**se ~** vr to have a bathe, swim.

baignoire f bathtub.

bâiller vi to yawn.

bain m bath; bathe, swim.

baiser m kiss:—vt to kiss.

baisse f fall, drop.

baisser vi to fall, drop vt to lower.

bal m dance.

balai m broom, brush.

balance f balance; scales.

balançoire f swing; seesaw.

balayer vt to sweep, brush.

balbutier vt to stammer, mumble.

balcon m balcony.

baleine f whale.

balle f bullet; ball.

ballon m ball; balloon.

balustrade f balustrade; handrail.

bambou m bamboo.

banal adj banal, trite:—**~ement** adv tritely.

banane f banana.

bancaire adj banking, bank.

bandage m bandage.

bande f band; tape.

bandeau m headband; blindfold.

bander vt to bandage; stretch.

bandit m bandit.

banlieue f suburbs.

bannière f banner.

bannir vt to banish.

banque f bank; banking.

banquette f seat, stool.

banquier m banker.

baptiser vt to baptise.

bar m bar.

barbare adj barbarian; barbaric.

barbe f beard.

barème m list, schedule.

baril m barrel, cask.

baromètre m barometer.

barque f small boat.

barre f bar, rod.

barrer vt to bar, block.

barricader vt to barricade:—**se ~** vr to barricade o.s.

barrière f barrier; fence.

bas adj low, base:—n stocking; sock.

bascule f weighing machine, scales.

base f base; basis.

baser vt to base:—**se baser sur** vr to depend on, rely on.

basse f (mus) bass; shoal, reef.

bassesse f meanness; vulgarity.

bassin m pond, pool; dock.

bataille f battle.

batailler vi to battle.

bateau m boat, ship.

bâtiment m building.

bâtir vt to build.

bâton m stick, staff.

batte *f* bat; beating.

batterie *f* battery.

battre *vt* to beat, defeat.

baume *m* balm, balsam.

bavard *m*, **-e** *f* chatterbox:—*adj* talkative, loquacious.

bavardage *m* chatting, gossiping.

bavarder *vi* to chat, gossip.

bazar *m* bazaar; general store.

béat *adj* blessed; complacent.

béatitude *f* beatitude; bliss.

beau, *f* **belle** *adj* beautiful, lovely.

beaucoup *adv* a lot, a great deal:—~ **de monde** a lot of people.

beauté *f* beauty, loveliness.

beaux-arts *m pl* fine art.

bébé *m* baby.

bec *m* beak, bill.

bégayer *vi* to stammer, stutter.

beige *adj* beige:—*m* beige.

bêler *vi* to bleat.

Belge *mf* Belgian.

belge *adj* Belgian.

Belgique *f* Belgium.

belligérant *m*, **-ante** *f* belligerent:—*adj* belligerent.

bénédiction *f* benediction, blessing.

bénéfice *m* profit; benefit.

bénéficier *vi* to benefit; enjoy.

bénin, *f* **bénigne** *adj* benign; harmless.

bénir *vt* to bless.

bénit *adj* consecrated, holy.

béquille *f* crutch; prop.

berceau *m* cradle.

bercer *vt* to rock, cradle.

béret *m* beret.

berge *f* riverbank; barge.

berger *m* shepherd:**-ère** *f* shepherdess.

besogne *f* work; job.

besoin *m* need; want:—**avoir ~ de** to need.

bête *adj* stupid, silly:—**~ment** *adv* stupidly, foolishly:—*f* animal.

bêtise *f* stupidity, foolishness.

béton *m* concrete.

beurre *m* butter.

biberon *m* baby's bottle.

bible *f* bible.

bibliographie *f* bibliography.

bibliothécaire *mf* librarian.

bibliothèque *f* library; bookcase.

bicyclette *f* bicycle.

bidon *m* tin, can; flask.

bien *adv* well; properly; very:—*n* property, estate.

bien-être *m* well-being.

bienfaiteur *m* benefactor, **-trice** *f* benefactress.

bienheureux *adj* blessed; lucky; happy.

bientôt *adv* soon.

bienvenu *adj* welcome.

bière *f* beer; coffin.

bifteck *m* steak.

bigot *adj* bigoted.

bijou *m* jewel.

bijouterie *f* jewellery.

bilan *m* balance sheet; assessment.

bilingue *adj* bilingual.

billet *m* ticket; note.

billetterie *f* cash dispenser.

billion *m* billion.

binaire *adj* binary.

biodégradable *adj* biodegradable.

biographie *f* biography.

biologie *f* biology.

biologiste *mf* biologist.

bipède *m* biped.

biscuit *m* cake; biscuit.

bisexuel *adj* bisexual.

bissextile *adj* bissextile, leap (year).

bitumer *vt* to asphalt, tarmac.

bizarre *adj* bizarre, strange:—**~ment** *adv* strangely, oddly.

blague *f* joke, trick.

blaguer *vi* to joke.

blagueur *m*, **-euse** *f* joker, wag:—*adj* jokey, teasing.

blaireau *m* badger.

blâme *m* blame, rebuke.

blâmer *vt* to blame, rebuke.

blanc *adj*, *f* **blanche** white:—*m* white; blank:—*mf* white person:—*f* minim.

blancheur *f* whiteness.

blanchir *vi* to turn white:—*vt* to whiten.

blanchisserie *f* laundry.

blasphème *m* blasphemy.

blé *m* wheat.

blêmir *vi* to turn pale.

blessé *adj* injured, wounded.

blesser *vt* to injure, wound.

bleu *adj* blue:—*n* blue; bruise.

bleuir *vi* to turn blue:—*vt* to make blue.

bloc *m* block, group, unit.

blond *adj* blond, fair.

blondir *vi* to turn blond, turn golden:—*vt* to bleach.

bloquer *vt* to block, blockade.

blouse *f* blouse; overall.

bœuf *m* ox, bullock.

boire *vt* to drink:—*vi* to drink, tipple.

bois *m* wood.

boisson *f* drink.

boîte *f* box.

boiter *vi* to limp.

boiteux *adj* lame.

bol *m* bowl.

bombarder *vt* to bombard, bomb.

bombe *f* bomb.

bon *adj*, *f* **bonne** good:—*m* slip, coupon, bond.

bonbon *m* sweet, candy.

bond *m* leap; bounce.

bondir *vi* to jump, leap; to bounce.

bonheur *m* happiness; luck.

bonhomme *m*, *pl* **bonshommes** chap, fellow.

bonifier *vt* to improve:—**se ~** *vr* to improve.

bonjour *m* hello, good morning.

bonsoir *m* good evening.

bonté *f* goodness, kindness.

bord *m* side, edge.

border *vt* to edge, border.

borner *vt* to restrict, limit.

botanique *f* botany:—*adj* botanical.

botaniste *f* botanist.

botte *f* boot.

bouche *f* mouth.

bouché *adj* cloudy, overcast.

bouche-à-bouche *m* kiss of life.

bouchée *f* mouthful.

boucher *vt* to butcher:—*m*, **-ère** *f* butcher.

boucherie *f* butcher's; butchery.

bouchon *m* cork.

boudeur *adj* sullen, sulky.

boudin *m* pudding.

boue *f* mud.

bouée *f* buoy.

bouger *vi* to move:—*vt* to move, shift.

bougie *f* candle.

bouillir *vi* to boil.

bouilloire *f* kettle.

boulanger *m*, **-ère** *f* baker.

boulangerie *f* bakery.

boule *f* ball, bowl.

boulevard *m* boulevard.

bouleversement *m* confusion, disruption.

bouleverser *vt* to confuse, disrupt.

boulon *m* bolt.

bourdon *m* bumblebee.

bourdonner *vi* to buzz, hum.
bourg *m* market-town.
bourgeois *m*, **-e** *f* bourgeois, middle-class person:—*adj* bourgeois, middle-class.
bourse *f* purse; stock exchange.
boursier *m*, **-ière** *f* broker; speculator.
bousculer *vt* to jostle, hustle.
bout *m* end; piece, scrap.
bouteille *f* bottle.
boutique *f* shop, store.
bouton *m* button.
boutonner *vt* to button.
boxe *f* boxing.
boxer *vi* to box.
boycotter *vt* to boycott.
bracelet *m* bracelet.
braguette *f* fly (trousers).
brancher *vt* to connect, link.
bras *m* arm.
brasse *f* breaststroke.
brasser *vt* to brew; to mix.
brasserie *f* bar; brewery.
brave *adj* brave, courageous.
braver *vt* to brave, defy.
brèche *f* breach, gap.
bredouiller *vi* to stammer, mumble.
bref *adj*, *f* **brève** brief, concise:—**en ~** *adv* in short.
brevet *m* licence, patent.
bric-à-brac *m* bric-a-brac.
bricolage *m* DIY, odd jobs.
bricoler *vi* to do odd jobs.
bride *f* bridle.
brider *vt* to restrain, restrict.
brièveté *f* brevity.
brillant *adj* brilliant, shining.
briller *vi* to shine.
brique *f* brick, slab.
brise *f* breeze.

briser *vt* to smash, shatter.
broche *f* brooch.
brochure *f* brochure, pamphlet.
bronze *m* bronze.
bronzer *vi* to get a tan.
brosse *f* brush.
brosser *vt* to brush.
brouette *f* wheelbarrow.
brouillard *m* fog, mist.
brouter *vt* to graze.
bruine *f* drizzle.
bruit *m* noise, sound.
bruitage *m* sound-effects.
brûler *vt vi* to burn.
brûlure *f* burn.
brume *f* haze, mist.
brun *m* dark-haired man, **brune** *f* brunette:—*adj* brown.
brusque *adj* brusque, abrupt.
brut *adj* crude, raw.
brutal *adj* brutal, rough.
brutalité *f* brutality.
brute *f* brute; animal.
bruyant *adj* noisy.
bûche *f* log.
bûcheron(ne) *m(f)* woodcutter, lumberjack.
budget *m* budget.
buée *f* condensation; steam.
buffet *m* sideboard, buffet.
bulbe *m* bulb.
bulletin *m* bulletin.
bureau *m* office; desk.
bureaucrate *mf* bureaucrat.
bus *m* bus.
buste *m* bust, chest.
but *m* objective, goal.
buvable *adj* drinkable.
buvette *f* refreshment-room.
buveur *m*, **-euse** *f* drinker.

C

ça *pron* that; it:—**~ va?** How goes it?:—**~ alors!** you don't say!

cabaret *m* cabaret; tavern.

cabine *f* cabin, cab; cockpit.

cabinet *m* surgery; office, study.

câble *m* cable.

cacahouète *f* peanut.

cacao *m* cocoa.

caché *adj* hidden, secluded.

cacher *vt* to hide, conceal.

cadavre *m* corpse.

cadeau *m* present.

cadenasser *vt* to padlock.

cadet *m*, **-ette** *f* youngest child.

cadre *m* frame; context; scope.

caduc *adj f* **caduque** null and void; obsolete.

café *m* coffee.

cafétéria *f* cafeteria.

cafetière *f* coffeepot.

cage *f* cage.

cahier *m* notebook.

caillou *m* stone; pebble.

caisse *f* box; till; fund.

caissier *m*, **-ière** *f* cashier.

calcul *m* sum, calculation.

calculatrice, calculette *f* calculator.

calculer *vt* to calculate, reckon:—*vi* to budget carefully.

caleçon *m* shorts, pants.

calendrier *m* calendar.

calibre *m* calibre, bore.

calmant *m* tranquilliser, sedative:—*adj* tranquillising.

calme *m* calm, stillness:—*adj* calm, still.

calmer *vt* calm, soothe, pacify.

calorie *f* calorie.

camarade *mf* companion, friend.

camaraderie *f* camaraderie, friendship.

cambrioler *vt* to burgle.

caméra *f* camera.

camion *m* lorry.

camionneur *m* lorry driver, trucker.

camouflage *m* camouflage.

camp *m* camp.

campagnard *m* countryman, **-e** *f* countrywoman:—*adj* country, rustic.

campagne *f* country, countryside.

camper *vi* to camp.

canal *m* canal, channel.

canapé *m* sofa, settee.

cancer *m* cancer.

cancéreux *adj* cancerous.

candidat *m*, **-e** *f* candidate.

candide *adj* frank, ingenuous.

canne *f* cane, rod.

canoë *m* canoe.

canon *m* cannon, gun.

cantatrice *f* singer.

cantine *f* canteen.

caoutchouc *m* rubber.

cap *f* cape; course.

capable *adj* capable, competent.

capacité *f* capacity.

capitaine *m* captain.

capital *adj* capital, cardinal, major:—*m* capital, stock.

capitale *f* capital (letter, city).

capitaliste *mf* capitalist.

capituler vt to capitulate.

capoter vt to capsize, overturn.

caprice m caprice, whim.

capricieux adj capricious.

capsule f capsule.

captif m:—**ve** f captive:—adj captive.

captiver vt to captivate, enthrall.

captivité f captivity.

capture f capture.

capturer vt to capture.

car conj for; because:—m bus; van.

caractère m character, disposition.

caractériser vt to characterise.

caractérisque f characteristic, feature:—adj characteristic.

carat m carat.

caravane f caravan.

carbone m carbon.

carburant m motor-fuel.

cardiaque adj cardiac.

carence f deficiency; insolvency.

caressant adj affectionate.

caresse f caress.

caresser vt to caress, fondle.

cargaison f cargo, freight.

caricature f caricature.

caricaturer vt to caricature.

caritatif adj charitable.

carnaval m carnival.

carnet m notebook; logbook.

carnivore mf carnivore:—adj carnivorous.

carotte f carrot.

carreau m tile; pane.

carrefour m crossroads.

carrière f career.

carrosserie f bodywork, coachwork.

carte f card; map.

cartilage m cartilage.

carton m cardboard.

cartonner vt to bind (book).

cas m case; circumstance.

cascade f waterfall.

case f square; box.

casier m compartment; filing cabinet.

casino m casino.

casque m helmet.

cassant adj brittle.

casse-croûte m invar snack.

casser vt to break:—**se ~** vr to break.

casserole f saucepan.

cassette f cassette; cash-box.

catalogue m catalogue.

cataloguer vt to catalogue.

catastrophe f catastrophe.

catastrophique adj catastrophic.

catégorie f category.

catégorique adj categorical.

cathédrale f cathedral.

catholique adj Catholic.

cauchemar m nightmare.

cause f cause, reason.

causer vt to cause; to chat:—vi to talk, chat.

cavalerie f cavalry.

cavalier m, -**ière** f rider.

cave f cellar.

caverne f cave, cavern.

cavité f cavity.

ce adj **cet** (bef. vowel and mute h), f **cette**, pl **ces** this, these:—**cet homme-là** that man:—pron:—**c'est le facteur** it's the postman:—**~ sont mes lunettes** these are my glasses.

ceci pron this.

céder vi to give in:—vt to give up, transfer.

ceinture f belt, girdle.

cela pron that:—emphasis **qui ~?** who? (do you mean)?:—**comment ~?** how? (do you mean?).

célèbre adj famous.

célébrer *vt* to celebrate.

célébrité *f* fame, celebrity.

célibataire *mf* single person:—*adj* single, unmarried.

cellule *f* cell, unit.

celluloïde *m* celluloid.

celui *pron*, *f* **celle** this one, *pl* **ceux** these ones.

cendre *f* ash.

censure *f* censorship.

cent *adj* a hundred:—**tu as ~ fois raison** you are absolutely right:—*m* a hundred:—~ **pour ~** per cent.

centenaire *m* centenarian:—*adj* a hundred years old.

centigrade *m* centigrade.

centigramme *m* centigram.

centime *m* centime.

centimètre *m* centimetre.

central *adj* central.

centre *m* centre.

cependant *conj* however.

cercle *m* circle, ring.

céréale *f* cereal.

cérébral *adj* cerebral.

cérémonie *f* ceremony.

certain *adj* certain, sure:—~**s** *pn* some, certain.

certificat *m* certificate.

certifier *vt* to certify; to guarantee.

certitude *f* certainty, certitude.

cervelle *f* brain.

cesser *f* to cease, stop.

cessez-le-feu *m* cease-fire.

cet *adj f* **cette** *see* **ce.**

ceux *see* **ce.**

chacun *pron* each one:—~**e d'entre elles** each of them.

chagrin *m* sorrow, chagrin.

chaîne *f* chain.

chair *f* flesh.

chaise *f* chair.

châlet *m* chalet.

chaleur *f* heat.

chaleureux *adj* warm, cordial.

chambre *f* room.

chameau *m* camel.

champ *m* field.

champignon *m* mushroom.

champion *m*, **-onne** *f* champion.

championnat *m* championship.

chance *f* luck.

chanceler *vi* to stagger, totter.

chanceux *adj* lucky, fortunate.

changement *m* change, changing.

changer *vi* to change:—*vt* to change.

chanson *f* song.

chantage *m* blackmail.

chanter *vi*, *vt* to sing.

chanteur *m*, **-euse** *f* singer.

chantier *m* building site.

chaos *m* chaos.

chapeau *m* hat.

chapelle *f* chapel.

chapitre *m* chapter.

chaque *adj* each.

charbon *m* coal.

charge *f* load; responsibility.

charger *vt* to load:—**se ~ de** to take responsibility for, attend to.

charisme *m* charisma.

charitable *adj* charitable, kind.

charité *f* charity.

charme *m* charm.

charmer *vt* to charm, beguile.

charpente *f* structure, framework.

charpentier *m* carpenter.

charrue *f* plough.

chasse-neige *m invar* snowplough.

chasser *vt* to hunt, chase.

châssis *m* chassis.

chat *m*, **chatte** *f* cat.

château m castle, château.

châtiment m chastisement, punishment.

chaud adj warm, hot.

chaudière f boiler.

chauffage m heating.

chauffer vi to heat:—vt to heat up.

chauffeur m driver.

chaumière f cottage.

chaussée f road, street.

chaussette f sock.

chaussure f shoe.

chauve-souris f bat.

chef m head, boss; chef.

chef-d'œuvre m masterpiece.

chemin m way, road:—~ **de fer** railway.

cheminée f chimney.

chemise f shirt.

chêne m oak.

chèque m cheque.

chéquier m chequebook.

cher adj f **chère** dear, expensive.

chercher vt to look for.

chéri m, **-ie** f darling:—adj cherished.

cheval m horse.

cheveu m hair.

cheville f ankle.

chèvre f goat.

chez prép at home:—**je rentre ~ moi** I'm going home.

chic m style, stylishness.

chien m, **chienne** f dog.

chiffre m figure.

chimie f chemistry.

chimiste mf chemist.

chimpanzé m chimpanzee.

chirurgie f surgery.

chirurgien m surgeon.

choc m shock, crash.

chocolat m chocolate.

choir vi to fall.

choisir vt to choose.

choix m choice.

chômage m unemployment.

chômeur m, **-euse** f unemployed person.

choquer vt to shock.

chose f thing, matter, object.

chou m cabbage.

chouette f owl.

chrétien m, **-ienne** f Christian, adj christian.

christianisme m Christianity.

chronologie f chronology.

chuchoter vi to whisper.

chuinter vi to hiss.

chute f fall, drop.

chuter vi to fall.

ci adv:—**ces fleurs-ci** these flowers:—**ci-joint** enclosed.

cible f target.

cicatrice f scar.

cidre m cider.

ciel m, pl **cieux, ciels** sky.

cierge m candle.

cigare m cigar.

cigarette f cigarette.

cil m eyelash.

ciment m cement.

cimetière m cemetery.

cinéma m cinema.

cingler vt to lash, sting.

cinq m five.

cinquante m fifty.

cinquième mf fifth, adj fifth.

cirage m polish.

circonférence f circumference.

circonspect adj circumspect.

circonstance f circumstance.

circuit m circuit, tour.

circulaire adj circular.

circulation f circulation; traffic.

circuler vi to circulate, move.

cirer *vt* to polish.

cirque *m* circus.

ciseau *m* chisel; scissor(s).

citadelle *f* citadel.

citadin(e) *m(f)* city dweller:—*adj* town, urban.

citation *f* citation, summons.

cité *f* city.

citer *vt* to quote, cite.

citoyen *m*, **-enne** *f* citizen.

citron *m* lemon.

civil *adj* civil:—**~ement** *adv* civilly.

civilisation *f* civilisation.

civiliser *vt* to civilise.

clair *adj* clear, bright:—**~ement** *adv* clearly.

clameur *f* clamour.

clandestin *adj* clandestine.

claque *f* slap, smack.

claquer *vi* to bang, slam.

clarifier *vt* to clarify:—**se ~** *vr* to become clear.

clarté *f* light, brightness.

classe *f* class, standing.

classer *vt* to file, classify.

classification *f* classification.

classique *adj* classical, standard.

clause *f* clause.

claustrophobie *f* claustrophobia.

clavier *m* keyboard.

clé, clef *f* key.

cliché *m* cliché; negative.

client *m*, **-e** *f* client.

cligner *vi* to blink.

clignoter *vi* to blink, flicker.

climat *m* climate.

climatisation *f* air conditioning.

clinique *f* clinic.

clochard *m*, **-e** *f* down-and-out.

cloche *f* bell.

cloison *f* partition.

clore *vt* to close, conclude.

clou *m* nail.

clouer *vt* to nail.

coalition *f* coalition.

cochon *m*, **-onne** *f* pig.

code *m* code.

cœur *m* heart.

coffre *m* chest:—**~-fort** safe.

cohabitation *f* cohabitation.

cohérent *adj* coherent.

cohésion *f* cohesion.

coiffer *vt* to arrange so's hair:—**se ~** *vr* to do one's hair.

coiffeur *m*, **-euse** *f* hairdresser.

coin *m* corner.

coïncidence *f* coincidence.

col *m* neck.

colère *f* anger.

colis *m* parcel.

collaborateur *m*, **-trice** *f* collaborator, colleague.

collaborer *vi* to collaborate.

collection *f* collection.

collectionner *vt* to collect.

collège *m* college, school.

collègue *mf* colleague.

coller *vt* to stick, glue:—*vi* to stick, be sticky.

colline *f* hill.

collision *f* collision.

colonie *f* colony.

coloniser *vt* to colonise.

coloration *f* colouring, staining.

colorier *vt* to colour in.

coma *m* coma.

comateux *adj* comatose.

combat *m* combat, fight.

combattre *vt* to fight, combat:—*vi* to fight.

combien *adv* how much, how many:—**~ de temps** how much time.

combiner vt to combine.

combustible m fuel.

combustion f combustion.

comédie f comedy.

comédien m:**-ienne** f actor.

comète f comet.

comique adj comic:—**~ment** adv comically.

comité m committee.

commande f command, order.

commander vt vi to order, command.

comme conj as, like:—**~ ci ~ ça** so-so:—adv how.

commémorer vt to commemorate.

commencer vt to begin:-vi to begin, start.

comment adv how:—**~ dire?** how shall we say?

commentaire m comment; commentary.

commenter vt to comment.

commerçant m, **-e** f merchant, trader.

commerce m business, commerce.

commercial adj commercial:—**~ement** adv commercially.

commercialiser vt to market.

commettre vt to commit.

commission f commission, committee.

commodité f convenience.

commun adj common, joint.

communal adj common, communal.

commune f town, district.

communication f communication.

communiquer vt to communicate, transmit:—vi to communicate.

communiste mf communist.

compact adj compact, dense.

compagne f companion.

compagnon m companion.

comparable adj comparable.

comparaison f comparison.

comparer vt to compare.

compartiment m compartment.

compas m compass.

compassion f compassion.

compatible adj compatible.

compatriote mf compatriot.

compensation f compensation.

compenser vt to compensate; offset.

compétence f competence.

compétitif adj competitive.

compétitivité f competitiveness.

complaisant adj kind; complacent.

complément m complement; extension.

complet adj complete, full.

compléter vt to complete.

complexe adj complex, complicated.

complication f complication.

complice mf accomplice.

compliment m compliment.

compliquer vt to complicate.

comportement m behaviour; performance.

comporter vt to consist of:—**se ~** vr to behave.

composer vt to compose, make up:—**se ~** vr:—**se ~ de** to be made up of.

compréhensible adj comprehensible.

compréhensif adj comprehensive, understanding.

comprendre vt to understand; consist of.

compression f compression; reduction.

comprimer vt to compress; to restrain.

compromettre vt to compromise.

comptable mf accountant.

compter vt vi to count.

comptoir m counter, bar.

concentration f concentration.

concept m concept.

conception f conception, design.

concerner vt to concern, regard.

concert m concert.

concession f concession; privilege.

concevoir vt to imagine, conceive.

concierge mf caretaker, concierge.

conciliation f conciliation; reconciliation.

concilier vt to reconcile; to attract.

concision f conciseness, brevity.

conclure vt to conclude; to decide.

conclusion f conclusion.

concours m competition; conjuncture.

concret adj concrete, solid.

concubin m, **-e** f concubine; cohabitant.

concurrence f competition.

condamnation f condemnation; sentencing.

condamner vt to condemn; to sentence.

condensation f condensation.

condenser vt to condense, compress.

condition f condition, term.

conditionner vt to condition; to package.

conducteur m, **-trice** f driver; operator.

conduire vt vi to lead; to drive.

conduite f conduct; driving; running.

cône m cone.

conférence f conference.

confession f confession.

confiance f confidence, trust.

confidence f confidence; disclosure.

confidentiel adj confidential.

confier vt to confide, entrust:—**se ~** vr to confide in.

confiner vt to confine:—**se ~** to be confined.

confirmer vt to confirm:—**se ~** vr to be confirmed.

confiserie f confectionery.

confiture f jam.

conflit m conflict, contention.

confondre vt to confuse, mingle.

conforme adj consistent; true.

conformer vt to model:—**se ~** vr to conform.

confort m comfort.

confortable adj comfortable, cosy.

confronter vt to confront.

confus adj confused, indistinct.

confusion f confusion, disorder.

congédier vt to dismiss.

congeler vt to freeze.

congratuler vt to congratulate.

congrégation f congregation.

congrès m congress, conference.

conjurer vt to conspire; to implore.

connaissance f knowledge; consciousness.

connaisseur m, **-euse** f connoisseur; expert.

connaître vt to know, be acquainted with.

connecter vt to connect.

connexion f connection, link.

connu adj known; famous.

conquérir vt to conquer.

conquête f conquest.

conscience f consciousness; conscience.

consciencieux adv conscientious.

conscient adj conscious, aware.

consécutif adj consecutive.

conseil m advice, counsel.

conseiller vt to advise, counsel.

consentir vi to consent, acquiesce.

conséquence f consequence, result.

conséquent adj consequent, logical.

conservateur m, **-trice** f conservative; curator.

conservation f conservation.

conserver vt to keep, preserve:—**se ~** vr to keep.

considérable adj considerable; notable.

considération f consideration, respect.

considérer vt to consider, regard.

consistance f consistency; strength.

consister *vi:*—**~ en** to consist of.

consolation *f* consolation, solace.

consoler *vt* to console, comfort.

consolider *vt* to consolidate, reinforce.

consommateur *m*, **-trice** *f* consumer.

consommation *f* consumption; accomplishment.

consommer *vt* to consume, use.

conspirer *vi* to conspire, plot.

constant *adj* constant, continuous.

constat *m* report; acknowledgement.

constater *vt* to record; to verify.

constellation *f* constellation, galaxy.

consterner *vt* to dismay.

constipation *f* constipation.

constituer *vt* to constitute, form.

constitution *f* constitution, formation.

constructeur *m*, **-trice** *f* builder, maker.

construction *f* building, construction.

construire *vt* to construct, build.

consulat *m* consulate.

consultant *m*, **-e** *f* consultant.

consulter *vt* to consult, take advice from.

consumer *vt* to consume, spend.

contact *m* contact, touch.

contagieux *adj* contagious, infectious.

contaminer *vt* to contaminate, pollute.

conte *m* story, tale.

contempler *vt* to contemplate, meditate.

contemporain *adj* contemporary.

contenir *vt* to contain.

contentement *m* contentment, satisfaction.

contenter *vt* to please, satisfy.

contenu *m* contents, enclosure.

contester *vt* to contest, dispute.

contexte *m* context.

continent *m* continent.

continental *adj* continental.

continuation *f* continuation.

continuel *adj* continual, continuous.

continuer *vt* to continue, proceed with:—*vi* to continue, go on.

contour *m* contour, outline.

contra~eptif *adj* contraceptive.

contracter *vt* to contract, acquire:—**se ~** *vr* to contract, shrink.

contradiction *f* contradiction, discrepancy.

contraindre *vt* to constrain, compel.

contraire *m* opposite, contrary:—*adj* opposite, contrary.

contrarier *vt* to annoy; to oppose.

contraste *m* contrast.

contrat *m* contract, agreement.

contre *prép* against:—**par ~** on the other hand.

contre-attaquer *vi* to counter-attack.

contrebande *f* contraband, smuggling.

contrecœur:—**à ~** reluctantly.

contredire *vt* to contradict, refute.

contrefaire *vt* to counterfeit, forge.

contrepartie *f* compensation; consideration.

contresens *m* nonsense; misunderstanding; mistranslation.

contribuer *vt* *vi* to contribute.

contribution *f* contribution; tax.

contrôler *vt* to control, check.

contrôleur *m*, **-euse** *f* inspector; auditor.

controverse *f* controversy.

convaincre *vt* to convince, persuade.

convalescence *f* convalescence.

convenable *adj* fitting, suitable:—**~ment** *adv* suitably, fitly.

convenir *vi* to agree, accord.

convention *f* convention, agreement.

conventionnel *adj* conventional; contractual.

conversation *f* conversation, talk.

conversion *f* conversion.

convertir vt to convert:—**se ~** vr to be converted.

conviction f conviction.

convoi m convoy; train.

convoquer vt to convoke, convene.

coopération f cooperation.

coopérative f cooperative.

coopérer vi to cooperate, collaborate.

coordination f coordination; committee.

copain m friend, pal.

copie f copy, reproduction.

copier vt to copy, reproduce.

copilote m co-pilot.

coq m cock, rooster.

coquet adj stylish, smart.

coquin m, **-e** f naughty, mischievous.

corail m coral.

coran m Koran.

corbeille f basket.

corde f rope; string.

cordial adj cordial, warm.

cordialité f cordiality, warmth.

cordon m cord, string; cordon.

corne f horn, antler.

corneille f crow.

cornet m cornet, cone.

corporatif adj corporative, corporate.

corporation f corporation, guild.

corps m body, corpse.

corpulent adj corpulent.

correct adj correct, accurate.

correcteur m, **-trice** f examiner; proof-reader.

correction f correction; proofreading.

correspondance f correspondence, communication.

correspondre vi to correspond, communicate.

corridor m corridor, passage.

corriger vt to correct.

corroder vt to corrode.

corrompre vt to corrupt, debase.

corrosion f corrosion.

corruption f corruption, debasement.

corset m corset.

cortège m cortège, procession.

cosmétique m cosmetic.

cosmique adj cosmic.

cosmopolite adj cosmopolitan.

cosmos m cosmos.

costume m costume, dress.

côte f coast; rib; slope.

côté m side; point.

coteau m hill.

coter vt to quote; to classify.

coton m cotton.

cou m neck.

couche f layer, coat.

coucher vt to put to bed:—**se ~** vr to go to bed.

coucou m cuckoo.

coude m elbow.

coudre vt vi to sew.

couler vi to flow, run.

couleur f colour, shade.

coulisser vi to slide, run.

couloir m corridor, passage.

coup m blow; shot:—**tout à ~** suddenly:—**après ~** afterwards, after the event:—**~ de feu** shot:—**jeter un ~ d'œil** to glance.

coupable mf culprit:—adj guilty.

coupe f cut; cutting.

couper vt to cut, slice.

couple m couple, pair.

coupon m coupon, voucher, ticket.

cour f court, yard, courtyard.

courage m courage, daring.

courageux adj courageous.

courant adj current; present:—m stream, current.

courbe f curve; contour.

courber vt to curve, bend.

coureur m, **-euse** f runner.

courir vi to run, race.

couronne f crown, wreath.

courrier m mail, post.

cours m course; flow; path.

course f running; race; flight; journey.

coursier m, **-ière** f courier, messenger.

court adj short, brief.

court-circuiter vt to short-circuit.

courtier m, **-ière** f broker, agent.

courtois adj courteous.

cousin m, **-e** f cousin.

coussin m cushion, pillow.

coût m cost, charge.

couteau m knife.

coûter vi, vt to cost.

coûteux adj costly, expensive.

coutume f custom, habit.

couvent m convent.

couvercle m lid, cap.

couvert m shelter; cover; pretext:—adj covered; secret.

couverture f blanket; cover; roofing.

couvrir vt to cover.

crabe m crab.

cracher vt to spit.

craie f chalk.

craindre vt to fear.

crampe f cramp.

crâne m cranium, skull.

crapaud m toad.

craquement m crack, creaking, snap.

craquer vi to creak, squeak, crack.

cratère m crater.

cravate f tie.

créateur m, **-trice** f creator, author.

création f creation.

créature f creature.

crèche f creche; crib.

crédible adj credible.

crédit m credit, trust.

crédule adj credulous, gullible.

créer vt to create, produce.

crème f cream.

crémerie f dairy.

crêpe f pancake:—m crepe.

crépiter vi to crackle; to rattle.

crépuscule m twilight, dusk.

crête f crest, comb.

crétin m, **-e** f cretin, idiot.

creuser vi to dig, burrow:—vt to dig, hollow.

crevaison f puncture, flat.

crever vt to burst; to gouge:—vi to burst; to split.

cri m cry, howl, yell.

crible m riddle, sieve.

crier vi to cry, shout.

crime m crime, offence.

criminel m, **elle** f criminal:—adj criminal.

crise f crisis, attack.

cristal m crystal, glassware.

cristalliser vt to crystallise.

critère m criterion, standard.

critique adj critical, censorious:—f criticism; critique.

critiquer vt to criticise, censure.

crochet m hook, clip.

crocodile m crocodile.

croire vt to believe, think.

croiser vt to cross; to fold:—**se ~** vr to cross, intersect.

croisière f cruise.

croissance f growth, increase.

croître vi to grow, rise.

croix f cross.

croquer vt to crunch, munch.

croquette f croquette.

croquis m sketch, outline.

croustiller vi to be crusty, crispy.

croûte f crust.

croyance f belief.
croyant adj believing.
cru adj raw, uncooked:—m vineyard; wine.
cruauté f cruelty, inhumanity.
crucial adj crucial, decisive.
crucifix m crucifix.
crudité f crudity, coarseness.
cruel adj cruel.
crypter vt to encode, scramble.
cube m cube, block.
cueillir vt to pick, gather.
cuiller, cuillère f spoon, spoonful.
cuir m leather, hide.
cuire vi to cook.
cuisine f kitchen; cookery.
cuisiner vt vi to cook.
cuisinier m, **-ière** f cook.
cuisse f thigh.
cuisson f cooking, baking.
cuit adj cooked.
cul-de-sac m blind alley, cul-de-sac.
culminer vi to culminate, tower.
culotte f knickers; underpants; shorts.

culpabiliser vt to make someone feel guilty.
culte m cult, veneration.
cultivateur m, **-trice** f farmer.
cultiver vt to cultivate:—**se ~** vr to improve oneself.
culture f culture; cultivation.
culturel adj cultural.
cumuler vt to accumulate.
cupide adj greedy.
cure f cure; treatment.
curé m parish priest, parson.
curieux adj curious, inquisitive.
cuvette f basin, bowl.
cycle m cycle; stage.
cyclique adj cyclical.
cyclisme m cycling.
cycliste mf cyclist.
cyclone m cyclone.
cygne m swan.
cylindre m cylinder.
cynique adj cynical:—**~ment** adv cynically.
cynisme m cynicism.

D

dactylographe mf typist.
dactylographier vt to type.
dame f lady.
damier m draughtboard.
danger m danger, risk.
dangereux adj dangerous, risky.
dans prép in; into.
danse f dance; dancing.
danser vi to dance.
danseur m **-euse** f dancer.
dard m dart; sting.

date f date.
dater vt to date.
dauphin m dolphin.
davantage adv more.
de prép of; from:—**deux ~ plus** two more:—art some, any.
dé m die; thimble.
débâcle f disaster; collapse.
débarquer vt to land, unship:—vi to disembark, land.
débarrasser vt to clear, rid.

débat *m* debate; dispute, contest.

débattre *vt* to debate, discuss.

débile *adj* weak, feeble.

débilitant *adj* debilitating, weakening.

débiteur *m*, **-trice** *f* debtor.

débloquer *vt* to release, unlock.

déboiser *vt* to deforest.

débordant *adj* exuberant, overflowing.

déborder *vi* to overflow; to outflank.

debout *adv* upright, standing:—**être ~** to stand.

débris *m* debris, waste.

début *m* beginning, outset.

débuter *vi* to start, begin:—*vt* to lead, start.

décadence *f* decadence, decline.

décadent *adj* decadent.

décaféiné *adj* decaffeinated.

décaler *vt* to stagger; to shift.

décathlon *m* decathlon.

décéder *vi* to die.

déceler *vt* to detect; to disclose.

décembre *m* December.

décence *f* decency.

décennie *f* decade.

décent *adj* decent, proper.

décentraliser *vt* to decentralise.

déception *f* disappointment; deceit.

décès *m* death, decease.

décevoir *vt* to disappoint; to deceive.

déchaîner *vt* to unleash.

décharge *f* discharge; receipt.

décharger *vt* to unload, discharge.

déchet *m* loss, waste.

déchiffrer *vt* to decipher, decode.

déchirer *vt* to tear, rip.

décibel *m* decibel.

décidé *adj* decided; determined.

décimal *adj* decimal.

décision *f* decision.

déclarer *vt* to declare, announce.

déclencher *vt* to release, set off.

décliner *vi* to decline, refuse.

décollage *m* take-off, lift-off.

décoller *vi* to unpaste.

décolleté *adj* low-cut.

décomposer *vt* to decompose; to break up.

décompte *m* discount; deduction.

décongeler *vt* to thaw, defrost.

déconnecter *vt* to disconnect.

décontenancé *adj* embarrassed; disconcerted.

décor *m* scenery; setting.

décorateur *m*, **-trice** *f* decorator; set designer.

décoration *f* decoration, embellishment.

décorer *vt* to decorate, adorn.

découper *vt* to carve, cut up.

décourageant *adj* discouraging, disheartening.

décourager *vt* discourage, dishearten.

découvert *adj* uncovered; open.

découverte *f* discovery.

découvrir *vt* to discover.

décréter *vt* to decree, enact.

décrire *vt* to describe.

décroître *vi* to decrease, diminish.

déçu *adj* disappointed.

dédaigner *vt to* disdain, scorn.

dédaigneux *adj* disdainful, scornful.

dedans *adv* inside, indoors:—*m* inside:—**au ~ inside**.

dédier *vt* to consecrate, dedicate to.

dédommager *vt* to compensate, indemnify.

déduction *f* deduction.

déduire *vt* to deduct; to deduce.

défaire *vt* to undo, dismantle.

défaite *m* defeat, overthrow.

défaut *m* defect, fault.

défavorable *adj* unfavourable.

défection *f* defection.

défectueux *adj* defective, faulty.
défendeur *m*, **-deresse** *f* defendant.
défendre *vt* to defend, protect; to prohibit.
défense *f* defence; prohibition.
défi *m* defiance; challenge.
déficience *f* deficiency.
déficit *m* deficit, shortfall.
défier *vt* to challenge, defy.
défiler *vi* to parade, march.
définir *vt* to define, specify.
définitif *adj* definitive, final.
définition *f* definition.
déformation *f* deformation, distortion.
déformer *vt* to deform.
défouler *vt* to unwind, relax.
défunt *m*, **-e** *f* deceased:—*adj* late, deceased.
dégagement *m* freeing, clearance.
dégager *vt* to free, clear:—**se ~** *vr* to free oneself.
dégât *m* havoc, damage.
dégel *m* thaw.
dégénérer *vi* to degenerate, decline.
dégoût *m* disgust, distaste.
dégradation *f* degradation, debasement.
dégrader *vt* to degrade, debase.
degré *m* degree; grade.
déguiser *vt* to disguise:—**se ~** *vr* to disguise oneself.
dégustation *f* tasting, sampling.
dehors *adv* outside, outdoors:—**en ~ de** outside; apart from:—*m* outside, exterior.
déjà *adv* already.
déjeuner *vi* to lunch:—*m* lunch.
delà *adv*:—**au ~ de** beyond:—**par ~** beyond.
délai *m* delay; respite; time limit.
délaisser *vt* to abandon, quit.
délasser *vt* to refresh, relax:—**se ~** *vr* to rest, relax.

délayer *vt* to thin; to drag out.
délectation *f* delectation, delight.
délégation *f* delegation.
délégué *m*, **-e** *f* delegate:—*adj* delegated.
déléguer *vt* to delegate.
délibéré *adj* deliberate; resolute.
délicat *adj* delicate, dainty.
délicieux *adj* delicious, delightful.
délimiter *vt* to delimit, demarcate.
délinquant *m*, **-e** *f* delinquent, offender:—*adj* delinquent.
délire *m* delirium, frenzy.
délirer *vi* to be delirious.
délit *m* offence, misdemeanour.
délivrer *vt* to deliver; to release.
déloyal *adj* disloyal, unfaithful.
delta *m* delta.
demain *adv* tomorrow.
demande *f* request, petition; question.
demander *vt* to ask, request:—**se ~** *vr* to wonder.
démaquiller *vt* to remove make-up.
démarche *f* bearing; gait, walk.
déménager *vi* to move house.
dément *adj* mad, insane, crazy.
démentir *vt* to deny, refute.
demeure *f* residence, dwelling place.
demeurer *vi* to live at, reside, stay.
demi *adj* half:—**à ~** halfway:—*m* half.
demi-cercle *m* semicircle.
demi-douzaine *f* half-dozen.
demi-heure *f* half hour.
demi-lune *f* half-moon.
démilitariser *vt* to demilitarise.
démission *f* resignation.
démissionner *vi* to resign.
démocrate *mf* democrat.
démocratie *f* democracy.
démocratique *adj* democratic.
démodé *adj* old-fashioned, out-of-date.

demoiselle *f* young lady.

démolir *vt* to demolish, knock down.

démolition *f* demolition.

démonstration *f* demonstration; proof.

démonter *vt* to dismantle, take down, dismount.

démontrer *vt* demonstrate; to prove.

démoraliser *vt* to demoralise.

déni *m* denial, refusal.

dénier *vt* to deny, disclaim.

dénigrer *vt* to denigrate, disparage.

dénombrer *vt* to number, enumerate.

dénomination *f* denomination, designation.

dénoncer *vt* to denounce; to inform against.

dénonciation *f* denunciation.

dénoyauter *vt* to stone (fruit).

dense *adj* dense, thick.

densité *f* density, denseness.

dent *f* tooth.

dentelle *f* lace.

dentifrice *m* toothpaste.

dentiste *mf* dentist.

dénuder *vt* to bare, denude.

dépanner *vt* to repair, fix.

dépanneur *m*, **-euse** *f* breakdown mechanic.

départ *m* departure; start.

département *m* department.

dépasser *vt* to exceed; to go past.

dépêcher *vt* to dispatch, send:—**se ~** *vr* to hurry, rush.

dépendant *adj* dependent.

dépendre *vi* to depend on, be dependent on.

dépenser *vt* to expend, spend:—**se ~** *vr* to exert oneself.

dépérir *vi* to decline, waste away.

dépit *m* spite; grudge:—**en ~ de** in spite of.

déplacement *m* displacement; removal.

déplacer *vt* to displace; to move:—**se ~** *vr* to change residence.

déplaire *vi* to displease; to offend.

déplaisant *adj* disagreeable, unpleasant.

déplorable *adj* deplorable, disgraceful.

déployer *vt* to deploy; to display.

déportation *f* deportation, transportation.

déporter *vt* to deport, transport.

déposer *vt* to lodge, deposit.

dépôt *m* deposit; warehouse.

dépouillement *m* scrutiny, perusal; despoiling.

dépréciation *f* depreciation.

déprécier *vt* to depreciate.

dépression *f* depression, slump; dejection.

déprimant *adj* depressing.

déprimer *vt* to depress; to discourage.

depuis *prép* since, from; after.

déraillement *m* derailment.

dérangement *m* derangement; inconvenience.

déranger *vt* to upset, unsettle.

déraper *vi* to skid, slip.

dérision *f* derision, mockery.

dérisoire *adj* derisory; pathetic.

dériver *vi* to drift.

dernier *adj* last; latest; back:—*m*, **-ière** *f* last one; latter.

dernièrement *adv* recently; lately.

dérober *vt* to steal; to hide:—**se ~** *vr* to steal away, escape.

déroger *vi* to derogate; to detract.

déroulement *m* unfolding; progress, development.

dérouler *vt* to unwind, uncoil:—**se ~** *vr* to develop; to unfold.

dérouter *vt* to rout, overthrow.

derrière *prép* behind:—*adv*:—**par ~**

by the back:—*m* bottom; back:—**de ~** back, rear.

des *art* = de les:—*see* **un, une**.

dès *prép* from, since:—**~ que** when; as soon as.

désaccord *m* disagreement, discord.

désaffecté *adj* disused.

désagréable *adj* disagreeable, unpleasant.

désagréger *vt* to separate:—**se ~** *vr* to become separated.

désagrément *m* displeasure, annoyance.

désapprobation *f* disapproval.

désapprouver *vt* to disapprove, object.

désarmement *m* disarmament.

désarroi *m* disarray, confusion.

désastre *m* disaster.

désavantage *m* disadvantage; prejudice.

désavantager *vt* to disadvantage, handicap.

descendant *m*, **-e** *f* descendant.

descendre *vi* to descend, go down:—*vt* to take down.

descente *f* descent, way down.

descriptif *adj* descriptive, explanatory.

description *f* description.

désenchantement *m* disenchantment; disillusion.

déséquilibré *adj* unbalanced, unhinged.

désert *m* desert, wilderness:—*adj* deserted.

déserter *vt* to desert.

désespéré *adj* desperate, hopeless.

désespérer *vi* to despair, give up hope.

désespoir *m* despair, despondency.

déshabiller *vt* to undress:—**se ~** *vr* to undress.

déshériter *vt* to disinherit.

désignation *f* designation, nomination; name.

désigner *vt* to designate, indicate.

désillusionner *vt* to disillusion; to disappoint.

désinfectant *m* disinfectant:—*adj* disinfectant.

désintégration *f* disintegration.

désintégrer *vt* to split, break up:—**se ~** *vr* to disintegrate.

désintéressé *adj* disinterested, unselfish.

désir *m* desire, wish, longing.

désirable *adj* desirable.

désirer *vt* to desire, wish, long.

désobéir *vi* to disobey.

désolation *f* desolation; ruin; grief.

désolé *adj* desolate; disconsolate, grieved.

désordonné *adj* untidy; inordinate; reckless.

désordre *m* disorder, confusion, disturbance.

désorienté *adj* disorientated.

désormais *adv* from now on, henceforth.

dessécher *vt* to dry, parch:—**se ~** *vr* to dry out.

dessein *m* design, plan, scheme:—**à ~** intentionally.

desserrer *vt* to unscrew:—**se ~** *vr* to work loose.

dessert *m* dessert, sweet.

dessin *m* drawing, sketch; draft.

dessiner *vt* to draw, sketch; to design.

dessous *adv* under, beneath:—*m* underside, bottom.

dessus *adv* over, above:—*m* **~** top.

destin *m* destiny, fate, doom.

destinataire *mf* addressee, consignee.

destination *f* destination; purpose.

destiner *vt* to determine; to intend, destine, aim.

destruction *f* destruction.

détachable *adj* detachable.

détachement *m* detachment, indifference.

détacher *vt* to detach, unfasten.

détail *m* detail, particular.

détaillant *m*, **-e** *f* retailer.

détailler *vt* to detail; to sell retail.

détecter *vt* to detect.

détecteur *m* detector.

détection *f* detection.

détective *m* detective.

détendre *vt* to release, loosen.

détenir *vt* to detain; to hold.

détente *f* relaxation, easing.

détérioration *f* deterioration.

détériorer *vt* to damage, impair:—**se ~** *vr* to deteriorate, worsen.

détermination *f* determination; resolution.

déterminer *vt* to determine, decide.

détestable *adj* detestable, odious.

détester *vt* to detest, hate.

détonation *f* detonation, explosion.

détour *m* detour; curve; evasion.

détournement *m* diversion, rerouting.

détourner *vt* to divert, reroute.

détresse *f* distress, trouble.

detruire *vt* to destroy, demolish.

dette *f* debt.

deuil *m* mourning, bereavement, grief.

deux *adj* two:—*m* two:—**en moins de ~** in a jiffy.

deuxième *adj* second:—*mf* second.

dévaliser *vt* to burgle; to rifle.

dévaloriser *vt* to depreciate, reduce the value of.

dévaluation *f* devaluation.

devancer *vt* to outstrip, outrun; to precede.

devant *prép* in front of, before:—*adv* in front:—*m* front.

devanture *f* display; shop-front.

développement *m* development; growth; progress.

développer *vt* to develop, expand:—**se ~** *vr* to develop, grow.

devenir *vi* to become, grow.

dévêtir *vt* to undress:—**se ~** *vr* to get undressed.

déviation *f* deviation; diversion.

deviner *vt* to guess; to solve; to foretell.

devise *f* currency.

dévisser *vt* to unscrew, undo.

devoir *m* duty; homework:—*vt* to owe; to have to.

dévorer *vt* to devour, consume.

dévotion *f* devotion, piety.

dextérité *f* dexterity, adroitness.

diabétique *adj* diabetic.

diable *m* devil.

diagnostic *m* diagnosis.

diagnostiquer *vt* to diagnose.

diagonale *f* diagonal.

diagramme *m* diagram; graph.

dialecte *m* dialect.

dialogue *m* dialogue, conversation.

diamant *m* diamond.

diamètre *m* diameter.

dictateur *m*, **-trice** *f* dictator.

dictée *f* dictating; dictation.

dictionnaire *m* dictionary.

diesel *m* diesel.

diète *f* diet.

diététicien *m*, **-ienne** *f* dietician.

dieu *m* god.

diffamer *vt* to defame, slander.

différence *f* difference.

différencier *vt* to differentiate.

différent *adj* different; various.

différer *vt* to differ; to vary.

difficile *adj* difficult; awkward, tricky.

difficulté *f* difficulty; problem.

diffuser *vt* to diffuse, circulate, broadcast.

digérer *vt* to digest.

digestion *f* digestion.

digne *adj* worthy; dignified.

dignité *f* dignity.

dilapider *vt* to squander; to embezzle.

dilemme *m* dilemma.

diluer *vt* to dilute.

dimanche *m* Sunday.

dimension *f* dimension, size.

diminuer *vt* to diminish, reduce:—*vi* to diminish, lessen.

diminutif *m* diminutive.

diminution *f* reduction, lessening.

dîner *vi* to dine:—*m* dinner.

diocèse *m* diocese.

diplomate *m* diplomat.

diplomatie *f* diplomacy.

diplomatique *adj* diplomatic.

diplôme *m* diploma, certificate.

dire *vt* to say; to tell:—**se ~** to say to oneself; to call oneself:—*vr* **se ~ que** to be said that.

direct *adj* direct:—*m* express.

directeur *m*, **-trice** *f* director.

direction *f* direction, management.

diriger *vt* to run, direct:—**se ~** *vr*:—**se ~ vers** to head for, make for.

discerner *vt* to discern, distinguish.

disciple *m* disciple.

discipline *f* discipline.

discorde *f* discord, dissension.

discothèque *f* discotheque.

discours *m* speech, talking.

discréditer *vt* to discredit.

discret *adj* discreet.

discrétion *f* discretion, prudence.

discrimination *f* discrimination.

discriminer *vt* to distinguish; to discriminate.

disculper *vt* to excuse, exonerate.

discussion *f* discussion, debate.

discuter *vi*, *vt* to discuss, debate.

disgrâce *f* disgrace.

disparaître *vi* to disappear, vanish.

disparité *f* disparity, incongruity.

disparition *f* disappearance; death; extinction.

dispenser *vt* to dispense, exempt.

dispersion *f* dispersal, scattering.

disponible *adj* available; transferable.

disposer *vt* to arrange, dispose.

dispositif *m* device, mechanism.

disposition *f* arrangement, layout.

dispute *f* dispute, argument.

disque *m* disk; record.

disquette *f* diskette.

dissertation *f* dissertation.

dissidence *f* dissidence, dissent.

dissident *adj* dissident.

dissimuler *vt* to dissemble, conceal.

dissipation *f* dissipation, waste.

dissiper *vt* to dispel; to dissipate.

dissolution *f* dissolution.

dissoudre *vt* to dissolve.

dissuader *vt* to dissuade.

distance *f* distance, interval.

distant *adj* distant.

distiller *vt* to distil.

distillerie *f* distillery.

distinct *adj* distinct, different.

distinction *f* distinction.

distingué *adj* distinguished.

distinguer *vt* to distinguish; to discern.

distraire *vt* to distract; to amuse:—**se ~** *vr* to enjoy oneself.

distrait *adj* inattentive, absentminded.

distribuer *vt* to distribute.

distribution *f* distribution.

district *m* district.

divaguer *vi* to ramble, rave.

divergence *f* divergence.

diverger *vi* to diverge, differ.
divers *adj* diverse, varied.
diversification *f* diversification.
diversifier *vt* to vary, diversify:—**se ~** *vr* to diversify.
diversité *f* diversity, variety.
divertir *vt* to amuse, entertain:—**se ~** *vr* to amuse oneself.
divertissant *adj* amusing, entertaining.
divin *adj* divine, exquisite.
divinité *f* divinity.
diviser *vt* to divide, split.
division *f* division.
divorce *m* divorce.
divorcer *vi* to get divorced.
dix *adj, m* ten.
dix-huit *adj, m* eighteen.
dix-huitième *adj, mf* eighteenth.
dix-neuf *adj, m* nineteen.
dix-neuvième *adj, mf* nineteenth.
dix-sept *adj, m* seventeen.
dix-septième *adj, mf* seventeenth.
dixième *adj, mf* tenth.
docile *adj* docile, submissive.
docteur *m* doctor.
doctrine *f* doctrine.
document *m* document.
documentaire *adj* documentary.
documentation *f* documentation; information.
documenter *vt* to document.
dogmatique *adj* dogmatic.
doigt *m* finger.
doigté *m* touch; fingering technique.
domaine *m* domain, estate; sphere.
domestique *adj* domestic, household.
domestiquer *vt* to domesticate, tame.
domicile *m* domicile, address.
dominant *adj* dominant, prevailing.
domination *f* domination; to dominion.

dominer *vt* to dominate; to prevail:—**se ~** to control oneself.
dommage *m* damage; harm:—**c'est ~** it's a pity.
dompter *vt* to tame, train.
don *m* gift; talent.
donation *f* donation.
donc *conj* so, therefore, thus:—**pourquoi ~?** why was that?.
donné *adj* given; fixed:—**étant ~** seeing that, in view of.
donnée *f* datum.
donner *vt* to give:—*vi* to knock, beat.
donneur *m*, **-euse** *f* giver, donor; dealer.
dont *pron* whose, of which.
dormir *vi* to sleep, be asleep; to be still.
dortoir *m* dormitory.
dos *m* back; top; ridge.
dose *f* dose; amount; quantity.
dossier *m* dossier, file; case.
douane *f* customs.
douanier *adj* custom(s).
double *adj* double, duplicate, dual:—*m* copy, double.
doubler *vt vi* to double, duplicate.
douceur *f* softness, gentleness.
douche *f* shower.
doucher (se) *vr* to take a shower.
doué *adj* gifted, endowed with.
douleur *f* pain, ache; anguish.
douloureux *adj* painful, grievous.
doute *m* doubt, misgiving:—**sans ~** without doubt.
douter *vi* to doubt, question:—**se ~ que** to suspect that, expect that.
douteux *adj* doubtful, dubious.
doux *adj* (*f* **douce**) soft; sweet; mild.
douzaine *f* dozen.
douze *adj m* twelve.
douzième *adj* twelfth:—*mf* twelfth.

dragon *m* dragon.
dramatique *adj* dramatic.
dramaturge *mf* playwright.
drame *m* drama.
drap *m* sheet.
drapeau *m* flag.
drogue *f* drug.
drogué(e) *m(f)* drug addict:—*adj* drugged.
droguer *vt* to drug, administer drugs.
droit *adj* right; straight; sound; honest:—*adv* straight, straight ahead:—*m* right; law; tax.
droite *f* right side; right (wing); straight line.
droitier *adj* right-handed.
drôle *adj* funny, amusing; peculiar.
du *art* of the.
dû *adj* owed; due:—**~ment** *adv* duly.
dubitatif *adj* doubtful, dubious.

duc *m* duke, **duchesse** *f* duchess.
dune *f* dune.
duo *m* duo; duet.
duper *vt* to dupe, take in.
dupliquer *vt* to duplicate.
dur *adj* hard, tough; difficult.
durable *adj* durable, lasting.
durant *prép* during, for.
durcir *vt vi* to harden:—**se ~** *vr* to become hardened.
durée *f* duration, length.
durer *vi* to last.
duvet *m* down.
dynamique *f* dynamic; dynamics:—*adj* dynamic.
dynamite *f* dynamite.
dynamo *f* dynamo.
dynastie *f* dynasty.
dyslexie *f* dyslexia.
dyslexique *adj* dyslexic.

E

eau *f* water; rain.
eau-de-vie *f* brandy.
éblouir *vt* to dazzle; to fascinate.
ébriété *f* intoxication.
écart *m* distance; interval; discrepancy.
écarter *vt* to separate; to avert; to dismiss.
ecclésiastique *adj* ecclesiastical:—*m* ecclesiastic, clergyman.
échange *m* exchange, barter, trade.
échanger *vt* to exchange.
échantillon *m* sample.
échappement *m* exhaust; release.
échapper *vi* to escape, avoid, elude.
écharpe *f* scarf; arm-sling.

échauffer *vt* to heat, overheat; to excite.
échec *m* failure, defeat.
échelle *f* ladder; scale.
échelonner *vt* to grade; to stagger, set at intervals.
échine *f* backbone, spine.
écho *m* echo; rumour.
échoir *vi* to fall due; to befall.
éclair *m* flash; lightning flash; spark.
éclairage *m* lighting, light.
éclaircir *vt* to lighten, brighten up.
éclairer *vt* to light; clarify, explain.
éclat *m* brightness; splendour.
éclatement *m* explosion, bursting, rupture.

éclipse *f* eclipse.

éclipser *vt* to eclipse, overshadow.

écœurer *vt* to nauseate, disgust.

école *f* school, schooling; sect, doctrine.

écolier *m* schoolgirl, **-ière** *f* schoolgirl.

écologie *f* ecology.

écologiste *mf* ecologist.

économe *adj* thrifty.

économie *f* economy, thrift; economics.

économique *adj* economic.

économiser *vt* to economise, save.

Écossais *m* Scotsman, **-e** *f* Scotswoman.

écossais *adj* Scottish.

Écosse *f* Scotland.

écoulement *m* flow, discharge, outlet.

écouler *vt* to flow, discharge; to sell.

écouter *vt* to listen to, hear.

écran *m* screen.

écraser *vt* to crush; to run over:—**s'~** *vr* to crash.

écrire *vt* to write; to spell.

écriture *f* writing; handwriting; script.

écrivain *m* writer.

écrouler (s') *vr* to collapse, crumble.

écume *f* foam, froth; scum.

écureuil *m* squirrel.

édifice *m* edifice, building.

édifier *vt* to build, construct; to edify.

éditer *vt* to publish, produce; to edit.

éditeur *m* **-trice** *f* publisher; editor.

éducation *f* education; upbringing.

éduquer *vt* to educate; to bring up, raise.

effacer *vt* to efface, erase, wipe off.

effaroucher *vt* to frighten; to shock.

effectif *m* staff; size, complement:— *adj* effective, positive.

effectuer *vt* to effect, execute, carry out.

effet *m* effect; bill, note.

efficace *adj* effective; efficient.

efficacité *f* effectiveness, efficiency.

efforcer (s') *vr* to endeavour, do one's best.

effort *m* effort, exertion; stress, strain.

effrayer *vt* to frighten, scare.

effroi *m* terror, dismay.

effronté *adj* shameless, impudent, cheeky.

effroyable *adj* horrifying, appalling.

égal *adj* equal; even, level; equable.

égaler *vt* to equal, match.

égaliser *vt* to equalise; to level out.

égalité *f* equality; equableness; evenness.

égard *m* consideration, respect:—**à l'~ de** concerning, regarding.

égarer *vt* to mislead, lead astray:—**s'~** *vr* to get lost.

église *f* church.

égoïsme *m* selfishness, egoism.

égoïste *mf* egotist:—*adj* egotistic.

éjecter *vt* to eject, throw out.

élaborer *vt* to elaborate, develop.

élan *m* surge, momentum, speed; spirit, elan.

élargir *vt* to widen, stretch:—**s'~** *vr* to get wider.

élastique *adj* elastic; flexible:—*m* elastic, elastic band.

élection *f* election; choice.

électorat *m* electorate; constituency; franchise.

électricité *f* electricity.

électrique *adj* electric.

électroménager *m* household appliance.

élégance *f* elegance, stylishness.

élégant *adj* elegant, stylish.

élémentaire *adj* elementary; basic.

éléphant *m* elephant.

élève *mf* pupil, student.

élever *vt* to bring up, raise:—**s'~** *vr* to rise, go up.

éligible *adj* eligible.

élimination *f* elimination.

éliminer *vt* to eliminate, discard.

élire *vt* to elect.

élite *f* elite.

elle *pron* she; it; her:—**~même** herself.

élocution *f* elocution, diction.

éloigné *adj* distant, remote.

éloigner *vt* to move away:—**s'~** *vr* to go away.

éloquent *adj* eloquent.

émancipation *f* emancipation, liberation.

émanciper *vt* to emancipate:—**s'~** *vr* to become emancipated.

emballer *vt* to pack up, wrap up.

embarcation *f* boat, craft.

embargo *m* embargo.

embarquer *vt* to embark:—*vi* to embark.

embarras *m* embarrassment, confusion; trouble.

embarrasser *vt* to embarrass; to hamper.

embaucher *vt* to take on, hire.

embellir *vt* to beautify, make more attractive.

emblème *m* symbol, emblem.

embouteillage *m* traffic jam; bottling.

embrasser *vt* to kiss, embrace.

embrayage *m* clutch.

embryon *m* embryo.

embuscade *f* ambush.

émerger *vi* to emerge; to stand out.

émerveiller *vt* to astonish, amaze:—**s'~** *vr* to marvel at.

émettre *vt* to send out, emit, transmit.

émeute *f* riot.

émigration *f* emigration.

émigrer *vi* to emigrate.

éminent *adj* eminent, distinguished.

émission *f* sending out; transmission; broadcast; emission.

emménager *vi* to move in.

emmener *vt* to take away; to lead.

émoi *m* agitation, emotion.

émotion *f* emotion; commotion.

émouvoir *vt* to move, upset:—**s'~** *vr* to be moved.

empaqueter *vt* to parcel up, pack.

emparer (s') *vr* to seize, grab; to take possession of.

empêcher *vt* to prevent, stop.

empereur *m* emperor.

empiler *vt* to pile up, stack.

empire *m* empire; influence, ascendancy.

empirer *vi* to get worse, deteriorate.

emplacement *m* site, location.

emploi *m* use; job, employment.

employé *m*, **-e** *f* employee.

employer *vt* to use, spend; to employ.

employeur *m*, **euse** *f* employer.

empoisonner *vt* to poison.

emporter *vt* to take; to carry off.

emprisonner *vt* to imprison, trap.

emprunter *vt* to borrow; to assume; to derive.

ému *adj* moved, touched, excited.

en *prép* in; to; by; on:—**~ tant que** as:—*pn* from there; of it, of them:—**je n'~ veux plus** I don't want any more.

encadrer *vt* to frame; to train; to surround.

encaisser *vt* to collect, receive; to cash.

enceinte *f* pregnant.

encercler *vt* to encircle, surround.

enchaînement *m* linking; link; sequence.

enchaîner *vt* to chain.

enchanté *adj* enchanted, delighted.

enchanter *vt* to enchant, delight.

enclave *f* enclave.

encombrer *vt* to clutter, obstruct.

encore *adv* still; only; again; more:—**~ que** even though.

encouragement *m* encouragement.

encourager *vt* to encourage; to incite.

encre *f* ink.

encyclopédie *f* encyclopaedia.

endetter (s') *vr* to get into debt.

endommager *vt* to damage.

endormir *vt* to put to sleep:—**s'~** *vr* to fall asleep.

endosser *vt* to put on; to shoulder; to endorse.

endroit *m* place.

enduit *m* coating.

endurance *f* endurance, stamina.

endurcir *vt* to harden:—**s'~** *vr* to become hardened.

endurer *vt* to endure, bear.

énergie *f* energy; spirit, vigour.

énergique *adj* energetic, vigorous.

énerver *vt* to irritate, annoy:—**s'~** *vr* to get worked up.

enfance *f* childhood; infancy.

enfant *mf* child; native.

enfer *m* hell.

enfermer *vt* to lock up; to confine.

enfin *adv* at last; in short; after all.

enflammer *vt* to set on fire:—**s'~** *vr* to ignite.

enfler *vi* to swell up, inflate.

enfuir (s') *vr* to run away, flee.

engagement *m* agreement, commitment.

engager *vt* to bind; to involve:—**s'~** *vr* to undertake to.

engin *m* machine; instrument; contraption.

engouffrer *vt* to engulf.

engourdi *adj* numb; dull.

engraisser *vi* to get fatter.

énigme *f* enigma, riddle.

enivrer *vt* to intoxicate, make drunk:—**s'~** *vr* to get drunk.

enlever *vt* to remove; to abduct.

enneigé *adj* snowy, snowbound.

ennemi(e) *m(f)* enemy.

ennui *m* boredom, tedium, weariness.

ennuyer *vt* to bore, bother:—**s'~** *vr* to get bored.

énorme *adj* enormous, huge.

enquête *f* inquiry, investigation; survey.

enquêter *vi* to hold an inquiry; to investigate.

enraciner *vt* to implant, root.

enregistrer *vt* to record; to register.

enrichir *vt* to enrich, expand:—**s'~** *vr* to get rich.

enrober *vt* to wrap, cover, coat.

enrôler *vt* to enlist, enrol.

enrouler *vt* to roll up, wind up.

enseignant(e) *m(f)* teacher.

enseignement *m* education, training, instruction.

enseigner *vt* to teach.

ensemble *adv* together, at the same time:—*m* unity; whole.

ensoleillé *adj* sunny.

ensuite *adv* then, next, afterwards.

entasser *vt* to pile up, heap up.

entendement *m* understanding, comprehension.

entendre *vt* to hear; to intend, mean; to understand:—**s'~** *vr* to agree; to know how to.

entendu *adj* agreed:—**bien ~** of course.

enterrer *vt* to bury, inter.

entêté *adj* stubborn, obstinate.

enthousiasme *m* enthusiasm.

enthousiaste *adj* enthusiastic:—*mf* enthusiast.

entier *adj* entire, whole; intact.

entité *f* entity.

entourer vt to surround, frame, encircle:—vr:—**s'~ de** to surround oneself with.

entraider (s') vr to help one another.

entrain m spirit, liveliness.

entraîner vt to drag; to lead; to train:—**s'~** vr to train oneself.

entraîneur m trainer, coach.

entre prép between, among, into.

entrée f entry, entrance; insertion:—**d'~ de jeu** from the outset.

entremêler vt to intermingle, intermix.

entrepôt m warehouse, bonded warehouse.

entreprendre vt to embark upon, undertake.

entrepreneur m **-euse** f contractor; entrepreneur.

entreprise f company; venture, business.

entrer vi to enter, go in.

entretemps adv meanwhile.

entretenir vt to maintain, look after; to speak with.

entretien m upkeep, maintenance; conversation.

entrevue f meeting, interview.

énumérer vt to enumerate, list.

envahir vt to invade, overrun.

enveloppe f envelope; covering; exterior.

envelopper vt to envelop; to wrap up; to veil.

envers prép towards, to:—m:—**à l'~** inside out, upside down.

envie f desire, longing, inclination; envy.

envier vt to envy.

environ adv about, around:—**~s** mpl vicinity, neighbourhood.

environnement m environment.

environnemental adj environmental.

environner vt to surround, encircle.

envisager vt to view, envisage.

envoi m dispatch, remittance; kick-off.

envoyer vt to send, dispatch; hurl, fire.

épais adj thick; deep.

épaissir vi to thicken:—vt; **s'~** vr to get thicker.

épanouir vt to brighten; to open out:—**s'~** vr to bloom.

épargner vt to save; to spare.

épaule f shoulder.

épeler vt to spell.

éperdu adj distraught, overcome.

épice f spice.

épicier m, **-ière** f grocer.

épidémie f epidemic.

épier vt to spy on.

épine f spine; thorn; quill.

épingle f pin.

épiscopal adj episcopal.

épisode m episode.

épitaphe f epitaph.

éponge f sponge.

éponger vt to sponge, mop.

époque f time, epoch, age, period.

épouser vt to marry, wed; espouse.

épouvanter vt to terrify, appall.

époux m, **épouse** f spouse.

éprendre(s') vr to fall in love with.

épreuve f test; ordeal, trial; proof.

éprouver vt to feel, experience.

épuisement m exhaustion.

épuiser vt to exhaust, wear out.

épurer vt to purify, refine.

équateur m equator.

équation f equation.

équilibre m balance, equilibrium; harmony.

équilibrer vt to balance.

équipe f team, crew, gang, staff.

équipement *m* equipment; fitting out, fittings.

équiper *vt* to equip, fit out.

équitable *adj* equitable, fair.

équivalence *f* equivalence.

équivalent *adj* equivalent, same:—*m* equivalent.

équivoque *adj* equivocal, questionable.

ère *f* era.

érection *f* erection; establishment.

ergot *m* spur; lug.

ermite *m* hermit.

éroder *vt* to erode.

érotique *adj* erotic.

errer *vi* to wander, roam.

erreur *f* error, mistake, fault.

érudition *f* erudition, learning.

éruption *f* eruption.

escalade *f* climbing; escalation.

escalader *vt* to climb, scale.

escalier *m* stairs, steps.

escargot *m* snail.

esclavage *m* slavery, bondage.

esclave *mf* slave.

escompte *m* discount.

escompter *vt* to discount.

escorte *f* escort; retinue.

escorter *vt* to escort.

espace *m* space, interval.

espacer *vt* to space out.

espèce *f* sort, kind; species.

espérance *f* hope, expectation.

espérer *vt* to hope.

espion *m*, **-onne** *f* spy.

espionner *vt* to spy.

espoir *m* hope.

esprit *m* mind, intellect; spirit; wit.

esquisse *f* sketch, outline.

esquisser *vt* to sketch, outline.

esquiver *vt* to dodge; to shirk.

essai *m* test, trial; attempt; essay.

essayer *vt* to test, try, try on.

essence *f* petrol; essential oil.

essentiel *adj* essential, basic.

essieu *m* axle.

essuyer *vt* to wipe, mop:—**s'~** *vr* to wipe oneself.

est *m* east.

esthéticien(ne) *m(f)* beautician.

estimation *f* valuation; estimation, reckoning.

estimer *vt* to value, assess, estimate.

estival *adj* summer.

estivant *m*, **-e** *f* holidaymaker, summer visitor.

estomac *m* stomach.

et *conj* and.

établi *adj* established:—*m* workbench.

établir *vt* to establish **s'~** *vr* to become established.

établissement *m* establishing, building; establishment.

étage *m* floor, storey; stage, level.

étanche *adj* waterproof.

étang *m* pond.

étape *f* stage, leg; staging point.

état *m* state, condition; statement.

étayer *vt* to prop up, support.

été *m* summer.

éteindre *vt* to put out, extinguish.

étendre *vt* to spread, extend:—**s'~** *vr* to spread; to stretch out.

étendue *f* expanse, area; duration.

éternel *adj* eternal, everlasting.

éternité *f* eternity; ages.

éternuer *vi* to sneeze.

éthnique *adj* ethnic.

ethnologie *f* ethnology.

étinceler *vi* to sparkle, gleam.

étincelle *f* spark; gleam, glimmer.

étiquette *f* label, ticket; etiquette.

étoffe f material, fabric; stuff.
étoile f star.
étonnement m surprise, astonishment.
étonner vt to astonish, surprise:—**s'~** vr to be astonished.
étouffer vt to suffocate:—**s'~** vr to be suffocated, to swelter.
étourdi adj absentminded.
étourdir vt to stun, daze; to deafen.
étourdissement m blackout, dizzy spell.
étrange adj strange, funny.
étranger m, **-ère** f foreigner, stranger, alien:—adj foreign, strange, unknown.
étrangeté f strangeness, oddness.
étrangler vt to strangle, stifle:—**s'~** vr to strangle oneself, choke.
être vi to be:—**c'est-à-dire** namely, that is to say:—m being, person, soul.
étreindre vt to embrace, hug; to seize.
étroit adj narrow; strict.
étude f study; survey; office.
étudier vt to study, examine.
étymologie f etymology.
eu = p.p. **avoir** had.
eucalyptus m eucharist.
eucharistie f euphoria.
européen m, **-enne** f European:—adj European.
euthanasie f euthanasia.
eux pron they, them:—**c'est à ~** it's up to them; it's theirs:—**~mêmes** themselves.
évacuer vt to evacuate, clear.
évader (s') vr to escape.
évaluation f evaluation, appraisal.
évaluer vt to evaluate, appraise.
évanouir (s') vr to faint, pass out.
évanouissement m faint, blackout.
évaporation f evaporation.

évaporer (s') vr to evaporate.
évasion f escape; escapism.
éveiller vt to waken, arouse:—**s'~** vr to wake up.
événement m event, incident.
éventualité f eventuality, possibility.
éventuel adj possible.
évêque m bishop.
évidence f evidence, proof.
évident adj obvious, evident.
évier m sink.
éviter vt to avoid; to spare.
évoluer vi to evolve, develop.
évolution f evolution, development.
évoquer vt to evoke, recall.
exacerber vt to exacerbate, aggravate.
exact adj exact, accurate.
exagération f exaggeration.
exagéré adj exaggerated, excessive.
exagérer vt to exaggerate.
examen m examination, survey, investigation.
examiner vt to examine, survey.
exaspérer vt to exasperate.
excellent adj excellent.
exceller vi to excel.
excentrique adj eccentric.
excepté adj apart, aside:—prép except, but for.
exception f exception, derogation.
exceptionnel adj exceptional.
excès m excess, surplus.
excitant m stimulant:—adj exciting, stimulating.
exciter vt to excite, stimulate:—**s'~** vr to get excited.
exclamation f exclamation.
exclamer (s') vr to exclaim.
exclure vt to exclude, oust, expel.
exclusif adj exclusive.
exclusion f exclusion, suspension.

excursion *f* excursion, trip.

excuse *f* excuse, pretext.

excuser *vt* to excuse, forgive:—**s'~** *vr* to apologise for.

exécuter *vt* to execute, carry out, perform; to produce.

exécution *f* execution, carrying out, performance.

exemple *m* example, model, instance.

exercer *vt* to exercise, perform, fulfil:—**s'~** *vr* to practise.

exercice *m* exercise, practice, use; financial year.

exhaustif *adj* exhaustive.

exhiber *vt* to exhibit, show.

exhibition *f* exhibition, show; display.

exhorter *vt* to exhort, urge.

exiger *vt* to demand, require.

exiler *vt* to exile, banish:—**s'~** *vr* to go into exile.

existence *f* existence, life.

exister *vi* to exist; to be.

exonérer *vt* to exempt.

exotique *adj* exotic.

expansion *f* expansion, development.

expectative *f* expectation, hope.

expédier *vt* to send, dispatch; to dispose of.

expédition *f* dispatch; consignment.

expérience *f* experience; experiment.

expérimental *adj* experimental.

expérimentation *f* experimentation.

expérimenter *vt* to test; to experiment with.

expert *adj* expert, skilled in:—*m* expert; connoisseur; assessor.

expertise *f* expertise; expert appraisal.

explicatif *adj* explanatory.

explication *f* explanation, analysis.

explicite *adj* explicit.

expliquer *vt* to explain, account for; to analyse.

exploitation *f* working; exploitation; concern.

exploiter *vt* to work, exploit; run, operate.

explorer *vt* to explore.

exploser *vi* to explode.

explosion *f* explosion.

exportation *f* export, exportation.

exporter *vt* to export.

exposer *vt* to display; to expose.

exposition *f* display; exposition; exposure.

express *adj* fast:—*m* fast train.

expression *f* expression.

exprimer *vt* to express, voice:—**s'~** *vr* to express oneself.

expropriation *f* expropriation.

expulser *vt* to expel; to evict.

exquis *adj* exquisite.

extase *f* ecstasy; rapture.

extension *f* extension; stretching; expansion.

exténuer *vt* to exhaust:—**s'~** *vr* to exhaust oneself.

extérieur *m* exterior, outside:—*adj* outer, external, exterior.

exterminer *vt* to exterminate.

externe *adj* external, outer.

extinction *f* extinction, extinguishing.

extradition *f* extradition.

extraire *vt* to extract; to mine.

extraordinaire *adj* extraordinary.

extravagant *adj* extravagant, wild.

extraverti *m*, **-e** *f* extrovert:—*adj* extrovert.

extrême *adj* extreme.

extrémiste *mf, adj* extremist.

exubérance *f* exuberance.

exubérant *adj* exuberant.

F

fable *f* fable, story, tale.

fabricant *m*, -ante *f* manufacturer, maker.

fabrique *f* factory.

fabriquer *vt* to manufacture; to forge; to fabricate.

façade *f* façade, front.

face *f* face, side, surface, aspect:—en ~ opposite:—~ à facing.

fâcher *vt* to anger; to grieve:—se ~ *vr* to get angry.

fâcheux *adj* deplorable, regrettable.

facile *adj* easy; facile.

facilité *f* easiness, ease; ability; facility.

faciliter *vt* to make easier, facilitate.

façon *f* way, fashion; make; imitation:—de toute ~ at any rate.

façonner *vt* to shape, fashion.

facteur *m* postman.

facture *f* bill, invoice; construction, technique.

facturer *vt* to invoice, charge for.

faculté *f* faculty; power, ability; right.

fade *adj* insipid, bland, dull.

faible *adj* weak, feeble; slight, poor.

faiblesse *f* weakness, feebleness, faintness.

faillir *vi* to come close to; to fail:—j'ai failli tomber I almost fell.

faim *f* hunger; appetite; famine.

faire *vt* to do; to make:—rien à ~! nothing doing!:—s'en ~ to worry.

faisable *adj* feasible.

fait *m* event; fact; act.

falaise *f* cliff.

falloir *vi* to be necessary:—il faut que tu partes you must leave.

falsifier *vt* to falsify, alter.

familial *adj* family, domestic.

familiariser *vt* to familiarise:—se ~ *vr* to familiarise oneself.

familiarité *f* familiarity.

familier *adj* familiar; colloquial; informal.

famille *f* family.

famine *f* famine.

fanatique *adj* fanatic:—*mf* fanatic.

faner *vt* to fade:—se ~ *vr* to wither, fade.

fantaisie *f* whim, extravagance; imagination.

fantastique *adj* fantastic.

fantôme *m* ghost, phantom.

farce *f* joke, prank; farce.

farcir *vt* to stuff, cram.

fardeau *m* load, burden.

farine *f* flour.

farouche *adj* shy, timid; unsociable.

fascination *f* fascination.

fasciner *vt* to fascinate, bewitch.

fasciste *mf, adj* fascist.

fastidieux *adj* tedious, boring.

fatal *adj* fatal, deadly; fateful.

fatalité *f* fatality; inevitability.

fatigue *f* fatigue, tiredness.

fatiguer *vt* to tire; to overwork, strain:—se ~ *vr* to get tired.

faubourg *m* suburb.

faune *f* wildlife, fauna.

faussaire *mf* forger.

fausser *vt* to distort, alter; to warp.

faute f mistake, foul, fault:—**~ de mieux** for lack of anything better.

fauteuil m armchair.

fautif m, **-ive** f culprit:—adj at fault.

faux adj false, forged, fake; wrong; bogus.

faux-semblant m sham, pretence.

faveur f favour.

favorable adj favourable, sympathetic.

favori m, **-ite** f favourite:—adj favourite.

favoriser vt to favour, further.

fécond adj fertile; prolific, fruitful; creative.

féconder vt to impregnate; to fertilise, pollinate.

fédéral adj federal.

fédération f federation.

feindre vt to feign, pretend.

fêlé adj cracked, hare-brained.

félicitation f congratulation.

féliciter vt to congratulate.

femelle f female.

féminin adj feminine, female.

féministe mf adj feminist.

féminité f femininity.

femme f woman; wife.

fendre vt to split, cleave, crack:—**se ~** vr to crack.

fenêtre f window.

fente f crack, fissure; slot.

fer m iron, point, blade:—**~ à cheval** horseshoe.

férié adj holiday.

ferme adj firm, steady; definite:—f farm.

ferment m ferment, leaven.

fermentation f fermentation, fermenting.

fermer vt to close; block; turn off:—

se ~ vr to close, shut up; to close one's mind to.

fermeté f firmness, steadiness.

fermier m, **-ière** f farmer.

féroce adj ferocious, savage.

férocité f ferocity, fierceness.

ferroviaire adj railway.

fertile adj fertile, productive.

fertilité f fertility.

fervent adj fervent, ardent.

festin m feast.

festival m festival.

fête f feast, holiday.

fêter vt to celebrate, fête.

feu m fire; light; hearth:—**en ~** on fire.

feuille f leaf.

feuilleter vt to leaf through.

fiable adj reliable; dependable.

fiancer (se) vr to become engaged.

fiasco m fiasco.

fibre f fibre.

ficelle f string; stick (bread).

fiche f card; sheet; certificate.

ficher vt to file, put on file.

fictif adj fictitious; imaginary.

fiction f imagination, fiction.

fidèle adj faithful, loyal.

fidélité f fidelity, loyalty.

fier adj proud, haughty; noble.

fier (se) vr to trust, rely on.

fierté f pride; arrogance.

fièvre f fever, temperature; excitement.

figuratif adj figurative, representational.

figure f face; figure; illustration, diagram.

figurer vt to represent:—vi to appear, feature:—**se ~** vr to imagine.

fil m thread; wire; cord:—**~ de fer** wire.

file *f* line, queue:—**à la ~** in line, in succession.

filer *vt* to spin.

filière *f* path; procedures; network.

fille *f* daughter, girl.

fillette *f* (small) girl.

film *m* film, picture.

filmer *vt* to film.

fils *m* son.

filtre *m* filter.

fin *f* end, finish:—*adj* thin, fine; delicate.

final *adj* final.

finance *f* finance.

financer *vt* to finance.

financier *m*, **-ière** *f* financier.

finesse *f* fineness; neatness.

fini *adj* finished, over, complete.

finir *vt* to finish, complete:—*vi* to finish, end; to die.

fissure *f* crack, fissure.

fixe *adj* fixed, permanent, set:—**~ment** *adv* fixedly, steadily.

fixer *vt* to fix; to arrange.

flacon *m* bottle, flask.

flagrant *adj* flagrant, blatant.

flair *m* sense of smell, nose; intuition.

flambeau *m* torch; candlestick.

flamme *f* flame; fervour; ardour.

flanc *m* flank, side.

flâner *vi* to stroll; to lounge about.

flatter *vt* to flatter, gratify.

flatterie *f* flattery.

flèche *f* arrow.

fléchir *vi* to bend, yield, weaken:—*vt* to bend, sway.

fleur *f* flower.

fleurir *vi* to blossom, flower:—*vt* to decorate with flowers.

e *m* river.

lité *f* flexibility.

flexible *adj* flexible, pliant.

flocon *m* fleck, flake.

flore *f* flora.

flot *m* stream, flood; floodtide; wave.

flotte *f* fleet; rain.

flotter *vi* to float; to drift; to wander; to waver.

fluctuation *f* fluctuation.

fluide *adj* fluid, flowing.

flux *m* flood; flow; flux.

foi *f* faith, trust.

foie *m* liver.

foin *m* hay.

foire *f* fair, trade fair.

fois *f* time, occasion.

folie *f* madness, insanity; extravagance.

foncé *adj* dark, deep (colours).

fonction *f* post, duty; function.

fonctionnaire *mf* civil servant.

fonctionner *vi* to work, function, operate.

fond *m* bottom, back:—**au ~** basically, in fact:—**à ~** thoroughly, in depth.

fondamental *adj* fundamental, basic.

fondamentaliste *mf*:—*adj* fundamentalist.

fondateur *m*, **-trice** *f* founder.

fondation *f* foundation.

fonder *vt* to found; to base.

fondre *vi* to melt:—*vt* to melt; to cast.

fonds *m* business; fund; money; stock.

fontaine *f* fountain, spring.

football *m* football, soccer.

force *f* strength, force, violence, energy.

forcé *adj* forced; emergency:—**~ment** *adv* inevitably.

forcer *vt* to force:—*vi* to overdo:—**se ~** *vr* to force oneself to.

forêt *f* forest.

forger *vt* to forge, form, mould.

formalité *f* formality.

formation *f* formation; training.

forme *f* form, shape; mould; fitness.

formel *adj* definite, positive; formal.

former *vt* to form; to train:—**se ~** *vr* to form; to train oneself

formidable *adj* tremendous:—**~ment** *adv* tremendously.

formulaire *m* form.

formule *f* formula; phrase; system.

formuler *vt* to formulate; express.

fort *adj* strong; high; loud; pronounced:—*adv* loudly; greatly; most:—*m* fort; strong point, forte.

fortifier *vt* to fortify, strengthen:—**se ~** *vr* to grow stronger.

fortuit *adj* fortuitous, chance.

fortune *f* fortune, luck.

fosse *f* pit; grave.

fou *adj*, *f* **folle** mad, wild; tremendous; erratic.

foudre *f* lightning, thunderbolt.

foudroyer *vt* to strike (lightning).

fouiller *vt* to search, scour.

foulard *m* scarf.

foule *f* crowd; masses, heaps.

four *m* oven; furnace; fiasco.

fourgon *m* coach, wagon, van.

fourmi *f* ant.

fourmiller *vi* to swarm, teem.

fournir *vt* to supply, provide.

fournisseur *m*, **-euse** *f* purveyor, supplier.

fourrer *vt* to stuff; to line.

fourrure *f* coat, fur.

foyer *m* home; fireplace; focus.

fracas *m* crash; roar, din.

fraction *f* fraction, part.

fracture *f* fracture.

fragile *adj* fragile, delicate.

fragment *m* fragment.

fragmenter *vt* to break up:—**se ~** *vr* to fragment.

fraîcheur *f* freshness, coolness.

frais *mpl* expenses:—*adj*, *f* **fraîche** fresh, cool.

franc *adj*, *f* **franche** frank, open.

Français *m* Frenchman, **-e** *f* Frenchwoman.

français *adj* French:—*m* French.

France *f* France.

franchir *vt* to clear, get over, cross.

francophone *mf* French-speaker, *adj* French-speaking.

frange *f* fringe; threshold.

frapper *vt* to hit; to strike down:—*vi* to strike, knock.

fraternel *adj* fraternal.

fraternité *f* fraternity.

fraude *f* fraud, cheating.

frein *m* brake; check.

freiner *vi* to brake, slow down:—*vt* to slow down; to curb, check.

frémir *vi* to quiver, tremble.

frénétique *adj* frenetic.

fréquence *f* frequency.

fréquent *adj* frequent.

frère *m* brother.

friand *adj* partial to, fond of.

frigidaire *m* refrigerator.

frire *vt* to fry.

frisé *adj* curly, curly-haired.

frisson *m* shiver, shudder.

frissonner *vi* to shudder, tremble, shiver.

frite *f* chip.

frivole *adj* frivolous, shallow.

frivolité *f* frivolity.

froid *adj* cold, cool:—*m* cold; coolness; refrigeration.

froideur *f* coldness, chilliness.

fromage *m* cheese.
front *m* forehead; face; front.
frontière *f* border, frontier.
frotter *vt* to rub, scrape.
fructueux *adj* fruitful, profitable.
frugal *adj* frugal.
frugalité *f* frugality.
fruit *m* fruit, result.
frustration *f* frustration.
frustrer *vt* to frustrate, deprive.
fugitif *m*, **-ive** *f* fugitive:—*adj* fugitive, runaway.
fuir *vi* to avoid; to flee; to leak.
fuite *f* flight, escape; leak.
fumé *adj* smoked.
fumée *f* smoke; vapour.
fumer *vi* to smoke, steam, give off smoke:—*vt* to smoke.

fumeur *m*, **-euse** *f* smoker.
funérailles *fpl* funeral.
funéraire *adj* funeral, funerary.
fureur *f* fury; violence.
furieux *adj* furious, violent.
furtif *adj* furtive; stealthy.
fusée *f* rocket, missile.
fusil *m* rifle, gun.
fusiller *vt* to shoot.
fusion *f* fusion; melting; merger; blending.
fusionner *vt* to merge, combine.
futile *adj* futile.
futilité *f* futility.
futur *adj* future:—*m* intended, fiancé; future.
fuyard *m*, **-e** *f*:—*adj* runaway.

G

gâcher *vt* to mix; to waste.
gachette *f* trigger.
gadget *m* gadget; gimmick.
gage *m* security; pledge; proof.
gagnant *m*, **-e** *f* winner:—*adj* winning.
gagner *vt* to earn, to win:—*vi* to win.
gai *adj* cheerful, happy, gay.
gain *m* earnings; gain, profit, benefit; saving.
gala *m* official reception; gala.
galant *adj* gallant, courteous.
galaxie *f* galaxy.
galerie *f* gallery; tunnel.
galet *m* pebble.
Gallois *m* Welshman, **-e** *f* Welshwoman.

gallois *adj* Welsh:—*m* Welsh.
galop *m* gallop; canter.
galoper *vi* to gallop; to run wild.
gamin *m*, **-e** *f* kid, street urchin.
gamme *f* range; scale.
gant *m* glove.
gap *m* gap; difference, discrepancy.
garage *m* garage.
garagiste *mf* garage owner.
garantie *f* guarantee, surety.
garantir *vt* to guarantee, secure.
garçon *m* boy; assistant; waiter.
garde *f* custody; guard; surveillance:—*m* guard, warder.
garde-boue *m* mudguard.
garder *vt* to look after; to stay in; to keep on.

garde-robe *f* wardrobe.

gardien *m*, **-ienne** *f* guard, guardian, warden; protector.

gare *f* rail station; basin; depot.

gargouiller *vi* to gurgle; to rumble.

garnir *vt* to fit with; to trim, decorate.

garnison *f* (*mil*) garrison.

gaspiller *vt* to waste, squander.

gastronomie *f* gastronomy.

gâté *adj* ruined; spoiled.

gâteau *m* cake.

gâter *vt* to ruin; to spoil:—**se ~** *vr* to go bad, go off.

gauche *adj* left; awkward, clumsy:—*f* left; left wing.

gaucher *adj* left-handed.

gaz *m invar* gas; fizz; wind.

gazeux *adj* gaseous; fizzy.

gazon *m* lawn; turf.

géant *m* giant, **-e** *f* giantess.

gel *m* frost; gel.

geler *vi* to freeze, be frozen:—*vt* to freeze.

gémir *vi* to groan, moan.

gendarme *m* policeman; gendarme.

gendarmerie *f* police force, constabulary.

gêne *f* discomfort; trouble:—**être sans ~** to be inconsiderate.

généalogie *f* genealogy.

gêner *vt* to bother; to hinder; to make uneasy.

général *adj* general, broad; common:—*m* general.

généralisation *f* generalisation.

généraliser *vt* to generalise:—**se ~** *vr* to become widespread.

générateur *m* generator.

génération *f* generation.

générer *vt* to generate

généreux *adj* generous; noble; mag-

nanimous.

générosité *f* generosity; nobility; magnanimity.

génétique *adj* genetic.

génie *m* genius; spirit; genie.

genou *m* knee.

genre *m* kind, type; gender; genre.

gens *mpl* people, folk.

gentil *adj*, *f* **gentille** kind; good; pleasant.

géographie *f* geography.

géographique *adj* geographic.

géologie *f* geology.

géométrie *f* geometry.

géométrique *adj* geometric.

gérant *m*, **-e** *f* manager.

gérer *vt* to manage, administer.

germe *m* germ; seed.

geste *m* gesture; act, deed.

gesticuler *vi* to gesticulate.

gestion *f* management, administration.

ghetto *m* ghetto.

gicler *vi* to spurt, squirt.

gifler *vt* to slap, smack.

gilet *m* waistcoat.

girafe *f* giraffe.

gisement *m* deposit; mine; pool.

gîte *m* shelter; home; self-catering holiday cottage.

givre *m* frost, rime.

glace *f* ice; ice cream; mirror.

glacer *vt* to freeze; to chill; to glaze.

glaçon *m* icicle; ice cube.

glande *f* gland.

glaner *vt* to glean.

glissement *m* sliding; gliding; downturn, downswing.

glisser *vi* to slide, slip, skid.

global *adj* global, overall:—**~ement** *adv* globally.

globe *m* globe, sphere; earth.

gloire *f* glory; distinction; celebrity.

glorieux *adj* glorious.

glorifier *vt* to glory, honour:—**se ~** *vr* to glory in; to boast.

glossaire *m* glossary.

gluant *adj* sticky, gummy.

gobelet *m* beaker, tumbler.

golf *m* golf.

golfeur *m*, **-euse** *f* golfer.

gomme *f* gum; rubber, eraser.

gommer *vt* to rub out; to gum.

gonflable *adj* inflatable.

gonfler *vt* to pump up, inflate:—**se ~** *vr* to swell; to be puffed up.

gorge *f* throat.

gothique *m, adj* Gothic.

goudronner *vt* to tar.

goulu *adj* greedy, gluttonous.

goupille *f* pin.

gourde *f* gourd; flask.

gourmand *adj* greedy.

gourmet *m* gourmet.

goût *m* taste; liking; style.

goûter *vt* to taste; to appreciate:—*vi* to have a snack; to taste good:—*m* snack.

goutte *f* drop; gout.

gouvernail *m* rudder; helm.

gouvernement *m* government.

gouverner *vt* to govern, rule; to control; to steer.

grâce *f* grace;favour; mercy; pardon:—**~ à** thanks to.

gracieux *adj* gracious.

grade *m* rank; grade; degree.

graduel *adj* gradual; progressive.

graduer *vt* to step up; to graduate.

grain *m* grain, seed; bead.

graisse *f* grease, fat.

grammaire *f* grammar.

grammatical *adj* grammatical.

gramme *m* gram.

grand *adj* big; tall; great; leading:— **pas ~~chose** not up to much.

grand-mère *f* grandmother.

grand-parents *mpl* grandparents

grand-père *m* grandfather.

grandeur *f* size; greatness; magnitude.

grandir *vi* to grow bigger, increase: —*vt* to magnify; to exaggerate.

graphique *m* graph:—*adj* graphic.

gras *adj f* **grasse** fatty; fat; greasy; crude.

gratification *f* gratuity; bonus.

gratis *adv* free, gratis.

gratitude *f* gratitude, gratefulness.

gratuit *adj* free, gratuitous.

grave *adj* grave, solemn.

graver *vt* to engrave, imprint.

gravitation *f* gravitation.

gravité *f* gravity.

gravure *f* engraving, carving.

gré *m* liking, taste:—**au ~ de** depending on, at the mercy of:—**savoir ~** to be grateful.

greffer *vt* to transplant, graft.

grêle *f* hail.

grelotter *vi* to shiver.

grenier *m* attic, garret.

grenouille *f* frog.

grève *f* strike; shore.

griffe *f* claw.

griffer *vt* to scratch.

griffonner *vt* to scribble, jot down.

grillade *f* grill.

grille *f* railings; gate; grill.

grille-pain *m invar* toaster.

griller *vt* to toast, scorch; to put bars on:—*vi* to toast, grill.

grimace *f* grimace

grimper *vi* to climb up.
grippe *f* flu, influenza.
gris *adj* grey.
griser *vt* to intoxicate:—**se ~** *vr* to get drunk.
grogner *vi* to grumble, moan.
grommeler *vi* to mutter; to grumble:—*vt* to mutter.
gronder *vt* to scold:—*vi* to rumble, growl.
gros *adj*, *f* **grosse** big; fat; serious; coarse:—**en ~** in bulk:—*m* bulk; wholesale; fat man.
grossesse *f* pregnancy.
grosseur *f* thickness; weight; fatness.
grossir *vi* to get fatter; to swell, grow:—*vt* to magnify; to exaggerate.
grossiste *mf* wholesaler.
grotesque *adj* grotesque, ludicrous.
groupe *m* group; party; cluster.
grouper *vt* to group together; to bulk:—**se ~** *vr* to gather.
grue *f* crane.
guépard *m* cheetah.

guêpe *f* wasp.
guère *adv* hardly, scarcely.
guérir *vi* to get better; to heal:—*vt* to cure, heal:—**se ~** *vr* to get better; to recover from.
guérison *f* recovery; curing.
guerre *f* war; warfare.
guerrier *m*, **-ière** *f* warrior.
guetter *vt* to watch; to lie in wait for.
gueule *f* mouth; face; muzzle.
guichet *m* counter; ticket office, booking office.
guichetier *m*, **-ière** *f* counter clerk.
guide *m* guide.
guider *vt* to guide:—**se ~** *vr* to be guided by.
guidon *m* handlebars.
guillotine *f* guillotine.
guise *f* manner, way:—**en ~ de** by way of:—**à ta ~** as you please.
guitare *f* guitar.
guitariste *mf* guitarist.
gymnastique *f* gymnastics.
gynécologue, gynécologiste *mf* gynaecologist.

H

habile *adj* skilful, skilled.
habiliter *vt* to qualify; to authorise.
habiller *vt* to dress, clothe:—**s'~** *vr* to get dressed.
habitant(e) *m(f)* inhabitant; occupant; dweller.
habitation *f* dwelling; residence; house.
habiter *vi* to live:—*vt* to live in; to occupy.

habitude *f* habit, custom, routine.
habituel *adj* usual, customary.
habituer *vt* to accustom; to teach:—**s'~** *vr* to get used to.
hache *f* axe, hatchet.
haie *f* hedge.
haine *f* hatred.
haïr *vt* to hate, detest.
hâle *m* tan, sunburn.

haleine *f* breath, breathing.

haleter *vi* to pant, gasp for breath.

hall *m* hall, foyer.

halle *f* covered market; hall.

hallucination *f* hallucination.

halte *f* stop, break; stopping place.

hameçon *m* fish-hook.

hanche *f* hip; haunch.

handicap *m* handicap.

hanter *vt* to haunt.

harceler *vt* to harass; to pester; to plague.

hardi *adj* bold, daring; brazen.

hargne *f* spite.

haricot *m* bean.

harmonie *f* harmony; wind section.

harmoniser *vt* to harmonise:—**s'~** *vr* to be in harmony.

harpe *f* harp.

hasard *m* chance; accident; hazard; risk.

hasardeux *adj* hazardous, risky.

hâte *f* haste; impatience.

hâter *vt* to hasten; to quicken:—**se ~** *vr* to hurry.

hâtif *adj* precocious; early; hasty.

hausse *f* rise, increase.

hausser *vt* to raise; to heighten.

haut *adj* high, tall; upper; superior.

haut-parleur *m* loudspeaker.

hauteur *f* height; elevation; haughtiness; bearing.

hebdomadaire *adj*:—*m* weekly.

hélice *f* propeller; helix.

hélicoptère *m* helicopter.

hémisphère *m* hemisphere.

hémophile *adj* haemophiliac.

herbe *f* grass:—**en ~** under grass.

herboriste *mf* herbalist.

héréditaire *adj* hereditary.

hérédité *f* heredity; heritage; right of inheritance.

hérisser *vt* to bristle; to spike.

hérisson *m* hedgehog.

héritage *m* inheritance; heritage, legacy.

hériter *vi* to inherit.

héritier *m* heir, **-ière** *f* heiress.

hermétique *adj* hermetic.

hernie *f* hernia, rupture.

héroïne *f* heroine; heroin.

héroïque *adj* heroic.

héroïsme *m* heroism.

héros *m* hero.

hésitation *f* hesitation.

hésiter *vi* to hesitate.

hétérosexuel *adj* heterosexual.

heure *f* hour; time of day:—**de bonne ~** early.

heureux *adv* lucky; happy.

heurter *vt* to strike, hit; to jostle.

hibernation *f* hibernation.

hibou *m* owl.

hier *adv* yesterday.

hilarité *f* hilarity, laughter.

hippopotame *m* hippopotamus.

hirondelle *f* swallow.

hisser *vt* to hoist, haul up.

histoire *f* history; story; business:— **~ de dire** just to say.

historien *m*, **-ienne** *f* historian.

historique *adj* historic; historical.

hiver *m* winter.

hivernal *adj* winter; wintry.

hocher *vt* to nod; to shake one's head.

homard *m* lobster.

homicide *m* homicide

homme *m* man.

homogène *adj* homogeneous.

homologuer *vt* to ratify; to approve.

homosexuel(le) *m(f)* homosexual.

honnête *adj* honest; decent; honourable.

honnêteté *f* honesty, decency.

honneur *m* honour; integrity; credit:—**en l'~ de** in honour of.

honorable *adj* honourable; reputable.

honorer *vt* to honour; to esteem.

honte *f* shame, disgrace.

honteux *adj* shameful; disgraceful.

hôpital *m* hospital.

horaire *m* timetable:—*adj* hourly.

horizon *m* horizon.

horizontal *adj* horizontal.

horloge *f* clock.

hormone *f* hormone.

horreur *f* horror.

horrible *adj* horrible; dreadful.

horrifier *vt* to horrify.

hors *prép* outside; beyond; save; except.

hors-d'œuvre *m invar* hors d'œuvre, starter.

hospice *m* home, asylum; hospice.

hospitalier *adj* hospital; hospitable.

hospitaliser *vt* to hospitalise.

hospitalité *f* hospitality.

hostile *adj* hostile.

hostilité *f* hostility.

hôte *m*, **hôtesse** *f* host; landlord.

hôtel *m* hotel.

hôtelier *m*, **-ière** *f* hotelier:—*adj* hotel.

houle *f* swell.

huer *vt* to boo.

huile *f* oil; petroleum.

huit *adj, m* eight.

huitième *adj* eighth:—*mf* eighth.

huître *f* oyster.

humain *adj* human; humane:—*m* human.

humanitaire *adj* humanitarian.

humanité *f* humanity.

humble *adj* humble; modest.

humeur *f* mood, humour; temper.

humide *adj* humid.

humidité *f* humidity.

humilier *vt* to humiliate.

humilité *f* humility.

humour *m* humour.

hurler *vi*:—*vt* to roar, yell.

hutte *f* hut.

hybride *adj m* hybrid.

hydraulique *adj* hydraulic.

hygiène *f* hygienics; hygiene.

hygiénique *adj* hygienic.

hymne *m* hymn.

hypermarché *m* hypermarket.

hypnose *f* hypnosis

hypnotiser *vt* to hypnotise.

hypocondriaque *mf adj* hypochondriac.

hypocrisie *f* hypocrisy.

hypocrite *mf* hypocrite:—*adj* hypocritical.

hypothèque *f* mortgage.

hypothéquer *vt* to mortgage.

hypothèse *f* hypothesis; assumption.

hypothétique *adj* hypothetical.

hystérie *f* hysteria.

hystérique *mf* hysterical:—*adj* hysteric.

I

iceberg *m* iceberg.
idéal *adj:*—*m* ideal.
idée *f* idea.
identifier *vt* to identify:—**s'~** *vr* to identify with.
identique *adj* identical.
identité *f* identity; similarity.
idiot *m*, **-e** *f* idiot, fool:—*adj* idiotic, stupid.
ignorance *f* ignorance.
ignorant *adj* ignorant; unacquaint-ed; uninformed.
ignorer *vt* to be ignorant of; to be unaware of; to ignore.
il *pron* he, it.
île *f* island, isle.
illégal *adj* illegal; unlawful.
illégitime *adj* illegitimate; unwarranted.
illicite *adj* illicit.
illogique *adj* illogical.
illusion *f* illusion
illustration *f* illustration.
illustrer *vt* to illustrate.
image *f* image, picture; reflection.
imagination *f* imagination.
imaginer *vt* to imagine; to suppose.
imbécile *mf* idiot, imbecile:—*adj* stupid, idiotic.
imitation *f* imitation; mimicry; forgery.
imiter *vt* to imitate.
immatriculation *f* registration.
immédiat *adj* immediate; instant.
immense *adj* immense, boundless.
immeuble *m* building; block of flats; real estate.

immigrant *m*, **-e** *f* immigrant.
immigration *f* immigration.
imminent *adj* imminent, impending.
immobilier *adj* property:—*m* property business.
immobiliser *vt* to immobilise; to bring to a standstill.
immoral *adj* immoral.
immortel *adj* immortal.
immunité *f* immunity.
impair *adj* odd, uneven.
imparfait *adj* imperfect.
impartial *adj* impartial.
impartialité *f* impartiality.
impassible *adj* impassive.
impatience *f* impatience.
impatient *adj* impatient.
imperceptible *adj* imperceptible.
impersonnel *adj* impersonal.
impertinence *f* impertinence.
impertinent *adj* impertinent.
imperturbable *adj* unshakeable; imperturbable.
impétueux *adj* impetuous.
impitoyable *adj* merciless, pitiless.
implacable *adj* implacable.
implantation *f* implantation; establishment; introduction.
implanter *vt* to introduce; to establish; to implant.
implication *f* implication; involvement.
implicite *adj* implicit.
impliquer *vt* to imply; to necessitate; to implicate.
impoli *adj* impolite, rude.

impolitesse *f* impoliteness, rudeness.

importance *f* importance, significance; size.

important *adj* important, significant; sizeable.

importation *f* import, importation.

importer *vt* to import:—*vi* to matter:—**n'importe qui** anybody:—**n'importe quoi** anything.

imposer *vt* to impose, lay down.

impossibilité *f* impossibility.

impossible *adj* impossible.

impôt *m* tax, duty.

imprégner *vt* impregnate; to permeate; to imbue.

impression *f* feeling, impression.

impressioniste *mf*:—*adj* impressionist.

impressionner *vt* to impress; to upset.

imprévisible *adj* unforeseeable; unpredictable.

imprévu *adj* unforeseen, unexpected.

imprimer *vt* to print.

imprimeur *m* printer.

improbable *adj* improbable, unlikely.

improviser *vt* to improvise.

imprudent *adj* careless, imprudent.

impudence *f* impudence; shamelessness.

impuissant *adj* powerless, helpless.

impulsif *adj* impulsive.

inacceptable *adj* unacceptable.

inaccessible *adj* inaccessible.

inactif *adj* inactive, idle.

inactivité *f* inactivity.

inadmissible *adj* inadmissible.

inanimé *adj* inanimate; unconscious.

inaperçu *adj* unnoticed.

inattendu *adj* unexpected, unforeseen.

incapable *adj* incapable; incompetent.

incapacité *f* incompetence; disability.

incarcérer *vt* to incarcerate.

incendie *m* fire, blaze.

incertain *adj* uncertain, unsure.

incessant *adj* incessant, ceaseless.

incident *m* incident, point of law.

inciter *vt* to incite, urge.

inclure *vt* to include; to insert.

incommoder *vt* to disturb, bother.

incomparable *adj* incomparable.

incompatible *adj* incompatible.

incompréhensible *adj* incomprehensible.

inconfortable *adj* uncomfortable; awkward.

incongru *adj* unseemly; incongruous.

inconnu *m*, **-e** *f* stranger, unknown person:—*m* unknown:—*adj* unknown.

inconscience *f* unconsciousness; thoughtlessness.

inconscient *adj* unconscious; thoughtless, reckless:—*m* subconscious, unconscious.

inconsidéré *adj* inconsiderate; thoughtless.

incontestable *adj* incontestable, unquestionable.

inconvénient *m* drawback, inconvenience.

incorporer *vt* to incorporate, integrate.

incorrect *adj* faulty, incorrect.

incroyable *adj* incredible; unbelievable.

indécis *adj* indecisive; unsettled; undefined.

indéfini *adj* undefined; indefinite:—**~ment** *adv* indefinitely.

indemne *adj* unharmed, unhurt.

indemnité *f* compensation; indemnity.

indéniable *adj* undeniable, indisputable.

indépendant *adj* independent.

indéterminé *adj* undetermined; unspecified.

index *m* index; index finger.

indication *f* indication; piece of information; instruction.

indice *m* indication; clue; sign.

indifférent *adj* indifferent; immaterial.

indigène *mf* native; local:—*adj* indigenous, native.

indigestion *f* indigestion.

indigne *adj* unworthy; undeserving.

indiquer *vt* to indicate, point out; to tell.

indirect *adj* indirect; circumstantial; collateral.

indiscret *adj* indiscreet; inquisitive.

indispensable *adj* indispensable; essential.

indisponible *adj* unavailable.

individu *m* individual.

individuel *adj* individual.

indulgent *adj* indulgent; lenient.

industrie *f* industry; dexterity, ingenuity.

industriel *m*, **-elle** *f* industrialist, manufacturer:—*adj* industrial.

inédit *adj* unpublished; original.

inefficace *adj* ineffective; inefficient.

inégal *adj* unequal; uneven; irregular.

inépuisable *adj* inexhaustible.

inertie *f* inertia, apathy.

inévitable *adj* inevitable, unavoidable.

inexact *adj* inexact, inaccurate.

inexplicable *adj* inexplicable.

infaillible *adj* infallible.

infantile *adj* infantile, childish.

infecter *vt* to infect; to contaminate:—**s'~** *vr* to become infected.

infection *f* infection.

inférieur *adj* inferior; lower.

infériorité *f* inferiority.

infester *vt* to infest; overrun.

infidèle *adj* unfaithful, disloyal.

infini *adj* infinite; interminable.

infirme *adj* feeble; crippled, disabled.

infirmier *m*, **-ière** *f* nurse.

infirmité *f* disability; infirmity.

inflation *f* inflation.

inflexible *adj* inflexible, rigid.

influence *f* influence.

influencer *vt* to influence, sway.

information *f* piece of information; information; inquiry.

informatique *f* computing; data processing:—*adj* computer.

informer *vt* to inform, tell.

ingénieur *m* engineer.

ingénieux *adj* ingenious, clever.

ingénu *adj* ingenuous, naive.

ingrédient *m* ingredient; component.

initial *adj* initial.

initiative *f* initiative; enterprise.

initier *vt* to initiate.

injecter *vt* to inject.

injure *f* injury; insult.

injuste *adj* unjust, unfair.

injustice *f* injustice.

inné *adj* innate, inborn.

innocence *f* innocence.

innocent *m*, **-e** *f* innocent person; simpleton:—*adj* innocent.

innovation *f* innovation.

inondation f inundation.

inouï adj unprecedented, unheard of.

inquiet adj worried, anxious, uneasy.

inscription f inscription; registration; matriculation.

inscrire vt to inscribe; to register:—s'~ vr to join.

insecte m insect.

insensible adj insensible, insensitive.

insérer vt to insert.

insinuer vt to insinuate, imply.

insipide adj insipid, tasteless.

insister vi to insist, be insistent; to stress.

insolent adj insolent; brazen.

insomnie f insomnia.

insoutenable adj unbearable; untenable.

inspecter vt to inspect, examine.

inspection f inspection.

inspiration f inspiration; suggestion.

inspirer vt to inspire; to breathe in.

instable adj unstable; unsettled.

installation f installation; installing.

installer vt to install; to fit out.

instant m moment, instant.

instinct m instinct.

instinctif adj instinctive.

institut m institute; school.

institution f institution; establishment.

instruction f instruction; education; inquiry.

instruire vt to instruct; to teach; to conduct an inquiry.

instrument m instrument, implement.

insuffisant adj insufficient, inadequate.

insulte f insult.

insulter vt to insult, affront.

insupportable adj unbearable, intolerable.

intact adj intact.

intégral adj integral, complete.

intégrer vt to integrate:—s'~ vr to become integrated; to fit in.

intégrité f integrity.

intellectuel m, **-uelle** f intellectual:—adj intellectual, mental.

intelligence f intelligence; understanding.

intelligent adj intelligent.

intelligible adj intelligible.

intense adj intense; severe.

intensifier vt to intensify:—s'~ vr to intensify.

intensité f intensity; severity.

intention f intention; purpose, intent.

intercepter vt to intercept.

interdire vt to forbid, ban, prohibit.

intéressant adj interesting; attractive, worthwhile.

intéresser vt to interest; to affect:—s'~ vr:—s'~ à to be interested in.

intérêt m interest; significance, importance.

interférence f interference; conjunction.

intérieur adj interior, internal, inland.

interlocuteur m, **-trice** f interlocutor, speaker.

intermittent adj intermittent, sporadic.

international adj international.

interne adj internal:—mf boarder; house doctor.

interprète mf interpreter.

interpréter vt to interpret; to perform.

interrogation *f* interrogation, questioning; question.

interroger *vt* to question; to interrogate:—**s'~** *vr* to wonder.

interrompre *vt* to interrupt, break.

interruption *f* interruption, break.

intervalle *m* interval; space, distance.

intervenir *vi* to intervene; to take part in.

intervention *f* intervention; operation.

intime *adj* intimate; private:—*mf* close friend.

intimider *vt* to intimidate.

intimité *f* intimacy; privacy.

intolérance *f* intolerance.

intolérant *adj* intolerant.

intrépide *adj* intrepid, fearless.

introduction *f* introduction; launching; institution.

introduire *vt* to introduce, insert; to present.

introverti *m*, **-e** *f* introvert:—*adj* introverted.

intuitif *adj* intuitive.

intuition *f* intuition.

inutile *adj* useless; unavailing; pointless.

invalide *adj* disabled; invalid.

invariable *adj* invariable; unvarying.

invasion *f* invasion.

inventer *vt* to invent; to devise; to make up.

invention *f* invention; inventiveness.

inverse *adj* opposite:—*m* opposite, reverse.

inversion *f* inversion; reversal.

investissement *m* investment; investing.

invincible *adj* invincible, indomitable.

invisible *adj* invisible; unseen.

invitation *f* invitation.

inviter *vt* to invite, ask.

involontaire *adj* involuntary; unintentional.

invoquer *vt* to invoke; to call up; to plead.

invraisemblable *adj* unlikely, improbable.

invulnérable *adj* invulnerable.

Irlandais *m* Irishman, **-e** *f* Irishwoman.

irlandais *adj* Irish.

Irlande *f* Ireland.

ironique *adj* ironic:—**~ment** *adv* ironically.

irrationnel *adj* irrational.

irréel *adj* unreal.

irrégularité *f* irregularity; variation; unevenness.

irrégulier *adj* irregular; varying; uneven.

irremplaçable *adj* irreplaceable.

irrésistible *adj* irresistible:—**~ment** *adv* irresistibly.

irresponsable *adj* irresponsible

irrigation *f* irrigation.

irriter *vt* to irritate; to provoke.

isoler *vt* to isolate; to insulate.

issue *f* outlet; solution; outcome.

ivre *adj* drunk, inebriated.

ivrogne *mf* drunkard.

J

jadis *adv* formerly, long ago.

jalousie *f* jealousy, envy.

jaloux *adj* jealous, envious.

jamais *adv* never, not ever:—**à ~** for ever.

jambe *f* leg.

jambon *m* ham.

janvier *m* January.

jardin *m* garden.

jardinier *m*, **-ière** *f* gardener.

jargon *m* jargon, slang; gibberish.

jaune *adj* yellow:—*m* yellow.

jaunir *vi* to yellow, turn yellow:—*vt* to make yellow.

jazz *m* jazz.

je, j' *pron* I.

jetable *adj* disposable.

jetée *f* pier.

jeter *vt* to throw.

jeton *m* token; counter.

jeu *m* play; game; gambling:—**~ de mots** pun.

jeudi *m* Thursday.

jeune *adj* young:—*m* youth, young man:—*f* young girl.

jeûne *m* fast.

jeunesse *f* youth, youthfulness.

joaillerie *f* jewelling; jewellery.

joie *f* joy, happiness; pleasure.

joindre *vt* to join, link.

jointure *f* joint (*anat*).

joli *adj* pretty; good, handsome.

jonction *f* junction.

joue *f* cheek

jouer *vi* to play; to gamble; to act.

jouet *m* toy.

joueur *m*, **-euse** *f* player; gambler.

jouir *vi* to enjoy; to delight in.

jouissance *f* enjoyment; use.

jour *m* day; daylight:—**tous les ~s** every day:—**à ~** up to date:—**~ férié** public holiday:—**mise à ~** updating; update.

journal *m* newspaper; bulletin:—**~ télévisé** television news.

journaliste *mf* journalist.

journée *f* day; day's work.

jovial *adj* jovial, jolly.

joyau *m* jewel, gem.

joyeux *adj* joyful.

judaïsme *m* Judaism.

judiciaire *adj* judicial, legal.

judicieux *adj* judicious.

juge *m* judge.

jugement *m* judgment.

juger *vt* to judge; to decide; to consider.

juif *m* Jew; Jewish:—**juive** *f* Jewess; Jewish.

juillet *m* July.

juin *m* June.

jumeau *m*, **-elle** *f* twin:—*adj* twin; double.

jumelle(s) *f(pl)* binoculars.

jungle *f* jungle.

jupe *f* skirt.

jurer *vt* to swear, pledge.

juridiction *f* jurisdiction; court of law.

juridique *adj* legal, juridical.

jury *m* jury; board of examiners.

jus *m* juice.

jusque, jusqu' *prép* to, as far as; until.

juste *adj* just, fair; exact; sound.

justesse *f* accuracy; aptness; soundness.

justice *f* justice, fairness.

justification *f* justification; proof.

justifier *vt* to justify, prove.

juteux *adj* juicy; lucrative.

juvénile *adj* young, youthful.

K

kaléidoscope *m* kaleidoscope.

kangourou *m* kangaroo.

karaté *m* karate.

képi *m* kepi.

kermesse *f* fair; bazaar.

kidnapper *vt* to kidnap, abduct.

kidnappeur *m*, **-euse** *f* kidnapper.

kilogramme *m* kilogramme.

kilomètre *m* kilometre.

kiosque *m* kiosk, stall.

klaxon *m* horn.

klaxonner *vi* to sound one's horn.

koala *m* koala.

L

la *art pn see* **le**.

là *adv* there; over there; then:—**par ~** that way;—**~dedans** inside, in there:—**~dessous**, under there:—**~dessus** on that; thereupon:—**~haut** up there:—**celui~** that one.

label *m* label; seal.

labeur *m* labour, toil.

laborantin(e) *m(f)* laboratory assistant.

laboratoire *m* laboratory.

lac *m* lake.

lacer *vt* to lace up; to tie up.

lâche *adj* slack; lax; cowardly.

lâcher *vt* to loosen; to release.

laid *adj* ugly, unsightly.

laideur *f* ugliness, unsightliness.

laine *f* wool.

laisser *vt* to leave; to let:—**~ tomber** to drop.

laisser-passer *m invar* pass, permit.

lait *m* milk

laitue *f* lettuce.

lame *f* blade; strip; metal plate.

lamentable *adj* lamentable, distressing.

lamenter (se) *vr* to lament, bewail.

lampe *f* lamp, light; bulb.

lance *f* lance, spear.

lancement *m* launching; starting up; throwing.

lancer *vt* to throw; to launch.

langage *m* language, speech.

langoureux *adj* languid, languorous.

langouste *f* spiny lobster.

langue *f* tongue; language.

langueur *f* languor.

lanterne *f* lantern; lamp.

lapin *m*, **-e** *f* rabbit.

large *adj* wide; generous; lax; great.

largeur *f* width, breadth.

larme *f* tear.

las *adj*, *f* **lasse** weary, tired.

lasser *vt* to tire:—**se ~** *vr* to grow tired of.

latéral *adj* lateral, side.

latin *adj* Latin:—*m* Latin.

latitude *f* latitude; margin.

lavabo *m* washbasin.

lavage *m* washing; bathing.

laver *vt* to wash; to cleanse:—**se ~** *vr* to wash oneself.

laxatif *adj* laxative:—*m* laxative.

le *art*, *f* **la**, *devant voyelle* **l'**, *pl* **les** the:—*pron* him, her, them.

leçon *f* lesson; reading; class.

lecteur *m*, **-trice** *f* reader.

lecture *f* reading; perusal.

légal *adj* legal, lawful.

légalité *f* legality, lawfulness.

légendaire *adj* legendary.

légende *f* legend; inscription.

léger *adj* light; inconsiderate.

légèreté *f* lightness; thoughtlessness.

législatif *adj* legislative:—*m* legislature.

législation *f* legislation, laws.

légitime *adj* legitimate, lawful.

légitimité *f* legitimacy.

légume *m* vegetable.

lendemain *m* next day, day after.

lent *adj* slow; tardy; sluggish.

lenteur *f* slowness.

lequel *pron*, *f* **laquelle**, *pl* **lesquels**, **lesquelles** who, whom, which.

leste *adj* nimble, agile:—**~ment** *adv* nimbly.

léthargie *f* lethargy.

léthargique *adj* lethargic.

lettre *f* letter, note; literature:—**suivre à la ~** to carry out to the letter.

leur *pron* them:—**le ~**, **la ~**, **les ~s** theirs.

lever *vt* to lift, raise; to levy:—**se ~** *vr* to get up.

levier *m* lever.

lèvre *f* lip.

lexique *m* vocabulary, lexis.

lézard *m* lizard.

liaison *f* connection; liaison, link.

libéral *adj* liberal:—*m* liberal.

libération *f* release, liberation.

libérer *vt* to release; to liberate.

liberté *f* liberty, freedom.

libraire *mf* bookseller.

librairie *f* bookshop; bookselling.

libre *adj* free; independent.

licence *f* degree; permit; licentiousness.

licenciement *m* redundancy; dismissal.

licencier *vt* to make redundant; to dismiss.

lien *m* bond; link, connection; tie.

lier *vt* to bind; to link:—**se ~** *vr*:—**se ~ avec** to make friends.

lieu *m* place; occasion:—**avoir ~** to take place:—**au ~ de** instead of.

lièvre *m* hare.

ligne *f* line; row; range.

lignée *f* lineage; offspring.

ligue *f* league.

lime *f* file.

limitation *f* limitation, restriction.

limite *f* boundary, limit:—**à la ~** ultimately.

limiter vt to limit, restrict.

limonade f lemonade.

limpide adj limpid, clear.

linéaire adj linear.

linge m linen; washing.

lingerie f linen room; underwear, lingerie.

linguiste mf linguist.

lion m lion, **lionne** f lioness

liquéfier vt to liquefy:—**se ~** vr to liquefy.

liqueur f liqueur; liquid.

liquide m liquid.

liquider vt to wind up; to eliminate

lire vt to read.

lisible adj legible; readable.

lisse adj smooth, glossy.

lisser vt to smooth, gloss.

liste f list; schedule.

lit m bed; layer.

litige m lawsuit; dispute.

litre m litre.

littéral adj literal.

littérature f literature; writing.

littoral m coast:—adj coastal.

livraison f delivery; number, issue.

livre m book:—f pound (weight, currency).

livrer vt to deliver, hand over; to give away.

livreur m delivery man, **-euse** f delivery woman.

local adj local.

localité f locality; town.

locataire mf tenant; lodger.

location f renting; lease, leasing.

loge f lodge; dressing room; box.

logement m housing; accommodation.

loger vt to accommodate; to billet:—vi to live in.

logiciel m software.

logique f logic:—adj logical.

logo m logo.

loi f law; act, statute; rule.

loin adv far, a long way:—m distance; background:—**au ~** in the distance:—**de ~** from a distance.

lointain adj distant, remote:—m distance; background

loisir m leisure, spare time.

long adj, f **longue** long, lengthy.

longévité f longevity.

longitude f longitude.

longtemps adv for a long time.

longueur f length.

loquace adj loquacious, talkative.

lors adv then **~ de** at the time of:—**dès ~** from that time.

lorsque conj when.

lot m prize; lot; portion.

loterie f lottery; raffle.

lotion f lotion.

louange f praise, commendation.

louer vt to rent, lease; to book.

loup m wolf.

lourd adj heavy; sultry.

lourdeur f heaviness.

loyal adj loyal, faithful.

loyauté f loyalty

loyer m rent.

lucide adj lucid, clear.

lucidité f lucidity, clearness.

lueur f glimmer, gleam; glimpse.

lugubre adj lugubrious, gloomy.

lui pron him, her, it:—**c'est à ~** it is his:—**~-même** himself, herself, itself.

luire vt to shine, gleam.

lumière f light; daylight; lamp; insight.

lumineux adj luminous; illuminated.

lunaire adj lunar, moon.

lundi *m* Monday.
lune *f* moon.
lunette *f* telescope; sight:—**~s** glasses.
lutte *f* struggle; contest; strife.
lutter *vi* to struggle, fight.
luxe *m* luxury, excess.

luxeux *adj* luxurious.
lycée *m* secondary school.
lyncher *vt* to lynch.
lyre *f* lyre.
lyrique *adj* lyric.
lyrisme *m* lyricism.

M

mâcher *vt* to chew.
machinal *adj* mechanical, automatic.
machine *f* machine; engine; apparatus.
machinerie *f* machinery, plant.
mâchoire *f* jaw.
maçon *m* builder, mason.
madame *f* Madam; Mrs; lady.
mademoiselle *f* Miss; young lady.
magasin *m* shop, store; warehouse.
magazine *m* magazine.
magicien(ne) *m(f)* magician.
magie *f* magic
magistrat *m* magistrate.
magnanime *adj* magnanimous.
magnétique *adj* magnetic.
magnétophone *m* tape recorder.
magnifique *adj* magnificent; sumptuous.
mai *m* May.
maigre *adj* thin; meagre, scarce.
maigrir *vi* to get thinner; to waste away.
maillot *m* jersey; leotard.
main *f* hand:—**avoir la ~** to have the lead.
main-d'œuvre *f* workforce.
maintenance *f* maintenance, servicing.

maintenant *adv* now:—**à partir de ~** from now on.
maintenir *vt* to keep.
maintien *m* maintenance; preservation; keeping up.
maire *m* mayor, **-esse** *f* mayoress.
mais *conj* but.
maison *f* house; home; building; premises.
maître *m* **-esse** *f* master; ruler; lord; proprietor.
maîtresse *f* mistress; teacher
maîtrise *f* mastery; control; expertise.
majoritaire *adj* majority.
majorité *f* majority.
mal *adv* wrong, badly:—*m* evil, wrong; harm; pain.
malade *adj* sick, ill; diseased:—*mf* invalid, sick person.
maladie *f* illness; malady, complaint; disorder.
maladroit *adj* clumsy, awkward.
malchanceux *adj* unlucky, unfortunate.
mâle *m* male:—*adj* male; manly, virile.
malentendu *m* misunderstanding.
malgré *prép* in spite of; despite.

malheur *m* misfortune; calamity.

malheureux *adj* unfortunate; unlucky; unhappy.

malhonnête *adj* dishonest, crooked; uncivil.

malicieux *adj* malicious, spiteful; mischievous.

malnutrition *f* malnutrition.

malsain *adj* unhealthy, unwholesome; immoral.

maltraiter *vt* to abuse; to handle roughly.

malveillant *adj* malevolent, spiteful.

maman *f* mother, mummy, mum.

mammifère *m* mammal.

manche *f* sleeve; game, round:—*m* handle, shaft.

mangeable *adj* edible.

manger *vt* to eat; to consume, squander

maniable *adj* handy, workable.

manier *vt* to handle; to manipulate.

manière *f* manner, way, style.

manifeste *adj* manifest, evident, obvious:—*m* manifesto.

manifester *vt* to display, make known; to demonstrate.

manipulation *f* handling; manipulation.

manipuler *vt* to handle; to manipulate

manœuvre *f* manoeuvre, operation; scheme:—*m* labourer.

manœuvrer *vt* to manoeuvre:—*vi* to manoeuvre, move.

manque *m* lack, shortage; shortcoming, deficiency.

manquer *vt* to miss; to fail; to be absent.

manteau *m* coat; mantle, blanket; cloak.

manuel *m* manual, handbook:—*adj* manual.

manufacture *f* factory; manufacture.

manufacturier *m* **-ière** *f* factory owner; manufacturer:—*adj* manufacturing.

manuscrit *m* manuscript; typescript:—*adj* handwritten.

maquillage *m* make-up.

marathon *m* marathon.

marbre *m* marble; marble statue.

marchand(e) *m(f)* merchant:—*adj* market, trade.

marchandise *f* merchandise, commodity; goods.

marche *f* walk; journey; progress; movement:—**mettre en ~** to start up; to turn on.

marché *m* market; transaction, contract.

marcher *vi* to walk, march; to progress; to work.

mardi *m* Tuesday.

marée *f* tide.

marge *f* margin; latitude, freedom; mark-up.

marginal *adj* marginal.

mari *m* husband.

mariage *m* marriage.

marié *m* bridegroom:—*adj* married.

marier *vt* to marry; blend, harmonise:—**se ~** *vr* to get married.

marin *m* sailor.

marine *f* navy; seascape; marine.

maritime *adj* maritime; seaboard.

marque *f* mark, sign; brand; make.

marquer *vt* to mark; to note down; to score.

mars *m* March.

marteau *m* hammer; knocker.

masculin *adj* masculine.

masque *m* mask; facade, front.

massage *m* massage.

masse f mass, heap; bulk; mob.

masser vt to mass, assemble; to massage.

masseur m masseur, **euse** f masseuse.

massif adj massive, solid, heavy:—m massif; clump.

match m match; game.

matelas m mattress.

matérialiser (se) ~ vr to materialise.

matériaux mpl material, materials.

matériel adj material, physical; practical.

maternel adj maternal, motherly.

maternité f motherhood; pregnancy; maternity hospital.

mathématicien(ne) m(f) mathematician.

mathématique adj mathematical:—f mathematics.

matière f material, matter; subject:— ~ **première** raw material.

matin m morning; dawn.

matrice f womb; mould; matrix.

maturité f maturity; prime.

maussade adj sulky, sullen.

mauvais adj bad; wicked; faulty; hurtful; poor.

maximum m maximum.

me, m' pn me; myself.

mécanicien(ne) m(f) mechanic; engineer.

mécanique f mechanics:—adj mechanical.

méchant adj spiteful; wicked; mischievous.

méconnu adj unrecognised; misunderstood.

mécontentement m discontent; displeasure.

médecin m doctor, physician.

médecine f medicine

médical adj medical.

médiocre adj mediocre; indifferent.

méditation f meditation.

méditer vi to meditate:—vt to contemplate, have in mind.

méfier (se) vr to mistrust, distrust; to be suspicious.

meilleur adj better, preferable:—**le ~, la ~e** the best.

mélancolique adj melancholy; melancholic.

mélange m mixture.

mélanger vt to mix, blend; to muddle.

mêler vt to mix; to combine:—**se ~** vr to mix, mingle

mélodie f melody, tune.

membre m member; limb.

même adv even:—**tout de ~** nevertheless, all the same:—adj same, identical:—pn:—**le/la ~, les ~s** the same one(s).

mémoire f memory:—m memorandum, report.

mémorable adj memorable.

menace f threat; intimidation; danger.

menacer vt to threaten, menace; to impend.

ménage m housework, housekeeping; household.

ménager vt to treat with caution; to manage; to arrange:—adj household, domestic.

ménagère f housewife.

mendiant(e) m(f) beggar, mendicant.

mener vt to lead, guide; to steer; to manage.

ménopause f menopause.

mensonge m lie, falsehood; error, illusion.

menstruation f menstruation.

mental *adj* mental.

menteur *m* -**euse** *f* liar:—*adj* lying, deceitful.

mention *f* mention; comment; grade.

mentionner *vt* to mention.

mentir *vi* to lie, tell lies; to be deceptive.

menton *m* chin.

menu *m* menu; meal:—*adj* slender, thin; petty, minor.

mépriser *vt* to scorn, despise.

mer *f* sea; tide.

merci *m* thank you:—*f* mercy:—**sans ~** merciless.

mercredi *m* Wednesday.

mère *f* mother.

méridien *m* meridian; midday.

mériter *vt* to deserve, merit.

merveilleux *adj* marvellous, wonderful.

message *m* message.

messager *m* -**ère** *f* messenger.

messe *f* mass

mesure *f* measure; gauge; measurement:—**au fur et à ~** as; one by one:—**dans la mesure où** insofar as:—**en ~** in time.

mesurer *vt* to measure; to assess; to limit:—**se ~** *vr* to try one's strength.

métal *m* metal.

métaphore *f* metaphor.

météore *m* meteor.

météoroloque, météorologiste *mf* meteorologist.

méthode *f* method, way.

méthodique *adj* methodical.

métier *m* job; occupation:—**~ à tisser** weaving loom.

mètre *m* metre.

métro *m* underground, metro.

métropole *f* metropolis.

mettre *vt* to put, place; to put on:—**~ en marche** to start up:—**se ~ à** to begin to:—**se ~ en route** to start off.

meuble *m* piece of furniture.

meurtrier *m* murderer, -**ière** *f* murderess.

mi- *adj* half:—**à ~chemin** halfway:—**~clos** half-closed:—**à ~jambe** up to the knees:—**à ~voix** in a low voice.

miauler *vi* to mew.

micro-onde *f* microwave:—*m* **micro-ondes** microwave oven.

micro-ordinateur *m* microcomputer.

microbe *m* germ, microbe.

microfilm *m* microfilm.

microphone *m* microphone.

microscope *m* microscope.

midi *m* midday, noon.

miel *m* honey.

mien *pron*, *f* **mienne**:—**le ~, la mienne, les ~s, les miennes** mine, my own.

mieux *m* improvement:—**le ~** the best:—**de ~ en ~** better and better.

migraine *f* headache; migraine.

migrateur *m* migrant.

migration *f* migration.

milieu *m* middle, centre; medium; environment.

militaire *m* serviceman:—*adj* military, army.

militant(e) *m*(*f*) *adj* militant.

militer *vi* to militate; to be a militant.

mille *m adj* one thousand.

milliard *m* thousand million; milliard.

millième *m adj* thousandth.

millier *m* thousand.

million *m* million.

millionnaire *adj* millionaire; worth millions:—*mf* millionaire.

mime *m* mime:—*mf* mimic.

mimer *vt* to mime; to mimic, imitate.

mince *adj* thin, slender; meagre, trivial.

mincir *vi* to get slimmer, get thinner.

mine *f* expression; appearance; mine:— **avoir bonne ~** to look good.

minéral *adj* mineral; inorganic:—*m* mineral.

mineur(e) *m(f)* minor:—*adj* minor:— *m* miner.

mini-jupe *f* miniskirt.

miniature *f* miniature.

minimal *adj* minimal, minimum.

minimum *m* minimum.

ministère *m* ministry; agency.

ministre *m* minister; clergyman.

minorité *f* minority.

minuit *m* midnight.

minute *f* minute, moment.

minutieux *adj* meticulous; minute.

miracle *m* miracle, wonder.

miraculeux *adj* miraculous.

mirage *m* mirage.

miroir *m* mirror, reflection.

mise *f* putting, placing; stake; deposit; investment:—**~ en scène** production, staging:—**~ en liberté** release:—**~ en ordre** ordering, arrangement:—**~ en œuvre** implementation.

misérable *adj* miserable; destitute; pitiable.

misère *f* misery; poverty; destitution.

mission *f* mission, assignment.

missionnaire *m* missionary.

mitigé *adj* mitigated; lukewarm.

mitoyen *adj* common; semi-detached.

mixer *vt* to mix; to blend.

mixte *adj* mixed; joint; combined.

mobile *adj* moving; movable:—*m* motive; moving body.

mobilier *m* furniture.

mobilité *f* mobility.

mode *f* fashion; custom:—*m* form, mode; way.

modèle *m* model; pattern; design; example.

modeler *vt* to model; to shape.

modem *m* modem.

modération *f* moderation; diminution.

modéré *adj* moderate

modérer *vt* to moderate.

moderne *adj* modern, up-to-date.

moderniser *vt* to modernise.

modeste *adj* modest, simple; unassuming.

modestie *f* modesty.

modification *f* modification, alteration.

modifier *vt* to modify, alter.

moelle *f* marrow; core.

mœurs *fpl* morals; customs.

moi *pn* me, I:—**c'est à ~** it is mine, it is my turn:—**~-même** myself.

mois *m* month.

moisson *f* harvest.

moissonner *vt* to reap, mow.

moite *adj* moist, damp.

moitié *f* half.

molécule *f* molecule.

moment *m* moment, instant, while; time; opportunity.

momentané *adj* momentary; brief.

mon *pron*, *f* **ma**, *pl* **mes** my.

monastère *m* monastery.

mondain *adj* worldly, mundane; society, fashionable.

monde *m* world, earth; society, company.

mondial *adj* world, worldwide.

moniteur *m* **-trice** *f* instructor, coach; supervisor.

monnaie f currency; coin; change.
monopole f monopoly.
monopoliser vt to monopolise.
monotone adj monotonous
monsieur m sir, gentleman, Mr, pl **messieurs** gentlemen, Messrs.
monstre m monster.
mont m mountain; mount.
montage m assembly; setting up; editing.
montagne f mountain.
montagneux adj mountainous.
montée f climb, climbing; ascent; rise.
monter vi to go up, ascend; get into (vehicle):—vt to go up; to carry/ bring up.
montre f watch.
montrer vt to show, point to; prove.
monument m monument, memorial.
moquer (se) vr to make fun, jeer, laugh at.
moqueur m **-euse** f mocker, scoffer:—adj mocking.
moral adj moral, ethical; intellectual.
moralité f morals, morality.
morceau m piece, morsel, fragment; extract.
mordre vt to bite, gnaw; to grip.
morose adj sullen, morose.
mort m dead man, **-e** f dead woman:—adj dead:—f death.
mortalité f mortality; death rate.
mortel adj mortal; fatal.
mortuaire adj mortuary; funeral.
mosquée f mosque
mot m word; saying:—~**s croisés** crossword.
moteur m engine, motor:—adj motor, driving.

motif m motive, grounds; motif, design.
motivation f motivation.
motiver vt to justify; to motivate.
moto f motorbike.
mou adj (f **molle**) soft; gentle; muffled.
mouche f fly.
moucher (se) vr to blow one's nose.
mouchoir m handkerchief.
moudre vt to mill, grind.
mouiller vt to wet; to water down:— **se ~** vr to get wet.
moule m mould:—f mussel.
mouler vt to mould; to model.
moulin m mill.
mourir vi to die.
mousser vi to froth, foam
mousseux adj sparkling; frothy:—m sparkling wine.
moustache f moustache; whiskers.
moustique m mosquito.
mouton m sheep; mutton.
mouvement m movement, motion; animation.
mouvoir vt to drive, power:—**se ~** vr to move.
moyen m means; way:—adj average, medium, moderate:—~ **âge** Middle Ages.
moyenne f average.
muet(te) m(f) mute:—adj dumb; silent, mute.
multicolore adj multicoloured.
multiple adj numerous, multiple:—m multiple.
multiplication f multiplication.
multiplier (se) vr to multiply, increase.
municipal adj municipal; local.

municipalité *f* town, municipality.
munir *vt* to provide, equip with:—**se ~** *vr* to equip oneself.
mur *m* wall.
mûr *adj* ripe, mature; worn out.
mûrir *vi* to ripen, mature.
murmure *m* murmur; muttering; grumbling.
murmurer *vi* to murmur.
muscle *m* muscle.
musculaire *adj* muscular.
musée *m* art gallery, museum.
musicien(ne) *m(f)* musician:—*adj* musical.

musique *f* music.
musulman(e) *m(f) adj* Moslem.
muter *vt* to transfer, move.
myope *mf* short-sighted person:—*adj* short-sighted.
myopie *f* short-sightedness, myopia.
mystère *m* mystery.
mystérieux *adj* mysterious.
mystifier *vt* to mystify; to hoax.
mystique *adj* mystical:—*mf* mystic.
mythe *m* myth.
mythique *adj* mythical.
mythologie *f* mythology.

N

nager *vi* to swim.
nageur *m*, **-euse** *f* swimmer; rower.
naissance *f* birth, extraction; dawn, beginning.
naître *vi* to be born; to arise, spring up.
naïveté *f* naïvety, artlessness, gullibility.
narcotique *m* drug, narcotic:—*adj* narcotic.
narrateur *m*, **-trice** *f* narrator.
nasal *adj* nasal.
natalité *f* birth rate.
nation *f* nation.
national *adj* national; domestic.
nationaliste *mf* nationalist:—*adj* nationalist.
nationalité *f* nationality.
nature *f* nature; kind, sort; temperament.
naturel *adj* natural; bodily; native;

unsophisticated:—**~lement** *adv* naturally; of course.
nautique *adj* nautical.
navigation *f* sailing, navigation.
navire *m* ship, vessel.
ne *adv* no, not.
né *adj* born
néanmoins *adv* nevertheless.
nécessaire *adj* necessary; requisite; indispensable.
nécessité *f* necessity; need; inevitability.
nécessiter *vt* to require, necessitate.
négatif *adj* negative.
négligent *adj* negligent, careless; nonchalant.
négliger *vt* to neglect; to be negligent about.
négociation *f* negotiation.
négocier *vi* to negotiate; to trade:—*vt* to negotiate.

neige f snow.

neiger vi to snow, be snowing.

nerf m nerve.

nerveux adj nervous; vigorous; excitable.

net adj, f **nette** clean; clear; plain; sharp; net.

nettoyage m cleaning; clearing up.

nettoyer vt to clean; to ruin, clean out.

neuf adj nine:—m nine.

neutre adj neutral; neuter.

neuvième adj ninth:—mf ninth.

neveu m nephew.

nez m nose; flair:—**avoir du ~** to have flair.

niais adj silly, simple, inane.

nid m nest; den; berth.

nièce f niece.

nier vt to deny; to repudiate.

niveau m level; standard; par; gauge.

noble adj noble, dignified.

noce f wedding, wedding feast; marriage ceremony.

nocif adj noxious, harmful.

nocturne adj nocturnal, night.

Noël m Christmas.

nœud m knot, bow; crux.

noir adj black; dark:—m black; darkness; black man

noircir vt to blacken; to dirty:—**se ~** vr to darken, grow black.

noix f walnut

nom m name; fame; noun

nombre m number, quantity.

nombreux adj numerous, frequent.

nommer vt to appoint; nominate.

non adv no; not.

non-sens m nonsense.

nonchalant adj nonchalant.

nord m north, northerly (wind)

normal adj normal, usual; standard-sized.

norme f norm; standard.

nostalgique adj nostalgic.

notable adj notable; noteworthy.

note f note; minute; mark; bill.

noter vt to note down; to notice; to mark.

notice f note; directions; instructions.

notion f notion, idea.

notoire adj notorious; well-known, acknowledged.

notre adj (pl **nos**) ours, our own.

nôtre poss pn:—**le ~, la ~, les ~s** ours, our own.

nouer vt to tie, knot.

nourrir vt to feed, provide for; to stoke:—**se ~** vr to feed o.s.

nourriture f food; sustenance.

nous pron we; us:—**c'est à ~** it's ours; it's our turn:—**~-mêmes** ourselves.

nouveau adj new; recent; additional.

nouvelle f piece of news; short story.

novembre m November.

novice mf novice, beginner.

noyer vt to drown; to flood:—**se ~** vr to drown.

nu adj naked, nude; plain, unadorned.

nuage m cloud.

nucléaire adj nuclear:—m nuclear energy.

nudité f nakedness, nudity.

nuire vi to harm, injure; to prejudice.

nuisible adj harmful; noxious.

nuit f night, darkness.

nul adj no; nil; null and void:—**~lement** adv not at all.

numérique adj numerical; digital.

numéro m number; issue.

numéroter vt to number.

nylon m nylon.

71

O

obéir *vt* to obey, be obedient; to comply.

obéissant *adj* obedient.

obèse *adj* obese.

objecter *vt* to object.

objectif *adj* objective, unbiased:—*m* objective, target.

objection *f* objection.

objet *m* object, thing; purpose; matter.

obligation *f* obligation, duty; bond.

obligatoire *adj* obligatory, compulsory.

obliger *vt* to oblige, require; to bind.

oblitérer *vt* to obliterate; to cancel (stamp).

obscène *adj* obscene.

obscur *adj* obscure, dark, gloomy.

obscurcir *vt* to darken; to obscure:— **s'~** *vr* to get dark.

obscurité *f* obscurity; darkness.

observation *f* observation; remark.

observatoire *m* observatory.

observer *vt* to observe.

obsession *f* obsession.

obstacle *m* obstacle, hindrance.

obstination *f* obstinacy, stubbornness.

obstiné *adj* obstinate, stubborn.

obstiner (s') *vr* to insist, persist.

obtenir *vt* to obtain.

occasion *f* occasion, opportunity; bargain.

occidental *adj* western.

occupant *m*, **-e** *f* occupant, occupier.

occupation *f* occupation; occupancy.

occuper *vt* to occupy:—**s'~** *vr* to keep busy.

océan *m* ocean.

octobre *m* October.

odeur *f* smell, odour.

odieux *adj* hateful, obnoxious.

odorat *m* smell (sense).

œil *m* (*pl* **yeux**) eye; look; bud.

œuf *m* egg.

œuvre *f* work; action, deed; production.

offense *f* offence; injury.

offenser *vt* to offend:—**s'~** *vr* to take offence.

offensif *adj* offensive.

office *m* office; duty; function.

officiel *adj* official.

officier *m* officer.

officieux *adj* officious; unofficial.

offre *f* offer, tender, bid.

offrir *vt* to offer.

oie *f* goose.

oignon *m* onion; bulb.

oiseau *m* bird.

oisif *adj* idle.

oisiveté *f* idleness.

olive *f* olive.

olivier *m* olive tree.

olympique *adj* Olympic.

ombre *f* shade, shadow.

omelette *f* omelette.

omettre *vt* to omit.

omission *f* omission.

omniprésent *adj* omnipresent.

on *pn* one; someone, anyone.

once *f* ounce.
oncle *m* uncle.
onde *f* wave.
onduler *vi* to undulate; to ripple.
onéreux *adj* onerous; costly.
ongle *m* nail; claw, talon; hoof.
onze *adj* eleven:—*m* eleven.
onzième *adj* eleventh:—*mf* eleventh.
opaque *adj* opaque; impenetrable.
opéra *m* opera.
opération *f* operation, performance.
opérationnel *adj* operational.
opérer *vt* to operate.
opiniâtre *adj* stubborn; persistent.
opinion *f* opinion, view.
opportun *adj* timely, opportune.
opposant *m*, **-e** *f* opponent:—*adj* opposing.
opposé *adj* opposite:—*m* opposite:—**à l'~** contrary to.
opposer *vt* to oppose.
opposition *f* opposition; conflict.
oppresser *vt* to oppress, weigh down.
oppressif *adj* oppressive.
optimiste *mf* optimist:—*adj* optimistic.
option *f* option, choice.
optionnel *adj* optional.
opulent *adj* opulent, wealthy.
or *m* gold:—*conj* now.
orage *m* storm.
orageux *adj* stormy.
oral *adj* oral, verbal.
orange *f* orange:—*adj* orange.
orateur *m*, **-trice** *f* orator.
orbite *f* orbit; socket; sphere.
orchestre *m* orchestra.
ordinaire *adj* ordinary:—*m* usual routine:—**d'~, à l'~** ordinarily, usually.
ordinateur *m* computer.
ordonner *vt* to order.

ordre *m* order, command; class.
ordure *f* filth; rubbish.
oreille *f* ear; hearing.
oreiller *m* pillow.
organe *m* organ; instrument; medium.
organique *adj* organic.
organisateur *m*, **-trice** *f* organiser.
organisation *f* organisation.
organiser *vt* to organise, arrange.
orgueil *m* pride, arrogance.
orgueilleux *adj* proud, arrogant.
orient *m* orient, east.
oriental *adj* eastern, oriental.
orienter *vt* to orientate.
original *adj* original, novel:—*m* original.
originalité *f* originality.
origine *f* origin:—**à l'~** originally.
originel *adj* original, primitive.
orner *vt* to adorn, decorate.
orphelin *m*, **-e** *f* orphan.
orteil *m* toe.
orthodoxe *adj* orthodox:—*mf* orthodox.
os *m* bone
oser *vt* to dare.
ossature *f* skeleton; framework.
ostensible *adj* open, conspicuous.
otage *m* hostage.
ôter *vt* to take away.
ou *conj* or
où *adv* where, in which; *pron* where.
oubli *m* forgetfulness; oblivion.
oublier *vt* to forget.
ouest *m* west; *adj* west.
oui *adv* yes.
ouïe *f* hearing.
ouragan *m* hurricane, whirlwind.
ours *m*, **-e** *f* bear.
outil *m* tool, implement.
outillage *m* (set of) tools; equipment.

outiller *vt* to equip; to provide with tools.

outrage *m* outrage, insult, wrong.

outre *prép* as well as, besides:—**en ~** moreover.

ouvert *adj* open; exposed; frank.

ouverture *f* opening.

ouvrable *adj* working, business.

ouvrage *m* work; piece of work.

ouvrier *m*, **-ière** *f* worker:—*adj* labour.

ouvrir *vt* to open; to unlock; to broach.

oxygène *m* oxygen.

ozone *f* ozone.

P

pacifier *vt* to pacify.

pacifique *adj* peaceful.

pacte *m* pact, treaty.

page *f* page; passage.

paiement *m* payment

païen(ne) *m(f)* pagan:—*adj* pagan.

paille *f* straw.

pain *m* bread; loaf; bar

pair *adj* even:—*m* peer; par.

paire *f* pair

paisible *adj* peaceful; calm.

paix *f* peace; stillness.

palais *m* palace.

pâle *adj* pale, pallid.

pâleur *f* paleness, pallor.

pâlir *vi* to turn pale; to dim; to fade.

pallier *vt* to palliate; to offset.

palme *f* palm leaf; palm.

palmier *m* palm tree.

palpable *adj* palpable.

palper *vt* to feel, touch; to palpate.

palpiter *vi* to palpitate; to beat; to race.

panache *m* panache; gallantry

pancarte *f* sign, notice; placard.

panda *m* panda.

panique *f* panic.

paniquer *vi* to panic.

panne *f* breakdown; fault.

panneau *m* panel; sign, notice.

pansement *m* dressing, bandage.

panser *vt* to dress, bandage.

pantalon *m* trousers.

pantomime *f* pantomime; mime.

pantoufle *f* slipper.

papa *m* dad; daddy.

pape *m* pope.

papeterie *f* stationery.

papier *m* paper.

papillon *m* butterfly.

Pâques *fpl* Easter.

paquet *m* packet, pack.

par *prép* by, with, through; from; along:—**~-ci**, **~-là** here and there.

parachever *vt* to perfect; to complete.

parachute *m* parachute.

parade *f* parade, show; parry.

paradis *m* paradise; gallery.

paradoxal *adj* paradoxical.

paradoxe *m* paradox.

paragraphe *m* paragraph.

paraître *vi* to appear; to seem.

parallèle *adj* parallel.

paralyser *vt* to paralyse.

paralysie *f* paralysis.

paranoïaque *adj* paranoid.

parapluie *m* umbrella.

parasite *m* parasite, sponger.

parasol *m* parasol; sunshade.

parc *m* park; grounds; depot.

parce que *conj* because

parcelle *f* particle; parcel.

parcourir *vt* to travel through.

pardon *m* pardon, forgiveness.

pardonner *vt* to pardon.

pare-brise *m invar* windscreen.

pare-chocs *m invar* bumper.

pareil(le) *m(f)* equal; match:—*adj* like, similar; identical.

parent(e) *m(f)* relative, relation; (*pl*) parents.

parental *adj* parental.

parenté *f* relationship, kinship.

paresse *f* laziness.

paresseux *adj* lazy.

parfaire *vt* to perfect.

parfait *adj* perfect, flawless.

parfois *adv* sometimes.

parfumer *vt* to perfume.

pari *m* bet, wager.

parier *vt* to bet, wager.

parking *m* car park; parking.

parlement *m* Parliament.

parlementaire *adj* parliamentary:— *mf* MP.

parler *vi* to talk, speak:—*vt* to speak.

parmi *prép* among.

paroi *f* wall; surface.

parole *f* word; speech; voice; lyrics.

parquer *vt* to park.

parrain *m* godfather; patron.

parrainer *vt* to sponsor, propose.

part *f* part; share; portion:—**prendre ~ à** to participate in:—**autre ~** elsewhere:—**nulle ~** nowhere.

partage *m* sharing, distribution.

partager *vt* to divide up.

partenaire *mf* partner.

parti *m* party; match.

partial *adj* partial, biased.

participant(e) *m(f)* participant, member.

participation *f* participation.

participer *vi* to participate.

particulier *adj* particular, specific:— *m* person, private individual.

partie *f* part; subject; party.

partiel *adj* part, partial.

partir *vi* to leave.

partisan(e) *m(f)* partisan.

partout *adv* everywhere.

parvenir *vi*:—**~ à** to reach.

pas *m* step; pace:—*adv* no, not.

passable *adj* passable, tolerable.

passage *m* passage; transit.

passager *m* **-ère** *f* passenger:—*adj* passing, transitory.

passant(e) *m(f)* passer-by.

passe *f* pass; permit; channel.

passé *m* past.

passe-temps *m invar* pastime

passeport *m* passport.

passer *vi* to pass:—**se ~** *vr* to take place.

passion *f* passion.

passionné *adj* passionate.

passionner (se) *vr* to be fascinated by, have a passion for.

passivité *f* passivity.

paternel *adj* paternal, fatherly.

paternité *f* paternity; fatherhood.

pathétique *adj* pathetic.

patience *f* patience.

patient *adj* patient.

patin *m* skate.

patiner *vi* to skate; to slip; to spin.

patineur *m* **-euse** *f* skater.

pâtisserie *f* cake shop, confectioner's.

pâtissier *m* **-ière** *f* pastry cook, confectioner.

patrie *f* homeland, country.

patriotisme *m* patriotism.

patron(ne) *m(f)* owner, boss.

patronner *vt* to patronise.

patte *f* leg, paw, foot.

paume *f* palm.

paupière *f* eyelid.

pause *f* pause; half-time.

pauvre *adj* poor; indigent:—*mf* pauper.

paye *f* pay, wages.

payer *vt* to pay.

pays *m* country; region.

paysage *m* landscape; scenery.

paysan *m* countryman **-anne** *f* countrywoman.

péage *m* toll; tollgate.

peau *f* skin; hide, pelt.

pêche *f* peach; fishing.

pécher *vi* to sin.

pêcher *vt* to fish; to catch.

pécheur *m* **-eresse** *f* sinner

pêcheur *m* fisherman.

pédale *f* pedal; treadle.

pédaler *vi* to pedal.

pédestre *adj* pedestrian.

peigne *m* comb.

peigner (se) *vr* to comb one's hair.

peindre *vt* to paint.

peine *f* effort; pain; punishment.

peiner *vi* to toil; to struggle.

peintre *m* painter.

peinture *f* painting; paintwork.

peler *vi* to peel.

pèlerinage *m* pilgrimage.

peloton *m* pack; platoon.

pelouse *f* lawn.

pénaliser *vt* to penalise.

pencher *vi* to lean:—**se ~** *vr* to bend down.

pendant *prép* during; for:—**~ que** while.

pendre *vi* to hang.

pendule *f* clock:—*m* pendulum.

pénétrer *vi* to enter, penetrate:—*vt* to penetrate.

pénible *adj* hard, tiresome.

péninsule *f* peninsula.

pénis *m* penis.

pénitencier *m* prison, penitentiary.

pensée *f* thought.

penser *vt* to think, suppose, believe: —*vi* to think.

pension *f* pension; boarding house.

pensionnaire *mf* boarder; lodger.

pente *f* slope; gradient.

Pentecôte *f* Pentecost.

pépère *m* granddad, grandpa.

percée *f* opening, breach.

perception *f* perception.

percer *vt* to pierce.

percevoir *vt* to perceive; to collect.

percussion *f* percussion.

percuter *vt* to strike.

perdant(e) *m(f)* loser.

perdre *vt* to lose.

père *m* father; sire.

perfection *f* perfection.

perfectionnement *m* perfection.

perfectionner *vt* to perfect.

perfectionniste *mf* perfectionist:— *adj* perfectionist.

performance *f* performance.

performant *adj* high-performance

péril *m* peril, danger.

périmètre *m* perimeter.

période *f* period; epoch, era.

périodique *adj* periodic.

péripétie *f* event, episode.

périphérie *f* periphery.

périphérique *adj* peripheral

périple *m* voyage; journey.
périr *vi* to perish, die.
permanence *f* permanence.
permanent *adj* permanent.
perméable *adj* permeable.
permettre *vt* to allow, permit.
permis *adj* permitted:—*m* permit, licence.
permission *f* permission; leave.
permuter *vt* to permutate.
perpendiculaire *adj* perpendicular.
perpétuel *adj* perpetual.
perpétuité *f* perpetuity.
perplexe *adj* perplexed, confused.
perplexité *f* perplexity, confusion.
perquisition *f* search.
perroquet *m* parrot.
persécuter *vt* to persecute.
persécution *f* persecution.
persévérance *f* perseverance.
persévérer *vi* to persevere; to persist in.
persil *m* parsley.
persistance *f* persistence.
persister *vi* to persist, keep up.
personnage *m* character, individual.
personnalité *f* personality.
personne *f* person; self; appearance:—**en ~** in person:—*pron* anyone, anybody; nobody.
personnel *adj* personal.
perspective *f* perspective; view; angle.
perspicace *adj* perspicacious.
persuader *vt* to persuade; to convince.
persuasion *f* persuasion; conviction.
perte *f* loss, losing; ruin.
pertinent *adj* pertinent.
perturber *vt* to disrupt, disturb.
pervers *adj* perverse; perverted.

perversité *f* perversity.
pesanteur *f* gravity; heaviness.
peser *vt* to weigh.
pessimisme *m* pessimism.
pessimiste *mf* pessimist:—*adj* pessimistic.
peste *f* pest, nuisance; plague.
petit *adj* small, tiny; slim; young.
petit-fils *m* grandson.
petite-fille *f* granddaughter.
petitesse *f* smallness; meanness.
pétition *f* petition.
petits-enfants *mpl* grandchildren.
pétrifié *adj* petrified.
pétrole *m* oil, petroleum.
peu *adv* little, not much, few:—**un petit ~** a little bit:—**quelque ~** a little:—**pour ~ que** however little:—**~ de** little, few.
peuple *m* people, nation; crowd.
peupler *vt* to populate, stock; to plant.
peur *f* fear, terror, apprehension:—**avoir ~** to be afraid.
peut-être *adv* perhaps.
phare *m* lighthouse; headlight.
pharmaceutique *adj* pharmaceutical.
pharmacie *f* pharmacy; pharmacology.
pharmacien(ne) *m(f)* pharmacist.
phase *f* phase, stage.
phénoménal *adj* phenomenal.
phénomène *m* phenomenon.
philosophe *mf* philosopher.
philosophie *f* philosophy.
philosophique *adj* philosophical.
phobie *f* phobia.
phonétique *f* phonetics:—*adj* phonetic.
photo *f* photo.
photocopie *f* photocopy.
photogénique *adj* photogenic.

photographe *mf* photograph.
photographie *f* photography.
photographier *vt* to photograph.
phrase *f* sentence; phrase.
physicien(ne) *m(f)* physicist.
physiologique *adj* physiological.
physionomie *f* countenance, physiognomy.
physiothérapie *f* physiotherapy.
physique *f* physics:—*adj* physical.
pianiste *mf* pianist.
piano *m* piano.
pic *m* peak.
pictural *adj* pictorial.
pièce *f* piece; room; document.
pied *m* foot; **à ~ on** foot.
piège *m* trap; pit; snare.
piéger *vt* to trap, set a trap.
pierre *f* stone.
piété *f* piety.
piéton *m* pedestrian.
pieu *m* post, stake, pile.
pieux *adj* pious, devout.
pigment *m* pigment.
pile *f* pile; battery.
piler *vt* to crush, pound.
pilier *m* pillar.
pilote *m* pilot; driver.
piloter *vt* to pilot, fly; to drive.
pilule *f* pill.
piment *m* pepper.
pin *m* pine.
pinceau *m* brush, paintbrush.
pincer *vt* to pinch.
pingouin *m* penguin.
pinte *f* pint.
piolet *m* ice axe.
pionnier *m* pioneer.
pipe *f* pipe.
pique-nique *m* picnic.
pique-niquer *vi* to picnic.

piquer *vt* to sting.
piqûre *f* prick; sting; bite.
pirate *m* pirate.
pire *adj* worse:—**le ~** the worst.
pis-aller *m invar* last resort, stopgap.
piscine *f* swimming pool.
piste *f* track; clue.
pistolet *m* pistol, gun.
piteux *adj* pitiful, pathetic.
pitié *f* pity, mercy.
pittoresque *adj* picturesque.
pivoter *vi* to revolve, pivot.
placard *m* poster, notice.
place *f* place; square; seat:—**à la ~ de** instead of.
placer *vt* to place; to invest.
placide *adj* placid, calm.
plafond *m* ceiling; roof.
plage *f* beach.
plaider *vt* to plead.
plaie *f* wound, cut.
plaignant(e) *m(f)* plaintiff.
plaindre *vt* to pity:—**se ~** *vr* to complain.
plaine *f* plain.
plainte *f* complaint.
plaire *vi* to please:—**se ~** *vr* to enjoy.
plaisant *adj* pleasant, agreeable.
plaisanter *vi* to joke, jest.
plaisir *m* pleasure.
plan *m* plan; plane, level.
planche *f* plank, board.
plancher *m* floor.
planer *vi* to glide, soar.
planète *f* planet.
planeur *m* glider.
planifier *vt* to plan.
plante *f* plant.
planter *vt* to plant.
plaque *f* sheet, plate; plaque.

plastique *m* plastic:—*adj* plastic.
plat *adj* flat; straight; dull:—*m* plate; course.
plateau *m* tray; turntable; plateau.
plâtre *m* plaster.
plâtrer *vt* to plaster.
plébiscite *m* plebiscite.
plein *adj* full; entire.
pleur *m* tear, sob:—**en ~s** in tears.
pleurer *vi* to cry, weep.
pleuvoir *vi* to rain.
pli *m* fold; crease; envelope.
pliant *adj* collapsible, folding.
plier *vt* to fold; to bend.
plissement *m* creasing, folding.
plisser *vt* to pleat, fold.
plomb *m* lead; sinker; fuse.
plomber *vt* to weight; to fill.
plomberie *f* plumbing.
plongée *f* diving, dive.
plongeon *m* dive.
plonger *vi* to dive; to plunge.
plongeur *m* **-euse** *f* diver.
pluie *f* rain; shower.
plume *f* feather.
plupart *f* most; majority.
pluriel *m* plural:—*adj* plural.
plus *adv* more, most:—**~ grand que** bigger than:—**de ~ en ~** more and more:—**de ~** moreover:—**non ~** neither, not either.
plusieurs *adj* several.
plutôt *adv* rather, quite, fairly.
pluvieux *adj* rainy, wet.
pneu *m* tyre.
pneumonie *f* pneumonia.
poche *f* pocket; pouch; bag.
poêle *m* stove:—*f* frying pan.
poème *m* poem.
poète *m* poet.
poids *m* weight, influence.

poignée *f* handful:—**~ de mains** handshake.
poil *m* hair; bristle.
poinçon *m* hallmark.
poinçonner *vt* to hallmark.
poing *m* fist:—**coup de ~** punch.
point *m* point; full stop:—**mettre au ~** to finalise; to perfect:—**être sur le ~ de** to be about to:—**à~** medium, just right:—**~ de vue** point of view.
pointe *f* point, head; spike:—**sur la ~ des pieds** on tiptoe.
pointu *adj* pointed, sharp.
poire *f* pear.
poireau *m* leek.
pois *m* pea.
poison *m* poison.
poisson *m* fish.
poitrine *f* chest, breast; bosom.
poivre *m* pepper.
poivrer *vt* to pepper.
polaire *adj* polar.
pôle *m* pole; centre.
polémique *f* controversy:—*adj* controversial.
poli *adj* polite; polished, smooth.
police *f* police.
policier *m* policeman, **-ière** *f* policewoman.
polir *vt* to polish; to refine.
politesse *f* politeness, courtesy.
politicien(ne) *m(f)* politician.
politique *f* politics; policy:—*adj* political.
politiser *vt* to politicise.
polluer *vt* to pollute.
pollution *f* pollution.
polyglotte *adj* polyglot:—*mf* polyglot.
pomme de terre *f* potato.
pomme *f* apple.

pompe f pump.

pomper vt to pump.

pompeux adj pompous; pretentious.

pompier m fireman.

poncer vt to sand down, rub down.

ponctualité f punctuality.

ponctuel adj punctual.

ponctuer vt to punctuate.

pondre vt to lay; to produce.

pont m bridge; deck; axle.

ponton m pontoon; landing stage.

populaire adj popular.

popularité f popularity.

population f population.

porc m pig; pork.

porche m porch.

pore m pore.

poreux adj porous.

port m port; pass; wearing.

portatif adj portable.

porte f door; gate; threshold.

porte-avions m invar aircraft carrier.

porte-clefs, porte-clés m invar key ring.

porte-parole m invar spokesperson.

portée f reach, range; significance:—**à la ~ de** within reach:—**hors de ~** out of reach.

portefeuille m wallet; portfolio.

porter vt to carry; to take; to wear.

porteur m **-euse** f porter; carrier:— adj booster; strong, buoyant.

portière f door.

portion f portion, share.

portrait m portrait.

pose f pose, posture; setting.

poser vt to put; to install:—**se ~** vr to land, settle.

positif adj positive, definite.

position f position; situation; state; stance.

positionner vt to position, locate.

posséder vt to possess.

possesseur m possessor, owner.

possession f possession.

possibilité f possibility; potential.

possible adj possible; potential:—m faire son ~ to do one's best.

postal adj postal, mail.

poste f post office, post:—m position; job.

poster vt to post, mail; to position.

postérieur adj subsequent.

postérité f posterity; descendants.

postier m **-ière** f post office worker.

postuler vt to apply for; to postulate.

posture f posture, position.

pot m jar; pot; can.

pot-de-vin m bribe.

potable adj drinkable; passable.

potage m soup.

poteau m post, stake.

potentiel adj potential:—m potential

poterie f pottery.

potier m potter.

poubelle f dustbin.

pouce m thumb; big toe; inch.

poudre f powder, dust.

poudrer vt to powder.

poule f hen, fowl.

poulet m chicken.

pouls m pulse.

poumon m lung.

poupon m baby.

pouponnière f creche.

pour prép for; to; in favour of; in order:—**~ que** in order that.

pourboire m tip.

pourcentage m percentage.

pourparlers mpl talks, negotiations.

pourquoi adv why:—**~ pas?** why not?:—m reason, question.

pourri *adj* rotten.

pourrir *vi* to rot.

pourriture *f* rot, rottenness.

poursuite *f* pursuit; prosecution.

poursuivre *vt* to pursue; to prosecute.

pourtant *adv* however, yet, nevertheless.

pourvoir *vt* to provide, equip.

pourvu *conj*:—**~ que** provided that.

poussée *f* pressure; thrust.

pousser *vt* to push:—*vi* to push; to grow.

poussière *f* dust.

poussiéreux *adj* dusty.

pouvoir *vi* can, be able; may:—*m* power; authority.

pragmatique *adj* pragmatic.

prairie *f* meadow, prairie.

praticable *adj* practicable; passable.

pratique *f* practice; exercise; observance:—*adj* practical.

pratiquer *vt* to practise, exercise; to carry out.

pré *m* meadow.

préalable *adj* preliminary.

préavis *m* notice, advance warning.

précaire *adj* precarious.

précaution *f* precaution; care.

précédent *adj* previous:—*m* precedent.

précéder *vt* to precede.

prêcher *vt* to preach.

précieux *adj* precious.

précipice *m* precipice.

précipitation *f* haste, violent hurry.

précipiter *vt* to hasten, precipitate.

précis *adj* precise, exact.

préciser *vt* to specify:—**se ~** *vr* to become clear.

précision *f* precision.

précoce *adj* precocious.

précurseur *m* precursor.

prédateur *m* predator.

prédécesseur *m* predecessor.

prédiction *f* prediction.

prédire *vt* to predict, foretell.

prédominance *f* predominance.

prédominer *vi* to predominate.

préfabriqué *adj* prefabricated.

préférable *adj* preferable.

préféré(e) *m(f)* favourite.

préférence *f* preference.

préférer *vt* to prefer.

préjudice *m* loss; damage.

préjudiciable *adj* prejudicial.

préjudicier *vt* to be prejudicial.

préjugé *m* prejudice.

préliminaire *m* preliminary:—*adj* preliminary.

prématuré *adj* premature.

préméditation *f* premeditation.

premier *m* first:—*adj* first; primary

prémonition *f* premonition.

prénatal *adj* prenatal.

prendre *vt* to take:—**se ~** *vr* to consider oneself.

prénom *m* first name, forename.

préoccuper *vt* to preoccupy:—**se ~** *vr* to concern oneself.

préparation *f* preparation.

préparer *vt* to prepare.

prérogative *f* prerogative.

près *adv* near; almost:—**de ~** closely:—**à peu ~** just about.

prescrire *vt* to prescribe.

présence *f* presence.

présent *m* present:—*adj* present:—*m* present:—**à ~** just now.

présentation *f* presentation; introduction.

présenter *vt* to introduce; to present.

préservatif *m* condom.
préserver *vt* to preserve.
présidence *f* presidency.
président(e) *m(f)* president.
présider *vt* to preside, chair.
présomption *f* presumption.
présomptueux *adj* presumptuous.
presque *adv* almost.
presse *f* press.
pressentiment *m* presentiment.
pressentir *vt* to have a presentiment of.
presser *vt* to press; to hurry up:—**se ~** *vr* to hurry.
pression *f* pressure.
pressoir *m* press (wine, cider)
prestation *f* benefit; payment.
prestige *m* prestige.
présumer *vt* to presume.
prêt *adj* ready; prepared:—*m* loan.
prêt-à-porter *m* ready-to-wear.
prétendant(e) *m(f)* candidate.
prétendre *vt* to claim; to want; to intend.
prétendu *adj* so-called, supposed.
prétentieux *adj* pretentious.
prétention *f* pretension, claim.
prêter *vt* to lend; to attribute.
prétexte *m* pretext, excuse.
prêtre *m* priest.
preuve *f* proof, evidence.
prévaloir *vi* to prevail.
prévenant *adj* considerate.
prévenir *vt* to prevent; to warn.
prévention *f* prevention.
prévisible *adj* foreseeable.
prévision *f* prediction; forecast.
prévoir *vt* to anticipate; to plan.
prévoyance *f* foresight.
prévoyant *adj* provident.
prévu *adj* provided for.

prier *vi* to pray.
prière *f* prayer; entreaty.
primaire *adj* primary.
primate *m* primate.
prime *f* premium, subsidy.
primer *vi* to dominate:—*vt* to outdo.
primitif *adj* primitive.
primordial *adj* primordial.
prince *m* prince.
princesse *f* princess.
principal *m* principal:—*adj* main, principal.
principe *m* principle; origin.
printanier *adj* spring.
printemps *m* spring.
prioritaire *adj* priority.
priorité *f* priority.
prise *f* hold, grip; catch; plug; dose —**~ de sang** blood sample:—**~ de courant** plug, power point:—**~ de conscience** awareness, realisation.
prison *f* prison; jail.
prisonnier *m* **-ière** *f* prisoner:—*adj* captive.
privation *f* deprivation.
privatiser *vt* to privatise.
privé *adj* private; unofficial.
priver *vt* to deprive.
privilège *m* privilege.
privilégié *adj* privileged, favoured.
privilégier *vt* to favour.
prix *m* price, cost; prize.
probabilité *f* probability.
probable *adj* probable, likely.
problématique *adj* problematical.
problème *m* problem, issue.
procédé *m* process; behaviour.
procéder *vi* to proceed.
procédure *f* procedure; proceedings.
procès *m* proceedings; lawsuit.
procès-verbal *m* minutes; report.

procession f procession.
prochain adj next; imminent:—m neighbour.
proche adj nearby; close.
proclamation f proclamation.
proclamer vt to proclaim, declare.
procurer vt to procure.
procureur m prosecutor.
prodigieux adj prodigious.
producteur m -trice f producer.
productif adj productive.
production f production.
productivité f productivity.
produire vt to produce.
produit m product; yield.
profane adj secular, profane.
professeur m teacher, professor.
profession f profession; occupation.
professionnel(le) m(f) professional; skilled worker:—adj professional.
profil m profile, outline.
profiler vt to profile.
profit m profit; advantage.
profitable adj profitable.
profiter vi to profit.
profond adj deep, profound.
profondeur f depth; profundity.
profusion f profusion.
programme m programme.
programmer vt to programme; to schedule.
progrès m progress; improvement; advance.
progresser vi to progress; to advance.
progression f progress.
prohiber vt to prohibit, ban.
proie f prey, victim.
projection f projection, casting.
projet m plan; draft.
projeter vt to plan; to cast, project.

prolétaire mf proletarian.
prolifération f proliferation.
proliférer vi to proliferate.
prolongement m continuation, extension.
prolonger vt to prolong.
promenade f walk, stroll.
promener (se) vr to go for a walk.
promeneur m -euse f walker.
promesse f promise.
promettre vt to promise.
promotion f promotion.
promouvoir vt to promote.
prompt adj prompt.
prononcer vt to pronounce.
prononciation f pronunciation.
pronostic m forecast; prognosis.
pronostiquer vt to forecast, prognosticate.
propagande f propaganda.
propagation f propagation.
propager vt to propagate.
prophète m prophet.
prophétique adj prophetic.
prophétiser vt to prophesy.
propice adj propitious.
proportion f proportion, ratio.
proportionnel adj proportional.
propos m talk, remarks; intention:— à ~ de about, on the subject of.
proposer vt to propose.
proposition f proposition.
propre adj clean; own; suitable.
propreté f cleanliness; tidiness.
propriétaire mf owner; landlord.
propriété f ownership; suitability.
propulser vt to propel, power.
propulsion f propulsion.
prorogation f prorogation.
proroger vt to prorogue.
proscrire vt to proscribe.

prose f prose.
prospecter vt to prospect.
prospecteur m **-trice** f prospector.
prospectus m leaflet; prospectus.
prospère adj prosperous.
prospérer vi to prosper, flourish.
prospérité f prosperity.
prostituée f prostitute.
prostitution f prostitution.
protagoniste m protagonist
protection f protection.
protéger vt to protect.
protestant(e) m(f) Protestant:—adj Protestant.
protestation f protest.
protester vi to protest; to affirm.
prototype m prototype.
prouesse f prowess.
prouver vt to prove; to demonstrate.
provenir vi to come from.
proverbe m proverb.
province f province.
provincial adj provincial
provision f provision; supply.
provisoire adj provisional, temporary.
provocation f provocation.
provoquer vt to provoke; to cause.
proximité f proximity.
prudence f prudence, care.
prudent adj prudent, careful.
pseudonyme m pseudonym.
psychanalyser vt to psychoanalyse
psychanalyste mf psychoanalyst.
psychiatre mf psychiatrist
psychiatrie f psychiatry.
psychique adj psychic.
psychisme m psyche, mind.

psychologie f psychology.
psychologique adj psychological.
psychologue mf psychologist:—adj psychological.
psychosomatique adj psychosomatic.
puberté f puberty.
public adj, f **publique** public:—m public, audience.
publicité f publicity.
publier vt to publish.
puce f flea.
pudique adj modest; chaste.
puer vi to stink:—vt to stink.
puéril adj puerile, childish.
puérilité f puerility, childishness.
puis adv then, next.
puisque conj since; as.
puissance f power, strength.
puissant adj powerful.
puits m well; shaft.
pulmonaire adj pulmonary, lung.
pulsation f pulsation.
pulvériser vt to pulverise; to powder.
punir vt to punish.
punition f punishment.
pupille f pupil; ward.
pupitre m desk; console.
pur adj pure; neat.
pureté f purity, pureness.
purifier vt to purify, cleanse.
puritain(e) m(f) adj puritan.
pur-sang m invar thoroughbred.
putréfier vt to putrefy, rot.
pyjama m pyjamas.
pylône m pylon.
pyramide f pyramid.

Q

quai *m* quay, wharf; platform.
qualificatif *adj* qualifying.
qualification *f* qualification.
qualifier *vt* to describe; to qualify.
qualitatif *adj* qualitative.
qualité *f* quality; skill; position.
quand *conj* when, while.
quant *prép*:—~ **à lui** as for him/it.
quantifier *vt* to quantify.
quantitatif *adj* quantitative.
quantité *f* quantity, amount.
quarante *adj, m inv* forty.
quarantième *adj, mf* fortieth.
quart *m* quarter; watch.
quartier *m* district; quarter.
quasi *adv* almost, nearly.
quatorze *adj m* fourteen.
quatorzième *adj mf* fourteenth.
quatre *adj m* four.
quatre-vingt(s) *adj m* eighty.
quatre-vingt-dix *adj m* ninety.
quatre-vingtième *adj mf* eightieth.
quatrième *adj mf* fourth.
que *conj* that; than:—*pron* that;
whom; what; which.
quel, *f* **quelle** *adj* who, what, which.
quelconque *adj* some, any; least, indifferent.

quelqu'un, *f* **-une** someone *pl*
quelques-uns, -unes *pron* some.
quelque *adj* some:—~ **part** somewhere.
quelque chose *pron* something.
quelquefois *adv* sometimes
querelle *f* quarrel; row; debate.
quereller (se) *vr* to quarrel.
question *f* question; issue.
questionnaire *m* questionnaire.
questionner *vt* to question.
quête *m* quest, search.
queue *f* tail; stalk; queue.
qui *pn* who, whom; which.
quiconque *pn* whoever, whosoever.
quiétude *f* quiet; peace.
quincaillerie *f* hardware, ironmon-
gery.
quintuple *adj* quintuple:—*m* quintuple.
quintupler *vi* to quintuple.
quinzaine *f* about fifteen; fortnight.
quinze *adj, m* fifteen.
quinzième *adj, mf* fifteenth.
quitter *vt* to leave.
quoi *pn* what:—~ **que** whatever.
quoique *conj* although, though.
quotidien *adj* daily:—*m* everyday life.

R

rabais *m* reduction, discount.

rabaisser *vt* to humble.

rabattre *vt* to close; to reduce.

rabbin *m* rabbi.

raccommoder *vt* to mend, repair.

raccord *m* join; link; pointing.

raccorder *vt* to link up.

raccourci *m* shortcut.

raccourcir *vt* to shorten.

raccrocher *vt* to ring off, hang up.

race *f* race; stock; breed.

rachat *m* repurchase, purchase.

racheter *vt* to repurchase.

racial *adj* racial.

racine *f* root:—~ **carrée** square root.

raciste *mf* racist:—*adj* racist.

raconter *vt* to tell, recount.

radar *m* radar.

rade *f* harbour, roads.

radiateur *m* radiator; heater.

radiation *f* radiation.

radical *adj* radical.

radieux *adj* radiant, dazzling.

radio *f* radio; X-ray.

radio-taxi *m* radio taxi.

radioactif *adj* radioactive.

radiodiffuser *vt* to broadcast (radio).

radiographie *f* radiography; X-ray photography.

radiologue *mf* radiologist.

radis *m* radish.

radoucir *vt* to soften.

rafale *f* gust, blast; flurry.

raffermir *vt* to harden.

raffinage *m* refining.

raffiné *adj* refined, sophisticated.

raffiner *vt* to refine.

raffoler *vi*:—~ **de** to be crazy about.

rafraîchir *vt* to cool, freshen.

rafraîchissant *adj* refreshing, cooling.

rage *f* rage, fury; mania; rabies.

raid *m* raid; trek.

raide *adj* stiff; steep; broke.

raideur *f* stiffness; steepness.

raidir *vt* to stiffen.

raie *f* line; furrow; scratch.

rail *m* rail; railway.

railler *vt* to scoff at, mock.

raillerie *f* mockery, scoffing.

raisin *m* grape.

raison *f* reason; motive; ratio:— **avoir** ~ to be right:—**en** ~ **de** because of.

raisonnable *adj* reasonable, sensible.

raisonnement *m* reasoning.

raisonner *vi* to reason; to argue.

rajeunir *vt* to rejuvenate.

rajuster *vt* to readjust.

ralenti *adj* slow:—*m* slow motion:— **au** ~ ticking over, idling.

ralentir *vi* to slow down.

ralentissement *m* slowing down.

râler *vi* to groan, moan.

rallier *vt* to rally; to win over.

rallumer *vt* to relight.

ramadan *m* Ramadan.

ramassage *m* gathering.

ramasser *vt* to collect, gather.

rame *f* oar; underground train.

rameau *m* branch.

ramener *vt* to bring back, restore.
ramer *vi* to row.
rameur *m*, **euse** *f* rower.
ramollir (se) *vr* to soften.
ramoner *vt* to sweep.
rampe *f* ramp, slope; gradient.
ramper *vi* to crawl, slither.
rance *adj* rancid, rank.
rançon *f* ransom.
rancune *f* grudge, rancour.
randonnée *f* drive; ride; ramble.
randonneur *m*, **-euse** *f* hiker, rambler.
rang *m* row, line; rank; class.
rangée *f* row, range, tier.
ranger *vt* to arrange.
ranimer *vt* to reanimate.
rapatriement *m* repatriation.
rapatrier *vt* to repatriate.
rapide *adj* rapid, quick.
rapidité *f* rapidity, quickness.
rapiécer *vt* to patch up.
rappel *m* recall; reminder
rappeler *vt* to recall; to remind:—**se ~**
  vr to remember.
rapport *m* report; relation; reference.
rapporter *vt* to report; to bring back.
rapporteur *m*, **-euse** *f* reporter.
rapprochement *m* reconciliation.
rapprocher (se) *vr* to approach; to be
  reconciled.
raquette *f* racket.
rare *adj* rare; odd.
raréfier (se) *vr* to rarefy.
rareté *f* rarity; scarcity.
ras *adj* close-shaven, shorn.
raser *vt* to shave off; to raze:—**se ~** *vr*
  to shave.
rasoir *m* razor.
rassemblement *m* assembling; crowd.
rassembler *vt* to rally:—**se ~** *vr* to
  gather, assemble.

rasseoir (se) *vr* to sit down again.
rassurant *adj* reassuring, comforting.
rassurer *vt* to reassure.
rat *m* rat.
raté *m* **-e** *f* failure:—*m* misfire.
rater *vt* to miss; to fail:—*vi* to misfire.
ratification *f* ratification.
ratifier *vt* to ratify, confirm.
ration *f* ration, allowance.
rationnel *adj* rational.
rationner *vt* to ration.
rattacher *vt* to refasten; to attach; to
  link.
rattraper *vt* to catch again; to recover.
rature *f* deletion, erasure.
raturer *vt* to delete, erase.
rauque *adj* hoarse, raucous.
ravage *m* havoc; devestation.
ravager *vt* to ravage; devastate.
ravin *m* ravine, gully.
ravir *vt* to delight.
raviser (se) *vr* to change one's mind.
ravissant *adj* ravishing, delightful.
ravitaillement *m* revictualling.
ravitailler *vt* to revictual.
raviver *vt* to revive.
rayer *vt* to scratch; to cross out.
rayon *m* ray, beam; spoke; shelf.
rayonnement *m* radiance.
rayonner *vi* to radiate, shine.
rayure *f* stripe; streak; groove.
réaccoutumer (se) *vr* to become
  reaccustomed.
réacteur *m* reactor; jet-engine.
réaction *f* reaction.
réactionnaire *adj* reactionary:—*mf* reactionary.
réagir *vi* to react.
réalisateur *m*, **-trice** *f* director, film-
  maker.
réalisation *f* realisation.

réaliser *vt* to realise:—**se ~** *vr* to be realised, come true.

réalisme *m* realism.

réalité *f* reality.

réanimation *f* resuscitation.

réanimer *vt* to reanimate.

réapparaître *vi* to reappear.

rebelle *mf* rebel:—*adj* rebel, rebellious.

rebeller (se) *vr* to rebel.

rébellion *f* rebellion.

reboiser *vt* to reafforest.

rebondir *vi* to rebound.

rebondissement *m* rebound.

rebut *m* scrap; repulse, rebuff.

receler *vt* to harbour.

récent *adj* recent; new.

réceptif *adj* receptive.

réception *f* reception, welcome.

réceptionniste *mf* receptionist.

récession *f* recession.

recette *f* recipe; formula; receipt.

receveur *m*, **-euse** *f* recipient; collector.

recevoir *vt* to receive.

rechange *m* spare.

recharge *f* reloading.

rechargeable *adj* reloadable.

recharger *vt* to reload.

réchauffer *vt* to reheat.

rêche *adj* rough, harsh.

recherche *f* search; research.

rechercher *vt* to seek; to investigate.

rechute *f* relapse; lapse.

récidiver *vi* to reoffend; to recur.

récif *m* reef.

récipient *m* container, receptacle.

réciproque *adj* reciprocal, mutual.

récit *m* account, story.

récitation *f* recitation.

réciter *vt* to recite.

réclamation *f* complaint; claim.

réclamer *vt* to claim.

réclusion *f* reclusion.

récolte *f* harvest; collection.

récolter *vt* to harvest; to collect.

recommandation *f* recommendation.

recommander *vt* to recommend; to register (letter).

recommencement *m* renewal.

recommencer *vi* to begin again.

récompense *f* reward; award.

réconciliation *f* reconciliation.

réconcilier *vt* to reconcile.

réconfort *m* comfort.

réconfortant *adj* comforting; tonic.

réconforter *vt* to comfort.

reconnaissance *f* recognition.

reconnaissant *adj* grateful.

reconnaître *vt* to recognise; to acknowledge; to be grateful.

reconsidérer *vt* to reconsider.

reconstituer *vt* to reconstitute.

reconstitution *f* reconstitution.

reconstruire *vt* to rebuild.

record *m* record.

recourbé *adj* curved, hooked.

recourir *vi* to run again.

recours *m* recourse; appeal.

récréatif *adj* recreative.

récréation *f* recreation.

récrimination *f* recrimination.

récriminer *vi* to recriminate.

recrue *f* recruit.

recrutement *m* recruitment.

recruter *vt* to recruit.

rectangle *m* rectangle.

rectangulaire *adj* rectangular.

rectification *f* rectification.

rectifier *vt* to rectify.

rectiligne *adj* rectilinear.

reçu *pp* **recevoir** accepted, successful:—*m* receipt.

recueil *m* collection, miscellany.
recueillir *vt* to gather:—**se ~** *vr* to collect one's thoughts.
reculer *vi* to fall back.
récupération *f* recovery.
récupérer *vt* to recover.
recycler *vt* to recycle.
rédacteur *m*, **-trice** *f* editor.
rédaction *f* drafting, drawing up.
rédemption *f* redemption.
redevance *f* rent; tax; fees.
rédiger *vt* to compile; to draft.
redire *vt* to repeat.
redoutable *adj* redoubtable, formidable.
redouter *vt* to dread, fear.
redresser *vt* to rectify; to true.
réduction *f* reduction.
réduire *vt* to reduce.
réduit *adj* reduced:—*m* retreat; recess.
rééducation *f* re-education.
rééduquer *vt* to re-educate.
réel *adj* real, genuine.
réélire *vt* to re-elect.
refaire *vt* to redo; to remake.
réfectoire *m* refectory.
référence *f* reference.
référendum *m* referendum.
réfléchir *vi* to think, reflect.
reflet *m* reflection.
refléter *vt* to reflect, mirror.
réflexe *m* reflex.
réflexion *f* thought, reflection:—**~ faite** all things considered.
réforme *f* reform.
réformer *vt* to reform.
réfraction *f* refraction.
réfréner *vt* to curb.
réfrigérateur *m* refrigerator.
réfrigérer *vt* to refrigerate.
refroidir *vt* to cool:—*vi* to get cold.

refuge *m* refuge.
réfugié(e) *m(f)* refugee:—*adj* refugee.
réfugier (se) *vr* to take refuge.
refus *m* refusal.
refuser *vt* to refuse.
réfuter *vt* to refute.
regagner *vt* to regain.
régaler *vt* to regale.
regard *m* look; glance.
regarder *vt* to look at.
régénération *f* regeneration.
régénérer *vt* to regenerate, revive.
régie *f* administration.
régime *m* system, régime.
région *f* region, area.
régional *adj* regional.
régir *vt* to govern, rule.
registre *m* register, record.
règle *f* rule; order.
règlement *m* regulation, rules.
réglementation *f* regulations; control.
réglementer *vt* to regulate.
régler *vt* to pay; to regulate.
règne *m* reign.
régner *vi* to reign.
régresser *vi* to regress.
régression *f* regression.
regret *m* regret.
regretter *vt* to regret, be sorry; to miss.
regroupement *m* reassembly
regrouper *vt* to reassemble:—**se ~** *vr* to assemble.
régulariser *vt* to regularise.
régularité *f* regularity.
régulier *adj* regular; consistent.
réhabilitation *f* rehabilitation.
réhabiliter *vt* to rehabilitate.
réhabituer (se) *vr* to reaccustom oneself.
rein *m* kidney.
réincarnation *f* reincarnation.

reine *f* queen.

réinsertion *f* reinsertion.

réintégrer *vt* to reinstate.

réitérer *vt* to reiterate.

rejet *m* rejection.

rejeter *vt* to reject.

rejoindre *vt* to rejoin.

rejouer *vt* to replay.

réjouir *vt* to delight:—**se ~** *vr* to rejoice.

réjouissance *f* rejoicing.

relâche *f* intermission, respite.

relâchement *m* relaxation.

relâcher (se) *vr* to relax; to become lax.

relais *m* relay.

relatif *adj* relative.

relation *f* relation; reference.

relaxation *f* relaxation.

relaxer (se) *vr* to relax.

relayer *vt* to relieve; to relay.

relecture *f* rereading.

reléguer *vt* to relegate.

relève *f* relief.

relevé *m* statement; bill.

relever *vt* to raise again; to rebuild.

relief *m* relief; contours; depth.

relier *vt* to link up; to bind.

religieux *m* monk, **-euse** *f* nun:—*adj* religious.

religion *f* religion.

relire *vt* to reread.

reluire *vi* to gleam, shine.

remaniement *m* recasting; revision.

remanier *vt* to recast; to amend.

remarquable *adj* remarkable.

remarque *f* remark, comment.

remarquer *vt* to remark; to notice.

remboursement *m* reimbursement.

rembourser *vt* to reimburse.

remède *m* remedy, cure.

remédier *vi* ~ **à** to remedy, cure.

remerciement *m* thanks; thanking.

remercier *vt* to thank.

remettre *vt* to replace:—**se ~** *vr* to recover.

réminiscence *f* reminiscence.

remise *f* delivery; remittance:—**~ en état** repairing:—**~ à neuf** restoration:—**~ en question** calling into question:—**~ en cause** calling into question.

remmener *vt* to take back.

remonter *vi* to go up again:—*vt* to take up.

remorque *f* trailer; towrope.

remorquer *vt* to tow.

remorqueur *m* tug.

rempart *m* rampart; defence.

remplaçant *m*, **-e** *f* replacement.

remplacer *vt* to replace.

remplir *vt* to fill.

remporter *vt* to take away.

remue-ménage *m invar* commotion; hullabaloo.

remuer *vi* to move; to fidget.

rémunération *f* remuneration.

rémunérer *vt* to remunerate, pay.

renaissance *f* rebirth, Renaissance.

renaître *vi* to be reborn.

renard *m* fox.

rencontre *f* meeting, encounter.

rencontrer *vt* to meet; to find.

rendement *m* yield; output.

rendez-vous *m* appointment; date; meeting place.

rendormir (se) *vr* to go back to sleep.

rendre *vt* to render; to give back:—**se ~** *vr* to surrender.

renfermer *vt* to contain, hold.

renflouer *vt* to refloat.

renforcer *vt* to strengthen.

renfort *m* reinforcement.
renifler *vt* to sniff.
renom *m* renown, fame.
renommée *f* renowned.
renoncement *m* renouncement.
renoncer *vi* to renounce.
renonciation *f* renunciation.
renouer *vt* to tie again.
renouveau *m* spring.
renouveler *vt* to renew.
renouvellement *m* renewal.
rénovation *f* renovation.
rénover *vt* to renovate.
renseignement *m* information.
renseigner *vt* to inform.
rentable *adj* profitable.
rente *f* rent; profit.
rentrer *vi* to re-enter; to return home.
renversement *m* reversal.
renverser *vt* to reverse; to overturn.
renvoi *m* sending back; dismissal.
renvoyer *vt* to send back;to dismiss.
réorganisation *f* reorganisation.
réorganiser *vt* to reorganise.
répandre *vt* to pour out.
répandu *adj* widespread.
réparation *f* repairing; restoration.
réparer *vt* to repair; to restore.
repartir *vi* to set off again.
répartir *vt* to share out.
répartition *f* sharing out.
repas *m* meal.
repeindre *vt* to repaint.
repentir (se) *vr* to repent, rue.
répercussion *f* repercussion.
répercuter (se) *vr* to reverberate; to echo.
repère *m* line, mark.
repérer *vt* to spot, pick out.
répertorier *vt* to itemise; to index.
répéter *vt* to repeat.

répétitif *adj* repetitive.
répétition *f* repetition; rehearsal.
répit *m* respite, rest.
repli *m* fold, coil, meander.
replier *vt* to fold up.
réplique *f* reply, retort.
répliquer *vt* to reply.
répondeur *m* answering machine.
répondre *vt* to answer, reply.
réponse *f* response, reply.
report *m* postponement, deferment.
reporter *vt* to take back:—*m* reporter.
repos *m* rest; landing.
reposer *vt* to put back:—**se ~** *vr* to rest oneself.
repoussant *adj* repulsive; repellent.
repousser *vt* to repel.
reprendre *vt* to retake, recapture.
représentant *m* representative.
représentation *f* representation; performance.
représenter *vt* to represent.
répressif *adj* repressive.
répression *f* repression.
réprimander *vt* to reprimand.
réprimer *vt* to repress.
reprise *f* resumption:—**à plusieurs ~s** several times.
reproche *m* reproach.
reprocher *vt* to reproach, blame.
reproduction *f* reproduction.
reproduire *vt* to reproduce.
reptile *m* reptile.
républicain *m*, **-e** *f* republican:—*adj* republican.
république *f* republic.
répudier *vt* to repudiate.
répugnance *f* repugnance.
répugnant *adj* repugnant.
réputation *f* reputation; character; fame.

réputé *adj* reputable, renowned.

requérir *vt* to request.

requête *f* request.

réquisition *f* requisition.

réseau *m* network, net.

réservation *f* reservation.

réserve *f* reserve; reservation.

réservé *f* reserved.

réserver *vt* to reserve.

réservoir *m* tank; reservoir.

résidence *f* residence.

résidentiel *adj* residential

résider *vi* to reside.

résignation *f* resignation.

résistance *f* resistance.

résistant *adj* resistant.

résister *vi* to resist, withstand.

résolu *adj* resolved, determined.

résolution *f* resolution; solution.

résonner *vi* to resonate.

résoudre *vt* to solve; to resolve.

respect *m* respect, regard.

respectable *adj* respectable.

respecter *vt* to respect.

respectif *adj* respective.

respectueux *adj* respectful.

respiration *f* respiration.

respiratoire *adj* respiratory.

respirer *vi* to breathe, respire.

responsabilité *f* responsibility.

responsable *adj* responsible; liable:— *mf* official, manager.

ressemblance *f* resemblance.

ressembler *vi* to resemble.

ressentiment *m* resentment.

ressentir *vt* to feel, experience.

resserrement *m* contraction.

resserrer *vt* to tighten.

ressort *m* spring.

ressortissant *m*, **-e** *f* national.

ressource *f* resource; resort.

ressusciter *vi* to reawaken.

restant *m* rest, remainder.

restaurant *m* restaurant.

restauration *f* restoration; catering.

restaurer *vt* to restore:—**se ~** *vr* to take refreshment.

reste *m* rest, remainder:—**du ~** besides.

rester *vi* to stay; to be left.

restituer *vt* to return; to refund.

restitution *f* restitution.

restreindre *vt* to restrict.

restrictif *adj* restrictive.

restriction *f* restriction, limitation.

résultat *m* result; profit.

résulter *vi:*—**~ de** to result from.

résumé *m* summary.

résumer *vt* to sum up.

résurrection *f* resurrection.

rétablir *vt* to re-establish, restore.

rétablissement *m* re-establishment, restoring.

retard *m* lateness; delay.

retardé *adj* backward, slow.

retarder *vt* to delay.

retenir *vt* to hold back, retain.

réticence *f* reticence.

réticent *adj* reticent.

retirer (se) *vr* to retire, withdraw.

rétorquer *vt* to retort.

retour *m* return; recurrence.

retourner *vi* to return, go back.

rétracter *vt* to retract.

retrait *m* retreat; withdrawal.

retraite *f* retreat; retirement.

retraité(e) *m(f)* pensioner:—*adj* retired.

rétrécissement *m* narrowing; shrinking.

rétribuer *vt* to remunerate.

rétribution *f* retribution.

rétroactif *adj* retroactive.
rétroaction *f* retroaction.
rétrograde *adj* reactionary.
rétrograder *vi* to go backward.
rétrospectif *adj* retrospective.
retrouver *vt* to find again; to recover:—**se ~** *vr* to meet up.
réunifier *vt* to reunify.
réunir (se) *vr* to meet; to assemble.
réussir *vi* to succeed.
réussite *f* success.
revanche *f* revenge:—**en ~** on the other hand.
rêve *m* dream, dreaming; illusion.
réveil *m* awaking; alarm clock.
réveiller *vt* to wake:—**se ~** *vr* to awaken.
révélation *f* revelation.
révéler *vt* to reveal.
revendeur *m*, **-euse** *f* retailer.
revendiquer *vt* to claim; to demand.
revendre *vt* to resell
revenir *vi* to come back, reappear.
revenu *m* income, revenue.
rêver *vi* to dream; to muse.
réverbère *m* street lamp.
révérer *vt* to revere.
rêverie *f* reverie, musing.
revers *m* back, reverse.
réversible *adj* reversible.
rêveur *m*, **-euse** *f* dreamer:—*adj* dreamy.
revigorer *vt* to invigorate.
revirement *m* reversal; turnaround.
réviser *vt* to review; to revise.
révision *f* revision.
revivre *vi* to relive.
révocation *f* removal; revocation.
revoir *vt* to see again.
révolte *f* revolt, rebellion.
révolter (se) *vr* to rebel, revolt.

révolu *adj* past, bygone.
révolution *f* revolution.
révolutionnaire *mf* revolutionary:—*adj* revolutionary.
révoquer *vt* to revoke.
revue *f* review.
rez-de-chaussée *m invar* ground floor.
rhabiller (se) *vr* to dress again.
rhétorique *f* rhetoric:—*adj* rhetorical.
rhinocéros *m* rhinoceros.
rhum *m* rum.
rhume *m* cold.
riant *adj* smiling; cheerful.
riche *adj* rich, wealthy.
richesse *f* richness; wealth.
ride *f* wrinkle; ripple; ridge.
rideau *m* curtain.
ridicule *adj* ridiculous.
ridiculiser *vt* to ridicule.
rien *pron* nothing:—**de ~** don't mention it:—*m* nothingness; mere nothing.
rieur *adj* cheerful; laughing.
rigide *adj* rigid.
rigidité *f* rigidity.
rigoureux *adj* rigorous, harsh.
rigueur *f* rigour; harshness.
rime *f* rhyme.
rimer *vi* to rhyme (with)
rincer *vt* to rinse out; to rinse.
riposter *vi* to answer back, retaliate.
rire *vi* to laugh; to smile:—*m* laughter, laugh.
risée *f* laugh; ridicule.
risible *adj* laughable.
risque *m* risk, hazard.
risquer *vt* to risk; to venture.
rivage *m* shore
rival *m*, **-e** *f* rival:—*adj* rival.
rivaliser *vi* to rival.

rivalité f rivalry.

rive f shore, bank.

riverain adj riverside, lakeside.

rivière f river.

riz m rice.

robe f dress; gown:—**~ de chambre** dressing gown.

robinet m tap.

robot m robot.

robuste adj robust.

roc m rock.

rocher m rock, boulder.

roder vt to grind.

rôder vi to roam; to prowl.

rôdeur m, **-euse** f prowler.

rognon m kidney.

roi m king

rôle m role, character; roll, catalogue.

roman m novel; romance.

romancier m, **-ière** f novelist.

romantique adj romantic.

rompre vt to break:—vi to break; to burst.

rond m circle, ring; round:—adj round; chubby.

rond-point m roundabout.

ronde f patrol; round; beat.

ronflement m snore, snoring.

ronfler vi to snore.

ronronner vi to purr; to hum.

rose f rose:—adj pink:—m pink.

rosée f dew.

rossignol m nightingale.

rotation f rotation; turnover.

rôti m joint, roast.

rôtir vt to roast.

rôtisserie f rotisserie, steakhouse.

roue f wheel.

rouge adj red:—m red.

rouge-gorge m robin.

rougeur f redness, blushing.

rougir vi to blush, go red:—vt to redden.

rouille f rust.

rouiller vi to rust.

roulement m rotation; movement.

rouler vt to wheel:—vi to drive.

roulotte f caravan.

route f road; way; direction.

routier adj road:—m lorry driver; transport cafe.

routine f routine.

routinier adj humdrum, routine.

roux m, **rousse** f redhead:—adj red, auburn.

royal adj royal, regal.

royaume m kingdom.

ruban m ribbon; tape.

rubis m ruby.

rubrique f column; rubric.

rude adj rough; hard; unrefined.

rudesse f roughness; harshness.

rudiment m rudiment; principle.

rudimentaire adj rudimentary.

rue f street.

ruelle f alley.

rugir vi to roar.

rugissement m roar, roaring.

ruine f ruin; wreck.

ruiner vt to ruin.

ruineux adj ruinous; extravagant.

ruisseau m stream, brook.

ruisseler vi to stream, flow.

rumeur f rumour; murmur.

rupture f break, rupture.

rural adj rural, country.

ruse f cunning, slyness.

rusé adj cunning, crafty.

rustique adj rustic.

rythme m rhythm; rate, speed.

rythmique adj rhythmic.

S

sable *m* sand.

sablé *adj* sandy, sanded.

sabotage *m* sabotage.

saboter *vt* to sabotage.

saboteur *m* **-euse** *f* saboteur.

sac *m* bag:—~ **à main** handbag.

saccade *f* jerk, jolt.

saccharine *f* saccharin.

sachet *m* bag; sachet; packet.

sacré *adj* sacred.

sacrifice *m* sacrifice.

sacrifier *vt* to sacrifice.

sacrilège *m* sacrilege.

sadique *adj* sadistic:—*mf* sadist.

safran *m* saffron.

saga *f* saga.

sagace *adj* sagacious, shrewd.

sage *adj* wise; well-behaved:—*m* sage, wise man.

sage-femme *f* midwife.

sagesse *f* wisdom, sense; good behaviour.

saignant *adj* bleeding.

saigner *vi* to bleed.

saillant *adj* protruding.

saillir *vi* to gush out; to project.

sain *adj* healthy; sound; sane.

saint(e) *m(f)* saint:—*adj* holy, saintly.

sainteté *f* saintliness; holiness.

saisie *f* seizure.

saisir *vt* to seize.

saison *f* season.

saisonnier *adj* seasonal.

salade *f* salad.

salaire *m* salary, pay; reward.

salarié(e) *m(f)* salaried employee:—*adj* salaried.

sale *adj* dirty, filthy; obscene.

salé *adj* salty, salted.

saler *vt* to salt, add salt.

saleté *f* dirt; rubbish; obscenity.

salière *f* saltcellar.

salir *vt* to make dirty:—**se ~** *vr* to get dirty.

salive *f* saliva.

salle *f* room; hall:—~ **de séjour** living room:—~ **à manger** dining room:—~ **de bain** bathroom.

salon *m* lounge; exhibition.

salubre *adj* healthy, salubrious.

saluer *vt* to greet; to salute.

salut *m* safety; welfare; salute.

salutation *f* salutation, greeting.

samedi *m* Saturday.

sanctifier *vt* to sanctify, bless.

sanction *f* sanction; approval.

sanctionner *vt* to punish; to sanction.

sanctuaire *m* sanctuary.

sandale *f* sandal.

sang *m* blood; race; kindred

sanglant *adj* bloody, gory.

sanglot *m* sob.

sangloter *vi* to sob.

sanguinaire *adj* sanguinary, blood-thirsty.

sanitaire *adj* health, sanitary.

sans-abris *mf invar* homeless person.

santé *f* health, healthiness.

saper *vt* to undermine, sap.

sapeur-pompier *m* fireman.

sapin *m* fir tree, fir.

sarcasme *m* sarcasm.

sarcastique *adj* sarcastic.

sardine *f* sardine.

sardonique *adj* sardonic

satellite *m* satellite.

satiété *f* satiety:—**à ~** ad nauseam.

satin *m* satin.

satire *f* satire, lampoon.

satirique *adj* satirical.

satisfaction *f* satisfaction.

satisfaire *vt* to satisfy.

satisfaisant *adj* satisfying.

saturation *f* saturation.

saturé *adj* saturated.

saturer *vt* to saturate.

sauce *f* sauce, dressing.

saucisse *f* sausage.

sauf *prép* save, except; unless:—*adj* safe, unhurt.

saumon *m* salmon.

saut *m* jump, bound; waterfall.

sauter *vi* to jump; to blow up.

sauvage *adj* savage; unsociable.

sauvegarde *f* safeguard; backup.

sauvegarder *vt* to safeguard.

sauver *vt* to save.

sauvetage *m* rescue; salvage.

sauveteur *m* rescuer.

savant *adj* learned; expert:—*m* scientist, scholar.

saveur *f* flavour; savour.

savoir *vt* to know; to be able:—*m* learning, knowledge.

savoir-faire *m* know-how.

savon *m* soap.

savonner *vt* to soap, lather.

savoureux *adj* tasty, savoury.

scandale *m* scandal.

scandaleux *adj* scandalous.

scandaliser *vt* to scandalise.

scaphandre *m* diving suit.

sceau *m* seal.

sceller *vt* to seal.

scénario *m* scenario; screenplay.

scénariste *mf* scriptwriter.

scène *f* stage; scenery, scene.

scepticisme *m* scepticism.

sceptique *adj* sceptical:—*mf* sceptic.

schéma *m* diagram, sketch; outline.

schizophrène *mf* schizophrenic:—*adj* schizophrenic.

schizophrénie *f* schizophrenia.

scie *f* saw; bore.

sciemment *adv* knowingly, on purpose.

science *f* science; skill; knowledge.

science-fiction *f* science fiction.

scientifique *adj* scientific.

scintillant *adj* sparkling, glistening.

scintiller *vi* to sparkle, glisten.

scolaire *adj* school; academic.

scolarité *f* schooling.

scooter *m* scooter.

score *m* score.

scout *m* scout, boy scout.

script *m* printing; script.

scrupule *m* scruple, doubt.

scrupuleux *adj* scrupulous.

sculpter *vt* to sculpt; to carve.

sculpteur *m* sculptor.

sculpture *f* sculpture.

se *pron* oneself, himself, herself, itself, themselves.

séance *f* meeting, session; seat.

seau *m* bucket, pail.

sec *adj, f* **sèche** dry, arid.

séchage *m* drying; seasoning.

sèche-cheveux *m invar* hair-drier

sécher *vi* to dry.

sécheresse *f* drought.

second *adj* second.

secondaire *adj* secondary.

seconde f second.

secouer vt to shake, toss.

secourir vt to help, assist.

secouriste mf first-aid worker.

secours m help, assistance; relief; rescue.

secousse f jolt, bump.

secret m secret:—adj secret; discreet.

secrétaire mf secretary:—m writing desk.

sécrétion f secretion.

secte f sect.

secteur m sector, section.

section f section, division; branch.

séculaire adj secular.

sécuritaire adj security.

sécurité f security; safety.

sédatif m sedative:—adj sedative.

sédiment m sediment.

séduction f seduction; captivation

séduire vt to seduce; to charm, captivate.

segment m segment.

segmenter vt to segment.

ségrégation f segregation.

seigneur m lord, nobleman.

sein m breast, bosom; womb:—**au ~ de** within.

séisme m earthquake, seism.

seize adj, m sixteen.

seizième adj, mf sixteenth.

séjour m stay, sojourn.

séjourner vi to stay, sojourn.

sel m salt; wit.

sélectif adj selective.

sélection f choosing, selection.

sélectionner vt to select, pick.

selle f saddle.

selon prép according to.

semaine f week.

semblable adj like, similar.

semblant m appearance, look.

sembler vi to seem, appear.

semence f seed.

semer vt to sow.

semestre m half-year; semester.

semestriel adj half-yearly; semest-ral.

séminaire m seminary; seminar.

sénat m senate.

sénateur m senator.

sénile adj senile.

sénilité f senility.

sens m sense; judgement; meaning; direction.

sensation f sensation, feeling.

sensationnel adj sensational.

sensé adj sensible.

sensibiliser vt to make sensitive to.

sensibilité f sensitivity.

sensible adj sensitive; perceptive.

sensualité f sensuality.

sensuel adj sensual.

sentence f sentence.

sentier m path, track.

sentiment m sentiment; feeling.

sentimental adj sentimental.

sentir vt to feel; to perceive.

séparation f separation.

séparatiste mf separatist.

séparer vt to separate:—**se ~** vr to separate.

sept adj, m seven.

septembre m September

septième adj, mf seventh.

sépulture f sepulture, burial.

séquence f sequence.

serein adj serene, calm.

sérénité f serenity, calmness.

sergent m sergeant.

série f series.

sérieux adj serious.

seringue f syringe.

serment *m* oath.

séropositif *adj* HIV positive, seropositive.

serpent *m* serpent, snake.

serpenter *vi* to meander, wind.

serre *f* greenhouse; claw.

serrer *vt* to tighten.

serrure *f* lock.

sérum *m* serum.

servante *f* servant.

serveur *m* waiter, **-euse** *f* waitress.

service *m* service; function.

serviette *f* towel; serviette.

servile *adj* servile, slavish.

servilité *f* servility.

servir *vi* to be of use:—*vt* to serve:— **se ~ de** to make use of.

servitude *f* servitude.

session *f* session, sitting.

seuil *m* threshold.

seul *adj* alone; single.

sévère *adj* severe, austere.

sévérité *f* severity; strictness

sexe *m* sex.

sexiste *mf* sexist:—*adj* sexist.

sexualité *f* sexuality.

sexuel *adj* sexual.

sexy *adj* sexy.

short *m* shorts.

si *adv* so, so much; yes:—*conj* if; whether.

SIDA *m* AIDS.

sidérurgiste *mf* steel worker.

siècle *m* century.

siège *m* seat; head office.

siéger *vi* to sit; to be located.

sien *pron*, *f* **sienne**:—**le ~ his**, its, his own, its own, **la sienne** her, its, her own, its own, **les ~s**, **les siennes** their, their own.

siffler *vi* to whistle; to hiss.

sigle *m* abbreviation; acronym.

signal *m* signal, sign.

signaler *vt* to signal, indicate.

signature *f* signature; signing.

signe *m* sign; mark.

signer *vt* to sign.

signet *m* bookmark.

significatif *adj* significant.

signification *f* significance.

signifier *vt* to mean, signify.

silence *m* silence.

silencieux *adj* silent; still.

silhouette *f* silhouette.

similaire *adj* similar.

similarité *f* similarity.

simple *adj* simple; mere; single.

simplicité *f* simplicity.

simplification *f* simplification.

simplifier *vt* to simplify.

simulation *f* simulation.

simuler *vt* to simulate.

simultané *adj* simultaneous.

sincère *adj* sincere, honest.

sincérité *f* sincerity, honesty.

singe *m* monkey.

singularité *f* singularity.

singulier *adj* singular, peculiar.

sinistre *m* disaster; accident:—*adj* sinister.

sinistré(e) *m(f)* disaster victim.

sinon *conj* otherwise, if not; except.

sinueux *adj* sinuous, winding.

site *m* setting, beauty spot.

sitôt *adv* as soon:—**~ que** as soon as.

situation *f* situation, position.

situer *vt* to site, situate.

six *adj*, *m* six.

sixième *adj*, *mf* sixth.

ski *m* ski, skiing.

skier *vi* to ski.

skieur *m* **-euse** *f* skier.

slip *m* briefs; panties.

snob *adj* snobbish.

snobisme *m* snobbishness.

sobre *adj* sober, temperate.

sobriété *f* sobriety, temperance.

sociable *adj* sociable; social.

social *adj* social.

socialiste *mf* socialist:—*adj* socialist.

société *f* society; company.

sociologique *adj* sociological.

sociologue *mf* sociologist.

sœur *f* sister; nun.

sofa *m* sofa.

soi *pn* one(self); self:—**~même** one-self, himself, herself, itself.

soie *f* silk.

soif *f* thirst

soigner *vt* to look after.

soigneux *adj* neat; careful.

soin *m* care.

soir *m* evening; night.

soit *conj* either; or; whether:—*adv* granted; that is to say.

soixante *adj, m* sixty.

soixantième *adj, mf* sixtieth.

sol *m* ground; floor; soil.

soldat *m* soldier

solde *f* pay:—*m* balance.

solder *vt* to pay; to settle.

soleil *m* sun, sunshine; sunflower.

solennel *adj* solemn.

solidarité *f* solidarity.

solide *adj* solid; sound.

solidifier *vt* to solidify.

solitaire *mf* recluse:—*adj* solitary, lone.

solitude *f* solitude; loneliness.

solution *f* solution.

solvable *adj* solvent.

sombre *f* dark; gloomy.

sommaire *m* summary:—*adj* basic, summary.

sommeil *m* sleep; sleepiness.

sommeiller *vi* to slumber.

sommet *m* summit; crest.

somnambule *mf* sleepwalker:—*adj* sleepwalking.

somnifère *m* sleeping pill.

somnoler *vi* to doze.

somptueux *adj* sumptuous, lavish.

son *m* sound:—*adj, f* **sa**; *pl* **ses** his, her, its.

songe *m* dream.

songer *vt* to dream.

sonner *vi* to ring.

sonore *adj* resonant, deep-toned.

sophistiqué *adj* sophisticated.

sordide *adj* sordid, squalid.

sort *m* fate, destiny, lot.

sorte *f* sort, kind.

sortie *f* exit, way out; trip; sortie.

sortir *vi* to go out.

sot *adj* (*f* **sotte**) silly, foolish.

sottise *f* stupidity; stupid remark.

souci *m* worry; concern.

soucier *vr*:—**se ~ de** to care about.

soucieux *adj* concerned, worried.

soudain *adj* sudden, unexpected.

souder *vt* to solder; to weld.

souffle *m* blow, puff; breath.

souffler *vi* to blow; to breathe.

souffrance *f* suffering; pain

souffrir *vi* to suffer.

souhait *m* wish.

souhaiter *vt* to wish for, desire.

soulagement *m* relief.

soulager *vt* to relieve, soothe.

soulever *vt* to lift:—**se ~** *vr* to rise; to revolt.

soulier *m* shoe.

souligner *vt* to underline.

soumettre *vt* to subdue.

soumission *f* submission.

soupape *f* valve.

soupçon *m* suspicion.

soupçonner *vt* to suspect.

soupçonneux *adj* suspicious.

soupe *f* soup.

soupir *m* sigh; gasp.

soupirer *vi* to sigh; to gasp.

souple *adj* supple; pliable.

souplesse *f* suppleness.

source *f* source.

sourcil *m* eyebrow.

sourd(e) *m(f)* deaf person:—*adj* deaf; muted.

sourd(e)-muet(te) *m(f)* deaf-mute:— *adj* deaf and dumb.

souriant *adj* smiling, cheerful.

sourire *m* smile, grin.

souris *f* mouse.

sournois *adj* deceitful.

sous *prép* under, beneath, below.

sous-alimenté *adj* undernourished.

sous-développé *adj* underdeveloped.

sous-entendre *vt* to imply.

sous-estimer *vt* to underestimate.

sous-marin *m* submarine:—*adj* under-water.

sous-titre *m* subtitle.

sous-titrer *vt* to subtitle.

sous-traitant *m* subcontractor.

sous-traiter *vt* to subcontract.

souscrire *vi* to subscribe.

soustraction *f* subtraction.

soustraire *vt* to subtract.

soute *f* hold; baggage hold.

soutenir *vt* to sustain.

souterrain *adj* underground.

soutien *m* support.

soutien-gorge *m* bra.

souvenir *m* memory; recollection.

souvenir (se) *vr* to remember

souvent *adv* often, frequently.

souverain(e) *m(f)* sovereign:—*adj* sovereign.

spacieux *adj* spacious, roomy.

spaghettis *mpl* spaghetti.

spasme *m* spasm.

spécial *adj* special.

spécialiser *vt* to specialise.

spécieux *adj* specious.

spécification *f* specification.

spécifier *vt* to specify.

spécifique *adj* specific.

spécimen *m* specimen.

spectacle *m* spectacle, scene.

spectaculaire *adj* spectacular.

spectateur *m* -trice *f* spectator.

spectre *m* ghost.

spéculateur *m* -trice *f* speculator.

spéculer *vi* to speculate.

sphère *f* sphere.

spiritualité *f* spirituality.

spirituel *adj* witty; spiritual.

splendeur *f* splendour, brilliance.

splendide *adj* splendid.

spontané *adj* spontaneous.

sport *m* sport.

sportif *m* sportsman, **-ive** *f* sports-woman:—*adj* sports.

square *m* square.

squelette *m* skeleton.

stabiliser *vt* to stabilise.

stabilité *f* stability.

stable *adj* stable.

stade *m* stadium; stage.

stage *m* training course.

stagiaire *mf* trainee.

standard *adj* standard.

star *f* star.

starter *m* choke.

station *f* station; stage.

stationnaire *adj* stationary.

stationnement *m* parking.

stationner vi to park.

station-service f service station.

statique adj static.

statistique f statistics:—adj statistical.

statue f statue.

statuer vt to rule.

statut m statute.

statutaire adj statutory.

stencil m stencil.

sténodactylo mf shorthand typist.

sténographie f shorthand.

stéréotype m stereotype.

stérile adj sterile, infertile.

stériliser vt to sterilise.

stérilité f sterility.

stimulant adj stimulating:—m stimulant.

stimulation f stimulation.

stimuler vt to stimulate.

stipuler vt to stipulate.

stock m stock, supply.

stocker vt to stock, stockpile.

stoïque adj stoical.

stop m stop; stop sign.

stopper vt to stop.

store m blind, shade.

stratégie f strategy.

stratégique adj strategic.

stress m stress.

stressant adj stessful.

strict adj strict, severe.

strident adj strident, shrill.

structural adj structural.

structure f structure.

studieux adj studious.

studio m studio; film theatre.

stupéfier vt to stupefy; to astound.

stupeur f amazement; stupor.

stupide adj stupid, foolish.

stupidité f stupidity.

style m style; stylus.

styliste mf designer; stylist.

stylo m pen.

suave adj suave, smooth.

subconscient m subconscious:—adj subconscious.

subir vt to sustain; to undergo.

subit adj sudden.

subjectif adj subjective.

subjectivité f subjectivity.

subjuguer vt to subjugate.

sublime adj sublime.

submerger vt to submerge.

subséquent adj subsequent.

subside m grant.

subsistance f subsistence.

subsister vi to subsist.

substance f substance.

substantiel adj substantial.

substantif m noun, substantive.

substituer vt to substitute.

substitut m substitute.

substitution f substitution.

subtil adj subtle.

subtilité f subtlety.

subvention f grant, subsidy.

subventionner vt to subsidise.

subversif adj subversive.

succéder vi:—~ à to succeed, follow.

succès m success; hit.

successeur m successor.

succession f succession.

succinct adj succinct.

succomber vi to succumb.

succulent adj succulent, delicious.

sucursale f branch.

sucer vt to suck.

sucre m sugar.

sud m south.

suer vi to sweat, perspire.

sueur f sweat.

suffire vi to suffice.

suffisant *adj* sufficient, adequate.

suffoquer *vi* to choke, suffocate.

suffrage *m* suffrage; vote.

suggérer *vt* to suggest.

suggestion *f* suggestion.

suicide *m* suicide.

suicider (se) *vr* to commit suicide.

suite *f* continuation; series:—**tout de ~** at once:—**et ainsi de ~** and so on.

suivant *adj* following, next:—*prép* according to.

suivi *m* follow-up.

suivre *vt* to follow:—**~ son cours** to take its course:—**à suivre** to be continued.

sujet *m* subject, topic:—*adj* subject.

super *adj* ultra, super.

superbe *adj* superb.

superficie *f* area, surface.

superficiel *adj* superficial.

superflu *adj* superfluous.

supérieur *adj* upper; superior.

supériorité *f* superiority.

superlatif *m* superlative:—*adj* superlative.

superstitieux *adj* superstitious.

superstition *f* superstition.

superviser *vt* to supervise.

supplanter *vt* to supplant.

supplément *m* supplement.

supplémentaire *adj* supplementary.

support *m* support, prop; stand.

supporter *vt* to support; to endure.

supposer *vt* to suppose.

suppression *f* suppression.

supprimer *vt* to suppress.

suprématie *f* supremacy.

suprême *adj* supreme.

sur *prép* on; over, above; into; out of, from.

sûr *adj* sure, certain; secure:—**~ de soi** self-assured:—**bien ~** of course.

surabondance *f* overabundance.

suranné *adj* outmoded, outdated.

surcharge *f* surcharge.

surcroît *m* surplus:—**de ~** in addition.

surdité *f* deafness.

surélever *vt* to raise, heighten.

surestimer *vt* to overestimate.

sûreté *f* safety; guarantee.

surface *f* surface.

surgeler *vt* to deep-freeze.

surgir *vi* to appear; to arise.

surlendemain *m* day after tomorrow.

surmonter *vt* to surmount.

surnaturel *adj* supernatural.

surnom *m* nickname.

surnommer *vt* to nickname.

surpasser *vt* to surpass, outdo.

surplomber *vt* to overhang.

surplus *m* surplus.

surpopulation *f* overpopulation.

surprenant *adj* surprising.

surprendre *vt* to surprise.

surprise *f* surprise.

sursaut *m* start, jump.

sursauter *vi* to start, jump.

surtaxe *f* surcharge.

surtout *adv* especially; above all.

surveillance *f* surveillance.

surveiller *vt* to watch; to supervise.

survenir *vi* to take place, occur.

survie *f* survival.

survivant(e) *m(f)* survivor:—*adj* surviving.

survivre *vi* to survive.

survoler *vt* to fly over.

susceptible *adj* susceptible:—**être ~ de** to be likely to.

susciter *vt* to arouse, incite.

suspect(e) *m(f)* suspect.

suspecter *vt* to suspect.
suspendre *vt* to hang up; to suspend.
suspension *f* suspension.
suspicieux *adj* suspicious.
suspicion *f* suspicion.
susurrer *vt* to whisper.
svelte *adj* svelte, slim.
syllabe *f* syllable.
symbole *m* symbol
symbolique *adj* symbolic; token.
symboliser *vt* to symbolise.
symétrie *f* symmetry.
symétrique *adj* symmetrical.
sympathie *f* liking; sympathy.
sympathique *adj* likeable, nice; friendly.

symphonie *f* symphony.
symptôme *m* symptom.
synagogue *f* synagogue.
synchroniser *vt* to synchronise.
syndical *adj* trade-union.
syndicaliste *mf* trade unionist:—*adj* trade union.
syndicat *m* trade union; association.
synonyme *m* synonym:—*adj* synonymous.
synthèse *f* synthesis.
synthétique *adj* synthetic.
systématique *adj* systematic.
système *m* system.

T

tabac *m* tobacco.
table *f* table:—~ **ronde** round-table conference.
tableau *m* table; chart.
tablette *f* bar; tablet.
tablier *m* apron; overall.
tabouret *m* stool.
tache *f* mark; stain; spot.
tâche *f* task, assignment; work.
tacite *adj* tacit.
taciturne *adj* taciturn, silent.
tact *m* tact.
tactile *adj* tactile.
tactique *f* tactics:—*adj* tactical.
taille *f* height, stature, size.
tailler *vt* to cut; to carve.
taire(se) *vr* to be quiet.
talent *m* talent, ability.
talentueux *adj* talented.
talon *m* heel; crust; spur.

tambour *m* drum; barrel.
tamis *m* sieve; riddle.
tamiser *vt* to sieve; to sift.
tampon *m* stopper, plug; tampon.
tandem *m* tandem; duo.
tandis *conj*:—~ **que** while; whereas.
tangible *adj* tangible.
tank *m* tank.
tanner *vt* to tan, weather.
tant *adv* so much:—~ **que** as long as:—~ **mieux** that's a good job:—~ **pis** too bad.
tante *f* aunt.
tantôt *adv* sometimes; this afternoon; shortly.
tapage *m* din, uproar, racket.
tape *f* slap.
taper *vt* to beat; to slap; to type.
tapis *m* carpet; rug; cloth.
tapisser *vt* to wallpaper; to cover.

tapisserie *f* tapestry.

taquin *adj* teasing.

taquiner *vt* to tease; to plague.

tard *adv* late.

tarder *vi* to delay, put off; to dally.

tardif *adj* late; tardy.

tarif *m* tariff; price-list.

tarir (se) *vr* to dry up.

tarte *f* tart, flan.

tartre *m* tartar; fur, scale.

tas *m* heap, pile; lot, set.

tasse *f* cup; coffee cup.

tassement *m* settling, sinking.

tasser *vt* to heap up:—**se ~** *vr* to sink; subside.

tâter *vt* to feel, try.

tatonner *vi* to feel one's way.

tatouer *vt* to tattoo.

taudis *m* hovel, slum.

taureau *m* bull.

taux *m* rate; ratio:—**~ de change** exchange rate.

taverne *f* tavern.

taxation *f* taxation, taxing.

taxe *f* tax; duty; rate.

taxer *vt* to tax.

taxi *m* taxi.

te *pn* you, yourself.

technicien(ne) *m(f)* technician.

technique *f* technique:—*adj* technical.

technologie *f* technology.

technologique *adj* technological.

teindre *vt* to dye.

teint *m* complexion, colouring.

teinter *vt* to tint; to stain.

teinture *f* dye; dyeing.

tel *adj* such; like, similar:—**~ quel** such as it is:—**en tant que ~** as such.

télé *f* TV, telly.

télécommande *f* remote control.

télécopie *f* facsimile transmission; fax.

télégramme *m* telegram; cable.

télégraphier *vt* to telegraph, cable.

télépathie *f* telepathy.

téléphérique *m* cableway; cable-car.

téléphone *m* telephone.

téléphoner *vi* to telephone.

télescope *m* telescope.

télescopique *adj* telescopic.

téléviseur *m* television set.

télévision *f* television.

télex *m* telex.

tellement *adj* so, so much:—**~ de** so many, so much.

téméraire *adj* rash, reckless.

témoignage *m* testimony.

témoigner *vi* to testify.

témoin *m* witness.

tempérament *m* temperament.

température *f* temperature

tempête *f* tempest.

temple *m* temple.

temporaire *adj* temporary.

temps *m* time; while; tense; beat; weather:—**de ~ en ~** from time to time.

tenace *adj* tenacious, stubborn.

ténacité *f* tenacity; stubbornness.

tenaille *f* pincers; tongs.

tendance *f* tendency; trend.

tendancieux *adj* tendentious.

tendon *m* tendon, sinew.

tendre *adj* tender, soft; delicate.

tendresse *f* tenderness; fondness.

tendu *adj* tight; stretched; delicate

ténébreux *adj* dark, gloomy.

teneur *f* terms; content; grade.

tenir *vt* to hold, keep:—**~ à** to value, care about.

tennis *m* tennis:—**~ de table** table tennis.

tentation *f* temptation.

tentative *f* attempt, bid.

tente *f* tent.

tenter *vt* to tempt.

tenue *f* holding; deportment; dress, appearance.

terme *m* term; termination, end; word.

terminaison *f* ending.

terminal *adj* terminal:—*m* terminal.

terminer *vt* to finish off:—**se ~** *vr* to terminate.

terminologie *f* terminology.

terne *adj* colourless; drab.

terrain *m* ground, earth; site; field.

terrasse *f* terrace.

terre *f* earth; ground, land:—**mettre pied à ~** to land, alight.

terrestre *adj* land; terrestrial.

terreur *f* terror, dread.

terrible *adj* terrible, dreadful; terrific, great.

terrier *m* burrow; earth; terrier.

terrifiant *adj* terrifying, fearsome.

terrifier *vt* to terrify.

territoire *m* territory, area.

territorial *adj* land, territorial.

terroir *m* soil.

terroriser *vt* to terrorise.

terroriste *mf* terrorist:—*adj* terrorist.

test *m* test.

testament *m* will, testament.

tester *vt* to test; to make out one's will.

tête à tête *m* private conversation.

tête *f* head; top; sense:—**tenir ~** to cope:—**être en ~** to head.

tétine *f* teat; udder; dummy.

téton *m* breast.

têtu *adj* headstrong, stubborn.

texte *m* text; theme; passage.

textile *adj* textile.

textuel *adj* textual, literal.

texture *f* texture.

thé *m* tea.

théâtral *adj* theatrical, dramatic.

théâtre *m* theatre; drama.

thème *m* theme.

théologie *f* theology.

théorie *f* theory.

théorique *adj* theoretical.

thérapeute *mf* therapist.

thérapie *f* therapy.

thermique *adj* thermal; thermic.

thermomètre *m* thermometer.

thermos *f/m* thermos.

thèse *f* thesis.

thym *m* thyme.

ticket *m* ticket.

tiède *adj* lukewarm, tepid.

tien *poss pn*:—**le ~, la ~ne, les ~(ne)s** yours.

tiers *adj* third:—**~-monde** Third World:—*m* third; third party.

tigre *m* tiger.

timbre *m* stamp; postmark; bell.

timbrer *vt* to stamp; to postmark.

timide *adj* timid, shy.

timidité *f* timidity, shyness.

tintement *m* ringing toll.

tinter *vi* to ring, toll; to chime.

tir *m* shooting; shot:—**~ à l'arc** archery.

tirailler *vt* to tug; to pester.

tire-bouchon *m* corkscrew.

tirelire *f* moneybox.

tirer *vt* to pull; to draw.

tiret *m* dash; hyphen.

tireur *m* **-euse** *f* gunner; drawer (cheque).

tiroir *m* drawer.

tisser *vt* to weave.

tissu *m* texture, fabric; tissue.

titre *m* title; heading; right; deed:—**à ~ de** by right of.

tituber *vi* to stagger.

titulaire *mf* incumbent, holder:—*adj* titular.

toi *pn* you:—**~-même** yourself:—**c'est à ~** it's your's; it's your turn.

toile *f* cloth; canvas; sheet.

toilette *f* cleaning, grooming:—**faire sa ~** to wash oneself.

toit *m* roof; home.

tolérable *adj* tolerable, bearable.

tolérant *adj* tolerant.

tolérer *vt* to tolerate.

tomate *f* tomato.

tombe *f* tomb; grave.

tomber *vi* to fall:—**laisser ~** to drop.

tome *m* book; volume.

ton *adj*, *f* **ta**, *pl* **tes** your:—*m* tone; pitch; shade.

tondre *vt* to shear; mow.

tonifiant *m* tonic.

tonifier *vt* to tone up.

tonique *adj* tonic; fortifying:—*m* tonic.

tonne *f* ton, tonne.

tonneau *m* barrel, cask.

tonnerre *m* thunder.

topographie *f* topography.

toquade *f* infatuation; fad, craze.

toquer *vi* to tap, rap.

torche *f* torch.

torcher *vt* to wipe, mop up.

torchon *m* cloth; duster.

tordre *vt* to twist, contort.

tordu *adj* twisted, crooked.

torpeur *f* torpor.

torrent *m* torrent.

torrentiel *adj* torrential.

torride *adj* torrid; scorching.

torse *m* chest; torso.

torsion *f* twisting; torsion.

tort *m* fault; wrong; prejudice:—**avoir ~** to be wrong:—**faire du ~** to harm.

tortiller *vt* to twist:—**se ~** *vr* to wriggle.

tortionnaire *mf* torturer.

tortue *f* tortoise.

tortueux *adj* tortuous, winding.

torture *f* torture.

torturer *vt* to torture.

tôt *adv* early; soon:—**au plus ~** as soon as possible:—**plus ~** sooner.

total *adj* total.

totalitaire *adj* totalitarian.

totalité *f* totality.

touche *f* touch.

toucher *vt* to touch.

touffe *f* tuft, clump.

toujours *adv* always; still.

tour *f* tower:—*m* turn, round; circuit; tour; trick:—**~ à ~** by turns.

tourbillon *m* whirlwind.

tourbillonner *vi* to whirl, eddy.

tourisme *m* tourism.

touriste *mf* tourist.

touristique *adj* tourist.

tourment *m* torment, agony.

tourmenter *vt* to torment.

tournant *m* bend; turning point:—*adj* revolving.

tournée *f* tour; round.

tourner *vi* to turn:—**se ~** *vr* to turn round.

tournesol *m* sunflower.

tournevis *m* screwdriver.

tournoi *m* tournament.

tournure *f* turn; turn of phrase.

tousser *vi* to cough.

tout *adj* (*pl* **tous**, **toutes**) all; whole;

every:—~ **le monde** everybody:—
pn everything; all:—*m* whole:—*adv*
entirely, quite.

toutefois *adv* however.

toux *f* cough.

toxicomane *mf* drug addict.

toxique *adj* toxic.

trac *m* nerves, stage fright.

tracasser *vt* to worry; to harass.

trace *f* track; outline, trace.

tracer *vt* to trace.

tract *m* leaflet, tract.

tractation *f* transaction.

tracteur *m* tractor.

tradition *f* tradition.

traditionnel *adj* traditional; usual.

traducteur *m* **-trice** *f* translator.

traduction *f* translation.

traduire *vt* to translate.

trafic *m* traffic; trading.

trafiquer *vi* to traffic, trade.

tragédie *f* tragedy.

tragique *adj* tragic.

trahir *vt* to betray.

trahison *f* betrayal, treason.

train *m* train; pace, rate.

traîneau *m* sleigh, sledge.

traînée *f* trail, track; drag.

traîner *vi* to drag on, lag.

traire *vt* to milk.

trait *m* trait, feature; relation.

traite *f* trade; draft, bill; milking.

traité *m* treaty; treatise, tract.

traitement *m* treatment; salary.

traiter *vt* to treat; to process.

traiteur *m* caterer.

traître *m* traitor.

traîtrise *f* treachery.

trajet *m* distance; course.

tramer *vt* to plot; to weave.

trampoline *m* trampoline.

tranche *f* slice; edge; section.

trancher *vt* to cut, sever.

tranquille *adj* quiet, tranquil.

tranquilliser *vt* to reassure.

tranquillité *f* tranquillity.

transaction *f* transaction.

transatlantique *adj* transatlantic.

transcription *f* transcription.

transcrire *vt* to transcribe.

transe *f* trance.

tranférer *vt* to transfer.

transfert *m* transfer.

transformateur *m* transformer.

transformation *f* transformation.

transformer *vt* to transform.

transfusion *f* transfusion.

transgresser *vt* to transgress.

transgression *f* transgression.

transistor *m* transistor.

transiter *vi* to pass in transit.

transition *f* transition.

transitoire *adj* transitory.

transmettre *vt* to transmit.

transmissible *adj* transmissible.

transmission *f* transmission.

transparence *f* transparency.

transparent *adj* transparent.

transpercer *vt* to pierce.

transplanter *vt* to transplant.

transport *m* carrying; transport.

transporter *vt* to transport.

transporteur *m* haulier; carrier.

transposer *vt* to transpose.

transversal *adj* transverse.

trapèze *m* trapeze.

trapéziste *mf* trapeze artist.

trappe *f* trap door.

trappeur *m* trapper.

traquer *vt* to track; to hunt down.

traumatiser *vt* to traumatise.

travail *m pl* **travaux** work, labour.

travailler *vi* to work.

travailleur *m*, **-euse** *f* worker:—*adj* diligent; hard-working.

travers *m* breadth:—**à ~** through, across.

traversée *f* crossing; traverse.

traverser *vt* to cross, traverse.

trébucher *vi* to stumble.

trèfle *m* clover.

treillis *m* trellis; wire mesh.

treize *adj*, *m* thirteen.

treizième *adj*, *mf* thirteenth.

tremblement *m* trembling ~ **de terre** earthquake.

trembler *vi* to tremble, shake.

trémousser (se) *vr* to wriggle.

tremper *vt* to soak.

tremplin *m* springboard.

trentaine *f* about thirty.

trente *adj*, *m* thirty.

trentième *adj mf* thirtieth.

trépidant *adj* pulsating, quivering.

trépigner *vi* to stamp one's feet.

très *adv* very; most; very much.

trésor *m* treasure.

trésorier *m* **-ière** *f* treasurer.

tressaillir *vi* to thrill; to shudder.

tresse *f* plait, braid.

tresser *vt* to plait, braid.

trêve *f* truce; respite.

tri *m* sorting out; grading.

triangle *m* triangle.

triangulaire *adj* triangular.

tribal *adj* tribal.

tribu *f* tribe.

tribunal *m* court, tribunal.

tribune *f* gallery; rostrum.

tribut *m* tribute.

tricher *vi* to cheat.

tricheur *m*, **-euse** *f* cheater.

tricolore *adj* three-coloured, tricolour.

tricoter *vt* to knit.

tridimensionnel *adj* three-dimensional.

trier *vt* to sort out.

trilingue *adj* trilingual.

trimestre *m* quarter; term.

trimestriel *adj* quarterly; three-monthly.

trinquer *vi* to toast; to booze.

trio *m* trio.

triomphal *adj* triumphal.

triomphe *m* triumph, victory.

triompher *vi* to triumph.

triple *adj* triple, treble.

tripler *vi* to triple.

triste *adj* sad, melancholy.

tristesse *f* sadness.

trivial *adj* trivial; crude.

trivialité *f* triviality; crudeness.

troc *m* exchange; barter.

trois *adj*, *m* three.

troisième *adj*, *mf* third.

trombe *f*:—**~ d'eau** cloudburst.

trompe *f* trumpet; trunk.

tromper *vt* to deceive, trick:—**se ~** *vr* to be mistaken.

tromperie *f* deception, deceit.

trompette *f* trumpet.

trompeur *adj* deceitful; deceptive.

tronc *m* trunk, shaft.

trône *m* throne.

tronquer *vt* to truncate, curtail.

trop *adv* too; too much:—*m* **~** excess.

trophée *m* trophy.

tropical *adj* tropical.

tropique *m* tropic.

troquer *vt* to barter, swap.

trotter *vi* to trot; to toddle.

trottinette *f* scooter.

trottoir *m* pavement.

trou *m* hole; gap; cavity.

troublant *adj* disturbing.

trouble *adj* unclear, murky:—*m* trouble, disturbance.

troubler *vt* to trouble, disturb.

trouer *vt* to make a hole in.

troupe *f* troupe; troop.

troupeau *m* herd, drove.

trousse *f* case, kit; wallet.

trouver *vt* to find.

truc *m* (*fam*) trick; gadget.

truite *f* trout.

truquage *m* rigging, fiddling.

truquer *vt* to rig, fiddle.

tu *pn* you.

tube *m* tube, pipe; duct.

tuer *vt* to kill.

tuerie *f* slaughter.

tueur *m* **-euse** *f* killer.

tuile *f* tile.

tulipe *f* tulip.

tumeur *f* tumour.

tumulte *m* tumult, commotion.

tumultueux *adj* tumultuous.

tunnel *m* tunnel.

turbine *f* turbine.

turbulence *f* turbulence.

turbulent *adj* turbulent.

tutelle *f* guardianship.

tuteur *m* **tutrice** *f* guardian:—*m* stake, prop.

tutoyer *vt* to address s.o. as *tu*.

tuyau *m* pipe.

type *m* type; model; bloke, chap.

typhon *m* typhoon.

typique *adj* typical.

tyran *m* tyrant.

tyrannique *adj* tyrannical.

U

ulcère *m* ulcer.

ultérieur *adj* subsequent:—**~ement** *adv* later.

ultimatum *m* ultimatum.

ultime *adj* ultimate, final.

un, une *art* a, an; one—**l'~ l'autre, les ~s les autres** one another.

unanime *adj* unanimous.

unification *f* unification.

unifier *vt* to unify.

uniforme *adj* uniform.

uniformité *f* uniformity; regularity.

unilatéral *adj* unilateral.

union *f* union.

unique *adj* only, single; unique:—**~ment** *adv* only, solely, exclusively.

unir *vt* to unite.

unisson *m* unison.

unité *f* unity; unit.

univers *m* universe; world.

universel *adj* universal.

universitaire *adj* university:—*mf* academic.

université *f* university.

urbain *adj* urban, city.

urbanisme *m* town planning.

urgence *f* urgency.

urgent *adj* urgent.

urne *f* ballot box; urn.

usage *m* use; custom.

usager *m* **ère** *f* user.

usé *adj* worn; banal, trite.

user *vt* to use.

usine *f* factory.

ustensile *m* implement; utensil.

usuel *adj* ordinary; everyday:— **~lement** *adv* ordinarily.

usurper *vt* to usurp.

utérus *m* womb, uterus.

utile *adj* useful.

utilisateur *m*, **-trice** *f* user.

utiliser *vt* to use, utilise.

utilité *f* usefulness; use; profit.

utopie *f* utopia.

utopique *adj* utopian.

V

vacance *f* vacancy:—**~s** holiday, vacation.

vacancier *m*, **-ière** *f* holidaymaker.

vacant *adj* vacant.

vacarme *m* racket, row.

vaccin *m* vaccine.

vache *f* cow.

vagabond *m*, **-e** *f* tramp, vagabond.

vagin *f* vagina.

vague *adj* vague:—*m* vagueness:—*f* wave.

vaguer *vi* to wander, roam.

vaillant *adj* brave, courageous.

vain *adj* vain; shallow.

vaincre *vt* to defeat, overcome.

vainqueur *m* conqueror, victor.

vaisseau *m* vessel; ship.

vaisselle *f* crockery; dishes.

valable *adj* valid; worthwhile.

valeur *f* value, worth; security.

valider *vt* to validate.

valise *f* suitcase.

vallée *f* valley.

valoir *vt* to be worth.

valser *vi* to waltz.

vandale *mf* vandal.

vanité *f* vanity, conceit.

vaniteux *adj* vain, conceited.

vantard *adj* boastful, bragging.

vanter *vt* to praise, vaunt:—**se ~** *vr* to boast.

vapeur *f* haze, vapour.

vaporiser *vt* to spray.

variable *adj* variable, changeable.

variation *f* variation, change.

varié *adj* varied; variegated.

varier *vi* to vary.

variété *f* variety, diversity.

vaste *adj* vast, huge.

vaurien(ne) *m(f)* good-for-nothing.

vautrer (se) *vr* to wallow in.

veau *m* calf; veal.

vedette *f* star; leading light.

végétal *adj* vegetable.

végétarien(ne) *m(f)* vegetarian:—*adj* vegetarian.

végétatif *adj* vegetative.

véhémence *f* vehemence.

véhément *adj* vehement.

véhicule *m* vehicle.

veille *f* wakefulness; watch; eve.

veiller *vi* to stay up, sit up.

veine *f* vein; inspiration; luck.

vélo *m* cycle.

vélodrome *m* velodrome.

velours *m* velvet.

vendange *f* wine harvest; vintage.
vendangeur *m* **-euse** *f* grape-picker.
vendeur *m* **-euse** *f* seller, salesperson.
vendre *vt* to sell.
vendredi *m* Friday.
vénéneux *adj* poisonous.
vénérable *adj* venerable.
vénérer *vt* to venerate.
vengeance *f* vengeance.
venger *vt* to avenge.
venin *m* venom.
venir *vi* to come.
vent *m* wind; breath; vanity.
vente *f* sale; selling.
ventre *m* stomach, belly; womb.
ventriloque *mf* ventriloquist.
venue *f* coming.
ver *m* worm; grub.
véracité *f* veracity; truthfulness.
verbal *adj* verbal.
verbe *m* verb; word.
verdict *m* verdict.
verdure *f* greenery, verdure.
verge *f* stick, cane.
verger *m* orchard.
vérification *f* check; verification.
vérifier *vt* to verify; to audit.
véritable *adj* real, genuine.
vérité *f* truth; truthfulness.
vermine *f* vermin.
verni *adj* varnished.
vernis *m* varnish; glaze.
verre *m* glass; lens; drink.
verrou *m* bolt.
verrouiller *vt* to bolt; to lock.
vers *prép* towards; around:—*m* line, verse.
versatile *adj* versatile.
verser *vt* to pour.
version *f* version.
vert *m* green:—*adj* green.

vertèbre *f* vertebra.
vertical *adj* vertical.
vertu *f* virtue.
vertueux *adj* virtuous.
verve *f* verve, vigour.
veste *f* jacket.
vestiaire *m* cloakroom.
vestibule *m* hall, vestibule.
veston *m* jacket.
vêtement *m* garment.
vêtir (se) *vr* to dress oneself.
veto *m* veto.
veuf *m* widower:—*adj* widowed.
veuve *f* widow:—*adj* widowed.
vexer *vt* to annoy; to hurt.
viable *adj* viable.
viande *f* meat.
vice *m* vice; fault, defect.
victime *f* victim, casualty.
victoire *f* victory.
victorieux *adj* victorious.
vide *adj* empty, vacant:—*m* vacuum.
vidéo *f* video:—*adj invar* video.
vidéocassette *f* videocassette.
vider *vt* to empty.
vie *f* life:—**être en ~** to be alive.
vieillard *m* old man.
vieillesse *f* old age.
vieillir *vi* to get old.
vierge *f* virgin:—*adj* virgin; blank; unexposed.
vieux *adj*, *f* **vieille** old; obsolete.
vif *adj* lively; quick; eager.
vigilant *adj* vigilant.
vigne *f* vine; vineyard.
vigneron *m*, **-onne** *f* wine grower.
vignoble *m* vineyard.
vigoureux *adj* vigorous.
vigueur *f* vigour, strength.
vil *adj* vile; lowly.
villa *f* villa, detached house.

village m village.

villageois m, **-e** f village, rustic.

ville f town, city.

vin m wine.

vinaigre m vinegar.

vindicatif adj vindictive.

vingt adj, m twenty.

vingtaine f about twenty.

vingtième adj, mf twentieth.

vinicole adj wine, wine-growing.

viol m rape.

violation f violation.

violence f violence; force.

violent adj violent.

violer vt to violate; to rape.

violet adj violet:—m violet.

violeur m rapist.

violon m violin.

violoniste mf violinist.

vipère f viper, adder.

virage m turn, bend.

virer vt to transfer:—vi to turn.

virginité f virginity; purity.

viril adj virile; male, masculine.

virilité f virility; masculinity.

virtuel adj virtual.

virulence f virulence.

virulent adj virulent.

virus m virus.

vis f screw.

visa m stamp, visa.

visage m face; expression.

vis-à-vis prép opposite:—m encounter:—en ~ opposite each other.

viser vt to aim, target; to visa.

viseur m sights; viewfinder.

visibilité f visibility.

visible adj visible; evident.

vision f eyesight; vision.

visionnaire mf visionary:—adj visionary.

visite f visit; inspection; visitor.

visiter vt to visit.

visiteur m, **-euse** f visitor.

visqueux adj viscous, thick.

visser vt to screw on.

visuel adj visual.

vital adj vital.

vitalité f energy, vitality.

vitamine f vitamin.

vite adv quickly, fast.

vitesse f speed, swiftness; gear.

viticulteur m wine grower.

vitrail m stained-glass window.

vitre f pane, window.

vitreux adj glassy, vitreous.

vitrier m glazier.

vitrine f shop window.

vitupérer vi to vituperate.

vivace adj hardy, perennial.

vivacité f vivacity, liveliness.

vivant adj alive, living; lively.

vivement adv quickly; keenly.

vivifiant adj refreshing.

vivifier vt to enliven.

vivre vi to live.

vivres mpl victuals, supplies.

vocabulaire m vocabulary.

vocal adj vocal.

vocation f vocation, calling.

vœu m vow; wish.

vogue f fashion:—en ~ in fashion.

voici prép here is, here are; ago, past.

voie f way, road; means:—~ **ferrée** railway.

voilà prép there is, there are; ago.

voile f sail:—m veil.

voiler vt to veil.

voir vt to see:—avoir à ~ avec to have to do with.

voisin m, **-e** f neighbour:—adj neighbouring.

voisinage *m* neighbourhood.
voiture *f* car; carriage; cart.
voix *f* voice; vote.
vol *m* flight:—**à ~ d'oiseau** as the crow flies.
volant *m* steering wheel:—*adj* flying.
volatile *adj* volatile.
volcan *m* volcano.
volcanique *adj* volcanic.
volée *f* flight; volley.
voler *vi* to fly:—*vt* to steal; to rob.
volet *m* shutter; flap, paddle.
voleur *m*, **-euse** *f* thief.
volontaire *adj* voluntary.
volonté *f* will; willpower.
volontiers *adv* willingly.
volubile *adj* voluble.
volume *m* volume.
volumineux *adj* voluminous.
volupté *f* voluptuousness.
voluptueux *adj* voluptuous.
vomir *vi* to vomit.
vorace *adj* voracious.
voracité *f* voracity.
vos = *pl* **votre**.
votant *m*, **-e** *f* voter.

vote *m* vote; voting.
voter *vi* to vote.
votre *adj*, *pl* **vos** your, your own.
vôtre *poss pn*:—**le/la ~, les ~s** yours.
vouer *vt* to vow.
vouloir *vt* to want, wish.
voulu *adj* required; deliberate.
vous *pn* you, yourself.
voûte *f* vault.
vouvoyer *vt* to address someone as *vous*.
voyage *m* journey, trip; travelling.
voyager *vi* to travel, journey.
voyageur *m* **-euse** *f* traveller, passenger.
voyelle *f* vowel.
vrac *adv*:—**en ~** in bulk.
vrai *adj* true, genuine.
vraisemblable *adj* likely, probable.
vrille *f* tendril; spiral.
vu *adj* seen:—*prép* in view of.
vue *f* sight, eyesight.
vulgaire *adj* vulgar.
vulgarité *f* vulgarity, coarseness.
vulnérable *adj* vulnerable.

W X Y Z

wagon *m* wagon, truck.
wagon-restaurant *m* restaurant car.
W.-C. (water-closet) *mpl* lavatory.
week-end *m* weekend.
whisky *m* whisky.

xénophobe *mf* xenophobe:—*adj* xenophobic.
xénophobie *f* xenophobia.

xylophone *m* xylophone.

yacht *m* yacht.
yaourt *m* yoghurt.
yeux = *pl* **œil**.
yoga *m* yoga
yoghurt *m* = **yaourt**.
yogi *m* yogi.
yucca *m* yucca.

zèle *m* zeal.
zélé *adj* zealous.
zénith *m* zenith.
zéro *m* zero, nought, nothing.
zézayer *vi* to lisp.
zigzag *m* zigzag.
zigzaguer *vi* to zigzag.

zodiaque *m* zodiac.
zone *f* zone, area.
zoo *m* zoo.
zoologie *f* zoology.
zoologiste *mf* zoologist.
zut *interj* damn!, rubbish!

English-French Dictionary

A

a *art* un, une.

abacus *n* abaque, boulier *m*.

abandon *vt* abandonner, laisser.

abash *vt* couvrir de honte.

abate *vt* baisser:—*vi* baisser; se calmer.

abbey *n* abbaye *f*.

abbreviate *vt* abréger.

abbreviation *n* abréviation *f*.

abdicate *vt* abdiquer; renoncer à.

abdomen *n* abdomen *m*.

abduct *vt* kidnapper, enlever.

abeyance *n* suspension *f*.

abhor *vt* abhorrer, exécrer.

abhorrent *adj* exécrable.

abide *vt* supporter, souffrir.

ability *n* capacité, aptitude *f*.

abject *adj* misérable; abject.

able *adj* capable:—**to be ~** pouvoir.

abnegation *n* renoncement *m*.

abnormal *adj* anormal.

abnormality *n* anomalie *f*.

aboard *adv* à bord.

abode *n* domicile *m*.

abolish *vt* abolir, supprimer.

abolition *n* abolition.

abominable *adj* abominable.

aboriginal *adj* aborigène.

abort *vi* avorter.

abortion *n* avortement *m*.

abound *vi* abonder.

about *prep* au sujet de; vers:—*adv* çà et là:—**to be ~ to** être sur le point de.

above *prep* au-dessus de:—*adv* au-dessus:—**~ all** surtout, principalement.

abrasion *n* écorchure *f*.

abrasive *adj* abrasif.

abroad *adv* à l'étranger.

abrupt *adj* abrupt; brusque.

abscess *n* abcès *m*.

absence *n* absence *f*.

absent *adj* absent:—*vi* s'absenter.

absent-minded *adj* distrait.

absolute *adj* absolu.

absolve *vt* absoudre.

absorb *vt* absorber.

absorption *n* absorption *f*.

abstain *vi* s'abstenir.

abstinence *n* abstinence *f*.

abstinent *adj* abstinent.

abstract *adj* abstrait:—*n* abrégé *m*.

abstraction *n* abstraction *f*.

absurd *adj* absurde.

absurdity *n* absurdité *f*.

abundance *n* abondance *f*.

abundant *adj* abondant.

abuse *vt* abuser de:—*n* abus *m*.

abyss *n* abîme *m*.

academic *adj* universitaire; scolaire; théorique.

academy *n* académie *f*.

accelerate *vt* accélérer.

acceleration *n* accélération *f*.

accelerator *n* accélérateur *m*.

accent *n* accent *m*:—*vt* accentuer.

accept *vt* accepter.

acceptable *adj* acceptable.

acceptance *n* acceptation *f*.

access *n* accès *m*.

accessible *adj* accessible.

accident *n* accident *m*.

accidental *adj* accidentel.

acclaim *vt* acclamer.

accommodate *vt* loger; accommoder.

accommodation *n* logement *m*.

accompany *vt* accompagner.

accomplice *n* complice *mf*.

accomplish *vt* accomplir.

accomplishment *n* accomplissement *m*.

accord *n* accord *m*:—**of one's own ~** de son propre chef.

accordance *n*:—**in ~ with** conformément à.

according *prep* selon:—**~ as** selon que:—**~ly** *adv* en conséquence.

accost *vt* accoster.

account *n* compte *m*:—**on no ~** en aucun cas:—**on ~ of** en raison de:—*vt* **to ~ for** expliquer.

accountability *n* responsabilité *f*.

accountancy *n* comptabilité *f*.

accountant *n* comptable *mf*.

accumulate *vt* accumuler:—*vi* s'accumuler.

accumulation *n* accumulation *f*.

accuracy *n* exactitude *f*.

accurate *adj* exact.

accusation *n* accusation *f*.

accuse *vt* accuser.

accused *n* accusé(e) *m(f)*.

accustom *vt* accoutumer.

ace *n* as *m*.

ache *n* douleur *f*:—*vi* faire mal.

achieve *vt* réaliser; obtenir.

achievement *n* réalisation *f*.

acid *adj* acide:—*n* acide *m*.

acknowledge *vt* reconnaître.

acknowledgment *n* reconnaissance *f*.

acoustics *n* acoustique *f*.

acquaint *vt* informer, aviser.

acquaintance *n* connaissance *f*.

acquiesce *vi* acquiescer, consentir.

acquiescent *adj* consentant.

acquire *vt* acquérir.

acquisition *n* acquisition *f*.

acquit *vt* acquitter.

acrimonious *adj* acrimonieux.

across *adv* en travers:—*prep* à travers.

act *vt* jouer:—*vi* agir; jouer la comédie:—*n* acte *m*.

action *n* action *f*.

activate *vt* activer.

active *adj* actif.

activity *n* activité *f*.

actor *n* acteur *m*.

actress *n* actrice *f*.

actual *adj* réel; concret.

acute *adj* aigu; perspicace

ad lib *vt* improviser.

ad nauseam *adv* à satiété.

adamant *adj* inflexible.

adapt *vt* adapter, ajuster.

adaptable *adj* adaptable.

adaptation *n* adaptation *f*.

add *vt* ajouter.

addict *n* intoxiqué *m*, -e *f*.

addiction *n* dépendance *f*.

addition *n* addition *f*.

additional *adj* additionnel.

address *vt* adresser.

adept *adj* adroit.

adequate *adj* adéquat; suffisant.

adhere *vi* adhérer.

adhesion *n* adhésion *f*.

adhesive *adj* adhésif.

adjacent *adj* adjacent, contigu.

adjective *n* adjectif *m*.

adjoin *vi* être contigu.

adjourn *vt* reporter, remettre.

adjournment *n* ajournement *m*.

adjust *vt* ajuster, adapter.

adjustable *adj* ajustable.

adjustment *n* ajustement *m*; réglage *m*.

administer *vt* administrer.

administration *n* administration *f*.

administrative *adj* administratif.

admirable *adj* admirable.

admiral *n* amiral *m*.

admiration *n* admiration *f*.

admire *vt* admirer.

admirer *n* admirateur *m*, -trice *f*.

admission *n* admission, entrée *f*.

admit *vt* admettre:—**to ~ to** reconnaître.

admonish *vt* admonester.

admonition *n* admonestation.

adolescence *n* adolescence *f*.

adopt *vt* adopter.

adoption *n* adoption *f*.

adoptive *adj* adoptif.

adorable *adj* adorable.

adore *vt* adorer.

adorn *vt* orner.

adrift *adv* à la dérive.

adroit *adj* adroit, habile.

adulation *n* adulation *f*.

adult *adj* adulte:—*n* adulte *mf*.

adultery *n* adultère *m*.

advance *vt* avancer:—*vi* avancer:—*n* avance *f*.

advantage *n* avantage *m*:—**to take ~ of** profiter de.

advantageous *adj* avantageux.

a.m. *adv* du matin.

adventure *n* aventure *f*.

adventurous *adj* aventureux.

adversary *n* adversaire *mf*.

adverse *adj* défavorable.

adversity *n* adversité *f*.

advertise *vt* faire de la publicité pour.

advertisement *n* publicité *f*; annonce *f*.

advice *n* conseil *m*; avis *m*.

advise *vt* conseiller; aviser.

advisory *adj* consultatif.

advocacy *n* plaidoyer *m*.

advocate *n* avocat *m*:—*vt* plaider pour.

aerial *n* antenne *f*.

aerobics *npl* aérobic *m*.

aeroplane *n* avion *m*.

aeroplane *n* avion *m*.

aerosol *n* aérosol *m*.

affability *n* affabilité *f*.

affable *adj* affable.

affair *n* affaire *f*.

affect *vt* toucher; affecter.

affection *n* affection *f*.

affectionate *adj* affectueux.

affiliate *vt* affilier.

affinity *n* affinité *f*.

affirm *vt* affirmer, déclarer.

affirmative *adj* affirmatif.

afflict *vt* affliger.

affluent *adj* riche; abondant.

afford *vt* fournir:—**to be able to ~** avoir les moyens d'acheter.

affront *n* affront *m*, injure *f*:—*vt* affronter; insulter.

afloat *adv* à flot.

afraid *adj* apeuré:—**I am ~** j'ai peur.

after *prep* après:—*adv* après:—**~ all** après tout.

afterbirth *n* placenta *m*.

aftermath *n* conséquences *fpl*.

afternoon *n* après-midi *mf*.

afterward(s) *adv* ensuite.

again *adv* à nouveau.

against *prep* contre.

age *n* âge *m*:—*vt* vieillir.

agency *n* agence *f*.

agenda *n* ordre du jour *m*.

agent *n* agent *m*.

aggravate *vt* aggraver; énerver.

aggravation *n* aggravation *f*.

aggression *n* agression *f*.

aggressive *adj* agressif.

aggressor *n* agresseur *m*.

agile *adj* agile; adroit.

agility *n* agilité *f*; adresse *f*.

agitate *vt* agiter.

agitation *n* agitation *f*.

ago *adv*:—**how long ~?** il y a combien de temps?

agony *n* agonie *f*.

agree *vt* convenir:—*vi* être d'accord.

agreeable *adj* agréable.

agreed *adj* convenu:—**~!** *adv* d'accord!

agreement *n* accord *m*.

agricultural *adj* agricole.

agriculture *n* agriculture *f*.

ahead *adv* en avant.

aid *vt* aider, secourir:—*n* aide *f*.

AIDS *n* SIDA *m*.

ailment *n* maladie *f*.

aim *vt* pointer; viser.

air *n* air *m*.

air terminal *n* aérogare *f*.

air-conditioned *adj* climatisé.

air-conditioning *n* climatisation *f*.

aircraft *n* avion *m*.

airiness *n* aération, ventilation *f*.

airlift *n* pont aérien *m*.

airline *n* ligne aérienne *f*.

airmail *n*:—**by ~** par avion.

airport *n* aéroport *m*.

airsick *adj*:—**to be ~** avoir le mal de l'air.

airtight *adj* hermétique.

aisle *n* nef d'église *f*.

ajar *adj* entrouvert.

akin *adj* ressemblant.

alarm bell *n* sonnette d'alarme *f*.

alarm *n* alarme *f*:—*vt* alarmer; inquiéter.

alarmist *n* alarmiste *mf*.

albeit *conj* bien que.

album *n* album *m*.

alcohol *n* alcool *m*.

alcoholic *adj* alcoolisé:—*n* alcoolique *mf*.

ale *n* bière *f*.

alert *adj* vigilant:—*n* alerte *f*.

alertness *n* vigilance *f*.

alien *adj* étranger:—*n* étranger *m*, -ère *f*; extra-terrestre *mf*.

alienate *vt* aliéner.

alight *vi* mettre pied à terre:—*adj* en feu.

alike *adj* semblable, égal:—*adv* de la même façon.

alimentation *n* alimentation *f*.

alive *adj* en vie, vivant; actif.

all *adj* tout:—*adv* totalement:—**~ the same** cependant:—**~ the better** tant mieux:—**not at ~!** pas du tout!:—*n* tout *m*.

allege *vt* alléguer.

allegiance *n* loyauté, fidélité *f*.

allergy *n* allergie *f*.

alley *n* ruelle *f*.

alliance *n* alliance *f*.

allocate *vt* allouer.

allocation *n* allocation *f*.

allot *vt* assigner.

allow *vt* permettre; accorder.

allowance *n* allocation *f*; concession *f*.

allude *vi* faire allusion à.

allure *n* charme, attrait *m*.

allusion *n* allusion *f*.

allusive *adj* allusif.

ally *n* allié *m*, -e *f*:—*vt* allier.

almost *adv* presque.

alone *adj* seul:—*adv* seul.

along *adv* le long (de):—**~side** à côté.

aloud *adj* à voix haute.

alphabet *n* alphabet *m*.

alphabetical *adj* alphabétique.

already *adv* déjà.

also *adv* aussi.

altar *n* autel *m*.

alter *vt* modifier.

alteration *n* modification *f*.

alternate *adj* alterné:—*vt* alterner.

alternation *n* alternance *f*.

alternative *n* alternative *f*:—*adj* alternatif:—**~ly** *adv* sinon.

although *conj* bien que, malgré.

altitude *n* altitude *f*.

always *adv* toujours.

amalgamate *vt* amalgamer; *vi* s'amalgamer.

amalgamation *n* amalgamation *f*.

amass *vt* accumuler, amasser.

amateur *n* amateur *m*.

amaze *vt* stupéfier.

amazement *n* stupéfaction *f*.

ambassador *n* ambassadeur *m*.

ambidextrous *adj* ambidextre.

ambiguity *n* ambiguïté *f*.

ambiguous *adj* ambigu.

ambition *n* ambition *f*.

ambitious *adj* ambitieux.

ambulance *n* ambulance *f*.

ambush *n* embuscade *f*:—*vt* tendre une embuscade à.

ameliorate *vt* améliorer.

amelioration *n* amélioration *f*.

amend *vt* modifier; amender.

amendment *n* amendement *m*.

amenities *npl* commodités *fpl*.

America *n* Amérique *f*.

American *adj* américain.

amiability *n* amabilité *f*.

amiable *adj* aimable.

amicable *adj* amical.

amid(st) *prep* entre, parmi.

ammunition *n* munitions *fpl*.

amnesia *n* amnésie *f*.

amnesty *n* amnistie *f*.

among(st) *prep* entre, parmi.

amorous *adj* amoureux

amount *n* montant *m*:—*vi* se monter.

amphibian *n* amphibie *m*.

amplify *vt* amplifier.

amplitude *n* amplitude *f*.

amputate *vt* amputer.

amputation *n* amputation *f*.

amuse *vt* distraire, divertir.

amusement *n* distraction *f*.

amusing *adj* divertissant.

an *art* un, une.

anachronism *n* anachronisme *m*.

anaemic *adj* (*med*) anémique.

anaesthetic *n* anesthésique *m*.

analogy *n* analogie *f*.

analyse *vt* analyser.

analysis *n* analyse *f*.

analytical *adj* analytique.

anarchic *adj* anarchique.

anarchy *n* anarchie *f*.

anatomical *adj* anatomique

anatomy *n* anatomie *f*.

ancestor *n* ancêtre *mf*.

anchor *n* ancre *f*.

ancient *adj* ancien, antique

and *conj* et.

anecdote *n* anecdote *f*.

angel *n* ange *m*.

anger *n* colère *f*:—*vt* irriter.

angle *n* angle *m*:—*vi* pêcher à la ligne.

angler *n* pêcheur à la ligne *m*.

angry *adj* en colère, irrité.

anguish *n* angoisse *f*.

angular *adj* angulaire.

animal *n adj* animal *m*.

animate *vt* animer:—*adj* vivant.

animation *n* animation *f*.

animosity *n* animosité *f*.

ankle *n* cheville *f.*

annex *vt* annexer:—*n* annexe *f.*

annihilate *vt* annihiler, anéantir.

anniversary *n* anniversaire *m.*

annotate *vt* annoter.

annotation *n* annotation *f.*

announce *vt* annoncer.

announcement *n* annonce *f.*

annoy *vt* ennuyer.

annoyance *n* ennui *m.*

annual *adj* annuel

annul *vt* annuler.

anomaly *n* anomalie.

anonymity *n* anonymat *m.*

anonymous *adj* anonyme.

another *adj* un autre:—**one ~** l'un l'autre.

answer *vt* répondre à:—*n* réponse *f.*

ant *n* fourmi *f.*

antagonise *vt* provoquer.

antagonism *n* antagonisme *m.*

antarctic *adj* antarctique.

antenna *n* antenne *f.*

anterior *adj* antérieur.

anthem *n* hymne *m.*

anthology *n* anthologie *f.*

anthropology *n* anthropologie *f.*

antibiotic *n* antibiotique *m.*

anticipate *vt* prévoir.

anticipation *n* attente *f.*

antidote *n* antidote *m.*

antipathy *n* antipathie *f.*

antiquarian *n* antiquaire *mf.*

antique *n* antiquité *f.*

antiquity *n* antiquité *f.*

antithesis *n* antithèse *f.*

antler *n* corne *f.*

anxiety *n* anxiété *f*; désir *m.*

anxious *adj* anxieux.

any *adj pn* n'importe quel, n'importe quelle; un, une; tout:—**~body** quelqu'un; n'importe qui; personne:—**~thing** quelque chose; n'importe quoi; rien.

apart *adv* séparément.

apartment *n* appartement *m.*

apathetic *adj* apathique.

apathy *n* apathie *f.*

aperture *n* ouverture *f.*

apex *n* sommet *m*; apex *m.*

apologise *vt* excuser.

apology *n* apologie, défense *f.*

apostle *n* apôtre *m.*

appall *vt* horrifier, atterrer.

apparatus *n* appareil *m.*

apparent *adj* évident, apparent.

apparition *n* apparition, vision *f.*

appeal *vi* faire appel:—*n* (*law*) appel *m.*

appear *vi* paraître.

appearance *n* apparence *f.*

appellant *n* (*law*) appelant *m.*

append *vt* annexer.

appetising *adj* appétissant.

appetite *n* appétit *m.*

applaud *vt vi* applaudir.

applause *n* applaudissements *mpl.*

apple *n* pomme *f.*

apple tree *n* pommier *m.*

appliance *n* appareil *m.*

applicable *adj* applicable.

applicant *n* candidat *m*, -e *f.*

application *n* application *f.*

apply *vt* appliquer:—*vi* s'adresser.

appoint *vt* nommer.

appointment *n* rendez-vous *m*; nomination *f.*

apportion *vt* répartir.

apposite *adj* adapté.

appraisal *n* estimation *f.*

appraise *vt* évaluer.

appreciate *vt* apprécier.

appreciation *n* appréciation *f.*

appreciative *adj* reconnaissant.

apprehend *vt* appréhender.

apprehension *n* appréhension *f.*

apprentice *n* apprenti *m.*

approach *vi* approcher (s'):—*n* approche *f.*

appropriate *adj* approprié, adéquat.

approval *n* approbation *f.*

approve (of) *vt* approuver.

approximate *adj* approximatif.

approximation *n* approximation *f.*

April *n* avril *m.*

apron *n* tablier *m.*

apt *adj* idéal.

aqualung *n* scaphandre autonome *m.*

aquarium *n* aquarium *m.*

aquatic *adj* aquatique.

arable *adj* arable.

arbiter *n* arbitre *m.*

arbitrary *adj* arbitraire.

arbitrate *vt* arbitrer.

arbitration *n* arbitrage *m.*

arcade *n* galerie *f.*

arch *n* arc *m.*

archbishopric *n* archevêché *m.*

archeological *adj* archéologique.

archeology *n* archéologie *f.*

architect *n* architecte *mf.*

architecture *n* architecture *f.*

archives *npl* archives *fpl.*

arctic *adj* arctique.

ardent *adj* ardent.

ardour *n* ardeur *f.*

area *n* région *f*; domaine *m.*

argue *vi* se disputer.

argument *n* argument *m*; dispute *f.*

argumentative *adj* raisonneur.

arid *adj* aride.

aridity *n* aridité *f.*

arise *vi* se lever; survenir.

aristocracy *n* aristocratie *f.*

aristocrat *n* aristocrate *mf.*

arithmetic *n* arithmétique *f.*

arm *n* bras *m*; arme *f:—vt* armer:—*vi* (s')armer.

armament *n* armement *m.*

armchair *n* fauteuil *m.*

armful *n* brassée *f.*

armistice *n* armistice *m.*

armour *n* armure *f.*

armpit *n* aisselle *f.*

army *n* armée *f.*

aroma *n* arôme *m.*

aromatic *adj* aromatique.

around *prep* autour de:—*adv* autour.

arouse *vt* éveiller; exciter.

arrange *vt* arranger, organiser.

arrangement *n* arrangement *m.*

array *n* série *f.*

arrest *n* arrestation *f:—vt* arrêter.

arrival *n* arrivée *f.*

arrive *vi* arriver.

arrogance *n* arrogance *f.*

arrogant *adj* arrogant.

arrow *n* flèche *f.*

arsenal *n* (*mil*) arsenal *m.*

art gallery *n* musée d'art *m.*

art *n* art *m.*

artery *n* artère *f.*

artful *adj* malin, astucieux.

article *n* article *m.*

articulate *vt* articuler.

articulation *n* articulation *f.*

artificial *adj* artificiel.

artillery *n* artillerie *f.*

artisan *n* artisan *m.*

artist *n* artiste *mf.*

artistry *n* habileté *f.*

as *conj* comme; pendant que; aussi: — ~ **for**, ~ **to** quant à.

ascend *vi* monter.

ascension *n* ascension *f.*

ascent *n* montée *f.*

ascertain *vt* établir.

ascetic *adj* ascétique:—*n* ascète *mf.*

ash *n* (*bot*) frêne *m*; cendre *f.*

ashamed *adj* honteux.

ashore *adv* à terre:—**to go ~** débarquer.

ashtray *n* cendrier *m.*

aside *adv* de côté.

ask *vt* demander.

asleep *adj* endormi:—**to fall ~** s'endormir.

aspect *n* aspect *m.*

aspersion *n* calomnie *f.*

asphyxiate *vt* asphyxier.

asphyxiation *n* asphyxie *f.*

aspirant *n* aspirant *m*, -e *f.*

aspiration *n* aspiration *f.*

aspire *vi* aspirer, désirer.

aspirin *n* aspirine *f.*

assail *vt* assaillir, attaquer.

assailant *n* assaillant.

assassin *n* assassin *m.*

assassinate *vt* assassiner.

assault *n* assaut *m*:—*vt* agresser.

assemble *vt* assembler:—*vi* s'assembler.

assembly *n* assemblée *f.*

assent *n* assentiment *m*:—*vi* donner son assentiment.

assert *vt* soutenir; affirmer.

assertion *n* assertion *f.*

assess *vt* évaluer.

assessment *n* évaluation *f.*

assets *npl* biens *mpl.*

assign *vt* assigner.

assignment *n* allocation *f.*

assimilate *vt* assimiler.

assist *vt* assister, aider.

assistance *n* assistance, aide *f.*

assistant *n* aide *mf.*

associate *vt* associer:—*adj* associé: — *n* associé *m*, -e *f.*

association *n* association *f.*

assortment *n* assortiment *m.*

assume *vt* assumer; supposer.

assumption *n* supposition *f.*

assurance *n* assurance *f.*

assure *vt* assurer.

asthma *n* asthme *m.*

asthmatic *adj* asthmatique.

astonish *vt* surprendre.

astonishment *n* surprise.

astound *vt* ébahir.

astrologer *n* astrologue *mf.*

astrology *n* astrologie *f.*

astronomer *n* astronome *mf.*

astronomy *n* astronomie *f.*

astute *adj* malin.

asylum *n* asile, refuge *m.*

at *prep* à; en.

atheist *n* athée *mf.*

athlete *n* athlète *mf.*

athletic *adj* athlétique.

atlas *n* atlas *m.*

atmosphere *n* atmosphère *f.*

atom *n* atome *m.*

atomic *adj* atomique.

atrocious *adj* atroce.

atrocity *n* atrocité, énormité *f.*

attach *vt* joindre.

attachment *n* attachement *m.*

attack *vt* attaquer:—*n* attaque *f.*

attacker *n* attaquant *m*, -e *f.*

attain *vt* atteindre, obtenir.

attempt *vt* essayer:—*n* essai *m*, tentative *f.*

attend *vt* servir; assister à.

attendance *n* service *m*; assistance *f.*

attention *n* attention *f*; soin *m.*

attentive *adj* attentif:—**~ly** *adv* attentivement.

attic *n* grenier *m.*

attitude *n* attitude *f.*

attract *vt* attirer.

attraction *n* attraction *f*; attrait *m.*

attractive *adj* attrayant.

attribute *vt* attribuer:—*n* attribut *m*.

auction *n* vente aux enchères *f*.

audacious *adj* audacieux.

audacity *n* audace, témérité *f*.

audible *adj* audible.

audience *n* audience *f*.

audit *n* audit *m*:—*vt* vérifier.

auditor *n* auditeur *m*, -trice *f*.

augment *vt vi* augmenter.

August *n* août *m*.

aunt *n* tante *f*.

auspicious *adj* favorable, propice.

austere *adj* austère, sévère.

authentic *adj* authentique

authenticity *n* authenticité *f*.

author *n* auteur *m*.

authorisation *n* autorisation *f*.

authorise *vt* autoriser.

authoritarian *adj* autoritaire.

authority *n* autorité *f*.

autograph *n* autographe *m*.

automatic *adj* automatique.

autonomy *n* autonomie *f*.

autopsy *n* autopsie *f*.

autumn *n* automne *m*.

auxiliary *adj* auxiliaire.

available *adj* disponible.

avalanche *n* avalanche *f*.

avarice *n* avarice *f*.

avenge *vt* venger.

avenue *n* avenue *f*.

average *n* moyenne *f*, moyen terme *m*.

aversion *n* aversion *f*, dégoût *m*.

avert *vt* détourner, écarter.

avoid *vt* éviter; échapper à.

await *vt* attendre.

awake *vt* réveiller:—*vi* se réveiller:— *adj* éveillé.

award *vt* attribuer:—*n* prix *m*; décision *f*.

aware *adj* conscient; au courant.

awareness *n* conscience *f*.

away *adv* absent; loin.

awe *n* peur, crainte *f*.

awful *adj* horrible, terrible.

awkward *adj* gauche, maladroit

axe *n* hache *f*.

axis *n* axe *m*.

axle *n* axe *m*.

B

babble *vi* bavarder, babiller.

babe, baby *n* bébé *m*; nourrisson *m*.

babyhood *n* petite enfance *f*.

babyish *adj* enfantin; puéril.

bachelor *n* célibataire *m*.

back *n* dos *m*:—*adv* en arrière, à l'arrière:—*vt* soutenir.

backbone *n* colonne vertébrale.

backdate *vt* antidater.

backer *n* partisan *m*, -e *f*.

background *n* fond *m*.

backpack *n* sac à dos *m*.

back payment *n* rappel de salaire *m*.

backside *n* derrière *m*.

backward *adj* rétrograde:—*adv* en arrière.

bacon *n* lard *m*.

bad *adj* mauvais, de mauvaise qualité; méchant:—**~ly** *adv* mal.

badge *n* insigne *m*, badge *m*.

badness *n* mauvaise qualité *f*; méchanceté *f*.

baffle vt déconcerter, confondre.

bag n sac m; valise f.

baggage n bagages mpl; équipement m.

bait vt appâter:—n appât m.

bake vt faire cuire au four.

bakery n boulangerie f.

baker n boulanger m, -ère f.

baking n cuisson f; fournée f.

balance n balance f; équilibre m:—vt équilibrer.

balcony n balcon m.

bald adj chauve.

baldness n calvitie f.

ball n balle f; boule f; ballon m.

ballad n ballade f.

ballerina n ballerine f.

ballet n ballet m.

balloon n aérostat m.

ballot n scrutin m; vote m:—vi voter au scrutin secret.

balm, balsam n baume m.

bamboo n bambou m.

ban n interdiction f:—vt interdire.

banal adj banal.

banana n banane f.

band n bande f; orchestre m.

bandage n bande f, bandage m:—vt bander.

bang n claquement m, détonation f: — vt frapper violemment; claquer.

bangle n bracelet m.

banish vt bannir.

banishment n bannissement m.

bank n rive f; banque f; banc m.

banker n banquier m, -ière f.

banknote n billet de banque m.

bankrupt adj failli:—n failli m.

bankruptcy n banqueroute, faillite f.

banquet n banquet m.

baptise vt baptiser.

baptism n baptême m.

bar n bar m; barre f; obstacle m:—vt interdire; exclure.

barbarian n barbare mf:—adj barbare, cruel.

barbarity n barbarie, atrocité f.

barbecue n barbecue m.

barber n coiffeur (pour hommes) m.

bare adj nu; pur:—vt dénuder, découvrir.

barefoot(ed) adj aux pieds nus.

barely adv à peine, tout juste.

bareness n nudité f.

bargain n affaire f; contrat:—vi conclure un marché.

bark n écorce f; aboiement m:—vi aboyer.

barn n grange f; étable f.

barometer n baromètre m.

barracks npl caserne f.

barrage n barrage m.

barrel n tonneau, fût m.

barren adj stérile, infertile.

barricade n barricade f:—vt barricader.

barrier n barrière f; obstacle m.

barring adv excepté, sauf.

bartender n barman m.

barter vi faire du troc:—vt troquer, échanger.

base n base f; partie inférieure f:—vt fonder sur:—adj vil, abject.

basement n sous-sol m.

baseness n bassesse, vilenie f.

bashful adj timide, modeste.

basic adj fondamental, de base.

basin n cuvette f; lavabo m.

basis n base f; fondement m.

basket n panier m, corbeille f.

bass n (mus) contrebasse f.

bastard n, adj bâtard m.

baste vt arroser.

bat n chauve-souris f.

batch n fournée f.

bath n bain m.
bathe vt (vi) (se) baigner.
bathing suit n maillot de bain m.
bathroom n salle de bain f.
baths npl piscine f.
bathtub n baignoire f.
batter vt battre:—n pâte à frire f.
battery n pile, batterie f.
battle n bataille f:—vi se battre.
battlefield n champ de bataille m.
bawdy adj paillard.
bawl vi brailler, (fam) gueuler.
bay n baie f; laurier m.
bazaar n bazar m.
be vi être.
beach n plage f.
beacon n phare m.
bead n perle f.
beak n bec m.
beaker n gobelet m.
beam n rayon m; poutre f:—vi rayonner.
bean n haricot m.
bear n ours m.
bear vt porter, supporter.
bearable adj supportable.
beard n barbe f.
bearded adj barbu.
bearer n porteur m, -euse f.
beast n bête f; brute f.
beat vt battre:—vi battre:—n battement m; pulsation f.
beating n raclée f; battement m.
beautiful adj beau m belle f.
beautify vt embellir; décorer.
beauty n beauté f.
because conj parce que:—prép ~ of en raison de.
become vi devenir, se faire.
becoming adj convenable, seyant.
bed n lit m.
bedclothes npl couvertures et draps mpl.

bedroom n chambre f.
bedspread n dessus-de-lit m invar.
bee n abeille f.
beef n bœuf (viande) m.
beefsteak n bifteck m.
beeline n ligne droite f.
beer n bière f.
befit vt convenir à.
before adv prep avant; devant:—conj avant de, avant que.
beforehand adv à l'avance, au préalable.
beg vt mendier.
beggar n mendiant m, -e f.
begin vt vi commencer.
beginner n débutant m, -e f.
beginning n commencement.
behave vi se comporter, se conduire.
behaviour n conduite f.
behead vt décapiter.
behind prep derrière:—adv derrière, par-derrière, en arrière.
behold vt voir; contempler.
being n existence f, être m.
belated adj tardif.
belch vi éructer:—n éructation f, rot m.
belie vt démentir, tromper.
belief n foi, croyance f.
believable adj croyable.
believe vt croire:—vi penser, croire.
believer n croyant m, -e f.
belittle vt rabaisser.
bell n cloche f.
belligerent adj belligérant.
bellow vi beugler, mugir.
belly n ventre m.
belong vi appartenir à.
beloved adj chéri, bien-aimé.
below adv en dessous, en bas:—prep sous, au-dessous de.
belt n ceinture f.
bench n banc m.

bend vt courber:—vi se courber:—n courbe f.

beneath adv au-dessous:—prep sous, au-dessous de.

benefactor n bienfaiteur m, -trice f.

beneficent adj bienfaisant.

beneficial adj profitable, salutaire, utile.

beneficiary n bénéficiaire mf.

benefit n profit m; bienfait m:—vi bénéficier.

benevolence n bienveillance f.

benevolent adj bienveillant.

benign adj bienveillant, doux.

bequeath vt léguer à.

bequest n legs m.

bereavement n perte f; deuil m.

beret n béret m.

berserk adj fou furieux.

beseech vt supplier, implorer.

beset vt assaillir.

beside(s) prep à côté de; excepté:— adv de plus, en outre.

besiege vt assiéger.

best adj le meilleur, la meilleure:—adv le mieux:—n le meilleur, le mieux m.

bestial adj bestial, brutal.

bestiality n bestialité, brutalité f.

bestow vt accorder, conférer.

bet n pari m:—vt parier.

betray vt trahir.

betrayal n trahison f.

better adj adv meilleur, mieux:—vt améliorer.

between prep entre;* adv au milieu.

beverage n boisson f.

bewilder vt déconcerter.

bewilderment n perplexité f.

beyond prep au-delà de:—adv au-delà, plus loin.

bias n préjugé m; inclination f.

Bible n Bible f.

bibliography n bibliographie f.

bicycle n bicyclette f.

bid vt ordonner; offrir:—n offre, tentative f.

bide vt attendre, supporter.

biennial adj biennal, bisannuel.

big adj grand, gros; important.

bigness n grandeur, grosseur f.

bigot n fanatique mf.

bigoted adj fanatique.

bike n vélo m.

bikini n bikini m.

bilingual adj bilingue.

bill n bec (d'oiseau) m; addition f; billet m.

billet n logement m.

billion n mil milliard m.

bin n coffre m.

bind vt attacher; lier.

biochemistry n biochimie f.

binoculars npl jumelles f pl.

biographer n biographe mf.

biography n biographie f.

biological adj biologique.

biology n biologie f.

bird n oiseau m.

birth n naissance f.

birth certificate n extrait de naissance m.

birth control n limitation des naissances f.

birthday n anniversaire m.

biscuit n biscuit m.

bishop n évêque m.

bit n morceau m; peu m.

bite vt mordre:—n morsure f.

bitter adj amer, âpre; acerbe.

bitterness n amertume f.

bizarre adj étrange, bizarre.

black adj noir, obscur:—n noir m.

blackboard n tableau (noir) m.

blacken vt noircir, ternir.

blackleg n jaune m.

blackmail n chantage m:—vt faire chanter.

blackness n noirceur f.

blacksmith n forgeron m.

bladder n vessie f.

blade n lame f.

blame vt blâmer:—n faute f.

blameless adj irréprochable.

blanch vt blanchir.

bland adj affable, suave.

blank adj blanc; vide:—n blanc m.

blanket n couverture f.

blare vi retentir.

blaspheme vt blasphémer.

blasphemy n blasphème m.

blast n souffle d'air m; explosion f:—vt faire sauter.

blatant adj flagrant.

blaze n flamme f:—vi flamber.

bleach vt blanchir.

bleak adj morne, lugubre.

bleakness n froid m; austérité f.

bleat n bêlement m:—vi bêler.

bleed vi, vt saigner.

bleeding n saignement m.

blemish vt gâter:—n tache f.

blend vt mélanger.

bless vt bénir.

blessing n bénédiction f; bienfait m.

blight vt détruire.

blind adj aveugle:—vt aveugler; éblouir

blindly adv à l'aveuglette, aveuglément.

blindness n cécité f.

blink vi clignoter.

bliss n bonheur extrême m.

blissful adj heureux; béat.

blister n ampoule f.

blizzard n tempête de neige f.

bloated adj gonflé.

blob n goutte, tache f.

bloc n bloc m.

block n bloc m; pâté de maisons m: —~ (up) vt bloquer.

blockade n blocus m:—vt bloquer.

blond adj blond:—n blond m, -e f.

blood n sang m.

blood donor n donneur(-euse) de sang m(f).

blood group n groupe sanguin m.

bloodiness n (fig) cruauté f.

blood pressure n pression artérielle f.

bloodstream n système sanguin m.

bloodthirsty adj sanguinaire.

blood transfusion n transfusion sanguine f.

blood vessel n vaisseau sanguin m.

bloody adj sanglant, ensanglanté.

blossom n fleur f.

blot vt tacher; sécher:—n tache f.

blouse n chemisier m.

blow vi souffler; sonner:—vt souffler:—n coup m.

blubber n blanc de baleine m:—vi pleurnicher.

blue adj bleu.

blueprint n (fig) projet m.

bluff n esbrouffe f:—vt faire de l'esbrouffe.

bluish adj bleuâtre.

blunder n gaffe f:—vi faire une gaffe.

blunt adj émoussé:—vt émousser.

blur n tache f:—vt tacher.

blush n rougeur f:—vi rougir.

board n planche f; table f; conseil m: — vt monter à bord de.

boarder n pensionnaire mf.

boarding house n internat m; pension (de famille) f.

boast vi se vanter:—n vantardise f.

boastful *adj* vantard.

boat *n* bateau *m*; canot *mf*.

boating *n* canotage *m*.

bobsleigh *n* bobsleigh *m*.

bodily *adj adv* physique(ment).

body *n* corps *m*; cadavre *m*.

bodywork *n* (*auto*) carrosserie *f*.

bog *n* marécage *m*.

bogus *adj* faux.

boil *vi* bouillir:—*n* furoncle *m*.

boiler *n* casserole *f*; chaudière *f*.

boisterous *adj* bruyant; turbulent.

bold *adj* audacieux.

boldness *n* audace *f*.

bolt *n* verrou *m*:—*vt* verrouiller.

bomb *n* bombe *f*.

bombard *vt* bombarder.

bombardment *n* bombardement *m*.

bond *n* lien *m*; engagement *m*.

bone *n* os *m*:—*vt* désosser.

bonnet *n* bonnet *m*.

bonus *n* prime *f*.

bony *adj* osseux.

boo *vt* huer.

book *n* livre *m*.

bookcase *n* bibliothèque *f*.

bookkeeper *n* comptable *mf*.

bookkeeping *n* comptabilité *f*.

bookseller *n* libraire *mf*.

bookstore *n* librairie *f*.

bookworm *n* rat de bibliothèque *m*.

boom *n* essor *m*.

boot *n* botte *f*; coffre *m*.

booth *n* cabine *f*; baraque *f*.

border *n* bord *m*; frontière *f*:—*vt* border, avoisiner.

bore *vt* forer; ennuyer:—*n* perceuse *f*; raseur *m*.

boredom *n* ennui *m*.

boring *adj* ennuyeux.

born *adj* né.

borrow *vt* emprunter.

borrower *n* emprunteur *m*, -euse *f*.

bosom *n* sein *m*, poitrine *f*.

boss *n* chef *m*; patron(ne) *m(f)*.

botanic(al) *adj* botanique.

botany *n* botanique *f*.

botch *vt* cochonner.

both *pron* tou(te)s les deux, l'un(e) et l'autre:—*adj* les deux.

bother *vt* ennuyer.

bottle *n* bouteille *f*.

bottleneck *n* embouteillage *m*.

bottle-opener *n* ouvre-bouteille *m invar*.

bottom *n* fond *m*:—*adj* du bas; dernier.

bough *n* branche *f*; rameau *m*.

bounce *vi* rebondir; bondir.

bound *n* limite *f*; saut *m*:—*vi* bondir:—*adj* à destination de.

boundary *n* limite *f*; frontière *f*.

bourgeois *adj* bourgeois.

bout *n* attaque *f*; combat *m*.

bow *vi* se courber:—*n* salut *m*.

bow *n* arc *m*; nœud *m*.

bowels *npl* entrailles *fpl*.

bowl *n* bol *m*; boule *f*.

bowling *n* boules *fpl*.

bow tie *n* nœud papillon *m*.

box *n* boîte, caisse *f*; loge *f*:—*vt* mettre en boîte:—*vi* boxer.

boxer *n* boxeur *m*.

box office *n* guichet *m*.

boy *n* garçon *m*.

boycott *vt* boycotter:—*n* boycottage *m*.

boyfriend *n* petit ami *m*.

bra *n* soutien-gorge *m*.

bracelet *n* bracelet *m*

bracket *n* tranche *f*; parenthèse *f*; crochet *m*.

brag *n* fanfaronnade *f*:—*vi* fanfaronner.

braid *n* tresse *f*:—*vt* tresser.

brain n cerveau m; tête f.
brainwave n idée lumineuse f.
brainy adj intelligent.
brake n frein m:—vi freiner.
brake light n feu de stop m.
branch n branche f:—vi se ramifier.
brand n marque f.
brandy n cognac m.
brash adj grossier; impertinent.
brat n môme, gosse mf.
brave adj courageux, brave.
bravery n bravoure f; courage m.
brawl n bagarre, rixe f:—vi se bagarrer.
breach n brèche f; violation f.
bread n pain m:—**brown ~** pain bis m.
breadth n largeur f.
break vt casser; briser:—vi se casser: —n cassure, rupture f; interruption f.
breakdown n panne f; dépression nerveuse f.
breakfast n petit déjeuner m:—vi déjeuner.
breast n poitrine f, sein m.
breaststroke n brasse f.
breath n haleine f; respiration f.
breathe vt vi respirer; exhaler.
breathtaking adj stupéfiant.
breed n race, espèce f:—vt élever:—vi se reproduire.
breeder n éleveur m, -euse f.
breeze n brise f.
brevity n brièveté f; concision f.
brew vt brasser.
brewer n brasseur m.
brewery n brasserie f.
bribe n pot-de-vin m:—vt soudoyer.
brick n brique f.
bricklayer n maçon m.
bride n mariée f.
bridegroom n marié m.
bridge n pont m.

bridle n bride f; frein m.
brief adj bref, concis:—n résumé m.
briefcase n serviette f.
bright adj clair, brillant.
brighten vt faire briller:—vi s'éclairer.
brilliance n éclat m.
brilliant adj éclatant; génial.
bring vt apporter; amener.
brisk adj vif, rapide, frais.
bristle n poil m:—vi se hérisser.
brittle adj cassant, fragile.
broad adj large.
broadcast n émission f:—vt vi diffuser.
broaden vt élargir:—vi s'élargir.
broadness n largeur f.
broccoli n brocoli m.
brochure n brochure f, dépliant m.
broken adj cassé; interrompu.
broker n courtier m.
bronze n bronze m.
brooch n broche f.
brood vi couver; ruminer f.
broom n genêt m; balai m.
brother n frère m.
brother-in-law n beau-frère m.
brow n sourcil m; front m.
brown adj marron; brun:—n marron m:—vt brunir.
browse vt brouter:—vi paître.
bruise n bleu m, ecchymose f.
brush n brosse f; pinceau m.
brutal adj brutal.
brutality n brutalité f.
brute n brute f:—adj bestial.
bubble n bulle f:—vi bouillonner; pétiller.
bucket n seau m.
buckle n boucle f:—vt boucler:—vi se déformer.
budge vi bouger, remuer.
budget n budget m.

buffet n buffet m:—vt gifler.
bug n punaise f.
build vt construire, bâtir.
builder n constructeur m.
building n bâtiment m; immeuble, édifice m.
bulb n bulbe m; oignon m.
bulge vi se renfler:—n renflement m.
bulk n masse f; volume m.
bulky adj volumineux.
bull n taureau m.
bullet n balle f.
bulletproof adj pare-balles, blindé.
bullion n or en barre m.
bully n tyran m:—vt tyraniser.
bump n heurt m; bosse f:—vt heurter.
bumpy adj cahoteux, bosselé.
bun n petit pain m; chignon m.
bunch n botte f; groupe m.
bundle n paquet m, liasse f:—vt empaqueter.
bungle vt bousiller.
bunk n couchette f.
buoy n (mar) bouée f.
buoyancy n flottabilité f.
buoyant adj flottable; gai, enjoué.
burden n charge f:—vt charger.
bureau n commode f; bureau m.
bureaucrat n bureaucrate mf.

burial n enterrement m; obsèques fpl.
burly adj robuste.
burn vt vi brûler:—n brûlure f.
burning adj brûlant.
burst vi éclater:—**to ~ out laughing** éclater de rire.
bury vt enterrer, inhumer.
bus n (auto)bus m.
bush n buisson, taillis m.
business n entreprise f; commerce m.
businessman n homme d'affaires m.
businesswoman n femme d'affaires f.
bus-stop n arrêt d'autobus m.
busy adj occupé; actif.
but conj mais; sauf, excepté, seulement.
butcher n boucher m, -ère f:—vt abattre, massacrer.
butchery n boucherie f, carnage m.
butter n beurre m:—vt beurrer.
butterfly n papillon m.
button n bouton m:—vt boutonner.
buy vt acheter.
buyer n acheteur m, -euse f.
buzz n bourdonnement:—vi bourdonner.
by prep à côté de, près de; par.
bypass n route de contournement f.
by-product n sous-produit m.
by-road n chemin de traverse m.
byte n (comput) octet m.

C

cabbage n chou m.
cabin n cabine f; cabane f.
cabinet n meuble de rangement m; console f.
cable n câble m.

cache n cachette f.
cackle vi caqueter, jacasser.
cafe n café m.
cafeteria n cafétéria f.
caffein(e) n caféine f.

cage *n* cage *f*:—*vt* mettre en cage.
cake *n* gâteau *m*.
calamity *n* calamité *f*, désastre *m*.
calculate *vt* calculer, compter.
calculation *n* calcul *m*.
calendar *n* calendrier *m*.
calf *n* veau *m*.
calibre *n* calibre *m*.
call *vt* appeler; convoquer:—*n* appel *m*; cri *m*.
calligraphy *n* calligraphie *f*.
calling *n* profession, vocation *f*.
callous *adj* dur; insensible.
calm *n* calme *m*:—*adj* calme:—*vt* calmer.
calorie *n* calorie *f*.
camera *n* caméra *f*.
camouflage *n* camouflage *m*.
camp *n* camp *m*:—*vi* camper.
campaign *n* campagne *f*.
camper *n* campeur *m*, -euse *f*.
camping *n* camping *m*.
campsite *n* camping *m*.
campus *n* campus *m*.
can *v aux* pouvoir:—*n* boîte de conserve *f*.
canal *n* conduit *m*; canal *m*.
cancel *vt* annuler.
cancer *n* cancer *m*.
candid *adj* candide, simple.
candidate *n* candidat(e) *m(f)*.
candle *n* bougie *f*; cierge *m*.
candour *n* candeur *f*; sincérité *f*.
cane *n* canne *f*; bâton *m*.
cannon *n* canon *m*.
canoe *n* canoë *m*.
canon *n* canon *m*; règle *f*.
can opener *n* ouvre-boîte *m*.
canopy *n* baldaquin *m*.
cantankerous *adj* acariâtre.
canteen *n* cantine *f*.
canvas *n* toile *f*.
canvass *vt* sonder.

canvasser *n* prospecteur *m*, -trice *f*.
cap *n* casquette *f*.
capability *n* capacité, aptitude.
capable *adj* capable.
capacity *n* capacité; potentiel *m*.
cape *n* cap, promontoire *m*.
capital *adj* capital:—*n* capital *m*; capitale *f*.
capitalise *vt* capitaliser.
capitalist *n* capitaliste *mf*.
capital punishment *n* peine de mort.
capitulate *vi* capituler.
capitulation *n* capitulation *f*.
capricious *adj* capricieux.
capsize *vt* (*mar*) chavirer.
capsule *n* capsule *f*.
captain *n* capitaine *m*.
captivate *vt* captiver.
captivation *n* fascination *f*.
captive *n* captif *m*, -ive *f*, prisonnier *m*, -ière *f*.
captivity *n* captivité *f*.
capture *n* capture *f*:—*vt* capturer.
car *n* voiture *f*; wagon *m*.
caravan *n* caravane *f*.
carbohydrates *npl* hydrates de carbone *m pl*.
carcass *n* cadavre *m*.
card *n* carte *f*.
cardboard *n* carton *m*.
cardinal *adj* cardinal, principal:—*n* cardinal *m*.
card table *n* table de jeu *f*.
care *n* soin *m*; souci *m*:—*vi* se soucier de.
career *n* carrière *f*; cours *m*.
careful *adj* soigneux, consciencieux.
careless *adj* insouciant, négligent.
carelessness *n* négligence.
caress *n* caresse *f*:—*vt* caresser.
caretaker *n* concierge *mf*.
cargo *n* cargaison *f*.

caricature n caricature f:—vt caricaturer.

carnage n carnage m.

carnal adj charnel; sensuel.

carnival n carnaval m.

carnivorous adj carnivore.

carpenter n charpentier m.

carpentry n charpenterie f.

carpet n tapis m.

carriage n port m; voiture f.

carrier n porteur, transporteur m.

carrion n charogne f.

carrot n carotte f.

carry vt porter:—vi porter.

cart n charrette f.

cartel n cartel m.

cartilage n cartilage m.

cartoon n dessin animé m.

cartridge n cartouche f.

carve vt tailler, sculpter.

carving n sculpture f.

case n cas m; boîte f; étui m; enveloppe f.

cash n espèces fpl:—vt encaisser.

cashier n caissier m, -ière f.

casing n chambranle m.

casino n casino m.

cask n tonneau, fût m.

casket n cercueil m.

casserole n cocotte f.

cassette n cassette f.

cassette player magnétophone m.

cast vt jeter, lancer:—n moule m.

caste n caste f.

castigate vt punir.

castle n château m.

castrate vt castrer.

castration n castration f.

casual adj accidentel, fortuit.

cat n chat m, chatte f.

catalogue n catalogue m.

catapult n catapulte f.

cataract n cascade f; déluge m.

catastrophe n catastrophe f.

catch vt attraper, saisir:—n prise f.

catchword n slogan m.

catechism n catéchisme m.

categorical adj catégorique.

category n catégorie f.

caterer n fournisseur, traiteur m.

catering n restauration f.

caterpillar n chenille f.

cathedral n cathédrale f.

catholic adj n catholique mf.

cattle n bétail m.

cauliflower n chou-fleur m.

cause n cause f; raison f:—vt causer.

cauterise vt cautériser.

caution n prudence, précaution:—vt avertir.

cautious adj prudent, circonspect.

cavalry n cavalerie f.

cave n grotte f; caverne f.

cavern n caverne f.

cavity n cavité f.

cease vt cesser, arrêter.

ceaseless adj incessant, continuel.

cede vt céder.

ceiling n plafond m.

celebrate vt célébrer, fêter.

celebration n fête f.

celibate adj célibataire.

cell n cellule f.

cellar n cave f; cellier m.

cement n ciment m:—vt cimenter.

cemetery n cimetière m.

censor n censeur m.

censorship n censure f.

censure n censure:—vt censurer.

census n recensement m.

centenary n centenaire m:—adj centenaire.

centigrade n centigrade m.

centimetre n centimètre m.

central *adj* central.

centralise *vt* centraliser.

centre *n* centre *m*:—*vt* centrer.

century *n* siècle *m*.

cereal *n* céréal *f*.

ceremonial *adj n* cérémonial *m*; rituel *m*.

ceremony *n* cérémonie *f*.

certain *adj* certain, sûr.

certainty *n* certitude *f*.

certificate *n* certificat, acte *m*.

certification *n* authentification *f*.

certify *vt* certifier, assurer.

cessation *n* cessation *f*.

chafe *vt* irriter; frotter.

chagrin *n* dépit *m*.

chain *n* chaîne *f*:—*vt* enchaîner.

chair *n* chaise *f*:—*vt* présider.

chairman *n* président *m*.

chalk *n* craie *f*.

challenge *n* défi *m*:—*vt* défier.

chamber *n* pièce *f*; chambre *f*.

champagne *n* champagne *m*.

champion *n* champion *m*, -ionne *f*:—
vt défendre.

championship *n* championnat *m*.

chance *n* hasard *m*.

chancellor *n* chancelier *m*.

change *vt* changer:—*vi* changer, se
transformer:—*n* modification *f*;
change *m*.

changeable *adj* changeant.

channel *n* canal *m*:—*vt* canaliser.

chant *n* chant *m*.

chaotic *adj* chaotique.

chapel *n* chapelle *f*.

chapter *n* chapitre *m*.

character *n* caractère *m*; personnage *m*.

characteristic *adj* caractéristique.

charcoal *n* charbon de bois *m*.

charge *vt* charger; accuser:—*n* fardeau
m; accusation *f*.

chargeable *adj* passible.

charitable *adj* caritatif.

charity *n* charité, bienfaisance *f*.

charm *n* charme *m*:—*vt* charmer.

chart *n* carte (marine) *f*; diagramme *m*.

charter *n* charte *f*; privilège *m*:—*vt* affréter.

chase *vt* poursuivre:—*n* chasse *f*.

chaste *adj* chaste; pur.

chastise *vt* châtier, punir.

chastisement *n* châtiment *m*.

chastity *n* chasteté, pureté *f*.

chat *vi* causer:—*n* bavardage *m*.

chatter *vi* jacasser.

chauffeur *n* chauffeur *m*.

chauvinist *n* chauvin, -e *f*.

cheap *adj* bon marché.

cheapen *vt* baisser le prix de.

cheat *vt* tromper, frauder:—*n* tricheur
m -euse *f*.

check *vt.* vérifier; contrôler; réprimer,
enrayer; stopper; enregistrer: —*n*
contrôle *m*.

checkup *n* bilan de santé *m*.

cheek *n* joue *f*.

cheer *n* gaieté *f*; applaudissement *m*:
—*vt* réconforter.

cheerful *adj* gai, enjoué, joyeux.

cheerfulness *n* gaieté *f*; bonne humeur *f*.

cheese *n* fromage *m*.

chef *n* chef (de cuisine) *m*.

chemist *n* chimiste *mf*; pharmacien *m*,
-ienne *f*.

chemistry *n* chimie *f*.

cheque *n* chèque *m*.

cherish *vt* chérir, aimer.

chess *n* échecs *mpl*.

chest *n* poitrine *f*.

chew *vt* mâcher, mastiquer.

chick *n* poussin *m*.

chicken *n* poulet *m*.

chief *adj* principal, en chef:—*n* chef *m*.

chieftain *n* chef *m*.

child *n* enfant *m*.

childbirth *n* accouchement *m*.

childhood *n* enfance *f*.

childish *adj* enfantin.

children *npl* de **child**, enfants *mpl*.

chill *n* froid *m*:—*vt* refroidir.

chilly *adj* froid, très frais.

chimney *n* cheminée *f*.

chin *n* menton *m*.

chip *vt* ébrécher:—*n* fragment, éclat *m*; frite *f*.

chisel *n* ciseau *m*:—*vt* ciseler.

chivalrous *adj* chevaleresque.

chocolate *n* chocolat *m*.

choice *n* choix *m*, préférence.

choir *n* chœur *m*.

choke *vt* étrangler; étouffer.

choose *vt* choisir, élire.

chop *vt* trancher, hacher:—*n* côtelette *f*.

chore *n* corvée *f*; travail routinier *m*.

chorus *n* chœur *m*.

christen *vt* baptiser.

christening *n* baptême *m*.

Christian *adj n* chrétien *m*, -ne *f*.

Christmas *n* Noël *f*.

Christmas Eve *n* veille de Noël *f*.

chronic *adj* chronique.

chronicle *n* chronique *f*.

chronicler *n* chroniqueur *m*.

chronological *adj* chronologique

chronology *n* chronologie *f*.

chuckle *vi* rire, glousser.

chum *n* copain *m*, copine *f*.

church *n* église *f*.

cider *n* cidre *m*.

cigar *n* cigare *m*.

cigarette *n* cigarette *f*.

cinder *n* cendre *f*.

cinema *n* cinéma *m*.

circle *n* cercle *m*; groupe *m*:—*vt* encercler.

circuit *n* circuit *m*; tour *m*; tournée *f*.

circular *adj* circulaire:—*n* circulaire *f*.

circulate *vi* circuler.

circulation *n* circulation *f*.

circumference *n* circonférence *f*.

circumnavigation *n* circumnavigation *f*.

circumspect *adj* circonspect.

circumspection *n* circonspection *f*.

circumstance *n* circonstance, situation *f*.

circumvent *vt* circonvenir.

circus *n* cirque *m*.

citation *n* citation *f*.

cite *vt* citer.

citizen *n* citoyen *m*, -enne *f*.

city *n* ville *f*.

civic *adj* civique.

civil *adj* civil, courtois.

civilian *n* civil *m*, -e *f*.

civilisation *n* civilisation *f*.

civilise *vt* civiliser.

claim *vt* revendiquer, réclamer:—*n* demande *f*; réclamation *f*.

claimant *n* demandeur *m*.

clamour *n* clameur *f*.

clamp *n* attache *f*:—*vt* serrer.

clandestine *adj* clandestin.

clap *vt vi* applaudir.

clapping *n* applaudissements *mpl*.

clarification *n* clarification *f*.

clarify *vt* clarifier, éclaircir.

clarity *n* clarté *f*.

clash *vi* se heurter.

clasp *n* fermoir *m*; boucle *f*.

class *n* classe *f*; catégorie *f*:—*vt* classer.

classic(al) *adj* classique.

classification *n* classification *f*.

classify *vt* classifier.

classroom *n* salle de classe *f*.

clatter *vi* résonner; cliqueter.

claw n griffe f; serre f.

clean adj propre; net:—vt nettoyer.

cleaning n nettoyage m.

cleanliness n propreté, pureté f.

cleanse vt nettoyer.

clear adj clair; net:—vt clarifier.

cleft n fissure, crevasse f.

clemency n clémence f.

clement adj clément.

clergy n clergé m.

clergyman n ecclésiastique m.

clerical adj clérical.

clerk n employé m.

clever adj intelligent; habile.

click vt claquer.

client n client m, -e f.

cliff n falaise f.

climate n climat m.

climatic adj climatique.

climax n apogée m.

climb v vi grimper, escalader.

climber n alpiniste mf.

cling vi s'accrocher (à).

clinic n clinique f.

clip vt couper:—n clip m.

cloak n cape f:—vt masquer.

cloakroom n vestiaire m.

clock n horloge f.

clog n sabot m:—vi se boucher.

close vt fermer:—n fin f; conclusion f:—adj proche:—adv de près.

closeness n proximité f.

closure n fermeture f; clôture f.

cloth n tissu m; toile f.

clothe vt habiller, vêtir.

clothes npl vêtements mpl.

cloud n nuage m; nuée f.

cloudiness n nébulosité f.

cloudy adj nuageux.

clover n trèfle m.

clown n clown m.

club n matraque f; club m.

clue n indice m, indication f.

clumsiness n gaucherie f.

clumsy adj gauche, maladroit.

cluster n grappe f:—vt grouper.

clutch n prise f; embrayage m:—vt empoigner.

coach n autocar m; wagon m; entraîneur m:—vt entraîner.

coal n charbon m.

coalesce vi s'unir.

coalition n coalition f.

coarse adj rude; grossier.

coast n côte f.

coastal adj côtier.

coastguard n gendarmerie maritime f.

coastline n littoral m.

coat n manteau m; couche f:—vt enduire.

coating n revêtement m.

coax vt cajôler.

cobweb n toile d'araignée f.

cock n coq m.

cockpit n cabine de pilotage f.

cocoa n cacao m.

coconut n noix de coco f.

cocoon n cocon m.

cod n morue f.

code n code m.

coercion n coercition.

coexistence n coexistence f.

coffee n café m.

coffeepot n cafetière f.

coffer n coffre m; caisse f.

coffin n cercueil m.

cog n dent d'engrenage f.

cogency n puissance, force f.

cogent adj convaincant, puissant.

cognac n cognac m.

cognisance n connaissance f; compétence f.

cogwheel n roue dentée f.
cohabit vi cohabiter.
cohabitation n cohabitation f.
cohere vi se tenir; être cohérent.
coherent adj cohérent; logique.
cohesive adj cohésif.
coil n rouleau m:—vt enrouler.
coin n pièce de monnaie f.
coincide vi coïncider.
coincidence n coïncidence f.
colander n passoire f.
cold adj froid; indifférent:—n froid m; rhume m.
coldness n froideur f.
collaborate vi collaborer.
collaboration n collaboration f.
collapse vi s'écrouler:—n écroulement.
collapsible adj pliant.
collar n col m.
collate vt collationner.
collateral adj concomitant:—n nantissement m.
collation n collation f.
colleague n collègue mf.
collect vt rassembler; collectionner.
collection n collection f.
collective adj collectif.
collector n collectionneur m, -euse f.
college n collège m.
collide vi se heurter.
collision n collision f, heurt m.
colloquial adj familier.
colloquialism n expression familière f.
collusion n collusion f.
colonial adj colonial.
colonise vt coloniser.
colonist n colon m.
colony n colonie f.
colour n couleur f:—vt colorer:—vi se colorer.

colourful adj coloré.
colouring n teint m.
column n colonne f.
columnist n chroniqueur m.
coma n coma m.
comatose adj comateux.
comb n peigne m:—vt peigner.
combat n combat m:—vt combattre.
combatant n combattant m, -e f.
combination n combinaison f.
combine vt combiner:—vi s'unir.
combustion n combustion f.
come vi venir:—**to ~ across, ~ upon** vt rencontrer par hasard:—**to ~ round, ~ to** vi revenir à soi.
comedian n comédien m; comique m.
comedy n comédie f.
comet n comète f.
comfort n confort m:—vt réconforter; soulager.
comfortable adj confortable.
comic(al) adj comique.
command vt ordonner, commander:—n ordre m.
commander n commandant m.
commemorate vt commémorer.
commemoration n commémoration f.
commence vt vi commencer.
commencement n commencement m.
commend vt recommander.
commendation n louange f; recommandation f.
commensurate adj proportionné.
comment n commentaire m:—vt commenter.
commentary n commentaire m; observation f.
commentator n commentateur m, -trice f.
commerce n commerce m.
commercial adj commercial.

commiserate *vt* compatir avec.

commiseration *n* commisération, pitié *f*.

commission *n* commission *f*:—*vt* commissionner.

commit *vt* commettre; confier à; engager.

commitment *n* engagement *m*.

committee *n* comité *m*.

common *adj* commun; ordinaire.

common sense *n* bon sens *m*.

commonly *adv* communément, généralement.

commotion *n* vacarme *m*.

communicable *adj* communicable

communicate *vt* communiquer:—*vi* communiquer.

communication *n* communication *f*.

communion *n* communion *f*.

communist *n* communiste *mf*.

community *n* communauté *f*.

commutable *adj* interchangeable, permutable.

commute *vt* échanger.

compact *adj* compact, serré.

compact disc *n* disque compact *m*.

companion *n* compagnon *m*, compagne *f*.

company *n* compagnie; société *f*.

comparable *adj* comparable.

comparative *adj* comparatif.

compare *vt* comparer.

comparison *n* comparaison *f*.

compartment *n* compartiment *m*.

compass *n* boussole *f*.

compassion *n* compassion *f*.

compassionate *adj* compatissant.

compatibility *n* compatibilité *f*.

compatible *adj* compatible.

compatriot *n* compatriote *mf*.

compel *vt* contraindre, obliger, forcer.

compensate *vt* compenser.

compensation *n* compensation *f*.

compete *vi* rivaliser (avec).

competence *n* compétence *f*; aptitude *f*.

competent *adj* compétent.

competition *n* compétition *f*; concurrence *f*.

competitive *adj* concurrentiel, compétitif.

competitor *n* concurrent *m*, -e *f*.

complacency *n* suffisance *f*.

complacent *adj* suffisant.

complain *vi* se plaindre.

complaint *n* plainte *f*; réclamation *f*.

complement *n* complément *m*.

complementary *adj* complémentaire.

complete *adj* complet; achevé:—*vt* achever.

completion *n* achèvement *m*.

complex *adj* complexe.

complexion *n* teint *m*; aspect *m*.

complexity *n* complexité *f*.

compliance *n* conformité *f*; soumission *f*.

complicate *vt* compliquer.

complication *n* complication *f*.

complicity *n* complicité *f*.

compliment *n* compliment *m*:—*vt* complimenter.

comply *vi* se conformer.

component *adj* composant.

compose *vt* composer.

composer *n* compositeur *m*, -trice *f*.

composition *n* composition *f*.

composure *n* maîtrise de soi *f*.

compound *vt* composer:—*adj* *n* composé *m*.

comprehend *vt* comprendre.

comprehensible *adj* compréhensible.

comprehension *n* compréhension *f*.

comprehensive *adj* global; compréhensif.

compress *vt* comprimer.

comprise *vt* comprendre, embrasser.

compromise n compromis m:—vt compromettre.

compulsion n compulsion f.

compulsory adj obligatoire.

computer n ordinateur m.

computerise vt traiter par ordinateur, informatiser.

computer science n informatique f.

comrade n camarade mf.

comradeship n camaraderie f.

conceal vt cacher.

concealment n dissimulation f.

concede vt concéder, accorder.

conceit n vanité f.

conceive vt vi concevoir.

concentrate vt concentrer.

concentration n concentration f.

concept n concept m.

conception n conception f.

concern vt concerner:—n affaire f; souci m.

concerning prep en ce qui concerne, concernant.

concert n concert m.

concession n concession f.

conciliate vt concilier.

conciliation n conciliation f.

concise adj concis, succinct.

conclude vt conclure.

conclusion n conclusion.

conclusive adj décisif, concluant.

concoct vt confectionner.

concord n entente, harmonie f.

concordance n accord m.

concrete n béton m:—vt bétonner.

concur vi coïncider; s'entendre.

concurrence n consentement m.

concussion n commotion f.

condemn vt condamner.

condemnation n condamnation f.

condensation n condensation f.

condense vt condenser.

condescend vi condescendre.

condescension n condescendance f.

condition vt conditionner:—n condition, situation f; état m.

conditional adj conditionnel.

condolences npl condoléances fpl.

condom n préservatif m.

conduct n conduite f:—vt conduire.

conduit n conduit m; tuyau m.

cone n cône m.

confectioner n confiseur m, -euse f.

confectionery n confiserie f.

confer vt vi conférer.

conference n conférence f.

confess vt confesser:—vi se confesser.

confession n confession f.

confidant n confident m, -e f.

confide vt confier:—~ in se confier à.

confidence n confiance f; assurance f.

confident adj confiant, sûr (de soi).

confidential adj confidentiel.

confine vt limiter.

confinement n détention f; alitement m.

confirm vt confirmer; ratifier.

confirmation n confirmation f.

confiscate vt confisquer.

confiscation n confiscation f.

conflict n conflit m; lutte f.

conflicting adj contradictoire.

conform vi se conformer (à).

conformity n conformité f.

confront vt confronter.

confrontation n confrontation f.

confuse vt confondre.

confusion n confusion f; désordre m.

congeal vi se congeler.

congenial adj sympathique.

congenital adj congénital.

congestion n congestion f.

congratulate vt complimenter, féliciter.

congratulations *npl* félicitations *fpl*.

congregate *vt* rassembler, réunir.

congregation *n* assemblée *f*.

congress *n* congrès *m*; conférence *f*.

congruity *n* congruence *f*.

congruous *adj* congru, approprié.

conifer *n* conifère *m*.

conjecture *n* conjecture.

conjugal *adj* conjugal.

conjunction *n* conjonction *f*.

conjuncture *n* conjoncture *f*.

connect *vt* relier, joindre.

connection *n* liaison, connexion *f*.

connoisseur *n* connaisseur *m* -euse *f*.

conquer *vt* conquérir.

conqueror *n* conquérant *m*.

conquest *n* conquête *f*.

conscience *n* conscience *f*.

conscientious *adj* consciencieux.

conscious *adj* conscient.

consciousness *n* conscience *f*.

consecrate *vt* consacrer.

consecration *n* consécration *f*.

consecutive *adj* consécutif.

consensus *n* consensus *m*.

consent *n* consentement:—*vi* consentir.

consequence *n* conséquence *f*; importance *f*.

consequent *adj* consécutif.

conservation *n* conservation *f*.

conservative *adj* conservateur.

conserve *vt* conserver:—*n* conserve *f*.

consider *vt* considérer.

considerable *adj* considérable.

considerate *adj* prévenant, attentionné.

consideration *n* considération *f*.

consign *vt* confier, remettre.

consignment *n* expédition *f*.

consist *vi* consister (en).

consistency *n* consistance *f*.

consistent *adj* constant; cohérent.

consolation *n* consolation *f*; réconfort *m*.

console *vt* consoler.

consolidate *vt* consolider.

consolidation *n* consolidation *f*.

conspicuous *adj* voyant, manifeste.

conspiracy *n* conspiration *f*.

conspire *vi* conspirer.

constancy *n* constance *f*.

constant *adj* constant.

constellation *n* constellation *f*.

consternation *n* consternation *f*.

constitute *vt* constituer; établir.

constitution *n* constitution *f*.

constitutional *adj* constitutionnel.

constrain *vt* contraindre.

constraint *n* contrainte *f*.

constrict *vt* serrer; gêner.

construct *vt* construire, bâtir.

construction *n* construction *f*.

consulate *n* consulat *m*.

consult *vt* consulter.

consultation *n* consultation.

consume *vt* consommer.

consumer *n* consommateur *m* -trice *f*.

consumerism *n* consumérisme *m*.

consummate *vt* consommer:—*adj* accompli.

consummation *n* consommation *f*.

consumption *n* consommation *f*.

contact *n* contact *m*.

contagious *adj* contagieux.

contain *vt* contenir.

container *n* récipient *m*.

contaminate *vt* contaminer.

contamination *n* contamination *f*.

contemplate *vt* contempler.

contemplation *n* contemplation *f*.

contemporary *adj* contemporain.

contempt *n* mépris, dédain *m*.

contemptible *adj* méprisable.

contemptuous *adj* méprisant.

contend *vi* combattre.

content *adj* content, satisfait:—*vt* contenter, satisfaire:—*n* contentement *m*.

contention *n* querelle, altercation *f*.

contentment *n* contentement *m*, satisfaction *f*.

contest *vt* contester, discuter:—*n* concours *m*.

contestant *n* concurrent *m*, -e *f*.

context *n* contexte *m*.

continent *n* continent *m*.

continental *adj* continental.

contingency *n* contingence *f*.

contingent *n* contingent *m*:—*adj* contingent.

continual *adj* continuel.

continuation *n* continuation.

continue *vt vi* continuer.

continuous *adj* continu.

contort *vt* tordre, déformer.

contortion *n* contorsion *f*.

contour *n* contour *m*.

contraception *n* contraception *f*.

contraceptive *n* contraceptif *m*:—*adj* contraceptif.

contract *vt* contracter:—*n* contrat *m*.

contradict *vt* contredire.

contradiction *n* contradiction *f*.

contradictory *adj* contradictoire.

contraption *n* gadget, bidule (*fam*) *m*.

contrary *adj* contraire:—*n* contraire *m*.

contrast *n* contraste *m*:—*vt* contraster.

contravention *n* infraction *f*.

contribute *vt* contribuer.

contribution *n* contribution *f*.

contrite *adj* contrit, repentant.

contrivance *n* dispositif *m*; invention *f*.

control *n* contrôle *m*; maîtrise *f*:—*vt* maîtriser; contrôler.

controversial *adj* polémique.

controversy *n* polémique *f*.

contusion *n* contusion *f*.

conurbation *n* conurbation *f*.

convalescence *n* convalescence *f*.

convalescent *adj* convalescent.

convene *vt* convoquer.

convenience *n* commodité, convenance *f*.

convenient *adj* commode, pratique

convention *n* convention *f*.

conventional *adj* conventionnel.

converge *vi* converger.

convergence *n* convergence *f*.

convergent *adj* convergent.

conversant *adj* au courant; compétent.

conversation *n* conversation *f*.

converse *vi* converser.

conversion *n* conversion; transformation *f*.

convert *vt* convertir:—*n* converti *m*, -e *f*.

convey *vt* transporter.

conveyance *n* transport *m*; cession *f*.

convict *n* détenu *m*, -e *f*.

conviction *n* condamnation *f*; conviction *f*.

convince *vt* convaincre, persuader.

convivial *adj* jovial.

conviviality *n* jovialité *f*.

convoke *vt* convoquer.

convoy *n* convoi *m*.

convulse *vt* ébranler.

convulsion *n* convulsion *f*; bouleversement *m*.

convulsive *adj* convulsif.

cook *n* cuisinier *m*, -ière *f*:—*vt* cuire.

cooker *n* cuisinière *f*.

cookery *n* cuisine *f*.

cool *adj* frais:—*n* fraîcheur *f*:—*vt* rafraîchir.

coolness *n* fraîcheur *f*; sang-froid *m*.

cooperate *vi* coopérer.

cooperation n coopération f.

cooperative adj coopératif.

coordinate vt coordonner.

coordination n coordination f.

cope vi se débrouiller.

copious adj copieux.

copy n copie f:—vt copier.

copyright n droit d'auteur m.

coral n corail m.

cord n corde f, cordon m.

cordial adj cordial, chaleureux.

core n trognon m; noyau, centre, cœur m.

cork n bouchon m:—vt boucher.

corkscrew n tire-bouchon m.

corn n maïs m; grain m; blé m.

corner n coin m; angle m.

cornerstone n pierre angulaire f.

corollary n corollaire m.

coronation n couronnement m.

coroner n coroner m.

corporate adj en commun; d'entreprise.

corporation n corporation f; société par actions f.

corps n corps m.

corpse n cadavre m.

corpulent adj corpulent.

correct vt corriger; rectifier:—adj correct.

correction n correction f; rectification f.

corrective adj correcteur, correctif: —n correcteur m.

correctness n correction f.

correlation n corrélation f.

correlative adj corrélatif.

correspond vi correspondre.

correspondence n correspondance f.

correspondent adj correspondant: —n correspondant m, -e f.

corridor n couloir, corridor m.

corroborate vt corroborer.

corrode vt corroder.

corrosion n corrosion f.

corrosive adj n corrosif m.

corrupt vt corrompre:—adj corrompu.

corruption n corruption f; dépravation f.

cosmetic adj n cosmétique m.

cosmic adj cosmique.

cosmopolitan adj cosmopolite.

cost n prix, coût m:—vi coûter.

costly adj coûteux, cher.

costume n costume m.

cottage n cottage m.

cotton n coton m.

cotton wool n coton hydrophile m.

couch n canapé, divan m.

cough n toux f:—vi tousser.

council n conseil m.

counsel n conseil m; avocat m.

counsellor n conseiller m, -ère f.

count vt compter:—n compte m.

countenance n visage m.

counter n comptoir m; jeton m.

counteract vt contrecarrer.

counterbalance vt contrebalancer.

counterfeit vt contrefaire:—adj faux.

counterpart n contrepartie f.

countersign vt contresigner.

countrified adj rustique; campagnard.

country n pays m; patrie f:—adj rustique; campagnard.

countryman n campagnard m; compatriote m.

county n comté m.

couple n couple m:—vt unir, associer.

coupon n coupon m.

courage n courage m.

courageous adj courageux.

courier n messager m; guide m.

course n cours m; route f; chemin m: —of ~ bien sûr.

court n cour f; tribunal m:—vt courtiser. adj courtois

courtesy n courtoisie f.

courthouse n palais de justice m.

courtroom n salle de tribunal f.

cousin n cousin m, -e f.

cover n couverture f:—vt (re)couvrir.

covert adj voilé; caché.

cover-up n dissimulation f.

covet vt convoiter.

cow n vache f.

coward n lâche mf.

cowardice n lâcheté f.

cowboy n cowboy m.

coy adj timide; coquet; évasif.

coyness n timidité f; modestie f.

crab n crabe m.

crack n craquement m; fente f:—vt fêler:—vi se fêler; craquer.

crackle vi crépiter, pétiller.

cradle n berceau m:—vt bercer.

craft n habileté f; barque f.

craftsman n artisan m.

crafty adj astucieux, rusé.

cram vt bourrer:—vi s'entasser.

cramp n crampe f:—vt entraver.

crane n grue f.

crash vi s'écraser:—n fracas m; collision f.

crate n caisse f; cageot m.

crater n cratère m.

crawl vi ramper.

crayon n crayon m.

craze n manie f, engouement m.

craziness n folie f.

crazy adj fou.

creak vi grincer, craquer.

cream n crème f:—adj crème.

crease n pli m:—vt froisser.

create vt créer; causer.

creation n création f.

creature n créature f.

credence n croyance; créance f.

credibility n crédibilité f.

credible adj crédible.

credit n crédit m; honneur m.

creditable adj estimable, honorable.

credit card n carte de crédit f.

creep vi ramper.

cremate vt incinérer.

cremation n incinération, crémation f.

crematorium n crématoire m.

crest n crête f.

crevice n fissure, lézarde f.

crew n bande, équipe f; équipage m.

crib n berceau m; mangeoire f.

crime n crime m; délit m.

criminal adj criminel:—n criminel m, -elle f.

cripple n, adj invalide mf:—vt paralyser.

crisis n crise f.

criterion n critère m.

critic n critique m.

critic(al) adj critique.

criticise vt critiquer.

criticism n critique f.

croak vi coasser, croasser.

crockery n poterie f.

crocodile n crocodile m.

crook n (fam) escroc m.

crop n culture f; récolte f.

cross n croix f; croisement m:—adj fâché:—vt traverser, croiser.

crossbreed n hybride m.

crossing n traversée f; passage pour piétons m.

cross-reference n renvoi m, référence f.

crossroad n carrefour m.

crouch vi s'accroupir, se tapir.

crow n corbeau m.

crowd n foule f; monde m; vi s'entasser.

crown n couronne f:—vt couronner.

crucial adj crucial.

crucifix n crucifix m.

crude *adj* brut, grossier.

cruel *adj* cruel.

cruelty *n* cruauté *f*.

crumb *n* miette *f*.

crumble *vt* émietter; effriter:—*vi* s'émietter.

crunch *vt* croquer.

crush *vt* écraser; opprimer:—*n* cohue *f*.

crust *n* croûte *f*.

crutch *n* béquille *f*.

crux *n* cœur *m*.

cry *vt vi* crier; pleurer:—*n* cri *m*; sanglot *m*.

crystal *n* cristal *m*.

crystalline *adj* cristallin; pur.

crystallise *vi* se cristalliser.

cube *n* cube *m*.

cuddle *vt* embrasser.

cuff *n* manchette *f*.

culinary *adj* culinaire.

culminate *vi* culminer.

culpable *adj* coupable.

culprit *n* coupable *mf*.

cult *n* culte *m*.

cultivate *vt* cultiver.

cultivation *n* culture *f*.

culture *n* culture *f*.

cumbersome *adj* encombrant.

cumulative *adj* cumulatif.

cunning *adj* astucieux, rusé.

cup *n* tasse, coupe *f*.

cupboard *n* placard *m*.

curb *n* frein *m*:—*vt* freiner, juguler.

cure *n* remède *m*; cure *f*:—*vt* guérir.

curiosity *n* curiosité *f*.

curious *adj* curieux.

curl *n* boucle de cheveux *f*:—*vt* boucler.

curly *adj* frisé, bouclé.

currency *n* monnaie *f*; cours *m*.

current *adj* courant; actuel:—*n* courant *m*.

current affairs *npl* actualité *f*.

curse *vt* maudire.

curt *adj* succinct; sec.

curtain *n* rideau *m*.

curve *vt* courber:—*n* courbe *f*.

cushion *n* coussin *m*.

custodian *n* gardien *m*, -ienne *f*.

custom *n* coutume *f*, usage *m*.

customary *adj* habituel, coutumier.

customer *n* client *m*, -e *f*.

customs *npl* douane *f*.

customs officer *n* douanier *m*.

cut *vt* découper; couper:—*n* coup *m*; coupure *f*.

cutlery *n* couverts *mpl*.

cutting *n* coupure *f*.

cycle *n* cycle *m*; bicyclette *f*:—*vi* aller à bicyclette.

cycling *n* cyclisme *m*.

cyclist *n* cycliste *mf*.

cylinder *n* cylindre *m*; rouleau *m*.

cynic(al) *adj* cynique:—*n* cynique *mf*.

D

dad(dy) *n* papa *m*.

daily *adj* quotidien:—*adv* quotidiennement.

daintiness *n* élégance *f*; délicatesse *f*.

dainty *adj* délicat; élégant.

dairy *n* laiterie *f*.

dam n barrage m:—vt endiguer.

damage n dommage m; tort m:—vt endommager.

damnation n damnation f.

damp adj humide:—vt humidifier.

dampen vt humidifier.

dance n danse f; soirée dansante f:—vi, vt danser.

dancer n danseur m, -euse f.

danger n danger m.

dangerous adj dangereux.

dangle vi pendre.

dare vi oser:—vt défier.

daring n audace f:—adj audacieux.

dark adj sombre, obscur:—n obscurité f; ignorance f.

darken vt assombrir:—vi s'assombrir.

darkness n obscurité f.

darling n, adj chéri m, -e f.

dart n dard m.

dash vi se dépêcher.

data n données fpl.

data processing n traitement de données m.

date n date f; rendez-vous m.

dated adj démodé.

daughter n fille f:—~ **in-law** belle-fille f.

dawn n aube f.

day n jour m, journée f:—~ **by** ~ de jour en jour.

daylight n lumière du jour.

daze vt étourdir.

dazzle vt éblouir.

dead adj mortl.

deaden vt amortir.

deadline n date limite f.

deadlock n impasse f.

deadly adj mortel.

deaf adj sourd.

deafen vt assourdir.

deafness n surdité f.

deal n accord m; marché m:—**a great** ~ beaucoup:—vt distribuer.

dealer n commerçant m; trafiquant m.

dear adj ~**ly** adv cher.

dearness n cherté f.

death n mort f.

death certificate n acte de décès m.

death penalty n peine de mort f.

debar vt exclure.

debase vt dégrader.

debasement n dégradation f.

debatable adj discutable.

debate n débat m:—vt discuter; examiner.

debilitate vt débiliter.

debit n débit m:—vt débiter.

debt n dette f:—**get into** ~ s'endetter.

debtor n débiteur m, -trice f.

decade n décennie f.

decadence n décadence f.

decaffeinated adj décaféiné.

decay vi décliner; pourrir:—n pourrissement m.

deceased adj décédé.

deceit n tromperie f.

deceive vt tromper.

December n décembre m.

decency n décence f; pudeur f.

decent adj décent; bien, bon.

decide vt decider:—vi se décider.

decided adj décidé.

decimate vt décimer.

decipher vt déchiffrer.

decision n décision, détermination f.

decisive adj décisif.

deck n pont m:—vt orner.

declaration n déclaration f.

declare vt déclarer.

decode vt décoder.

decor n décor m; décoration f.

decorate vt décorer, orner.

decoration n décoration f.

decorative *adj* décoratif.

decoy *n* leurre *m*.

decrease *vt* diminuer:—*n* diminution *f*.

decree *n* décret *m*:—*vt* décréter; ordonner.

decrepit *adj* décrépit.

dedicate *vt* dédier; consacrer.

dedication *n* dédicace *f*; consacration *f*.

deduce *vt* déduire, conclure.

deduct *vt* déduire, soustraire.

deed *n* action *f*; exploit *m*.

deep *adj* profond.

deepen *vt* approfondir.

deepness *n* profondeur *f*.

default *n* défaut *m*:—*vi* manquer à ses engagements.

defeat *n* défaite *f*:—*vt* vaincre; frustrer.

defect *n* défaut *m*.

defective *adj* défectueux.

defend *vt* défendre; protéger.

defendant *n* accusé *m*, -e *f*.

defense *n* défense *f*; protection *f*.

defensive *adj* défensif.

defer *vt* déférer.

deference *n* déférence *f*.

defiance *n* défi *m*.

deficiency *n* défaut *m*; manque *m*.

deficient *adj* insuffisant.

define *vt* définir.

definite *adj* sûr; précis.

definition *n* définition *f*.

definitive *adj* définitif.

deflect *vt* dévier.

deform *vt* déformer.

deformity *n* déformité *f*.

defraud *vt* frauder.

deft *adj* habile.

degenerate *vi* dégénérer:—*adj* dégénéré.

degeneration *n* dégénération *f*.

degradation *n* dégradation *f*.

degrade *vt* dégrader.

degree *n* degré *m*; diplôme *m*.

dejected *adj* découragé.

dejection *n* découragement *m*.

delay *vt* retarder:—*n* retard *m*.

delegate *vt* déléguer:—*n* délégué *m*, -e *f*.

delegation *n* délégation *f*.

delete *vt* effacer.

deliberate *vt* examiner:—*adj* délibéré.

deliberation *n* délibération *f*.

delicacy *n* délicatesse *f*.

delicate *adj* délicat.

delicious *adj* délicieux.

delight *n* délice *m*:—*vt* enchanter.

delighted *adj* enchanté.

delightful *adj* charmant.

delinquency *n* délinquance *f*.

delinquent *n* délinquant *m*, -e *f*.

delirious *adj* délirant.

deliver *vt* livrer; délivrer.

delivery *n* livraison *f*.

delude *vt* tromper.

delusion *n* tromperie *f*; illusion *f*.

demand *n* demande *f*:—*vt* exiger; réclamer.

demanding *adj* exigeant.

demean *vi* s'abaisser.

demeanour *n* conduite *f*.

democracy *n* démocratie *f*.

democratic *adj* démocratique.

demolish *vt* démolir.

demolition *n* démolition *f*.

demonstrate *vt* démontrer, prouver: —*vi* manifester.

demonstration *n* démonstration *f*.

demonstrator *n* manifestant *m*, -e *f*.

demoralisation *n* démoralisation *f*.

demoralise *vt* démoraliser.

den *n* antre *m*.

denial *n* dénégation *f*.

denims *npl* jean *m*.

denomination n valeur f; dénomination f.
denote vt dénoter, indiquer.
denounce vt dénoncer.
dense adj dense, épais.
dentist n dentiste mf.
dentistry n dentisterie f.
denture n dentier m.
denunciation n dénonciation f.
deny vt nier.
deodorant n déodorant m.
depart vi partir.
department n département m; service m.
department store n grand magasin m.
departure n départ m.
depend vi dépendre.
dependable adj fiable; sûr.
dependent adj dépendant.
depict vt dépeindre, décrire.
deplorable adj déplorable.
deplore vt déplorer, lamenter.
depopulated adj dépeuplé.
deport vt déporter.
deportation n déportation f.
deportment n comportement m.
deposit vt déposer:—n dépôt m; caution f.
deposition n déposition f.
depot n dépôt m.
depreciate vi se déprécier.
depreciation n dépréciation f.
depress vt déprimer.
depression n dépression f.
deprivation n privation f.
deprive vt priver.
depth n profondeur f.
deputation n députation f.
depute vt députer, déléguer.
deputy n député m.
deranged adj dérangé.
derelict adj abandonné.

deride vt se moquer de.
derision n dérision f.
derivative n dérivé m.
derive vt vi dériver.
descend vi descendre.
descendant n descendant m, -e f.
descent n descente f.
describe vt décrire.
description n description f.
descriptive adj descriptif.
desert n désert m:—adj désert.
desert vt abandonner; déserter:—n mérite m.
desertion n désertion f.
deserve vt mériter.
design vt concevoir; dessiner:—n dessein m.
designate vt désigner.
desirable adj désirable.
desire n désir m:—vt désirer.
desist vi abandonner.
desk n bureau m.
desolate adj désert, désolé.
despair n désespoir m:—vi se désespérer.
desperate adj désespéré.
desperation n désespoir m.
despicable adj méprisable.
despise vt mépriser.
despite prep malgré.
despondency n abattement m.
despondent adj abattu.
dessert n dessert m.
destination n destination f.
destine vt destiner.
destiny n destin, sort m.
destitute adj indigent.
destitution n indigence f.
destroy vt détruire.
destruction n destruction f.
detach vt séparer, détacher.
detachable adj détachable.

detail n détail m:—**in ~** en détail:—vt détailler.

detain vt retenir; détenir.

detect vt détecter.

detection n détection f; découverte f.

detective n détective m.

detention n détention f.

deteriorate vt détériorer.

deterioration n détérioration f.

determination n détermination f.

determine vt déterminer, décider.

detest vt détester.

detestable adj détestable.

detour n déviation f.

detriment n détriment m.

devaluation n dévaluation f.

devastate vt dévaster.

devastation n dévastation f.

develop vt développer.

development n développement m.

deviate vi dévier.

deviation n déviation f.

device n mécanisme m.

devil n diable, démon m.

devise vt inventer; concevoir.

devoid adj dépourvu.

devote vt consacrer.

devoted adj dévoué.

devotion n dévotion f.

devour vt dévorer.

dew n rosée f.

dexterity n dextérité f.

diagnosis n (med) diagnostic m.

diagram n diagramme m.

dialect n dialecte m.

dialogue n dialogue m.

diamond n diamant m.

diary n journal m.

dictate vt dicter:—n ordre m.

dictionary n dictionnaire m.

die vi mourir.

diet n diète f; régime m:—vi être au régime.

differ vi différer.

difference n différence f.

different adj différent.

difficult adj difficile.

difficulty n difficulté f.

dig vt creuser.

digest vt digérer.

digestion n digestion f.

digestive adj digestif.

digit n chiffre m.

digital adj digital.

dignified adj digne.

dignity n dignité f.

digression n digression f.

dilemma n dilemme m.

diligence n assiduité f.

diligent adj assidu.

dilute vt diluer.

dim adj indistinct; faible; sombre.

dimension n dimension f.

diminish vt vi diminuer.

diminutive n diminutif m.

din n vacarme m.

dine vi dîner.

dinner n dîner m.

dint n:—**by ~ of** à force de.

dip vt tremper.

diploma n diplôme m.

diplomat n diplomate m.

diplomatic adj diplomatique.

dire adj atroce, affreux.

direct adj direct:—vt diriger.

direction n direction f; instruction f.

director n directeur m, -trice f.

directory n annuaire m.

dirt n saleté f.

dirty adj sale.

disability n incapacité f; infirmité f.

disabled adj infirme.

disadvantage n désavantage m:—vt désavantager.

disagree vi ne pas être d'accord.

disagreeable adj désagréable.

disagreement n désaccord m.

disallow vt rejeter.

disappear vi disparaître.

disappearance n disparition f.

disappoint vt décevoir.

disappointment n déception f.

disapproval n désapprobation f.

disapprove vt désapprouver.

disarm vt désarmer.

disaster n désastre m.

disastrous adj désastreux.

disbelief n incrédulité f.

discard vt jeter.

discern vt discerner, percevoir.

discerning adj perspicace.

disciple n disciple m.

discipline n discipline f:—vt discipliner.

disclose vt révéler.

disclosure n révélation f.

disco n discothèque f.

discomfort n incommodité f.

disconnect vt débrancher.

disconsolate adj inconsolable.

discontent n mécontentement m:—adj mécontent.

discontented adj mécontent.

discontinue vt interrompre.

discord n discorde f.

discount n escompte m:—vt escompter.

discourage vt décourager.

discouragement n découragement m.

discourse n discours m.

discourteous adj discourtois.

discover vt découvrir.

discovery n découverte f.

discredit vt discréditer.

discreet adj discret.

discrepancy n contradiction f.

discretion n discrétion f.

discretionary adj discrétionnaire.

discriminate vt distinguer; discriminer.

discrimination n discrimination f.

discuss vt discuter.

discussion n discussion f.

disdain vt dédaigner:—n dédain, mépris m.

disdainful adj dédaigneux.

disease n maladie f.

disembark vt vi débarquer.

disenchant vt désenchanter.

disenchanted adj désenchanté.

disengage vt dégager.

disfigure vt défigurer.

disgrace n honte f; scandale m:—vt déshonorer.

disgraceful adj honteux.

disguise vt déguiser:—n déguisement m.

disgust n dégoût m:—vt dégoûter.

dish n plat m; assiette f.

dishearten vt démoraliser.

dishonest adj malhonnête.

dishonesty n malhonnêteté f.

disillusion vt désillusionner.

disillusioned adj désillusionné.

disinfect vt désinfecter.

disinfectant n désinfectant m.

disinherit vt déshériter.

disintegrate vi se désintégrer.

disinterested adj désintéressé.

disk n disque m; disquette f.

dislike n aversion f:—vt ne pas aimer.

dislocate vt disloquer.

dislocation n dislocation f.

dislodge vt déloger.

disloyal adj déloyal.

dismantle vt démonter.

dismay n consternation f.

dismiss vt renvoyer; écarter.

dismissal n renvoi m; rejet m.

disobedience n désobéissance f.

disobedient adj désobéissant.

disobey vt désobéir.

disorder n désordre m.

disorderly adj en désordre, confus.

disorganization n désorganisation f.

disparage vt dénigrer.

disparity n disparité f.

dispatch vt envoyer:—n envoi m; dé-
pêche f.

dispel vt dissiper.

dispensary n dispensaire m.

dispense vt dispenser; distribuer.

disperse vt disperser.

displace vt déplacer.

display vt exposer:—n exposition f.

displeased adj mécontent.

displeasure n mécontentement m.

dispose vt disposer.

disposition n disposition f.

disprove vt réfuter.

dispute n dispute f; controverse f:—vt
mettre en cause.

disqualify vt rendre incapable.

dissatisfaction n mécontentement m.

dissatisfied adj mécontent.

disseminate vt disséminer.

dissension n dissension f.

dissent n dissension f.

dissertation n thèse f.

dissident n dissident m, -e f.

dissimilar adj dissemblable.

dissimilarity n dissemblance f.

dissipate vt dissiper.

dissipation n dissipation f.

dissolution n dissolution f.

dissolve vt dissoudre.

dissonance n dissonance f.

dissuade vt dissuader.

distance n distance f.

distant adj distant.

distaste n dégoût m.

distasteful adj désagréable.

distil vt distiller.

distinct adj distinct.

distinction n distinction f.

distinctive adj distinctif.

distinguish vt distinguer; discerner.

distort vt déformer.

distortion n distortion f.

distract vt distraire.

distracted adj distrait.

distraction n distraction f; confusion f.

distress n souffrance f:—vt désoler.

distribute vt distribuer, répartir.

distribution n distribution f.

district n district m.

disturb vt déranger.

disturbance n dérangement m; trouble
m.

disturbed adj troublé.

disturbing adj troublant.

disuse n désuétude f.

disused adj abandonné.

ditch n fossé m.

dive vi plonger.

diver n plongeur m, -euse f.

diverge vi diverger.

divergent adj divergent.

diverse adj divers, différent.

diversion n diversion f.

diversity n diversité f.

divert vt dévier; divertir.

divide vt diviser:—vi se diviser.

divine adj divin.

divinity n divinité f.

divisible adj divisible.

division n division f.

divorce n divorce m:—vi divorcer.

divorced *adj* divorcé.

divulge *vt* divulguer.

dizziness *n* vertige *m*.

dizzy *adj* pris de vertige.

do *vt* faire.

docile *adj* docile.

dock *n* dock *m*.

do-it-yourself *n* bricolage *m*.

doctor *n* docteur *m*.

doctrine *n* doctrine *f*.

document *n* document *m*.

documentary *adj* documentaire.

dodge *vt* esquiver.

dog *n* chien *m*.

dogmatic *adj* dogmatique.

doll *n* poupée *f*.

dolphin *n* dauphin *m*.

dome *n* dôme *m*.

domestic *adj* domestique.

domesticate *vt* domestiquer.

domesticity *n* domesticité *f*.

domicile *n* domicile *m*.

dominate *vi* dominer.

domination *n* domination *f*.

donate *vt* donner, faire don de.

donation *n* donation *f*.

donkey *n* âne *m*.

donor *n* donneur *m*; donateur *m*.

door *n* porte *f*.

doorway *n* entrée *f*.

dormant *adj* latent; dormant.

dormitory *n* dortoir *m*.

dosage *n* dose *f*; dosage *m*.

dose *n* dose *f*:—*vt* doser.

dossier *n* dossier *m*.

dot *n* point *m*.

double *adj* double:—*vt* doubler:—*n* double *m*.

double room *n* chambre pour deux *f*.

double-dealing *n* duplicité *f*.

doubt *n* doute *m*:—*vt* douter de.

doubtful *adj* douteux.

douse *vt* éteindre.

dove *n* colombe *f*.

down *n* duvet *m*:—*prep* en bas:—**upside ~** à l'envers.

down-to-earth *adj* pratique; terre à terre.

downfall *n* ruine *f*.

downhearted *adj* découragé.

downhill *adv* en descendant, dans la descente.

downstairs *adv* en bas.

dowry *n* dot *f*.

doze *vi* somnoler.

dozen *n* douzaine *f*.

drab *adj* gris; morne.

drag *vt* tirer:—*n* drague *f*; ennui *m*.

drain *vt* drainer; vider:—*n* tuyau d'écoulement *m*.

drama *n* drame *m*.

dramatic *adj* dramatique.

dramatist *n* dramaturge *mf*.

draught *n* courant d'air *m*.

draw *vt* tirer; dessiner.

drawback *n* désavantage.

drawer *n* tiroir *m*.

drawing *n* dessin *m*.

drawing room *n* salon *m*.

dread *n* terreur *f*:—*vt* redouter.

dreadful *adj* horrible.

dream *n* rêve *m*:—*vi*, *vt* rêver.

dreary *adj* triste, morne.

dress *vi* s'habiller:—*n* robe *f*.

dressing *n* pansement *m*; sauce *f*.

dressy *adj* élégant.

drift *vi* aller à la dérive.

drill *n* perceuse *f*; *vt* percer.

drink *vt vi* boire:—*n* boisson *f*.

drinker *n* buveur *m*, -euse *f*.

drip *vi* goutter:—*n* goutte *f*.

drive *vt vi* conduire.

driver *n* conducteur *m*, -trice *f*; chauffeur *m*.

driving licence *n* permis *m* de conduire.

drizzle *vi* pleuvasser.

drop *n* goutte *f*:—*vt* laisser tomber.

drought *n* sécheresse *f*.

drown *vt* noyer:—*vi* se noyer.

drowsiness *n* somnolence *f*.

drug *n* drogue *f*:—*vt* droguer.

drum *n* tambour *m*:—*vi* jouer du tambour.

drunk *adj* ivre.

drunken *adj* ivre.

drunkenness *n* ivresse *f*.

dry *adj* sec:—*vt* faire sécher:—*vi* sécher.

dryness *n* sécheresse *f*.

dual *adj* double.

dub *adj* doubler.

due *adj* dû, *f* due *n* droit *m*.

duel *n* duel *m*.

dull *adj* terne; insipide.

duly *adv* dûment.

dumb *adj* muet.

dump *n* tas *m*:—*vt* jeter.

duplicate *vt* dupliquer.

duplicity *n* duplicité *f*.

durability *n* durabilité *f*.

durable *adj* durable.

duration *n* durée *f*.

during *prep* pendant.

dusk *n* crépuscule *m*.

dust *n* poussière *f*:—*vt* épousseter.

dutiful *adj* obéissant, soumis.

duty *n* devoir *m*; obligation *f*.

dwarf *n* nain *m*, naine *f*:—*vt* rapetisser.

dwell *vi* habiter, vivre.

dwelling *n* habitation *f*; domicile *m*.

dye *vt* teindre:—*n* teinture *f*.

dying *p, adj* mourant.

dynamic *adj* dynamique.

dynasty *n* dynastie *f*.

E

each *pn* chacun:—~ **other** les un(e)s les autres.

eager *adj* enthousiaste.

eagerness *n* enthousiasme *m*.

eagle *n* aigle *m*.

ear *n* oreille *f*; ouïe *f*.

early *adj* premier:—*adv* tôt.

earn *vt* gagner.

earnest *adj* sérieux

earth *n* terre *f*:—*vt* brancher à la terre.

earthquake *n* tremblement de terre *m*.

ease *n* aise *f*; facilité *f*.

easiness *n* facilité *f*.

east *n* est *m*; orient *m*.

Easter *n* Pâques *fpl*.

eastern *adj* de l'est, oriental.

easy *adj* facile.

eat *vt vi* manger.

ebb *n* reflux *m*:—*vi* refluer.

eccentric *adj* excentrique.

eccentricity *n* excentricité *f*.

echo *n* écho *m*:—*vi* résonner.

eclipse *n* éclipse *f*:—*vt* éclipser.

ecology *n* écologie *f*.

economic *adj* économique

economist *n* économiste *mf*.

economise *vt* économiser.

economy *n* économie *f*.

ecstasy *n* extase *f.*
ecstatic *adj* extatique.
edge *n* fil *m*; pointe *f.*
edible *adj* mangeable.
edifice *n* édifice *m.*
edit *vt* diriger; rédiger.
edition *n* édition *f.*
editor *n* rédacteur *m*, -trice *f.*
educate *vt* éduquer; instruire.
education *n* éducation *f.*
efface *vt* effacer.
effect *n* effet *mf*:—**~s** *npl* biens *mpl*: — *vt* effectuer.
effective *adj* efficace; effectif.
effectiveness *n* efficacité *f.*
effectual *adj* efficace.
effeminate *adj* efféminé.
effervescence *n* effervescence *f.*
efficiency *n* efficacité *f.*
efficient *adj* efficace.
effort *n* effort *m.*
egg *n* œuf *m.*
ego(t)ist *n* égoïste *mf.*
ego(t)istical *adj* égoïste.
eight *adj n* huit *m.*
eighteen *adj n* dix-huit *m.*
eighteenth *adj n* dix-huitième *mf.*
eighth *adj n* huitième *mf.*
eightieth *adj n* quatre-vingtième *mf.*
eighty *adj n* quatre-vingt.
either *pn* n'importe lequel/laquelle: — *conj* ou, soit.
eject *vt* éjecter, expulser.
ejection *n* éjection, expulsion *f.*
elaborate *vt* élaborer:—*adj* élaboré.
elapse *vi* passer.
elastic *adj* élastique.
elbow *n* coude *m.*
elder *adj* aîné.
eldest *adj* aîné.
elect *vt* élire; choisir.

election *n* élection *f*; choix *m.*
electoral *adj* électoral.
electorate *n* électorat *m.*
electric(al) *adj* électrique.
electrician *n* électricien *m.*
electricity *n* électricité *f.*
electrify *vt* électriser.
electronic *adj* électronique.
elegance *n* élégance *f.*
elegant *adj* élégant.
element *n* élément *m.*
elementary *adj* élémentaire.
elephant *n* éléphant *m.*
elevate *vt* élever, hausser.
elevation *n* élévation *f*; hauteur *f.*
eleven *adj n* onze *m.*
eleventh *adj n* onzième *mf.*
eligibility *n* éligibilité *f.*
eligible *adj* éligible.
eliminate *vt* éliminer.
elocution *n* élocution *f.*
eloquence *n* éloquence *f.*
eloquent *adj* éloquent.
else *pn* autre.
elsewhere *adv* ailleurs.
elude *vt* éluder; éviter.
emaciated *adj* émacié.
emancipate *vt* émanciper.
emancipation *n* émancipation *f.*
embargo *n* embargo *m.*
embark *vt* embarquer.
embarkation *n* embarcation *f.*
embarrass *vt* embarrasser.
embarrassment *n* embarras *m.*
embassy *n* ambassade *f.*
emblem *n* emblème *m.*
embody *vt* incorporer; incarner.
embrace *vt* étreindre; comprendre.
embryo *n* embryon *m.*
emerald *n* émeraude *f.*
emerge *vi* émerger; apparaître.

emergency n urgence f.
emergency exit n sortie de secours f.
emigrate vi émigrer.
emigration n émigration f.
emission n émission f.
emit vt émettre.
emotion n émotion f.
emotional adj émotionnel.
emphasise vt souligner, accentuer.
emphatic adj emphatique.
empire n empire m.
employ vt employer.
employee n employé m, -e f.
employer n employeur m.
employment n emploi, travail m.
emptiness n vide m.
empty adj vide; vain:—vt vider.
emulate vt imiter.
enable vt permettre.
enamour vt s'éprendre de.
encamp vi camper.
encampment n campement m.
encase vt entourer.
enchant vt enchanter.
enchantment n enchantement m.
encircle vt encercler.
enclose vt entourer.
enclosure n clôture f.
encompass vt comprendre.
encounter n rencontre f:—vt rencontrer.
encourage vt encourager.
encouragement n encouragement m.
encyclopedia n encyclopédie f.
end n fin f; extrémité f:—**to the ~ that** afin que:—vt vi terminer.
endanger vt mettre en danger.
endeavour vi s'efforcer:—n effort m.
endorse vt endosser; approuver.
endorsement n endos m; approbation f.
endurable adj supportable.
endurance n endurance f.

endure vt supporter:—vi durer.
enemy n ennemi mf.
energetic adj énergique.
energy n énergie, force f.
enfeeble vt affaiblir.
enfold vt envelopper.
enforce vt mettre en vigueur.
engage vt aborder.
engaged adj fiancé; occupé.
engagement n engagement m.
engender vt engendrer.
engine n moteur m; locomotive f.
engineer n ingénieur m; mécanicien m.
engineering n ingénierie f.
enigma n énigme f.
enjoy vr:—**to ~ oneself** s'amuser.
enjoyable adj agréable; amusant.
enjoyment n plaisir m; jouissance f.
enlarge vt agrandir; étendre.
enlargement n agrandissement m.
enlist vt recruter.
enliven vt animer; égayer.
enmity n inimitié f; haine f.
enormous adj énorme.
enough adv suffisamment; assez:—n assez m.
enrich vt enrichir; orner.
enrichment n enrichissement m.
enrol vt enrôler; inscrire.
ensue vi s'ensuivre.
ensure vt assurer.
entail vt impliquer, entraîner.
enter vt entrer dans; inscrire.
enterprise n entreprise f.
enterprising adj entreprenant.
entertain vt divertir.
entertaining adj divertissant, amusant.
enthusiasm n enthousiasme m.
enthusiast n enthousiaste mf.
enthusiastic adj enthousiaste.
entire adj entier, complet.

entitle vt intituler.

entity n entité f.

entrance n entrée f; admission f.

entrant n participant m, -e f.

entreat vt implorer.

entrust vt confier.

entry n entrée f.

enumerate vt énumérer.

envelop vt envelopper.

envelope n enveloppe f.

envious adj envieux.

environment n environnement m.

environmental adj relatif à l'environnement.

envisage vt envisager.

envy n envie f:—vt envier.

epidemic adj épidémique:—n épidémie f.

episode n épisode m.

epitomise vt incarner; résumer.

equable adj uniforme.

equal adj égal; semblable:—n égal m, -e f:—vt égaler.

equalise vt égaliser.

equality n égalité f.

equanimity n équanimité f.

equate vt égaliser.

equator n équateur m.

equilibrium n équilibre m.

equip vt équiper.

equipment n équipement m.

equivalent adj n équivalent m.

equivocal adj équivoque.

equivocate vt équivoquer.

era n ère f.

eradicate vt supprimer.

eradication n suppression f.

erase vt effacer.

eraser n gomme f.

erect vt ériger:—adj droit, debout.

erode vt éroder; ronger.

erotic adj érotique.

err vi se tromper.

errand n message m.

erratic adj changeant; irrégulier.

erroneous adj erroné.

error n erreur f.

erudite adj érudit.

eruption n éruption f.

escalate vi monter en flèche.

escape vt éviter:—vi s'évader, s'échapper:—n évasion.

escort n escorte f:—vt escorter.

especial adj spécial.

essay n essai m.

essence n essence f.

essential n essentiel m:—adj essentiel.

establish vt établir.

establishment n établissement m.

estate n état m; biens mpl.

esteem vt estimer:—n estime f.

esthetic adj esthétique f.

estimate vt estimer; évaluer.

estimation n estimation.

estuary n estuaire m.

eternal adj éternel.

eternity n éternité f.

ethical adj éthique.

ethics npl éthique f.

ethnic adj ethnique.

etiquette n étiquette f.

evacuate vt évacuer.

evacuation n évacuation f.

evade vt éviter; échapper à.

evaluate vt évaluer.

evaporate vi s'évaporer.

evaporation n évaporation f.

evasion n dérobade f.

evasive adj évasif.

eve n veille f.

even adj pair:—adv même:—vt égaliser.

evening n soir m, soirée f.

evenness n égalité f; impartialité f.

event n événement m.

eventual adj final:—**ly** adv finalement, en fin de comptes.

eventuality n éventualité f.

ever adv toujours; jamais.

everlasting adj éternel.

every adj chacun, chacune:—**where** partout:—**thing** tout:—**one**, **body** tout le monde.

evict vt expulser.

eviction n expulsion f.

evidence n évidence f.

evident adj évident.

evil adj malveillant:—n mal m.

evocative adj évocateur.

evoke vt évoquer.

evolution n évolution f.

evolve vi évoluer.

exacerbate vt exacerber.

exact adj exact:—vt exiger.

exacting adj exigeant.

exaction n exaction f; extorsion f.

exactness n exactitude f.

exaggerate vt exagérer.

exaggeration n exagération f.

exalt vt exalter; élever.

examination n examen m.

examine vt examiner.

example n exemple m.

exasperate vt exaspérer.

exasperation n exaspération f.

excavate vt excaver, creuser.

excavation n excavation f.

exceed vt excéder, dépasser.

excel vt surpasser; vi exceller.

excellence n excellence f.

excellent adj excellent.

except vt excepter:—**(ing)** prep excepté, à l'exception de.

exception n exception f.

exceptional adj exceptionnel.

excess n excès m.

excessive adj excessif.

exchange vt échanger:—n échange m.

exchange rate n taux de change m.

excise n impôt m.

excitable adj excitable.

excite vt exciter; animer.

excited adj animé, enthousiaste.

excitement n animation f.

exciting adj passionnant; stimulant.

exclaim vi s'exclamer.

exclamation n exclamation f.

exclude vt exclure.

exclusion n exclusion f; exception f.

exclusive adj exclusif.

excommunicate vt excommunier.

exculpate vt disculper; justifier.

excursion n excursion f; digression f.

excusable adj excusable.

excuse vt excuser:—n excuse f.

execute vt exécuter.

execution n exécution f.

executive adj exécutif.

exemplary adj exemplaire.

exemplify vt exemplifier.

exempt adj exempt.

exemption n exemption f.

exercise n exercice m:—vt exercer.

exert vt employer, exercer.

exertion n effort m.

exhale vt exhaler.

exhaust n vt épuiser.

exhaustion n épuisement m.

exhaustive adj exhaustif.

exhibit vt exhiber.

exhibition n exposition, présentation f.

exhilarating adj stimulant.

exhilaration n joie f; stimulation f.

exhume vt exhumer, déterrer.

exile n exil m:—vt exiler, déporter.

exist vi exister.

existence *n* existence *f.*
existent *adj* existant.
exit *n* sortie *f:—vi* sortir.
exonerate *vt* disculper.
exoneration *n* disculpation *f.*
exorbitant *adj* exorbitant, excessif.
exotic *adj* exotique.
expand *vt* étendre.
expanse *n* étendue *f.*
expansion *n* expansion *f.*
expect *vt* attendre; espérer.
expectancy *n* attente *f;* espoir *m.*
expectation *n* expectative *f;* attente *f.*
expediency *n* convenance *f;* opportunité *f.*
expedient *adj* opportun.
expedite *vt* accélérer; expédier.
expedition *n* expédition *f.*
expel *vt* expulser.
expend *vt* dépenser; utiliser.
expense *n* dépense *f;* coût *m.*
expensive *adj* cher; coûteux.
experience *n* expérience *f;* pratique *f:—vt* ressentir; connaître.
experienced *adj* expérimenté.
experiment *n* expérience *f:—vi* expérimenter.
experimental *adj* expérimental.
expert *adj* expert.
expertise *n* habileté *f.*
explain *vt* expliquer.
explanation *n* explication *f.*
explanatory *adj* explicatif.
explicit *adj* explicite.
explode *vt* faire exploser:—*vi* exploser.
exploit *vt* exploiter:—*n* exploit *m.*
exploitation *n* exploitation *f.*
exploration *n* exploration *f.*
explore *vt* explorer; sonder.
explorer *n* explorateur *m,* -trice *f.*
explosion *n* explosion *f.*

explosive *adj n* explosif *m.*
export *vt* exporter.
exportation *n* exportation *f.*
exporter *n* exportateur *m,* -trice *f.*
expose *vt* exposer; dévoiler.
exposition *n* exposition *f.*
exposure *n* exposition *f;* temps de pose *m.*
expound *vt* exposer; interpréter.
express *vt* exprimer:—*adj* exprès:—*n* exprès *m;* (*rail*) rapide *m.*
expression *n* expression *f.*
expressive *adj* expressif.
expropriate *vt* exproprier.
expulsion *n* expulsion *f.*
exquisite *adj* exquis.
extemporise *vi* improviser.
extend *vt* étendre:—*vi* s'étendre.
extension *n* extension *f.*
extensive *adj* étendu.
extent *n* extension *f.*
extenuate *vt* atténuer.
exterior *adj n* extérieur *m.*
exterminate *vt* exterminer.
external *adj* externe.
extinct *adj* disparu; éteint.
extinction *n* extinction *f.*
extinguish *vt* éteindre.
extinguisher *n* extincteur *m.*
extort *vt* extorquer.
extortion *n* extorsion *f.*
extra *adv* particulièrement; *n* supplément *m.*
extract *vt* extraire:—*n* extrait *m.*
extraction *n* extraction *f;* origine *f.*
extraneous *adj* superflu; sans rapport.
extraordinary *adj* extraordinaire.
extravagance *n* extravagance *f.*
extravagant *adj* extravagant.
extreme *adj* extrême.
extremist *adj n* extrémiste *mf.*
extricate *vt* extirper, démêler.

extrovert *adj n* extraverti *m*, -e *f*.
exuberance *n* exubérance *f*.
exuberant *adj* exubérant.
eye *n* œil *m*:—*vt* regarder; lorgner.

eyebrow *n* sourcil *m*.
eyelash *n* cil *m*.
eyelid *n* paupière *f*.
eyesight *n* vue *f*.

F

fabric *n* tissu *m*.
fabricate *vt* fabriquer; inventer.
fabrication *n* fabrication *f*.
fabulous *adj* fabuleux.
face *n* visage *m*; mine *f*; apparence *f*:
    —*vt* faire face à.
facet *n* facette *f*.
facile *adj* facile.
facilitate *vt* faciliter.
facility *n* facilité *f*; équipement *m*.
facing *n* revers *m*:—*prep* en face de.
fact *n* fait *m*; réalité *f*:—**in ~** en fait.
factory *n* usine *f*.
factual *adj* factuel.
faculty *n* faculté *f*.
fail *vt* échouer à; omettre:—*vi* échouer;
    faiblir; manquer.
failure *n* faillite *f*; manquement *m*.
faint *vi* s'évanouir, défaillir:—*n* éva-
    nouissement *m*:—*adj* faible.
fair *adj* beau; blond; équitable; consi-
    dérable:—*n* foire *f*.
fairness *n* beauté *f*; justice *f*.
fair play *n* fair-play.
faith *n* foi *f*; croyance *f*; fidélité *f*.
faithful *adj* fidèle, loyal.
fake *n* falsification *f*:—*adj* faux:—*vt*
    falsifier.
fall *vi* tomber; baisser:—*n* chute *f*,
    automne *m*.
fallacy *n* erreur *f*, tromperie *f*.

fallibility *n* faillibilité *f*.
fallible *adj* faillible.
false *adj* faux.
false alarm *n* fausse alerte *f*.
falsify *vt* falsifier.
falter *vi* vaciller.
fame *n* réputation *f*; renommée.
familiar *adj* familier.
familiarise *vt* familiariser.
familiarity *n* familiarité *f*.
family *n* famille *f*.
famine *n* famine *f*.
famous *adj* célèbre, fameux.
fan *n* éventail *m*; ventilateur *m*:—*vt*
    éventer.
fancy *n* caprice *m*:—*vt* avoir envie de;
    s'imaginer.
fantastic *adj* fantastique; excentrique.
fantasy *n* fantaisie *f*.
far *adv* loin:—*adj* lointain, éloigné.
fare *n* prix (du voyage) *m*; tarif *m*; ré-
    gime alimentaire *m*.
farewell *n* adieu *m*.
farm *n* ferme *f*:—*vt* cultiver.
farmer *n* fermier *m*; agriculteur *m*.
farming *n* agriculture *f*.
fascinate *vt* fasciner, captiver.
fascination *n* fascination *f*; charme *m*.
fashion *n* manière, façon *f*; mode *f*: —
    vt façonner.
fashionable *adj* à la mode; chic.

fast *vi* jeûner:—*n* jeûne *m*:—*adj* rapide:—*adv* rapidement.

fasten *vt* attacher; fixer.

fast food *n* restauration rapide *f*.

fat *adj* gros, gras:—*n* graisse *f*.

fatal *adj* mortel.

fatality *n* fatalité *f*.

fate *n* destin, sort *m*.

father *n* père *m*.

fatherhood *n* paternité *f*.

fatigue *n* fatigue *f*:—*vt* fatiguer.

fatuous *adj* imbécile.

fault *n* défaut *m*, faute *f*; délit *m*.

faulty *adj* défectueux.

favour *n* faveur *f*:—*vt* favoriser.

favourable *adj* favorable.

favourite *n* favori *m*:—*adj* favori.

fax *n* fax *m*:—*vt* envoyer par fax.

fear *vt* craindre:—*n* crainte *f*.

fearful *adj* effrayant; craintif.

fearless *adj* intrépide, courageux.

feasibility *n* faisabilité *f*.

feasible *adj* faisable.

feast *n* banquet *m*; fête *f*.

feat *n* exploit *m*; prouesse *f*.

feather *n* plume *f*.

feature *n* trait *m*:—*vi* figurer.

February *n* février *m*.

fed-up *adj*:—**to be ~** en avoir marre.

fee *n* honoraires *mpl*.

feeble *adj* faible, frêle.

feebleness *n* faiblesse *f*.

feed *vt* nourrir:—*vi* manger; se nourrir.

feel *vt* sentir; toucher:—*n* sensation *f*.

feeling *n* sensation *f*; sentiment *m*.

feign *vt* feindre, simuler.

fellow *n* homme, type *m*.

female *n* femelle *f*:—*adj* femelle.

feminine *adj* féminin.

feminist *n* féministe *mf*.

fence *n* barrière *f*; clôture *f*.

ferment *n* agitation *f*:—*vi* fermenter.

ferocious *adj* féroce.

ferocity *n* férocité *f*.

ferry *n* bac *m*; ferry *m*:—*vt* transporter.

fertile *adj* fertile, fécond.

fertility *n* fertilité, fécondité *f*.

fervent *adj* fervent; ardent.

fervour *n* ferveur *f*.

festival *n* fête *f*; festival *m*.

festive *adj* de fête.

fetch *vt* aller chercher.

fetching *adj* charmant, séduisant.

feud *n* rivalité *f*.

fever *n* fièvre *f*.

feverish *adj* fiévreux.

few *adj* peu:—**a ~** quelques.

fibre *n* fibre *f*.

fickle *adj* volage, inconstant.

fiction *n* fiction *f*; invention *f*.

fictional *adj* fictif.

fictitious *adj* fictif, imaginaire.

fidelity *n* fidélité, loyauté *f*.

fidget *vi* s'agiter, remuer.

fidgety *adj* agité, remuant.

field *n* champ *m*; domaine *m*.

fiend *n* démon *m*.

fiendish *adj* diabolique.

fierce *adj* féroce; acharné.

fierceness *n* férocité, fureur *f*.

fifteen *adj n* quinze *m*.

fifteenth *adj n* quinzième *mf*.

fifth *adj n* cinquième *mf*.

fiftieth *adj n* cinquantième *mf*.

fifty *adj n* cinquante *m*.

fight *vt vi* combattre; lutter:—*n* combat *m*.

fighter *n* combattant *m*.

figure *n* figure *f*; image *f*; chiffre *m*.

file *n* file *f*; liste *f*; dossier *m*; fichier *m*:—*vt* enregistrer; classer.

fill *vt* remplir.

fillet *n* filet *m*.

film n pellicule f; film f:—vt filmer:—vi s'embuer.

filter n filtre m:—vt filtrer.

filth n immondice, ordure f.

filthy adj crasseux, dégoûtant.

fin n nageoire f.

final adj dernier; définitif.

finalise vt parachever.

finance n finance f.

financial adj financier.

financier n financier m.

find vt trouver:—n trouvaille f.

findings npl résultats mpl.

fine adj fin; pur; délicat:—n amende f.

finesse n finesse, subtilité f.

finger n doigt m:—vt manier.

fingernail n ongle m.

finish vt finir, terminer.

fir (tree) n sapin m

fire engine n voiture de pompiers f.

fire extinguisher n extincteur m.

fire n feu m; incendie m:—vt incendier:—vi s'enflammer.

fire station n caserne de pompiers f.

firearm n arme à feu f.

fireman n pompier m.

fireplace n cheminée f, foyer m.

fireproof adj ignifugé.

fireworks npl feu d'artifice m.

firm adj ferme:—n (com) compagnie f.

firmness n fermeté f; résolution f.

first adj premier:—adv premièrement.

first aid n premiers secours mpl.

first name n prénom m.

first-class adj de première classe.

first-hand adj de première main.

first-rate adj de première qualité.

fish n poisson m:—vi pêcher.

fisherman n pêcheur m.

fishing n pêche f.

fissure n fissure, crevasse f.

fist n poing m.

fit n accès m:—adj en forme; capable:—vt adapter:—vi (bien) aller.

fitness n forme physique f.

fitting adj qui convient, approprié: —n accessoire ml.

five adj n cinq m.

fix vt fixer, établir.

fixation n obsession f.

fixed adj fixe.

fizz(le) vi pétiller.

fizzy adj gazeux.

flabby adj mou, f molle, flasque.

flag n drapeau m:—vi s'affaiblir.

flagrant adj flagrant.

flair n flair m; talent m.

flake n flocon m:—vi s'effriter.

flamboyant adj flamboyant.

flame n flamme f; ardeur f.

flammable adj inflammable.

flank n flanc m.

flap n battement m; rabat m.

flare vi luire, briller:—n flamme f.

flash n éclat m:—vt allumer.

flask n flasque f; flacon m.

flat adj plat; insipide.

flatten vt aplanir; aplatir.

flatter vt flatter.

flattery n flatterie f.

flaunt vt étaler, afficher.

flavour n saveur m:—vt assaisonner.

flaw n défaut m; imperfection f.

fleck n petite tache f; particule f.

flee vt fuir de:—vi s'enfuir.

fleece n toison f.

fleet n flotte f; parc m.

fleeting adj fugace, fugitif.

flesh n chair f.

flex n cordon m:—vt fléchir.

flexibility n flexibilité f.

flexible adj flexible, souple.

flicker *vt* vaciller; trembloter.

flier *n* aviateur *m*, -trice *f*.

flight *n* vol *m*; fuite *f*; volée *f*.

flight attendant *n* steward *m*, hôtesse de l'air *f*.

flimsy *adj* léger; fragile.

flinch *vi* sourciller.

fling *vt* lancer, jeter.

flip *vt* lancer.

flippant *adj* désinvolte, cavalier.

flipper *n* nageoire *f*.

flirt *vi* flirter:—*n* charmeur *m*, -euse *f*.

flirtation *n* flirt *f*.

float *vt* faire flotter:—*vi* flotter:—*n* flotteur *m*; char (de carnaval) *m*.

flock *n* troupeau *m*; foule *f*:—*vi* affluer.

flood *n* inondation *f*; déluge *m*:—*vt* inonder.

floodlight *n* projecteur *m*.

floor *n* sol *m*; plancher *m*; étage *m*: —*vt* parqueter.

flop *n* four, fiasco *m*.

floppy *adj* lâche:—*n* disquette *f*.

flora *n* flore *f*.

floral *adj* floral.

florid *adj* fleuri.

florist *n* fleuriste *mf*.

flounder *n* flet *m*:—*vi* patauger.

flour *n* farine *f*.

flourish *vi* fleurir; prospérer.

flourishing *adj* florissant.

flout *vt* mépriser.

flow *vi* couler; circuler:—*n* flux *m*; écoulement *m*; flot *m*.

flower *n* fleur *f*:—*vi* fleurir.

flowery *adj* fleuri.

fluctuate *vi* fluctuer.

fluctuation *n* fluctuation *f*.

fluency *n* aisance *f*.

fluent *adj* coulant; facile.

fluff *n* peluche *f*.

fluid *adj n* fluide *m*.

fluke *n* veine *f*.

flurry *n* rafale *f*; agitation *f*.

flush *vi* rougir:—*n* rougeur *f*; éclat *m*.

flushed *adj* rouge.

fluster *vt* énerver.

flute *n* flûte *f*.

flutter *vi* voleter; s'agiter.

fly *vt* piloter:—*vi* voler; fuir:—*n* mouche *f*; braguette *f*.

flying *n* aviation *f*.

foam *n* écume *f*:—*vi* écumer.

foamy *adj* écumeux.

focus *n* foyer *m*; centre *m*.

foe *n* ennemi *m*, -e *f*.

fog *n* brouillard *m*.

foggy *adj* brumeux.

fold *n* pli *m*:—*vt* plier.

folder *n* chemise *f*; dépliant *m*.

folding *adj* pliant.

foliage *n* feuillage *m*.

folio *n* folio *m*.

folk *n* gens *mpl*.

folklore *n* folklore *m*.

follow *vt* suivre:—*vi* suivre, s'ensuivre.

follower *n* partisan *m*, -e *f*; adhérent *m*, -e *f*.

folly *n* folie, extravagance *f*.

fond *adj* affectueux:—**to be ~ of** aimer.

fondle *vt* caresser.

fondness *n* prédilection *f*; affection *f*.

food *n* nourriture *f*.

food processor *n* robot *m*.

foodstuffs *npl* denrées alimentaires *fpl*.

fool *n* imbécile *mf*:—*vt* duper.

foolhardy *adj* téméraire.

foolish *adj* idiot, insensé.

foolproof *adj* infaillible.

foolscap *n* papier ministre *m*.

foot n pied m.

football n football m; ballon de football m.

footballer n footballeur m, -euse f.

footbridge n passerelle f.

footnote n note (de bas de page) f.

footpath n sentier m.

footprint n empreinte (de pas) f.

footstep n pas m.

for prep pour; en raison de; pendant: — conj car:—**as ~ me** quant à moi.

foray n incursion f.

forbid vt interdire, défendre.

forbidding adj menaçant; sévère.

force n force f; puissance:—vt forcer, contraindre.

forceful adj énergique.

forceps n forceps m.

forcible adj énergique, vigoureux.

forearm n avant-bras m.

foreboding n pressentiment m.

forecast vt prévoir:—n prévision f.

forefinger n index m.

foregone adj passé; anticipé.

foreground n premier plan m.

forehead n front m.

foreign adj étranger.

foreigner n étranger m, -ère f.

foreman n contremaître m.

foremost adj principal.

forensic adj judiciaire.

forerunner n précurseur m.

foresee vt prévoir.

foresight n prévoyance f; prescience f.

forest n forêt f.

foretaste n avant-goût m.

foretell vt prédire.

forever adv toujours; un temps infini.

forewarn vt prévenir à l'avance.

foreword n préface f.

forfeit n amende f:—vt perdre.

forge n forge f:—vt forger.

forger n faussaire mf.

forgery n contrefaçon f.

forget vt vi oublier.

forgetful adj étourdi; négligent.

forgive vt pardonner.

forgiveness n pardon m.

fork n fourchette f; fourche f:—vi bifurquer.

forked adj fourchu.

form n forme f; formalité f; moule m:— vt former.

formal adj formel.

formality n formalité f.

format n format m:—vt formater.

formation n formation f.

formative adj formateur m, -trice f.

former adj précédent, ancien:—**~ly** adv autrefois, jadis.

formula n formule f.

forsake vt abandonner, renoncer à.

fort n fort m.

forthcoming adj prochain; sociable.

forthwith adv immédiatement, tout de suite.

fortieth adj n quarantième mf.

fortification n fortification f.

fortify vt fortifier, renforcer.

fortnight n quinze jours mpl:—adj **~ly** bimensuel:—adv **~ly** tous les quinze jours.

fortuitous adj fortuit; imprévu.

fortunate adj chanceux.

fortune n chance f, sort m; fortune f.

forty adj n quarante m.

forward adj avancé; précoce; présomptueux:—**~(s)** adv en avant:—vt transmettre.

forwardness n précocité f.

fossil n fossile m.

foster vt élever.

foster child n enfant adoptif m.

foul adj infect:—vt polluer.

found vt fonder, créer; établir.

foundation n foundation f; fondement m.

foundry n fonderie f.

fountain n fontaine f.

four adj n quatre m.

fourfold adj quadruple.

fourteen adj n quatorze m.

fourteenth adj n quatorzième mf.

fourth adj n quatrième mf:—n quart m.

fowl n volaille f.

fox n renard f.

foyer n vestibule m.

fracas n rixe f.

fraction n fraction f.

fracture n fracture f:—vt fracturer.

fragile adj fragile.

fragility n fragilité f.

fragment n fragment m.

fragmentary adj fragmentaire.

fragrance n parfum m.

fragrant adj parfumé, odorant.

frail adj frêle, fragile.

frailty n fragilité f; faiblesse f.

frame n charpente f; cadre m:—vt encadrer.

franchise n droit de vote m; franchise f.

frank adj franc, direct.

frankness n franchise f.

frantic adj frénétique.

fraternal adv fraternel.

fraternise vi fraterniser.

fratricide n fratricide mf.

fraud n fraude, tromperie f.

fraudulent adj frauduleux.

free adj libre; autonome; gratuit; dégagé:—vt affranchir; libérer; débarrasser.

freedom n liberté f.

freelance adj indépendant:—adv en indépendant.

freely adv librement; libéralement.

freewheel vi rouler au point mort.

free will n libre arbitre m.

freeze vi geler:—vt congeler; geler.

freezer n congélateur m.

freezing adj gelé.

freight n cargaison f; fret m.

freighter n affréteur m.

French fries npl frites fpl.

French window n porte-fenêtre f.

frenzied adj fou, frénétique.

frenzy n frénésie f; folie f.

frequency n fréquence f.

frequent adj fréquent:—vt fréquenter.

fresco n fresque f.

fresh adj frais; nouveau, récent.

freshen vt rafraîchir:—vi se rafraîchir.

freshly adv récemment.

freshness n fraîcheur f.

freshwater adj d'eau douce.

fret vi s'agiter, se tracasser.

friction n friction f.

Friday n vendredi m:—**Good ~** Vendredi Saint m.

friend n ami m, -e f.

friendliness n amitié, bienveillance f.

friendly adj amical.

friendship n amitié f.

fright n peur, frayeur f.

frighten vt effrayer.

frightened adj effrayé, apeuré.

frightful adj épouvantable.

frigid adj glacé; frigide.

fringe n frange f.

frisk vt fouiller.

frivolity n frivolité f.

frivolous adj frivole.

fro adv:—**to go to and ~** aller et venir.

frock n robe f.

frog n grenouille f.

frolic vi folâtrer.

from prep de; depuis; à partir de.

front n avant, devant m; front m:—adj de devant; premier.

front door n porte d'entrée f.

frontier n frontière f.

front-wheel drive n (auto) traction avant f.

frost n gel m; gelée f:—vt geler.

frostbite n engelure f.

frostbitten adj gelé.

frosty adj glacial; givré.

froth n écume f:—vi écumer.

frothy adj mousseux, écumeux.

frown vt froncer les sourcils.

frozen adj gelé.

frugal adj frugal; économique.

fruit n fruit m.

fruiterer n fruitier m, -ière f.

fruitful adj fécond, fertile; fructueux.

fruition n réalisation f.

fruitless adj stérile.

frustrate vt contrecarrer; annuler.

frustrated adj frustré.

frustration n frustration f.

fry vt frire.

frying pan n poêle f.

fudge n caramel m.

fuel n combustible, carburant m.

fuel tank n réservoir à carburant m.

fugitive adj n fugitif m, -ive f.

fulfil vt accomplir; réaliser.

fulfilment n accomplissement m.

full adj plein, rempli; complet:—adv pleinement, entièrement.

full moon n pleine lune f.

fullness n plénitude f; abondance f.

full-time adj à plein temps.

fully adv pleinement, entièrement.

fumble vi farfouiller.

fume vi rager, fumer.

fumigate vt fumiger.

fun n amusement m:—**to have ~** (bien) s'amuser.

function n fonction f.

functional adj fonctionnel.

fund n fonds m:—vt financer.

fundamental adj fondamental.

funeral service n office des morts m.

funeral n enterrement m.

funnel n entonnoir m; cheminée f.

funny adj amusant; curieux.

fur n fourrure f.

furious adj furieux; déchaîné.

furnace n fourneau m; chaudière f.

furnish vt meubler; fournir.

furniture n meubles mpl.

furrow n sillon m:—vt sillonner.

furry adj à poil.

further adj supplémentaire; plus lointain:—adv plus loin; en outre; de plus:—vt favoriser; promouvoir.

further education n formation continue f.

furthermore adv de plus.

furtive adj furtif; secret.

fury n fureur f; colère f.

fuse vi fondre, sauter:—n fusible m; amorce f.

fuse box n boîte à fusibles f.

fusion n fusion f.

fuss n tapage m.

fussy adj tatillon, chipoteur.

futile adj futile, vain.

futility n futilité f.

future adj futur:—n futur m; avenir m.

fuzzy adj flou, confus.

G

gabble *vi* baragouiner:—*n* charabia *m*.

gadget *n* gadget *m*.

gaiety *n* gaieté *f*.

gain *n* gain *m*; bénéfice *m*:—*vt* gagner.

gait *n* démarche *f*; maintien *m*.

galaxy *n* galaxie *f*.

gale *n* grand vent *m*.

gallant *adj* galant.

gallery *n* galerie *f*.

gallop *n* galop *m*:—*vi* galoper.

galore *adv* en abondance.

galvanise *vt* galvaniser.

gamble *vi* jouer; spéculer:—*n* risque *m*; pari *m*.

gambler *n* joueur *m*, -euse *f*.

gambling *n* jeu *m*.

game *n* jeu *m*; divertissement *m*:—*vi* jouer.

gang *n* gang *m*, bande *f*.

gangway *n* passerelle *f*.

gap *n* vide *m*; écart *m*.

garage *n* garage *m*.

garbage *n* ordures *fpl*.

garbage can *n* poubelle *f*.

garden *n* jardin *m*.

gardener *n* jardinier *m*, -ière *f*.

gardening *n* jardinage *m*.

garlic *n* ail *m*.

garment *n* vêtement *m*.

garnish *vt* garnir:—*n* garniture *f*.

garret *n* mansarde *f*.

garrulous *adj* locace, bavard.

garter *n* jarretelle *f*.

gas *n* gaz *m*; essence *f*.

gas cylinder *n* bouteille de gaz *f*.

gaseous *adj* gazeux.

gash *n* entaille *f*:—*vt* entailler.

gasoline *n* essence *f*.

gasp *vi* haleter.

gas station *n* poste d'essence *m*.

gassy *adj* gazeux.

gastronomic *adj* gastronomique.

gate *n* porte *f*; portail *m*.

gather *vt* rassembler; ramasser:—*vi* se rassembler.

gaudy *adj* criard.

gauge *n* calibre *m*:—*vt* calibrer.

gaunt *adj n* maigre *mf*.

gay *adj* gai; vif.

gaze *vi* contempler:—*n* regard *m*.

gear *n* équipement *m*, matériel *m*; vitesse *f*.

gearbox *n* boîte de vitesses *f*.

gem *n* pierre précieuse *f*; perle *f*.

gender *n* genre *m*.

gene *n* gène *m*.

genealogical *adj* généalogique.

genealogy *n* généalogie *f*.

general *adj* général:—**in ~** en général:—*n* général *m*.

generalisation *n* généralisation *f*.

generalise *vt* généraliser.

generation *n* génération *f*.

generator *n* générateur *m*.

generosity *n* générosité, libéralité *f*.

generous *adj* généreux.

genial *adj* bienveillant; doux.

genitals *npl* organes génitaux *mpl*.

genius *n* génie *m*.

gentle *adj* doux, *f* douce, modéré.

gentleman *n* gentleman *m*.

gentleness *n* douceur *f*.

genuine *adj* authentique; sincère.

genus *n* genre *m*.

geographer *n* géographe *mf*.

geography *n* géographie *f*.

geologist *n* géologue *mf*.

geology *n* géologie *f*.

geometry *n* géométrie *f*.

germinate *vi* germer.

gesticulate *vi* gesticuler.

gesture *n* geste *m*.

get *vt* avoir; obtenir:—*vi* devenir.

geyser *n* geyser *m*; chauffe-eau *m* invar.

ghost *n* fantôme, spectre *m*.

giant *n* géant *m*, -e *f*.

gibe *vi* se moquer:—*n* moquerie *f*.

giddiness *n* vertige *m*.

giddy *adj* vertigineux.

gift *n* cadeau *m*.

gifted *adj* talentueux; doué.

gigantic *adj* gigantesque.

gild *vt* dorer.

gills *pl* branchies *fpl*.

ginger *n* gingembre *m*.

ginger-haired *adj* roux, *f* rousse.

girl *n* fille *f*.

girlfriend *n* amie *f*; petite amie *f*.

gist *n* essence *f*.

give *vt* donner; remettre.

gizzard *n* gésier *m*.

glacial *adj* glacial.

glacier *n* glacier *m*.

glad *adj* joyeux, content.

gladden *vt* réjouir.

glamour *n* attrait *m*, séduction *f*.

glamorous *adj* attrayant, séduisant.

glance *vi* jeter un coup d'œil.

glare *n* éclat *m*:—*vi* éblouir.

glass *n* verre *m*:—**es** *pl* lunettes *fpl*.

glaze *vt* vitrer.

gleam *n* rayon *m*.

glee *n* joie *f*; exultation *f*.

glide *vi* glisser; planer.

glimmer *n* lueur *f*:—*vi* luire.

glimpse *n* aperçu *m*:—*vt* entrevoir.

glint *vi* briller, scintiller.

glitter *vi* luire, briller.

global *adj* global; mondial.

globe *n* globe *m*; sphère *f*.

gloom *n* obscurité *f*; mélancolie.

gloomy *adj* sombre, mélancolique.

glorious *adj* glorieux, illustre.

glory *n* gloire, célébrité *f*.

glove *n* gant *m*.

glow *vi* rougeoyer:—*n* rougeoiment *m*.

glue *n* colle *f*:—*vt* coller.

glum *adj* abattu, triste.

glutton *n* glouton *m*, -onne *f*.

gnome *n* gnome *m*.

go *vi* aller:—**~ away** s'en aller.

goal *n* but, objectif *m*.

gobble *vt* engloutir.

God *n* Dieu *m*.

godfather *n* parrain *m*.

godlike *adj* divin.

godmother *n* marraine *f*.

gold *n* or *m*.

golden *adj* doré; d'or.

goldsmith *n* orfèvre *m*.

golf *n* golf *m*.

golfer *n* golfeur *m*, -euse *f*.

gong *n* gong *m*.

good *adj* bon; valable:—*n* bien *m*:—**~s** *pl* biens *mpl*.

goodbye! *excl* au revoir!

good-looking *adj* beau.

goodness *n* bonté *f*; qualité *f*.

goodwill *n* bienveillance *f*.

goose *n* oie *f*.

gorge *n* gorge *f*:—*vt* engloutir, avaler.

gorgeous *adj* merveilleux.

gory *adj* sanglant.

gossip *n* potins *mpl*:—*vi* potiner.

govern *vt* gouverner, diriger.

government *n* gouvernement *m*.

governor *n* gouverneur *m*.

gown *n* toge *f*; robe *f*.

grab *vt* saisir.

grace *n* grâce *f*:—*vt* honorer.

graceful *adj* gracieux.

gradation *n* gradation *f*.

grade *n* grade *m*.

gradual *adj* graduel.

graduate *vi* obtenir son diplôme.

graft *n* greffe *f*:—*vt* greffer.

grain *n* grain *m*.

grammar *n* grammaire *f*.

grammatical *adj* grammatical.

grand *adj* grandiose; magnifique.

grandchild *n* petit-fils *m*; petite-fille *f*:—**grandchildren** *pl* petits-enfants *m pl*.

grandad *n* pépé *m*.

granddaughter *n* petite-fille *f*.

grandeur *n* grandeur *f*; pompe *f*.

grandfather *n* grand-père *m*.

grandma *n* mémé *f*.

grandmother *n* grand-mère *f*.

grandparents *npl* grands-parents *mpl*.

grandson *n* petit-fils *m*.

grandstand *n* tribune *f*.

granny *n* mémé *f*.

grant *vt* accorder:—*n* bourse *f*.

granulate *vt* granuler.

granule *n* granule *m*.

grape *n* raisin *m*.

grapefruit *n* pamplemousse *m*.

graph *n* graphe, graphique *m*.

graphic(al) *adj* graphique.

grasp *vt* saisir, empoigner; comprendre.

grass *n* herbe *f*.

grasshopper *n* sauterelle *f*.

grassy *adj* herbeux.

grate *n* grille *f*:—*vt* râper:—*vi* grincer.

grateful *adj* reconnaissant.

gratification *n* satisfaction *f*.

gratify *vt* satisfaire.

gratifying *adj* réjouissant.

gratis *adv* gratis, gratuitement.

gratitude *n* gratitude, reconnaissance *f*.

gratuitous *adj* gratuit; volontaire.

gratuity *n* gratification *f*.

grave *n* tombe *f*:—*adj* grave.

graveyard *n* cimetière *m*.

gravity *n* gravité *f*.

gravy *n* jus de viande *m*; sauce *f*.

graze *vt* paître:—*vi* paître.

grease *n* graisse *f*:—*vt* graisser.

great *adj* grand; important.

greatness *n* grandeur *f*; importance *f*.

greed *n* avidité *f*; gloutonnerie *f*.

greedy *adj* avide; glouton.

green *adj* vert:—*n* vert *m*; verdure *f*.

greenery *n* verdure *f*.

greenhouse *n* serre *f*.

greenish *adj* verdâtre.

greet *vt* saluer; accueillir.

greeting *n* salutation *f*; accueil *m*.

grey *adj* gris:—*n* gris *m*.

greyish *adj* grisâtre; grisonnant.

grid *n* grille *f*; réseau *m*.

grief *n* chagrin *m*, douleur.

grievance *n* grief *m*; doléance *f*.

grieve *vt* peiner:—*vi* se chagriner.

grievous *adj* douloureux; grave.

grill *n* gril *m*:—*vt* faire griller.

grim *adj* peu engageant.

grimace *n* grimace *f*; moue *f*.

grime *n* saleté *f*.

grind *vt* moudre.

grip *n* prise *f*; poignée *f*:—*vt* saisir, agripper.

groan *vi* gémir; grogner:—*n* gémissement *m*.

grocer *n* épicier *m*, -ière *f*.

groom n valet m; marié m:—vt panser; préparer.

groove n rainure f.

grope vt chercher à tâtons:—vi tâtonner.

gross adj gros; grossier.

grotesque adj grotesque.

ground n terre f, sol m; terrain:—vt fonder.

ground floor n rez-de-chaussée m.

groundless adj sans fondement.

group n groupe m:—vt regrouper.

grove n bosquet m.

grovel vi se traîner; ramper.

grow vt cultiver:—vi pousser.

grower n cultivateur m, -trice f.

growl vi grogner.

growth n croissance f.

grudge n rancune f.

gruelling adj difficile, pénible.

gruesome adj horrible.

grumble vi grogner; grommeler.

guarantee n garantie f:—vt garantir.

guard n garde f:—vt garder.

guardian n tuteur m, -trice f.

guardianship n tutelle f.

guess vt deviner:—vi deviner:—n conjecture f.

guest n invité m, invitée f.

guidance n guidage m; direction f.

guide vt guider, diriger:—n guide m.

guidebook n guide m.

guild n association f; corporation f.

guile n astuce f.

guilt n culpabilité f.

guilty adj coupable.

guise n apparence f.

guitar n guitare f.

gullibility n crédulité f.

gullible adj crédule.

gulp n gorgée f:—vi, vt avaler.

gum n gomme f:—vt coller.

gun n pistolet m; fusil m.

gunpowder n poudre à canon f.

gunshot n coup de feu m.

gurgle vi gargouiller.

gush vi jaillir; bouillonner:—n jaillissement m.

gust n rafale f; bouffée f.

gusto n plaisir m, délectation f.

gusty adj venteux.

gut n intestin m:—vt vider.

gutter n gouttière f; caniveau m.

guy n mec, type m.

guzzle vt bouffer, engloutir.

gymnasium n gymnase m.

gymnast n gymnaste mf.

gymnastic adj gymnastique:—~s npl gymnastique f.

gynecologist n gynécologue mf.

gypsy n gitan m, -e f.

H

habit n habitude f.

habitable adj habitable.

habitat n habitat m.

habitual adj habituel.

haemorrhage n hémorragie f.

haggard adj décharné hagard.

haggle vi marchander.

hail n grêle f:—vt saluer:—vi grêler.

hair n cheveu m; poil m.

haircut n coupe de cheveux f.

hairless *adj* chauve; sans poils.

hairstyle *n* coiffure *f*.

hairy *adj* chevelu; poilu.

hale *adj* vigoureux.

half *n* moitié *f*:—*adj* demi:—*adv* à moitié.

half-hearted *adj* peu enthousiaste.

half-hour *n* demi-heure *f*.

half-moon *n* demi-lune *f*.

halfway *adv* à mi-chemin.

hall *n* vestibule *m*.

hallow *vt* consacrer, sanctifier.

hallucination *n* hallucination *f*.

halt *vi* s'arrêter:—*n* arrêt *m*; halte *f*.

ham *n* jambon *m*.

hammer *n* marteau *m*:—*vt* marteler.

hammock *n* hamac *m*.

hamper *n* panier *m*:—*vt* entraver.

hand *n* main *f*:—*vt* donner, passer.

handbag *n* sac à main *m*.

handbrake *n* frein à main *m*.

handful *n* poignée *f*.

handicap *n* handicap *m*.

handicapped *adj* handicapé.

handkerchief *n* mouchoir *m*.

handle *n* manche *m*:—*vt* manier.

handlebars *npl* guidon *m*.

handrail *n* garde-fou *m*.

handsome *adj* beau.

handwriting *n* écriture *f*.

hang *vt* accrocher; pendre:—*vi* pendre.

hangover *n* gueule de bois *f*.

haphazard *adj* fortuit.

hapless *adj* malheureux.

happen *vi* se passer.

happening *n* événement *m*.

happily *adv* heureusement.

happiness *n* bonheur *m*.

happy *adj* heureux.

harass *vt* harceler.

harbour *n* port *m*:—*vt* héberger.

hard *adj* dur; pénible; sévère.

harden *vt vi* durcir.

hardiness *n* robustesse *f*.

hardly *adv* à peine:—~ **ever** presque jamais.

hardness *n* dureté *f*; difficulté *f*.

hard-up *adj* fauché.

hardy *adj* fort, robuste.

hare *n* lièvre *m*.

harm *n* mal *m*; tort *m*:—*vt* nuire à.

harmful *adj* nuisible.

harmonious *adj* harmonieux.

harmony *n* harmonie *f*.

harp *n* harpe *f*.

harsh *adj* dur; austère; rude.

harshness *n* aspérité, dureté *f*; austérité *f*.

harvest *n* moisson *f*:—*vt* moissonner.

harvester *n* moissonneur *m*, -euse *f*.

haste *n* hâte *f*.

hasten *vt* accélérer:—*vi* se dépêcher.

hasty *adj* hâtif; irréfléchi.

hat *n* chapeau *m*.

hatch *vt* couver; faire éclore:—*n* écoutille *f*.

hatchet *n* hachette *f*.

hate *n* haine *f*:—*vt* haïr, détester.

hatred *n* haine *f*.

haughtiness *n* orgueil *m*.

haughty *adj* orgueilleux.

haul *vt* tirer:—*n* prise *f*.

haunt *vt* hanter:—*n* repaire *m*.

have *vt* avoir; posséder.

haversack *n* sac à dos *m*.

havoc *n* ravages *mpl*.

hay *n* foin *m*.

hay fever *n* rhume des foins *m*.

hazard *n* risque, danger *m*:—*vt* risquer.

hazardous *adj* risqué, dangereux.

haze *n* brume *f*.

hazelnut *n* noisette *f*.

hazy *adj* brumeux.

he *pn* il.

head *n* tête *f*; chef *m*:—*vt* conduire.

headache *n* mal de tête *m*.

headland *n* promontoire *m*.

headlight *n* phare *m*.

headline *n* titre *m*.

headlong *adv* à toute allure.

headstrong *adj* têtu.

headwaiter *n* maître d'hôtel *m*.

heady *adj* capiteux.

heal *vt vi* guérir.

health *n* santé *f*.

healthiness *n* bonne santé *f*.

healthy *adj* en bonne santé; sain.

heap *n* tas *m*:—*vt* entasser.

hear *vt* entendre; écouter:—*vi* entendre.

hearing *n* ouïe *f*.

heart *n* cœur *m*.

heart failure *n* arrêt cardiaque *m*.

hearth *n* foyer *m*.

heartless *adj* cruel.

hearty *adj* cordial.

heat *n* chaleur *f*:—*vt* chauffer.

heater *n* radiateur *m*.

heathen *n* païen *m*, païenne *f*.

heating *n* chauffage *m*.

heatwave *n* onde de chaleur *f*.

heave *vt* lever; tirer.

heaven *n* ciel *m*.

heaviness *n* lourdeur *f*.

heavy *adj* lourd, pesant.

hectic *adj* agité.

hedge *n* haie *f*.

hedgehog *n* hérisson *m*.

heed *vt* tenir compte de:—*n* attention *f*.

heedless *adj* inattentif, étourdi.

heel *n* talon *m*.

hefty *adj* fort; gros.

height *n* hauteur *f*; altitude *f*.

heighten *vt* rehausser.

heinous *adj* atroce.

heir *n* héritier *m*.

helicopter *n* hélicoptère *m*.

hell *n* enfer *m*.

helmet *n* casque *m*.

help *vt* aider, secourir:—*n* aide *f*; secours *m*.

helper *n* aide *mf*.

helpful *adj* utile.

helpless *adj* impuissant.

hemisphere *n* hémisphère *m*.

hen *n* poule *f*.

henceforward *adv* dorénavant.

hen-house *n* poulailler *m*.

hepatitis *n* hépatite *f*.

her *pn* son, sa, ses; elle; la; lui.

herb *n* herbe *f*.

herbalist *n* herboriste *mf*.

herd *n* troupeau *m*.

here *adv* ici.

hereby *adv* par la présente.

hereditary *adj* héréditaire.

heredity *n* hérédité *f*.

heritage *n* patrimoine, héritage *m*.

hermit *n* ermite *m*.

hernia *n* hernie *f*.

hero *n* héros *m*.

heroic *adj* héroïque.

hers *pn* le sien, la sienne, le(s) sien(ne)s, à elle.

herself *pn* elle-même.

hesitate *vi* hésiter.

hesitation *n* hésitation *f*.

heterogeneous *adj* hétérogène.

heterosexual *adj n* hétérosexuel *m*, -elle *f*.

hiatus *n* (*gr*) hiatus *m*.

hiccup *n* hoquet *m*:—*vi* avoir le hoquet.

hide *vt* cacher:—*n* cuir *m*; peau *f*.

hideaway *n* cachette *f*.

hideous *adj* hideux; horrible.

hierarchy *n* hiérarchie *f*.

hi-fi n hi-fi f invar.
high adj haut; élevé.
highlight n point fort m.
highness n hauteur f; altesse f.
hike vi faire une randonnée.
hilarious adj hilarant; hilare.
hill n colline f.
hillside n coteau m.
hilly adj montagneux.
him pn lui; le.
himself pn lui-même; soi.
hinder vt gêner, entraver.
hindrance n gêne f, obstacle m.
hindsight n:—**with ~** rétrospectivement.
hint n allusion f:—vt insinuer; suggérer.
hip n hanche f.
hire vt louer:—n location f.
his poss adj son, sa, ses; poss pn le sien, la sienne, les sien(ne)s; à lui.
hiss vt vi siffler.
historian n historien m, -ienne f.
historic(al) adj historique.
history n histoire f.
hit vt frapper; atteindre.
hitch-hike vi faire du stop.
hoard n stock m; trésor caché m:—vt accumuler.
hoarse adj rauque.
hoarseness n voix rauque f.
hobby n passe-temps m invar.
hoist vt hisser:—n grue f.
hold vt tenir; détenir:—n prise f; pouvoir m.
holder n détenteur m, -trice f.
holdup n hold-up m.
hole n trou m.
holiday n jour de congé m:—**s** pl vacances fpl.
hollow adj creux:—n creux m:—vt creuser.
holocaust n holocauste m.

holy adj saint; bénit.
homage n hommage m.
home n maison f; domicile m.
homeless adj sans abri.
homely adj simple.
homesick adj nostalgique.
homesickness n nostalgie f.
homework n devoirs mpl.
homicide n homicide m; homicide mf.
homogeneous adj homogène.
homosexual adj n homosexuel m, -elle f.
honest adj honnête.
honesty n honnêteté f.
honey n miel m.
honor n honneur m:—vt honorer.
honorable adj honorable.
honorary adj honoraire.
hood n capot m; capuche f.
hoof n sabot m.
hook n crochet m; hameçon m:—vt accrocher.
hoop n cerceau m.
hooter n sirène f.
hop n saut m:—vi sauter.
hope n espoir m, espérance f:—vi espérer.
hopeful adj plein d'espoir; prometteur.
horizon n horizon m.
horizontal adj horizontal.
hormone n hormone f.
horn n corne f.
horoscope n horoscope m.
horrible adj horrible.
horrific adj horrible, affreux.
horrify vt horrifier.
horror n horreur f.
hors d'œuvre n hors-d'œuvre m invar.
horse n cheval m.
horseback adv:—**on ~** à cheval.
horseman n cavalier m.
horsepower n cheval-vapeur m; puissance en chevaux f.

horseshoe n fer à cheval m.
horticulture n horticulture f.
horticulturist n horticulteur m, -trice f.
hospitable adj hospitalier.
hospital n hôpital m.
hospitality n hospitalité f.
host n hôte m; hostie f.
hostage n otage m.
hostess n hôtesse f.
hostile adj hostile.
hostility n hostilité f.
hot adj chaud; épicé.
hotel n hôtel m.
hotelier n hôtelier m, -ière f.
hotheaded adj exalté.
hotplate n plaque chauffante f.
hour n heure f.
hour-glass n sablier m.
hourly adv toutes les heures.
house n maison f; maisonnée f:—vt loger.
houseboat n péniche f.
household n famille f, ménage m.
householder n propriétaire mf; chef de famille m.
housekeeper n gouvernante f.
housewife n ménagère f.
housework n travaux ménagers mpl.
housing n logement m.
hovel n taudis m.
hover vi planer.
how adv comme; comment:—~ do you do! enchanté.
however adv de quelque manière que; cependant, néanmoins.
howl vi hurler:—n hurlement m.
hub n centre m; moyeu m.
hue n teinte f; nuance f.
hug vt étreindre:—n étreinte f.
huge adj énorme.
huil n (mar) coque f.
hum vi chantonner.

human adj humain.
humane adj humain.
humanise vt humaniser.
humanist n humaniste mf.
humanity n humanité f.
humble adj humble:—vt humilier.
humdrum adj monotone.
humid adj humide.
humiliate vt humilier.
humiliation n humiliation f.
humility n humilité f.
humorous adj humoristique.
humour n sens de l'humour m, humour m.
hump n bosse f.
hundred adj cent:—n centaine f.
hundredth adj centième.
hunger n faim f:—vi avoir faim.
hungry adj affamé.
hunt vt chasser:—n chasse f.
hunter n chasseur m.
hurdle n haie f.
hurl vt jeter.
hurricane n ouragan m.
hurry vt presser:—vi se presser:—n hâte f.
hurt vt faire mal à; blesser:—n mal m.
hurtful adj blessant.
husband n mari m.
hut n cabane, hutte f.
hydrant n bouche d'incendie f.
hydraulic adj hydraulique.
hydroelectric adj hydroélectrique.
hygiene n hygiène f.
hygienic adj hygiénique.
hypochondriac adj n hypocondriaque mf.
hypocrisy n hypocrisie f.
hypocritical adj hypocrite.
hypothesis n hypothèse f.
hypothetical adj hypothétique.
hysterical adj hystérique.
hysterics npl hystérie f.

I

I *pn* je, j'; moi
ice *n* glace *f*:—*vt* glacer.
ice cream *n* glace *f*.
ice rink *n* patinoire *f*.
ice skating *n* patinage sur glace *m*.
icy *adj* glacé.
idea *n* idée *f*.
ideal *adj* idéal.
identical *adj* identique.
identification *n* identification *f*.
identify *vt* identifier.
identity *n* identité *f*.
idiot *n* imbécile *mf*.
idiotic *adj* idiot, bête.
idle *adj* désœuvré; au repos.
idleness *n* paresse *f*.
idler *n* paresseux *m*, -euse *f*.
idol *n* idole *f*.
idolise *vt* idôlatrer.
idyllic *adj* idyllique.
if *conj* si:—~ **not** sinon.
ignite *vt* allumer, enflammer.
ignoble *adj* ignoble; bas.
ignominious *adj* ignominieux.
ignorance *n* ignorance *f*.
ignorant *adj* ignorant.
ignore *vt* ne pas tenir compte de.
ill *adj* malade:—*n* mal *m*.
illegal *adj* illégal.
illegality *n* illégalité *f*.
illegible *adj* illisible.
illegitimacy *n* illégitimité *f*.
illegitimate *adj* illégitime.
illicit *adj* illicite.
illiterate *adj* analphabète.
illness *n* maladie *f*.

illogical *adj* illogique.
illuminate *vt* illuminer.
illusion *n* illusion *f*.
illusory *adj* illusoire.
illustrate *vt* illustrer.
illustration *n* illustration *f*.
illustrious *adj* illustre.
image *n* image *f*.
imaginary *adj* imaginaire.
imagination *n* imagination *f*.
imagine *vt* imaginer.
imbecile *adj* imbécile, idiot.
imitate *vt* imiter.
imitation *n* imitation *f*.
immaterial *adj* insignifiant.
immeasurable *adj* incommensurable.
immediate *adj* immédiat.
immense *adj* immense.
immigrant *n* immigrant *m*, -e *f*.
immigration *n* immigration *f*.
imminent *adj* imminent.
immobile *adj* immobile.
immobility *n* immobilité *f*.
immoderate *adj* immodéré.
immoral *adj* immoral.
immorality *n* immoralité *f*.
immortal *adj* immortel.
immune *adj* immunisé.
immunise *vt* immuniser.
immutable *adj* immuable.
impact *n* impact *m*.
impalpable *adj* impalpable.
impart *vt* communiquer.
impartial *adj* impartial.
impartiality *n* impartialité *f*.
impassive *adj* impassible.

impatience n impatience f.

impatient adj impatient.

impeccable adj impeccable.

impede vt empêcher; entraver.

impending adj imminent.

impenetrable adj impénétrable.

imperceptible adj imperceptible.

imperfect adj imparfait.

imperfection n imperfection f; défaut m.

impermeable adj imperméable.

impersonal adj impersonel.

impertinence n impertinence f.

impertinent adj impertinent.

impetuosity n impétuosité f.

impetuous adj impétueux.

implement n outil m; ustensile m.

implicate vt impliquer.

implication n implication f.

implicit adj implicite.

implore vt supplier.

imply vt supposer.

impolite adj impoli.

import vt importer:—n importation f.

importance n importance f.

important adj important.

impose vt imposer.

imposition n imposition f.

impossibility n impossibilité f.

impossible adj impossible.

impostor n imposteur m.

impotence n impotence f.

impotent adj impotent.

impoverish vt appauvrir.

impoverishment n appauvrissement m.

impracticable adj impraticable.

imprecise adj imprécis.

impress vt impressionner.

impression n impression f; édition f.

impressionable adj impressionnable.

impressive adj impressionnant.

imprint n empreinte f:—vt imprimer.

imprison vt emprisonner.

imprisonment n emprisonnement m.

improbability n improbabilité f.

improbable adj improbable.

improper adj indécent; impropre.

improve vt améliorer:—vi s'améliorer.

improvement n amélioration f.

improvise vt improviser.

imprudent adj imprudent.

impudent adj impudent.

impulse n impulsion f.

impulsive adj impulsif.

impunity n impunité f.

in prep dans; en.

inability n incapacité f.

inaccurate adj inexact.

inactive adj inactif.

inadequate adj inadéquat.

inadmissible adj inadmissible.

inane adj inepte.

inanimate adj inanimé.

inapplicable adj inapplicable.

inaudible adj inaudible.

incalculable adj incalculable.

incapable adj incapable.

incapacitate vt mettre dans l'incapa-cité.

incapacity n incapacité f.

incarcerate vt incarcérer.

incautious adj imprudent.

incentive n prime, aide f

inception n commencement m.

incessant adj incessant, continuel.

incidence n fréquence f.

incident n incident m.

incidental adj fortuit.

incisive adj incisif.

incite vt inciter, encourager.

inclination n inclination, propension f.

incline vt incliner:—vi s'incliner.

include vt inclure, comprendre.

including *prep* inclus, y compris.

incoherence *n* incohérence *f*.

incoherent *adj* incohérent.

income *n* revenu *m*; recettes *fpl*.

incomparable *adj* incomparable.

incompetence *n* incompétence *f*.

incompetent *adj* incompétent.

incomplete *adj* incomplet.

incomprehensible *adj* incompréhensible.

inconceivable *adj* inconcevable.

incongruity *n* incongruité *f*.

incongruous *adj* incongru.

inconsiderate *adj* inconsidéré.

inconsistent *adj* inconsistant.

inconspicuous *adj* discret.

incontrovertible *adj* incontestable.

inconvenience *n* inconvénient:—*vt* incommoder.

inconvenient *adj* incommode.

incorporate *vt* incorporer:—*vi* s'incorporer.

incorporation *n* incorporation *f*.

incorrect *adj* incorrect.

increase *vt vi* augmenter:—*n* augmentation *f*.

increasing *adj* croissant.

incredible *adj* incroyable.

incredulous *adj* incrédule.

incriminate *vt* incriminer.

incur *vt* encourir.

incurable *adj* incurable.

incursion *n* incursion *f*.

indebted *adj* endetté; redevable.

indecent *adj* indécent.

indecision *n* indécision, irrésolution *f*.

indecisive *adj* indécis, irrésolu.

indefatigable *adj* infatigable.

indefinite *adj* indéfini.

indemnify *vt* indemniser.

indemnity *n* indemnité *f*.

independence *n* indépendance *f*.

independent *adj* indépendant.

indeterminate *adj* indéterminé.

index *n* indice *m*.

indicate *vt* indiquer.

indication *n* indication *f*; indice *m*.

indifference *n* indifférence *f*.

indifferent *adj* indifférent.

indigenous *adj* indigène.

indigent *adj* indigent.

indigestion *n* indigestion *f*.

indignant *adj* indigné.

indignation *n* indignation *f*.

indirect *adj* indirect.

indiscreet *adj* indiscret.

indiscretion *n* indiscrétion *f*.

indispensable *adj* indispensable.

indisputable *adj* indiscutable.

indistinct *adj* indistinct.

indistinguishable *adj* indistinctible.

individual *adj* individuel:—*n* individu *m*.

individuality *n* individualité *f*.

indolence *n* indolence *f*.

indolent *adj* indolent.

indoors *adv* à l'intérieur.

induce *vt* persuader; provoquer.

inducement *n* encouragement *m*; incitation *f*.

indulge *vt* céder à; *vi* se permettre.

indulgent *adj* indulgent.

industrial *adj* industriel.

industrialise *vt* industrialiser.

industrious *adj* travailleur.

industry *n* industrie *f*.

inebriated *vt* ivre.

inedible *adj* non comestible.

inefficiency *n* inefficacité *f*.

inefficient *adj* inefficace.

ineligible *adj* inéligible.

inept *adj* inepte; déplacé.

inequality *n* inégalité *f*.
inertia *n* inertie *f*.
inestimable *adj* inestimable.
inevitable *adj* inévitable.
inexhaustible *adj* inépuisable.
inexpedient *adj* imprudent, inopportun.
inexpensive *adj* bon marché.
inexplicable *adj* inexplicable.
infallible *adj* infaillible.
infamous *adj* vil, infâme.
infancy *n* enfance *f*.
infant *n* bébé *m*; enfant *mf*.
infantile *adj* infantile.
infatuated *adj* fou.
infatuation *n* folie *f*; obsession *f*.
infect *vt* infecter.
infectious *adj* infectieux.
infer *vt* inférer.
inference *n* inférence *f*.
inferior *adj* inférieur.
inferiority *n* infériorité *f*.
infernal *adj* infernal.
infest *vt* infester.
infidelity *n* infidélité *f*.
infiltrate *vi* s'infiltrer.
infinite *adj* infini.
infinity *n* infini *m*; infinité *f*.
infirm *adj* infirme.
infirmity *n* infirmité *f*.
inflame *vt* enflammer:—*vi* s'enflammer.
inflammation *n* inflammation *f*.
inflatable *adj* gonflable.
inflate *vt* gonfler.
inflation *n* inflation *f*.
inflict *vt* infliger.
influence *n* influence *f*:—*vt* influencer.
influential *adj* influent.
influenza *n* grippe *f*.
inform *vt* informer.
informal *adj* informel.
informality *n* simplicité *f*.

information *n* information *f*.
infrequent *adj* rare.
infringe *vt* enfreindre.
infringement *n* infraction *f*.
infuriate *vt* rendre furieux.
ingenious *adj* ingénieux.
ingenuity *n* ingéniosité *f*.
ingenuous *adj* ingénu.
inglorious *adj* honteux.
ingot *n* lingot *m*.
ingratitude *n* ingratitude *f*.
ingredient *n* ingrédient *m*.
inhabit *vt vi* habiter.
inhabitable *adj* habitable.
inhabitant *n* habitant *m*, -e *f*.
inhale *vt* inhaler.
inherit *vt* hériter.
inheritance *n* héritage *m*.
inhibit *vt* inhiber.
inhibition *n* inhibition *f*.
inhospitable *adj* inhospitalier.
inhuman *adj* inhumain.
inhumanity *n* inhumanité.
inimical *adj* hostile, ennemi.
inimitable *adj* inimitable.
initial *adj* initial:—*n* initiale *f*.
initiate *vt* commencer; initier.
initiation *n* initiation *f*.
initiative *n* initiative *f*.
inject *vt* injecter.
injection *n* injection *f*.
injunction *n* injonction *f*.
injure *vt* blesser.
injury *n* blessure *f*; tort *m*.
injustice *n* injustice *f*.
ink *n* encre *f*.
inlet *n* entrée *f*; bras de mer *m*.
inn *n* auberge *f*; hôtel *m*.
innate *adj* inné.
inner *adj* intérieur.
innkeeper *n* aubergiste *mf*.

innocence n innocence f.
innocent adj innocent.
innocuous adj inoffensif.
innovate vt innover.
innuendo n allusion f; insinuation f.
innumerable adj innombrable.
inoculate vt inoculer.
inoffensive adj inoffensif.
inopportune adj inopportun.
inquest n enquête f.
inquire vt vi demander.
inquiry n enquête f.
inquisition n investigation f.
inquisitive adj curieux.
insane adj fou, f folle.
insanity n folie f.
insatiable adj insatiable.
inscribe vt inscrire.
inscription n inscription f.
inscrutable adj impénétrable.
insect n insecte m.
insecure adj peu assuré.
insecurity n insécurité f.
insemination n insémination f.
insensible adj inconscient.
insensitive adj insensible.
inseparable adj inséparable.
insert vt introduire, insérer.
insertion n insertion f.
inside n intérieur m:—adv à l'intérieur.
inside out adv à l'envers.
insidious adj insidieux.
insight n perspicacité f.
insignificant adj insignifiant.
insinuate vt insinuer.
insinuation n insinuation f.
insipid adj insipide.
insist vi insister.
insistence n insistance f.
insistent adj insistant.
insolence n insolence f.

insolent adj insolent.
inspect vt examiner, inspecter.
inspection n inspection f.
inspector n inspecteur m, -trice f.
instability n instabilité f.
instal vt installer.
installation n installation f.
instalment n installation f.
instance n exemple m.
instant adj instantané:—n instant.
instead (of) pr au lieu.
instigate vt inciter; susciter.
instinct n instinct m.
instinctive adj instinctif.
institute vt instituer.
institution n institution f.
instruct vt instruire.
instrument n instrument m.
insufficiency n insuffisance f.
insufficient adj insuffisant.
insular adj insulaire.
insulate vt isoler.
insulation n isolation f.
insult vt insulter:—n insulte f.
insurance n (com) assurance f.
insure vt assurer.
intact adj intact.
integrate vt intégrer.
integration n intégration f.
integrity n intégrité f.
intellect n intellect m.
intellectual adj intellectuel.
intelligence n intelligence f.
intelligent adj intelligent.
intelligible adj intelligible.
intend vt avoir l'intention de.
intense adj intense.
intensify vt intensifier.
intensity n intensité f.
intensive adj intensif.
intention n intention f, dessein m.

intentional *adj* intentionnel:—**ly** *adv* à dessein, intentionnellement.
intercede *vi* intercéder.
intercept *vt* intercepter.
interest *vt* intéresser:—*n* intérêt *m*.
interesting *adj* intéressant.
interfere *vi* s'ingérer.
interior *adj* intérieur.
interlock *vi* s'entremêler.
interlude *n* intermède *m*.
intermediary *n* intermédiaire *mf*.
intermediate *adj* intermédiaire.
interminable *adj* interminable.
intermingle *vt* entremêler:—*vi* s'entremêler.
intermittent *adj* intermittent.
intern *n* interne *mf*.
internal *adj* intérieur; interne.
international *adj* international.
interpret *vt* interpréter.
interpretation *n* interprétation *f*.
interpreter *n* interprète *mf*.
interrogate *vt* interroger.
interrogation *n* interrogatoire *m*.
interrupt *vt* interrompre.
interruption *n* interruption *f*.
intersect *vi* se croiser.
intersection *n* croisement *m*.
intertwine *vt* entrelacer.
interval *n* intervalle *m*; mi-temps *f*.
intervene *vi* intervenir.
intervention *n* intervention *f*.
interview *n* entrevue *f*; interview *f*.
interviewer *n* interviewer *m*.
intestine *n* intestin *m*.
intimacy *n* intimité *f*.
intimate *adj* intime *vt* insinuer.
intimidate *vt* intimider.
into *prep* dans, en.
intolerable *adj* intolérable.
intolerant *adj* intolérant.

intonation *n* intonation *f*.
intoxicate *vt* enivrer.
intoxication *n* ivresse *f*.
intricacy *n* complexité *f*.
intricate *adj* complexe.
intrigue *n* intrigue *f*:—*vi* intriguer.
intriguing *adj* intrigant.
intrinsic *adj* intrinsèque.
introduce *vt* introduire.
introduction *n* introduction *f*.
introvert *n* introverti *m*, -ie *f*.
intruder *n* intrus *m*, -e *f*.
intuition *n* intuition *f*.
intuitive *adj* intuitif.
inundate *vt* inonder.
invade *vt* envahir.
invader *n* envahisseur *m*, -euse *f*.
invalid *n* invalide *mf*.
invalidate *vt* invalider.
invaluable *adj* inappréciable.
invasion *n* invasion *f*.
invent *vt* inventer.
invention *n* invention *f*.
inventor *n* inventeur *m*, -trice *f*.
investigation *n* investigation *f*.
investigator *n* investigateur *m*, -trice *f*.
invincible *adj* invincible.
inviolable *adj* inviolable.
invisible *adj* invisible.
invitation *n* invitation *f*.
invite *vt* inviter.
invoice *n* facture *f*.
invoke *vt* invoquer.
involuntary *adj* involontaire.
involve *vt* impliquer, entraîner.
involvement *n* implication *f*.
irascible *adj* irascible.
irate *adj* irrité.
iron *n* fer *m*:—*adj* de fer.
ironic *adj* ironique.
irony *n* ironie *f*.

irrational *adj* irrationnel.
irreconcilable *adj* irréconciliable.
irregular *adj* irrégulier.
irregularity *n* irrégularité *f*.
irreparable *adj* irréparable.
irreplaceable *adj* irremplaçable.
irresistible *adj* irrésistible.
irresponsible *adj* irresponsable.
irreverence *n* irrévérence *f*.
irrigate *vt* irriguer.
irrigation *n* irrigation *f*.
irritability *n* irritabilité *f*.
irritable *adj* irritable.
irritate *vt* irriter.
irritation *n* irritation *f*.

island *n* île *f*.
isle *n* île *f*.
isolate *vt* isoler.
isolation *n* isolement *m*.
issue *n* sujet *m*, question *f*:—*vt* publier.
it *pn* il, elle; le, la; cela, ça, ce, c'.
itch *n* démangeaison *f*:—*vi* avoir des démangeaisons.
item *n* article *m*.
itinerant *adj* itinérant.
itinerary *n* itinéraire *m*.
its *pn* son, sa, ses.
itself *pn* lui-même, elle-même.
ivory *n* ivoire *m*.
ivy *n* lierre *m*.

J

jabber *vi* bafouiller.
jack *n* cric *m*; valet *m*.
jacket *n* veste *f*; couverture *f*.
jackpot *n* gros lot *m*.
jagged *adj* dentelé.
jail *n* prison *f*.
jailer *n* geôlier *m*, -ière *f*.
jam *n* confiture *f*; embouteillage *m*.
January *n* janvier *m*.
jar *vi* (*mus*) détonner:—*n* pot *m*.
jargon *n* jargon *m*.
jaw *n* mâchoire *f*.
jazz *n* jazz *m*.
jealous *adj* jaloux.
jealousy *n* jalousie *f*.
jeans *npl* jean *m*.
jeer *vi* railler:—*n* raillerie.
jelly *n* gelée *f*.
jeopardise *vt* mettre en péril.
jerk *n* secousse *f*.

jersey *n* jersey *m*.
jest *n* blague.
jester *n* bouffon *m*.
jet *n* avion à réaction *m*; jet *m*.
jettison *vt* se défaire de.
jewel *n* bijou *m*.
jewellery *n* bijouterie *f*.
Jewish *adj* juif.
jibe *n* raillerie, moquerie *f*.
jigsaw *n* puzzle *m*.
jinx *n* porte-malheur *m invar*.
job *n* travail *m*.
jockey *n* jockey *m*.
jocular *adj* joyeux; facétieux.
jog *vi* faire du jogging.
join *vt* joindre, unir.
joint *n* articulation *f*:—*adj* commun.
joke *n* blague:—*vi* blaguer.
joker *n* blagueur *m*, -euse *f*.
jolly *adj* gai, joyeux.

jostle *vt* bousculer.

journal *n* revue *f*.

journalism *n* journalisme *m*.

journalist *n* journaliste *mf*.

journey *n* voyage *m*:—*vi* voyager.

joy *n* joie *f*.

joyful *adj* joyeux.

jubilation *n* jubilation *f*.

jubilee *n* jubilé *m*.

Judaism *n* judaïsme *m*.

judge *n* juge *m*:—*vt* juger.

judgment *n* jugement *m*.

judicious *adj* judicieux.

judo *n* judo *m*.

jug *n* cruche *f*.

juggle *vi* jongler.

juice *n* jus *m*; suc *m*.

juicy *adj* juteux.

July *n* juillet *m*.

jumble *vt* mélanger:—*n* mélange *m*.

jump *vi* sauter:—*n* saut *m*.

June *n* juin *m*.

jungle *n* jungle *f*.

junior *adj* plus jeune.

jurisdiction *n* juridiction *f*.

juror *n* juré *m*.

jury *n* jury *m*.

just *adj* juste:—*adv* justement, exactement.

justice *n* justice *f*.

justification *n* justification *f*.

justify *vt* justifier.

juvenile *adj* juvénile.

juxtaposition *n* juxtaposition *f*.

K

kaleidoscope *n* kaléidoscope *m*.

kangaroo *n* kangourou *m*.

keen *adj* enthousiaste; vif.

keenness *n* enthousiasme *m*.

keep *vt* garder, conserver.

kernel *n* amande *f*; noyau *m*.

kettle *n* bouilloire *f*.

key *n* clé, clef *f*; (*mus*) ton *m*; touche *f*.

keyboard *n* clavier *m*.

key ring *n* porte-clefs *m invar*.

keystone *n* clef de voûte *f*.

kick *vi* (*vt*) donner un coup de pied (à).

kidnap *vt* kidnapper.

kidney *n* rein *m*; rognon *m*.

killer *n* assassin *m*.

killing *n* assassinat *m*.

kiln *n* four *m*.

kilo *n* kilo *m*.

kilogram *n* kilogramme *m*.

kilometre *n* kilomètre *m*.

kin *n* parents *mpl*.

kind *adj* gentil:—*n* genre *m*.

kindle *vt* allumer:—*vi* s'allumer.

kindliness *n* gentillesse, bonté *f*.

kindly *adj* bon, bienveillant.

kindness *n* bonté *f*.

king *n* roi *m*.

kingdom *n* royaume *m*.

kiss *n* baiser *m*:—*vt* embrasser.

kit *n* équipement *m*.

kitchen *n* cuisine *f*.

kitten *n* chaton *m*.

knack *n* don, chic *m*.

knead *vt* pétrir.

knee *n* genou *m*.

kneel *vi* s'agenouiller.

knife n couteau m.
knight n chevalier m.
knit vt vi tricoter.
knob n bouton m.
knock vt vi cogner, frapper:—n coup m.

knot n nœud m:—vt nouer.
know vt vi savoir; connaître.
know-how n savoir-faire m.
knowledge n connaissances fpl.
knowledgeable adj bien informé.
knuckle n articulation f.

L

label n étiquette f.
laboratory n laboratoire m.
laborious adj laborieux.
labour n travail m:—vi travailler.
labourer n ouvrier m.
lace vt lacer.
lacerate vt lacérer.
lack vt manquer de:—vi manquer:—n manque m.
lad n garçon m.
ladder n échelle f.
lady n dame f.
lag vi se laisser distancer.
lagoon n lagune f.
lair n repaire m.
lake n lac m.
lame adj boiteux.
lament vt se lamenter sur:—n lamentation f.
lamentable adj lamentable.
lamentation n lamentation f.
lamp n lampe f.
lance n lance f:—vt inciser.
lancet n bistouri m.
land n pays m; terre f:—vi atterrir.
landlord n propriétaire m.
landmark n point de repère m.
landscape n paysage m.
landslide n glissement de terrain m.

lane n allée, ruelle f; file f.
language n langue f; langage m.
languish vi languir.
lantern n lanterne f.
lapel n revers m.
lapse n laps m; défaillance f:—vi expirer.
larder n garde-manger m invar.
large adj grand:—**at ~** en liberté.
larva n larve f.
lascivious adj lascif.
lash n coup de fouet m:—vt fouetter.
last adj dernier:—vi durer.
last-minute adj de dernière minute.
late adj en retard; défunt:—adv tard:—**~ly** adv récemment.
latent adj latent.
lateral ad latérale.
lather n mousse f.
latitude n latitude f.
laudable adj louable.
laugh vi rire:—**to ~ at** vt rire de:—n rire m.
laughter n rires mpl.
launch vt lancer:—vi se lancer.
laundry n lessive f.
lava n lave f.
lavatory n toilettes fpl.
lavish adj prodigue:—vt prodiguer.

law n loi f; droit m.

lawful adj légal; légitime.

lawmaker n législateur m, -trice f.

lawn n pelouse f, gazon m.

lawyer n avocat m; notaire m.

lax adj relâché.

laxative n laxatif m.

lay vt mettre; pondre.

layer n couche f.

laziness n paresse f.

lazy adj paresseux.

lead n plomb m:—vt vi conduire, mener.

leader n chef m.

leadership n direction f.

leading adj principal; premier.

leaf n feuille f.

leaflet n feuillet m.

league n ligue f; lieue f.

leak n fuite f:—vi (mar) faire eau.

lean vi s'appuyer:—adj maigre.

leap vi sauter:—n saut m.

learn vt vi apprendre.

learning n érudition f.

lease n bail m:—vt louer.

leash n laisse f.

least adj moindre:—at ~ au moins.

leather n cuir m.

leave n permission f; congé m:—vt laisser.

lecture n conférence f:—vi faire une conférence.

lecturer n conférencier m, -ière f.

leeway n liberté d'action f.

left adj gauche.

left-handed adj gaucher.

left-luggage office n consigne f.

leftovers npl restes mpl.

leg n jambe f; patte f.

legal adj légal, légitime.

legalise vt légaliser.

legality n légalité, légitimité f.

legend n légende f.

legendary adj légendaire.

legible adj lisible.

legion n légion f.

legislate vi, vt légiférer.

legislation n législation f.

legislative adj législatif.

legislature n corps législatif m.

legitimacy n légitimité f.

legitimate adj légitime:—vt légitimer.

leisure n loisir m:—~ly adj tranquille.

lemon n citron m.

lemonade n limonade f.

lend vt prêter.

length n longueur f; durée f:—at ~ longuement.

lengthen vt allonger:—vi s'allonger.

lengthy adj long.

lenient adj indulgent.

lens n lentille f.

leotard n justaucorps m.

lesbian n lesbienne f.

less adj moins:—adv moins.

lessen vt vi diminuer.

lesser adj moindre.

lesson n leçon f.

let vt laisser, permettre.

lethal adj mortel.

lethargic adj léthargique.

lethargy n léthargie f.

letter n lettre f.

lettering n inscription f.

lettuce n salade f.

level adj plat, égal:—n niveau m:—vt niveler.

lever n levier m.

levity n légèreté f.

liability n responsabilité f.

liable adj sujet (à); responsable.

liaise vi effectuer une liaison.

liaison n liaison f.

liar n menteur m, -euse f.

liberal adj libéral; généreux.

liberate vt libérer.

liberation n libération f.

liberty n liberté f.

librarian n bibliothécaire mf.

library n bibliothèque f.

licence n licence f; permis m.

lick vt lécher.

lid n couvercle m.

lie n mensonge m:—vi mentir; être allongé.

lieu n:—**in ~ of** au lieu de.

life n vie f.

life jacket n gilet de sauvetage m.

lifeless adj mort; sans vie.

life sentence n condamnation à perpétuité f.

life-sized adj grandeur nature.

lift vt lever.

ligament n ligament m.

light n lumière f:—adj léger; clair: —vt allumer.

lighten vi s'éclaircir:—vt éclairer; éclaircir.

lighthouse n (mar) phare m.

lighting n éclairage m.

lightning n éclair m.

light year n année-lumière f.

like adj pareil:—adv comme:—vt vi aimer.

likelihood n probabilité f.

likely adj probable, vraisemblable.

liken vt comparer.

likeness n ressemblance f.

likewise adv pareillement.

liking n goût m.

limb n membre m.

limit n limite f:—vt limiter.

limitation n limitation f; restriction f.

limp vi boiter:—n boitement m:—adj mou.

line n ligne f, ride f:—vt rayer; rider.

linear adj linéaire.

liner n transatlantique m.

linger vi traîner.

linguist n linguiste mf.

linguistic adj linguistique.

link n chaînon m:—vt relier.

lion n lion m.

lip n lèvre f; bord m.

lip-read vi lire sur les lèvres.

lipstick n rouge à lèvres m.

liqueur n liqueur f.

liquid adj liquide:—n liquide m.

liquidise vt liquéfier.

liquor n spiritueux m.

lisp vi zézayer:—n zézaiement m.

list n liste f:—vt faire une liste de.

listen vi écouter.

literal adj littéral.

literary adj littéraire.

literature n littérature f.

litigation n litige m.

litigious adj litigieux.

litre n litre m.

litter n litière f; ordures fpl:—vt recouvrir.

little adj petit:—n peu m.

live vi vivre; habiter:—adj vivant.

livelihood n moyens de subsistance mpl.

liveliness n vivacité f.

lively adj vif.

liver n foie m.

livid adj livide; furieux.

living n vie f:—adj vivant.

living room n salle de séjour f.

load vt charger:—n charge f.

loaf n pain m.

loan n prêt m.

loathe vt détester.
loathing n aversion f.
lobster n langouste f.
local adj local.
locate vt localiser.
location n situation f.
lock n serrure f;—vt fermer à clé.
locker n casier m.
lockout n grève patronale f.
locomotive n locomotive f.
lodge vi se loger.
lodger n locataire mf.
log n bûche f.
logic n logique f.
logical adj logique.
loiter vi s'attarder.
lollipop n sucette f.
lonely adj seul, solitaire.
loneliness n solitude f.
long adj long, f longue:—vi désirer.
longevity n longévité f.
longing n désir m.
long-range adj à longue portée.
long-term adj à long terme.
look vi regarder; sembler:—n aspect m; regard m.
loop n boucle f.
loose adj lâché; desserré
loosen vt lâcher; desserrer.
loot vt piller:—n butin m.
loquacious adj loquace.
loquacity n loquacité f.
lose vt vi perdre.
loss n perte f.
lot n sort f; lot m:—**a ~** beaucoup.
lotion n lotion f.
loud adj fort, bruyant.
loudspeaker n haut-parleur m.

lounge n salon m.
lovable adj sympathique.
love n amour m:—vt aimer.
loveliness n beauté f.
lovely adj beau.
lover n amant m.
loving adj affectueux.
low adj bas:—vi meugler.
lower vt baisser.
lowly adj humble.
loyal adj loyal, fidèle.
loyalty n loyauté f; fidélité f.
lucid adj lucide.
luck n chance f.
luckless adj malchanceux.
lucky adj chanceux.
lucrative adj lucratif.
ludicrous adj absurde.
luggage n bagages mpl.
lukewarm adj tiède.
lull vt bercer:—n répit m.
luminous adj lumineux.
lump n bosse f; grosseur f.
lunch n déjeuner m.
lungs npl poumons mpl.
lure n leurre m; attrait m:—vt séduire, attirer.
lurk vi se cacher.
lush adj luxuriant.
lust n luxure f:—vi désirer.
lustre n lustre m.
luxuriance n luxuriance f.
luxuriant adj luxuriant.
luxurious adj luxueux.
luxury n luxe m.
lyrical adj lyrique.
lyrics npl paroles fpl.

M

macerate vt macérer.
machination n machination f.
machine n machine f.
machinery n machinerie f; mécanisme m.
mad adj fou, f folle; insensé.
madam n madame f.
madden vt rendre fou; rendre furieux.
madman n fou m.
madness n folie f.
magazine n magazine m, revue f; magasin m.
magic n magie f:—adj magique.
magnanimous adj magnanime.
magnet n aimant m.
magnetic adj magnétique.
magnetism n magnétisme m.
magnificence n magnificence f.
magnificent ad magnifique.
magnify vt grossir; exagérer.
magnitude n magnitude f.
maid n bonne f.
mail n courrier m.
mail train n (rail) train-poste m.
maim vt mutiler.
main adj principal; essentiel:—**in the ~** en général.
mainland n continent m.
main line n (rail) grande ligne f.
main street n rue principale f.
maintain vt maintenir; soutenir.
maintenance n entretien m.
majestic adj majestueux.
majesty n majesté f.
major adj majeur.
majority n majorité f.

make vt faire n marque f.
make-up n maquillage m.
malady n maladie f.
malaise n malaise m.
malaria n malaria f.
malcontent adj n mécontent m, -e f.
male adj mâle; masculin:—n mâle m.
malevolence n malveillance f.
malevolent adj malveillant.
malice n malice f.
malicious adj méchant.
malign adj nocif:—vt calomnier.
malleable adj malléable.
malnutrition n malnutrition f.
malpractice n négligence f.
maltreat vt maltraiter.
mammal n mammifère m.
man n homme m.
manage vt diriger; réussir:—vi réussir.
management n direction f.
manager n directeur m.
managing director n directeur général m.
mandate n mandat m.
mandatory n obligatoire.
manhandle vt maltraiter; manutentionner.
maniac n maniaque mf.
manic adj maniaque.
manifest adj manifeste:—vt manifester.
manifestation n manifestation f.
manipulate vt manipuler.
manipulation n manipulation f.
mankind n humanité f.
manliness n virilité f.
manly adj viril.

man-made *n* artificiel.

manner *n* manière *f*.

manoeuvre *n* manœuvre *f*.

manual *adj n* manuel *m*.

manufacture *n* fabrication *f*.

manufacturer *n* fabricant *m*.

manuscript *n* manuscrit *m*.

many *adj* beaucoup de:—**how ~?** combien?

map *n* carte *f*; plan *m*.

mar *vt* gâter, gâcher.

marble *n* marbre *m*:—*adj* marbré.

March *n* mars *m*.

march *n* marche *f*:—*vi* marcher.

margarine *n* margarine *f*.

margin *n* marge *f*; bord *m*.

marginal *adj* marginal.

marine *adj* marin.

maritime *adj* maritime.

mark *n* marque *f*; signe *m*:—*vt* marquer.

marker *n* marque *f*; marqueur *m*.

market *n* marché *m*.

marketable *adj* vendable.

marmalade *n* confiture d'oranges *f*.

marriage *n* mariage *m*.

marriageable *adj* mariable.

married *adj* marié; conjugal.

marry *vi* se marier.

marsh *n* marécage *m*.

marshy *adj* marécageux.

martial *adj* martial.

martyr *n* martyr *m*, -e *f*.

marvel *n* merveille *f*:—*vi* s'émerveiller.

marvellous *adj* merveilleux.

masculine *adj* masculin, viril.

mask *n* masque *m*:—*vt* masquer.

mason *n* maçon *m*.

mass *n* masse *f*; messe *f*; multitude *f*.

massacre *n* massacre *m*:—*vt* massacrer.

massage *n* massage *m*.

massive *adj* énorme.

mast *n* mât *m*.

master *n* maître *m*:—*vt* maîtriser.

mastermind *vt* diriger.

mastery *n* maîtrise *f*.

match *n* allumette *f*:—*vt* égaler.

matchless *adj* incomparable, sans pareil.

mate *n* camarade *mf*:—*vt* accoupler.

material *adj* matériel.

maternal *adj* maternel.

maternity hospital *n* maternité *f*.

mathematical *adj*mathématique.

mathematics *npl* mathématiques *fpl*.

matrimonial *adj* matrimonial.

matted *adj* emmêlé.

matter *n* matière, substance *f*:—*vi* importer.

mattress *n* matelas *m*.

mature *adj* mûr:—*vi* mûrir.

maturity *n* maturité *f*.

maximum *n* maximum *m*.

may *v aux* pouvoir:—**~be** peut-être.

May *n* mai *m*.

mayor *n* maire *m*.

maze *n* labyrinthe *m*.

me *pn* moi; me.

meadow *n* prairie *f*, pré *m*.

meagre *adj* pauvre.

meal *n* repas *m*.

mean *adj* avare, mesquin; moyen:—**~s** *npl* moyens *mpl*:—*vt vi* signifier.

meander *vi* serpenter.

meaning *n* sens *m*.

meanness *n* avarice, mesquinerie *f*.

meantime *adv* pendant ce temps-là.

measure *n* mesure *f*:—*vt* mesurer.

measurement *n* mesure *f*.

meat *n* viande *f*.

mechanic *n* mécanicien *m*.

mechanical *adj* mécanique.

mechanism *n* mécanisme *m*.

medal n médaille f.

media npl média mpl.

mediate vi agir en tant que médiateur.

mediator n médiateur m, -trice f.

medical adj médical.

medicinal adj médicinal.

medicine n médecine f.

mediocre adj médiocre.

meditate vi méditer.

meditation n méditation f.

meditative adj méditatif.

Mediterranean adj méditerranéen.

medium n milieu m; médium m:—adj moyen.

medium wave n ondes moyennes fpl.

meek adj doux.

meekness n douceur f.

meet vt rencontrer:—vi se rencontrer.

meeting n réunion f; congrès m.

melancholy n mélancolie f:—adj mélancolique.

mellow adj mûr; doux:—vi mûrir.

melody n mélodie f.

melon n melon m.

melt vt faire fondre:—vi fondre.

member n membre m.

memorable adj mémorable.

memorandum n mémorandum m.

memorise vt mémoriser.

memory n mémoire f; souvenir m.

menace n menace f.

mend vt réparer; raccommoder.

menial adj vil.

menstruation n menstruation f.

mental adj mental.

mentality n mentalité f.

mention n mention f:—vt mentionner.

menu n menu m.

mercantile adj commercial.

mercenary adj n mercenaire m.

merchandise n marchandise f.

merchant n négociant m, -e f.

merciful adj miséricordieux.

mercy n pitié f.

mere adj simple.

merge vt vi fusionner.

merger n fusion f.

merit n mérite m:—vt mériter.

merry adj joyeux.

mesh n maille f.

mesmerise vt hypnotiser.

mess n désordre m; confusion f.

message n message m.

messenger n messager m, -ère f.

metal n métal m.

metallic adj métallique.

meteorological adj météorologique.

meteorology n météorologie f.

meter n compteur m; mètre m.

method n méthode f.

methodical adj, ~ly adv méthodique(ment).

metropolitan adj métropolitain.

mew vi miauler.

microphone n microphone m.

microscope n microscope m.

mid adj demi; mi-.

midday n midi m.

middle adj moyen; du milieu:—n milieu m.

middling adj moyen.

midnight n minuit m.

midway adv à mi-chemin.

midwife n sage-femme f.

might n force f.

mighty adj fort, puissant.

migrate vi émigrer.

migration n émigration f.

mild adj doux; modéré.

mildness n douceur f.

mile n mille m.

militant adj militant.

militate vi militer.

milk n lait m:—vt traire.

milky adj laiteux.

mill n moulin m:—vt moudre.

millimetre n millimètre m.

million n million m.

millionaire n millionaire mf.

millionth adj n millionième mf.

mime n mime m.

mimic vt mimer.

mimicry n mimique f.

mince vt hacher.

mind n esprit m:—vt prendre soin de.

minded adj disposé.

mindful adj conscient; attentif.

mine pn le mien, la mienne, les mien(ne)s; à moi:—n mine f.

miner n mineur m.

mineral adj n minéral m.

mingle vt mêler.

miniature n miniature f.

minimise vt minimiser.

minimum n minimum m.

minister n ministre m:—vt servir.

ministry n ministère m.

minor adj mineur:—n mineur m, -e f.

minority n minorité f.

minus adv moins.

minute adj minuscule.

minute n minute f.

miracle n miracle m.

miraculous adj miraculeux.

mirage n mirage m.

mirror n miroir m.

misadventure n mésaventure f.

misbehave vi se conduire mal.

misbehaviour n mauvaise conduite f.

miscarriage n fausse couche f.

miscellaneous adj divers, varié.

miscellany n mélange, assortiment m.

mischief n mal, tort m.

mischievous adj mauvais; espiègle.

misconception n méprise f.

misconduct n mauvaise conduite f.

misdeed n méfait m.

misdemeanour n délit m.

miser n avare mf.

miserable adj malheureux.

misery n malheur m; misère f.

misfortune n infortune f.

misgovern vt mal gouverner.

mishap n mésaventure f.

misjudge vt méjuger.

mislead vt induire en erreur.

misogynist n misogyne mf.

misprint n coquille f.

Miss n Mlle, Mademoiselle f.

miss vt rater; s'ennuyer de.

missing adj perdu; absent.

mission n mission f.

mist n brouillard m.

mistake vt confondre:—vi se tromper:—n erreur f.

Mister n Monsieur m.

mistress n maîtresse f.

mistrust vt se méfier de:—n méfiance f.

misty adj brumeux.

misunderstanding n malentendu m.

misuse vt faire un mauvais usage de.

mitigate vt atténuer.

mitigation n atténuation f.

mix vt mélanger.

mixed adj mélangé; mixte.

mixture n mélange m.

moan n gémissement m:—vi gémir.

moat n fossé m.

mob n foule f; masse f.

mobile adj mobile.

mobilise vt mobiliser.

mobility n mobilité f.

mock vt se moquer de.

mockery n moquerie f.

mode n mode m.

model n modèle m:—vt modeler.

moderate adj modéré:—vt modérer.

moderation n modération f.

modern adj moderne.

modernise vt moderniser.

modest adj modeste.

modesty n modestie f.

modification n modification f.

modify vt modifier.

moist adj humide.

moisten vt humidifier.

moisture n humidité f.

molest vt importuner.

molten adj fondu.

moment n moment m.

momentary adj momentané.

monastery n monastère m.

monastic adj monastique.

Monday n lundi m.

monetary adj monétaire.

money n argent m; pièce de monnaie f.

monk n moine m.

monkey n singe m.

monopolise vt monopoliser.

monopoly n monopole m.

monotonous adj monotone.

monotony n monotonie f.

monster n monstre m.

monstrous adj monstrueux.

month n mois m.

monthly adj mensuel; adv mensuellement.

mood n humeur f.

moon n lune f.

moonlight n clair de lune m.

moped n vélomoteur m.

moral adj moral:—s npl moralité f.

morale n moral m.

morality n moralité f.

morbid adj morbide.

more adj adv plus:—~ and ~ de plus en plus.

moreover adv de plus, en outre.

morning n matin m:—good ~ bonjour.

morsel n bouchée f; morceau m.

mortal adj mortel:—n mortel m, -elle f.

mortality n mortalité f.

mortgage n hypothèque f:—vt hypothéquer.

mortuary n morgue f.

mosque n mosquée f.

most adj pn la plupart de:—ly adv surtout, essentiellement.

mother n mère f.

motherhood n maternité f.

mother-in-law n belle-mère f.

motherly adj maternel.

mother tongue n langue maternelle f.

motif n motif m.

motion n mouvement m.

motionless adj immobile.

motivated adj motivé.

motive n motif m.

motor n moteur m.

motorbike n moto f.

motor vehicle n automobile f.

motto n devise f.

mould n moule m:—vt mouler.

mound n monticule m.

mount n mont m:—vt gravir.

mountain n montagne f.

mountaineer n alpiniste mf.

mountainous adj montagneux.

mourn vt pleurer.

mourning n deuil m.

mouse n (pl mice) souris f.

moustache n moustache f.

mouth n bouche f; embouchure f.

mouthful n bouchée f.

movable adj mobile.

move *vt* déplacer:—*vi* bouger:—*n* mouvement *m*.

movement *n* mouvement *m*.

moving *adj* touchant, émouvant.

mow *vt* tondre.

Mrs *n* Mme, Madame *f*.

much *adj pn* beaucoup:—*adv* beaucoup, très.

mud *n* boue *f*.

muddy *adj* boueux.

multiple *adj* multiple.

multiplication *n* multiplication *f*.

multiply *vt* multiplier.

multitude *n* multitude *f*.

mumble *vt vi* grommeler.

munch *vt* mâcher.

mundane *adj* banal.

municipal *adj* municipal.

mural *n* mural *m*.

murder *n* meurtre *m*:—*vt* assassiner.

murderer *n* assassin, meurtrier *m*.

murky *adj* obscur.

murmur *n* murmure *m*:—*vt vi* murmurer.

muscle *n* muscle *m*.

muscular *adj* musculaire.

museum *n* musée *m*.

music *n* musique *f*.

musical *adj* musical; mélodieux.

musician *n* musicien *m*, -ienne *f*.

must *v aux* devoir.

musty *adj* moisi.

mute *adj* muet, silencieux.

mutilate *vt* mutiler.

mutilation *n* mutilation *f*.

mutter *vt vi* grommeler:—*n* grommellement *m*.

mutual *adj* mutuel, réciproque.

my *pn* mon, ma, mes.

myself *pn* moi-même.

mysterious *adj* mystérieux.

mystery *n* mystère *m*.

myth *n* mythe *m*.

mythology *n* mythologie *f*.

N

nag *vt* harceler.

nail *n* ongle *m*; clou *m*:—*vt* clouer.

naive *adj* naïf.

naked *adj* nu; dénudé; pur.

name *n* nom *m*:—*vt* nommer.

nap *n* sieste *f*, somme *m*.

nape *n* nuque *f*.

napkin *n* serviette *f*.

narrate *vt* narrer, raconter.

narrative *adj* narratif:—*n* narration *f*.

narrow *adj* étroit.

nasty *adj* méchant; mauvais.

nation *n* nation *f*.

national *adj* national.

nationalist *adj n* nationaliste *mf*.

nationality *n* nationalité *f*.

native *adj* natal:—*n* autochtone *mf*.

natural *adj* naturel.

naturalist *n* naturaliste *mf*.

nature *n* nature *f*; sorte *f*.

naughty *adj* méchant.

nausea *n* nausée.

nauseous *adj* écœurant.

navel *n* nombril *m*.

navigate *vi* naviguer.

navigation *n* navigation *f.*

navy *n* marine *f.*

near *prep* près de:—*adv* près; à côté:—*adj* proche.

nearly *adv* presque.

neat *adj* soigné; net.

necessary *adj* nécessaire.

necessitate *vt* nécessiter.

necessity *n* nécessité *f.*

neck *n* cou *m.*

necklace *n* collier *m.*

need *n* besoin *m*:—*vt* avoir besoin de.

needle *n* aiguille *f.*

needy *adj* nécessiteux.

negation *n* négation *f.*

negative *adj* négatif:—*n* négative *f.*

neglect *vt* négliger:—*n* négligence *f.*

negligence *n* négligence *f.*

negligent *adj* négligent.

negotiate *vt vi* négocier.

negotiation *n* négociation *f.*

Negro *adj* noir:—*n* Noire *m.*

neighbour *n* voisin *m*, -e *f.*

neighbouring *adj* voisin.

neither *conj* ni:—*pn* aucun(e), ni l'un(e) ni l'autre.

nephew *n* neveu *m.*

nerve *n* nerf *m*; courage *m.*

nervous *adj* nerveux.

nest *n* nid *m*; nichée *f.*

net *n* filet *m.*

net curtain *n* voile *m.*

nettle *n* ortie *f.*

network *n* réseau *f.*

neutral *adj* neutre.

neutrality *n* neutralité *f.*

never *adv* jamais.

nevertheless *adv* cependant, néanmoins.

new *adj* neuf; nouveau.

newborn *adj* nouveau-né, *f* nouveau-née.

news *npl* nouvelles, informations *fpl.*

newspaper *n* journal *m.*

New Year *n* Nouvel An *m*:—~'**s Day** *n* Jour du Nouvel An *m*:—~'**s Eve** Saint-Sylvestre *f.*

next *adj* prochain:—*adv* ensuite, après.

nibble *vt* mordiller.

nice *adj* gentil, *f* gentille; agréable.

niche *n* niche *f.*

nickname *n* surnom *m*:—*vt* surnommer.

niece *n* nièce *f.*

night *n* nuit *f*:—**good ~** bonne nuit.

nightly *adv* toutes les nuits:—*adj* nocturne.

nightmare *n* cauchemar *m.*

nimble *adj* léger; agile.

nine *adj n* neuf *m.*

nineteen *adj n* dix-neuf *m.*

nineteenth *adj n* dix-neuvième *mf.*

ninetieth *adj n* quatre-vingt-dixième *mf.*

ninety *adj n* quatre-vingt-dix *m.*

ninth *adj n* neuvième *mf.*

no *adv* non:—*adj* aucun; pas de.

noble *adj* noble:—*n* noble *mf.*

nobody *pn* personne.

nocturnal *adj* nocturne.

nod *n* signe de tête *m*:—*vi* faire un signe de la tête.

noise *n* bruit *m.*

noisiness *n* bruit, tapage *m.*

nominal *adj* nominal.

nominate *vt* nommer.

nomination *n* nomination *f.*

nonchalant *adj* nonchalant.

none *pn* aucun; personne.

nonentity *n* nullité *f.*

nonetheless *adv* cependant.

nonplussed *adj* perplexe.

nonsense *n* absurdité *f.*

nonsensical *adj* absurde.
nonstop *adj* direct.
noon *n* midi *m*.
nor *conj* ni.
normal *adj* normal.
north *n* nord *m*:—*adj* du nord.
northeast *n* nord-est *m*.
northern *adj* du nord.
northwest *n* nord-ouest *m*.
nose *n* nez *m*.
nostalgia *n* nostalgie *f*.
nostril *n* narine *f*.
not *adv* pas; non.
notable *adj* notable.
note *n* note *f*; billet *m*:—*vt* noter, marquer.
notebook *n* carnet *m*.
nothing *n* rien *m*.
notice *n* notice *f*; avis *m*:—*vt* remarquer.
noticeable *adj* visible.
notify *vt* notifier.
notion *n* notion *f*; idée *f*.
notoriety *n* notoriété *f*.
notorious *adj* notoire.
nourish *vt* nourrir, alimenter.
nourishment *n* nourriture *f*, aliments *mpl*.

novel *n* roman *m*.
novelty *n* nouveauté *f*.
November *n* novembre *m*.
novice *n* novice *mf*.
now *adv* maintenant.
nowadays *adv* de nos jours.
nowhere *adv* nulle part.
nuance *n* nuance *f*.
nuclear *adj* nucléaire.
nude *adj* nu.
nudity *n* nudité *f*.
nuisance *n* ennui *m*; gêne *f*.
null *adj* nul.
numb *adj* engourdi:—*vt* engourdir.
number *n* numéro, nombre *m*:—*vt* numéroter.
numbness *n* engourdissement *m*.
numeral *n* chiffre *m*.
numerical *adj* numérique.
nurse *n* infirmière *f*:—*vt* soigner.
nursery *n* crèche *f*.
nurture *vt* élever.
nut *n* noix *f*.
nutritious *adj* nutritif.
nylon *n* nylon *m*.

O

oak *n* chêne *m*.
oar *n* rame *f*.
oath *n* serment *m*.
obedience *n* obéissance *f*.
obedient *adj* obéissant.
obese *adj* obèse.
obesity *n* obésité *f*.
obey *vt* obéir à.
object *n* objet *m*:—*vt* objecter.
objection *n* objection *f*.

objective *adj n* objectif *m*.
obligation *n* obligation *f*.
obligatory *adj* obligatoire.
oblige *vt* obliger.
obliging *adj* obligeant.
oblique *adj* oblique.
oblivious *adj* oublieux.
obnoxious *adj* odieux.
obscene *adj* obscène.
obscure *adj* obscur:—*vt* obscurcir.

obscurity *n* obscurité *f.*
observant *adj* observateur.
observation *n* observation *f.*
observatory *n* observatoire *m.*
observe *vt* observer.
obsess *vt* obséder.
obsessive *adj* obsédant.
obsolete *adj* désuet.
obstacle *n* obstacle *m.*
obstinate *adj* obstiné.
obstruct *vt* obstruer; entraver.
obstruction *n* obstruction *f;* encombrement *m.*
obtain *vt* obtenir.
obtainable *adj* disponible.
obvious *adj* évident.
occasion *n* occasion *f:—vt* occasionner.
occasional *adj* occasionnel.
occupant *n* occupant *m,* -e *f.*
occupation *n* occupation *f;* emploi *m.*
occupy *vt* occuper.
occur *vi* se produire, arriver.
occurrence *n* incident *m.*
ocean *n* océan *m.*
oceanic *adj* océanique.
October *n* octobre *m.*
odd *adj* impair; étrange.
odious *adj* odieux.
odour *n* odeur *f;* parfum *m.*
of *prep* de; à.
off *adj* éteint; fermé; annulé.
offend *vt* offenser, blesser.
offense *n* offense *f;* injure *f.*
offensive *adj* offensant.
offer *vt* offrir:—*n* offre *f.*
office *n* bureau *m;* poste *m.*
officer *n* officier *m;* fonctionnaire *mf.*
official *adj* officiel:—*n* employé *m,* -e *f.*
officiate *vi* officier.
offset *vt* compenser; décaler.
offshore *adj* côtier.

offspring *n* progéniture *f.*
oil *n* huile *f:—vt* huiler.
oil painting *n* peinture à l'huile *f.*
oil tanker *n* pétrolier *m.*
ointment *n* onguent *m.*
OK, okay *excl* OK, d'accord.
old *adj* vieux, *f* vieille.
old age *n* vieillesse *f.*
olive *n* olivier *m;* olive *f.*
olive oil *n* huile d'olive *f.*
omelette *n* omelette *f.*
omission *n* omission *f;* négligence *f.*
omit *vt* omettre.
on *prep* sur, dessus; en; pour:—*adj* allumé, branché.
once *adv* une fois:—~ **more** encore une fois.
one *adj* un, une.
onerous *adj* lourd; onéreux.
oneself *pn* soi-même.
one-sided *adj* partial.
onion *n* oignon *m.*
onlooker *n* spectateur *m,* -trice *f.*
only *adj* seul, unique:—*adv* seulement.
onus *n* responsabilité *f.*
opaque *adj* opaque.
open *adj* ouvert; sincère, franc:—*vt* ouvrir; *vi* s'ouvrir.
opening *n* ouverture *f.*
openness *n* clareté *f.*
opera *n* opéra *m.*
operate *vi* fonctionner; opérer.
operation *n* fonctionnement *m;* opération *f.*
operator *n* opérateur *m,* -trice *f.*
opine *vt* être d'avis (que).
opinion *n* opinion *f;* jugement *m.*
opinion poll *n* sondage *m.*
opponent *n* opposant *m,* -e *f.*
opportune *adj* opportun.
opportunity *n* occasion *f.*

oppose vt s'opposer à.

opposing adj opposé.

opposite adj opposé:—adv en face: — prep en face de:—n contraire m.

opposition n opposition f.

oppress vt opprimer.

oppressive adj oppressif.

optimist n optimiste mf.

optimistic adj optimiste.

optimum adj optimum.

option n option f.

optional adj optionnel.

opulent adj opulent.

or conj ou.

oral adj oral, verbal.

orange n orange f.

orbit n orbite f.

orchestra n orchestre m.

ordain vt ordonner.

order n ordre m; commande f:—vt ordonner.

orderly adj ordonné; réglé.

ordinary adj ordinaire.

ore n minerai m.

organ n organe m.

organic adj organique.

organisation n organisation f.

organise vt organiser.

organism n organisme m.

oriental adj oriental.

orifice n orifice m.

origin n origine f.

original adj original.

originality n originalité f.

ornament n ornement m:—vt ornementer.

ornate adj ornementé.

orphan adj n orphelin m, -e f.

orthodox adj orthodoxe.

oscillate vi osciller.

other pn autre.

otherwise adv autrement.

ought v aux devoir; falloir.

our pn notre, pl nos.

ours pn le nôtre, la nôtre, les nôtres; à nous.

ourselves pn pl nous-mêmes.

out adv dehors; éteint.

outburst n explosion f.

outcome n résultat m.

outdo vt surpasser.

outdoor adj de plein air:—~s adv à l'extérieur.

outer adj extérieur.

outfit n tenue f; équipement m.

outgoing adj extroverti; sortant.

outlay n dépenses fpl, frais mpl.

outline n contour m; grandes lignes fpl.

outlook n perspective f.

output n rendement m; sortie f.

outrage n outrage m:—vt outrager.

outright adv absolument:—adj absolu.

outset n commencement m.

outside n surface f; extérieur m:—adv dehors:—prep en dehors de.

outstrip vt devancer; surpasser.

oval n, adj ovale m.

ovary n ovaire m.

oven n four m.

over prep sur, dessus; plus de; pendant:—adj fini.

overall adj total:—~s npl salopette f.

overbalance vi perdre l'équilibre.

overcast adj couvert.

overcharge vt surcharger.

overcoat n pardessus m.

overcome vt vaincre.

overdo vi exagérer.

overdraft n découvert m.

overdue adj en retard; arriéré.

overestimate vt surestimer.

overflow vi déborder:—n surplus m.

overhaul *vt* réviser:—*n* révision *f.*
overland *adj adv* par voie de terre.
overlap *vi* se chevaucher.
overlook *vt* donner sur; oublier; tolérer; négliger.
overnight *adv* pendant la nuit:—*adj* de nuit.
overpower *vt* dominer, écraser.
overrate *vt* surévaluer.
overrun *vt* envahir; infester; dépasser.
overseas *adv* à l'étranger; outremer:—*adj* étranger.
oversee *vt* inspecter, surveiller.
oversight *n* oubli *m;* erreur *f.*
oversleep *vi* se réveiller en retard.
overtake *vt* doubler.

overthrow *vt* renverser:—*n* renversement *m.*
overtime *n* heures supplémentaires *fpl.*
overturn *vt* renverser.
overwhelm *vt* écraser.
overwhelming *adj* écrasant.
overwork *vi* se surmener.
owe *vt* devoir.
owing *adj* dû:—~ **to** en raison de.
owl *n* chouette *f.*
own *adj* propre:—*vt* posséder.
owner *n* propriétaire *mf.*
ox *n* bœuf *m.*
oxygen *n* oxygène *m.*
oyster *n* huître *f.*
ozone *n* ozone *m.*

P

pace *n* pas *m;* allure *f:*—*vi* marcher.
pacific *adj* pacifique.
pacification *n* pacification *f.*
pacify *vt* pacifier.
pack *n* paquet *m;* bande *f:*—*vt* empaqueter:—*vi* faire ses valises.
package *n* paquet *m.*
packet *n* paquet *m.*
pact *n* pacte *m.*
pad *n* bloc *m;* tampon *m;* (*sl*) piaule *f:*—*vt* rembourrer.
paddle *vi* ramer:—*n* pagaie *f.*
pagan *adj vi* païen *m,* païenne *f.*
page *n* page *f;* page *m.*
pail *n* seau *m.*
pain *n* douleur *f;* peine *f:*—*vt* peiner.
pained *adj* peiné.
painful *adj* douloureux; pénible.
painstaking *adj* soigneux.

paint *vt* peindre.
painter *n* peintre *m.*
painting *n* peinture *f;* tableau *m.*
pair *n* pair *m.*
palatable *adj* savoureux.
palate *n* palais *m.*
pale *adj* pâle; clair.
palette *n* palette *f.*
pallet *n* palette *f.*
pallid *adj* pâle.
palpable *adj* palpable; évident.
palpitation *n* palpitation *f.*
pamper *vt* gâter, dorloter.
pamphlet *n* pamphlet *m;* brochure *f.*
pan *n* casserole *f;* poêle *f.*
panache *n* panache *m.*
pane *n* vitre *f.*
panel *n* panneau *m;* comité *m.*
pang *n* angoisse *f;* tourment *m.*

panic *adj n* (de) panique *f.*
pant *vi* haleter.
panther *n* panthère *f.*
pantry *n* placard *m.*
pants *npl* slip *m*; pantalon *m.*
paper *n* papier *m*; journal *m*:—*adj* en papier:—*vt* tapisser.
paperweight *n* presse-papiers *m.*
par *n* équivalence *f*; pair *m.*
parachute *n* parachute *m.*
parade *n* parade *f.*
paradise *n* paradis *m.*
paradox *n* paradoxe *m.*
paragraph *n* paragraphe *m.*
parallel *adj* parallèle:—*n* parallèle *f.*
paralyse *vt* paralyser.
paralysis *n* paralysie *f.*
paramount *adj* suprême, supérieur.
paranoid *adj* paranoïaque.
parasite *n* parasite *m.*
parcel *n* paquet *m*; parcelle *f*:—*vt* empaqueter.
parch *vt* dessécher.
pardon *n* pardon *m*:—*vt* pardonner.
parent *n* père *m*; mère *f*:—**~s** parents *mpl.*
park *n* parc *m*:—*vt* garer; *vi* se garer.
parking *n* stationnement *m.*
parking lot *n* parking *m.*
parliament *n* parlement *m.*
parody *n* parodie *f*:—*vt* parodier.
parry *vt* parer.
part *n* partie *f*; part *f*; rôle (d'acteur) *m*:—*vt* séparer; diviser:—*vi* se séparer; se diviser:—**~ly** *adv* en partie.
partial *adj* partial.
participate *vi* participer (à).
participation *n* participation *f.*
particle *n* particule *f.*
particular *adj* particulier:—*n* particulier *m*; particularité *f.*

partition *n* partition, séparation *f*:—*vt* partager,
partner *n* associé *m*, -e *f.*
party *n* parti *m*; fête *f.*
pass *vt* passer; dépasser:—*vi* passer:—*n* permis *m*; passage *m.*
passage *n* passage *m.*
passenger *n* passager *m*, -ère *f.*
passer-by *n* passant *m*, -e *f.*
passion *n* passion *f*; amour *m.*
passionate *adj* passionné.
passive *adj* passif.
passport *n* passeport *m.*
past *adj* passé:—*n* passé *m*:—*prep* audelà de; après.
paste *n* pâte *f*; colle *f*:—*vt* coller.
pastime *n* passe-temps *m invar.*
pastry *n* pâtisserie *f.*
pasture *n* pâture *f.*
patch *n* pièce *f*; terrain *m*:—*vt* rapiécer.
patent *adj* évident:—*n* brevet *m*:—*vt* faire breveter.
patentee *n* détenteur d'un brevet *m.*
paternal *adj* paternel.
paternity *n* paternité *f.*
path *n* chemin, sentier *m.*
pathetic *adj* pathétique.
patience *n* patience *f.*
patient *adj* patient:—**~ly** *adv* patiemment:—*n* patient *m*, -e *f.*
patrol *n* patrouille *f*:—*vi* patrouiller.
patron *n* protecteur *m*; client *m*, -e *f.*
patronise *vt* patronner, protéger.
pattern *n* motif *m*; modèle *m.*
pause *n* pause *f*:—*vi* faire une pause; hésiter.
pave *vt* paver; carreler.
pavement *n* trottoir *m.*
paw *n* patte *f*:—*vt* tripoter.
pay *vt* payer:—**to ~ back** *vt* rembourser:—*n* paie *f*; salaire *m.*

payable *adj* payable.

payment *n* paiement *m*.

pea *n* pois *m*.

peace *n* paix *f*.

peaceful *adj* paisible; pacifique.

peak *n* pic *m*; maximum *m*.

pear *n* poire *f*.

pearl *n* perle *f*.

peasant *n* paysan *m*, -anne *f*.

pebble *n* caillou *m*; galet *m*.

peculiar *adj* étrange, singulier.

peculiarity *n* particularité, singularité *f*.

pedal *n* pédale *f*:—*vi* pédaler.

pedestrian *n* piéton *m*, -onne *f*:—*adj* pédestre.

peel *vt* peler:—*n* peau *f*; pelure *f*.

peer *n* pair *m*.

peerless *adj* incomparable.

pelt *n* fourrure *f*.

pen *n* stylo *m*; plume *f*.

penalty *n* peine *f*; sanction *f*; amende *f*.

pencil *n* crayon *m*.

pendulum *n* pendule *m*.

penetrate *vt* pénétrer dans.

peninsula *n* péninsule *f*.

penitentiary *n* pénitencier *m*.

penknife *n* canif *m*.

penpal *n* correspondant *m*, -e *f*.

pension *n* pension *f*:—*vt* pensionner.

pensive *adj* pensif.

penultimate *adj* pénultième.

people *n* peuple *m*; nation *f*; gens *mpl*:—*vt* peupler.

pepper *n* poivre *m*:—*vt* poivrer.

per *prep* par.

per annum *adv* par an.

perceive *vt* percevoir.

percentage *n* pourcentage *m*.

perception *n* perception *f*; notion *f*.

perch *n* perche *f*.

percussion *n* percussion *f*.

perdition *n* perte, ruine *f*.

perennial *adj* perpétuel.

perfect *adj* parfait; idéal:—*vt* parfaire, perfectionner.

perfection *n* perfection *f*.

perform *vt* exécuter:—*vi* donner une représentation.

performance *n* exécution *f*; accomplissement *m*.

performer *n* exécutant *m*, -e *f*; acteur *m*, -trice *f*.

perfume *n* parfum *m*:—*vt* parfumer.

perhaps *adv* peut-être.

peril *n* péril, danger *m*.

perilous *adj* dangereux.

perimeter *n* périmètre *m*.

period *n* période *f*; époque *f*.

periodic *adj* périodique.

perish *vi* périr.

perishable *adj* périssable.

permanent *adj* permanent.

permissible *adj* permis.

permission *n* permission *f*.

permissive *adj* permissif.

permit *vt* permettre:—*n* permis *m*.

perpetrate *vt* perpétrer, commettre.

perpetual *adj* perpétuel.

perplex *vt* confondre, laisser perplexe.

persecute *vt* persécuter; importuner.

persecution *n* persécution *f*.

persevere *vi* persévérer.

persist *vi* persister.

persistence *adj* persistance *f*.

persistent *adj* persistant.

person *n* personne *f*.

personage *n* personnage *m*.

personal *adv* personnel.

personal computer *n* ordinateur individuel *m*.

personality *n* personnalité *f*.

personnel *n* personnel *m*.

perspective *n* perspective *f*.

perspiration *n* transpiration *f*.

perspire *vi* transpirer.

persuade *vt* persuader.

persuasion *n* persuasion *f*.

persuasive *adj* persuasif.

pertaining:—— to *prep* relatif à.

pertinent *adj* pertinent.

perturb *vt* perturber.

peruse *vt* lire; examiner attentivement.

perverse *adj* pervers, dépravé.

pessimist *n* pessimiste *mf*.

pest *n* insecte nuisible *m*; casse-pieds (*fam*) *mf invar*.

pester *vt* importuner, fatiguer.

pestilence *n* peste *f*.

pet *n* animal domestique *m*:—*vt* gâter.

petal *n* (*bot*) pétale *m*.

petition *n* pétition *f*.

petticoat *n* jupon *m*.

pettiness *n* insignifiance *f*.

petty *adj* mesquin; insignifiant.

phantom *n* fantôme *m*.

pharmacist *n* pharmacien *m*, -ienne *f*.

pharmacy *n* pharmacie *f*.

phase *n* phase *f*.

phenomenal *adj* phénoménal.

phenomenon *n* phénomène *m*.

philosopher *n* philosophe *mf*.

philosophical *adj* philosophique.

philosophise *vi* philosopher.

philosophy *n* philosophie *f*.

phobia *n* phobie *f*.

phone *n* téléphone *m*:—*vt* téléphoner à.

phone book *n* annuaire *m*.

phone call *n* coup de téléphone *m*.

photograph *n* photo(graphie) *f*:—*vt* photographier.

photographer *n* photographe *mf*.

photography *n* photographie *f*.

phrase *n* phrase *f*:—*vt* exprimer.

phrase book *n* guide de conversation *m*.

physical *adv* physique.

physician *n* médecin *m*.

physicist *n* physicien *m*, -ienne *f*.

physiotherapy *n* physiothérapie *f*.

physique *n* physique *m*.

pianist *n* pianiste *mf*.

piano *n* piano *m*.

pick *vt* choisir; cueillir:—*n* pic *m*; choix *m*.

picnic *n* pique-nique *m*.

pictorial *adj* pictural; illustré.

picture *n* image *f*; peinture *f*:—*vt* dépeindre.

pie *n* gâteau *m*; tarte *f*; pâté en croûte *m*.

piece *n* morceau *m*; pièce *f*.

pierce *vt* percer, transpercer.

piercing *adj* perçant.

pig *n* cochon *m*.

pigeon *n* pigeon *m*.

pile *n* tas *m*; pile *f*; amas *m*:—*vt* entasser.

pilgrim *n* pèlerin *m*.

pill *n* pilule *f*.

pillar *n* pilier *m*.

pillow *n* oreiller *m*.

pilot *n* pilote *m*:—*vt* piloter; (*fig*) mener.

pin *n* épingle *f*:—*vt* épingler.

pincers *n* pinces, tenailles *fpl*.

pine *n* (*bot*) pin *m*:—*vi* languir.

pineapple *n* ananas *m*.

pink *n*, *adj* rose *m*.

pint *n* pinte *f*.

pioneer *n* pionnier *m*.

pious *adj* pieux, dévot.

pipe *n* tube, tuyau *m*; pipe *f*.

pipeline *n* canalisation *f*.

piracy *n* piraterie *f*.

pirate *n* pirate *m*.

pistol *n* pistolet *m*.

pitch *n* lancement *m*:—*vt* lancer, jeter.

pitcher *n* cruche *f*.

pitiable *adj* pitoyable.

pitiful *adj* pitoyable.

pity *n* pitié *f:—vt* avoir pitié de.

placard *n* affiche *f.*

placate *vt* apaiser.

place *n* endroit, lieu *m:—vt* placer.

placid *adj* placide, calme.

plague *n* peste *f:—vt* tourmenter.

plain *adj* uni; simple; évident:—*n* plaine *f.*

plait *n* pli *m*; tresse *f:—vt* plier.

plan *n* plan *m:—vt* projeter.

plane *n* avion *m*; plan *m:—vt* aplanir.

planet *n* planète *f.*

plank *n* planche *f.*

planner *n* planificateur *m*, -trice *f.*

plant *n* plante *f*; usine *f:—vt* planter.

plantation *n* plantation *f.*

plaster *n* plâtre *m*; emplâtre *m:—vt* plâtrer.

plastic *adj* plastique.

plate *n* assiette *f*; plaque *f*; lame *f.*

platform *n* plateforme *f.*

platter *n* écuelle *f*; plat *m.*

plausible *adj* plausible.

play *n* jeu *m*; pièce *f* de théâtre:—*vt vi* jouer.

player *n* joueur *m*, -euse *f*; acteur *m*, -trice *f.*

playful *adj* enjoué, amusé.

playwright *n* dramaturge *mf.*

plea *n* appel *m*; excuse *f*, prétexte *m.*

plead *vt* plaider; prétexter.

pleasant *adj* agréable; plaisant.

please *vt* faire plaisir à.

pleased *adj* content.

pleasure *n* plaisir *m*; gré *m.*

pledge *n* promesse *f*; gage *m:—vt* engager.

plentiful *adj* copieux; abondant.

plenty *n* abondance *f.*

pliable *adj* pliant; souple.

pliers *npl* tenailles *fpl.*

plot *n* complot *m*; intrigue *f:—vt* tracer.

plough *n* charrue *f:—vt* labourer.

pluck *vt* tirer; arracher:—*n* courage *m.*

plug *n* bougie *f*; prise *f:—vt* boucher.

plumber *n* plombier *m.*

plump *adj* rondouillet, dodu.

plunge *vi* plonger; s'élancer.

plural *adj n* pluriel *m.*

plus *prep* plus.

pneumonia *n* pneumonie *f.*

poach *vt* pocher; braconner.

poacher *n* braconnier *m.*

pocket *n* poche *f:—vt* empocher.

poem *n* poème *m.*

poet *n* poète *m.*

poetry *n* poésie *f.*

poignant *adj* poignant.

point *n* pointe *f*; point *m:—vt* pointer.

pointed *adj* pointu; acéré.

poise *n* attitude *f*; équilibre *m.*

poison *n* poison *m:—vt* empoisonner.

poisonous *adj* vénéneux.

poke *vt* attiser.

poker-faced *adj* au visage impassible.

pole *n* pôle *m*; mât *m*; perche *f.*

police *n* police *f.*

policeman *n* agent de police *m.*

police station *n* commissariat *m.*

policy *n* politique *f.*

polish *vt* polir; cirer:—*n* poli *m.*

polished *adj* poli; ciré; élégant.

polite *adj* poli.

politeness *n* politesse.

political *adj* politique.

politician *n* homme (femme) politique *m(f).*

politics *npl* politique *f.*

pollute *vt* polluer.

pollution *n* pollution.

polytechnic n école d'enseignement technique f.

pompous adj pompeux.

pond n mare f; étang m.

ponder vt considérer.

pony n poney m.

pool n piscine f.

poor adj pauvre; mauvais

populace n populace f.

popular adj populaire.

popularity n popularité f.

populate vi peupler.

population n population f.

porch n porche m.

pork n porc m.

port n port m.

portable adj portable, portatif.

portion n portion, part f.

portrait n portrait m.

portray vt faire le portrait de; dépeindre.

pose n posture f; pose f:—vi, vt poser.

position n position f:—vt mettre en position.

positive adj positif; réel.

possess vt posséder.

possession n possession f.

possibility n possibilité f.

possible adj possible:—**~ly** adv peut-être.

post n courrier m; poste f; emploi m.

postage stamp n timbre m.

postcard n carte postale f.

poster n poster m.

posterior n postérieur m.

posthumous adj posthume.

postman n facteur m.

post office n poste f, bureau de poste m.

postpone vt remettre; différer.

posture n posture f.

pot n pot m; marmite f:—vt empoter.

potato n pomme de terre.

potent adj puissant.

potential adj potentiel.

potion n potion f.

pouch n sac m.

poultry n volaille f.

pound n livre f; livre sterling f:—vt concasser.

pour vt verser; servir:—vi couler; pleuvoir à verse.

poverty n pauvreté f.

powder n poudre f:—vt poudrer.

powdery adj poudreux.

power n pouvoir m; puissance f; force f:—vt propulser.

powerful adj puissant.

powerless adj impotent.

practicable adj praticable; faisable.

practical adj pratique.

practicality n faisabilité f.

practice n pratique f; usage m; entraînement m.

practise vt pratiquer:—vi s'exercer.

pragmatic adj pragmatique.

praise n louange f:—vt louer.

prance vi cabrioler.

prattle vi jacasser:—n jacasserie f.

prawn n crevette f.

pray vi prier.

prayer n prière f.

preach vt prêcher.

preacher n prédicateur m.

precarious adj précaire, incertain.

precaution n précaution f.

precede vt précéder.

precedent adj n précédent m.

precinct n limite f; enceinte f.

precious adj précieux.

precipitate vt précipiter:—adj précipité.

precise n précis, exact.

precision n précision, exactitude f.

precocious adj précoce, prématuré.

preconceive *vt* préconcevoir.
preconception *n* préjugé *m*; idée préconçue *f*.
predator *n* prédateur *m*.
predecessor *n* prédécesseur *m*.
predict *vt* prédire.
predictable *adj* prévisible.
prediction *n* prédiction *f*.
predominant *adj* prédominant.
predominate *vt* prédominer.
preface *n* préface *f*.
prefer *vt* préférer.
preferable *adj* préférable.
preference *n* préférence *f*.
preferential *adj* préférentiel.
prefix *vt* préfixer.
pregnancy *n* grossesse *f*.
pregnant *adj* enceinte.
prehistoric *adj* préhistorique.
prejudice *n* préjudice *m*; préjugé *m*: — *vt* préjudicier à.
prejudiced *adj* qui a des préjugés; partial.
prejudicial *adj* préjudiciable.
preliminary *adj* préliminaire.
premature *adj* prématuré.
premeditation *n* préméditation *f*.
premises *npl* locaux *mpl*.
premium *n* prix *m*; prime *f*.
premonition *n* prémonition *f*.
preparation *n* préparation *f*.
preparatory *adj* préparatoire.
prepare *vt* préparer:—*vi* se préparer.
preposterous *adj* ridicule, absurde.
prerogative *n* prérogative *f*.
prescribe *vt* prescrire.
prescription *n* prescription *f*.
presence *n* présence *f*.
present *n* cadeau *m*:—*adj* présent; actuel:—**~ly** *adv* actuellement:—*vt* présenter.
presentable *adj* présentable.

presenter *n* présentateur *m*, -trice *f*.
preservation *n* préservation *f*.
preserve *vt* préserver:—*n* conserve *f*; confiture *f*.
preside *vi* présider; diriger.
president *n* président *m*.
press *vt* appuyer sur:—*vi* se presser: —*n* presse *f*; pressoir *m*.
pressing *adj* pressant; urgent.
pressure *n* pression *f*.
prestige *n* prestige *m*.
presumable *adj* vraisemblable.
presume *vt* présumer, supposer.
presumption *n* présomption *f*.
pretence *n* prétexte *m*; simulation *f*.
pretend *vi* prétendre; faire semblant.
pretext *n* prétexte *m*.
pretty *adj* joli, mignon.
prevail *vi* prévaloir; prédominer.
prevalent *adj* prédominant.
prevent *vt* prévenir; empêcher.
prevention *n* prévention *f*.
previous *adj* précédent; antérieur:— **~ly** *adv* auparavant.
prey *n* proie *f*.
price *n* prix *m*.
prick *vt* piquer:—*n* piqûre *f*; pointe *f*.
pride *n* orgueil *m*; vanité *f*; fierté *f*.
priest *n* prêtre *m*.
priesthood *n* sacerdoce *m*, prêtrise *f*.
primacy *n* primauté *f*.
primarily *adv* principalement, surtout.
primary *adj* primaire; principal, premier.
primate *n* primate *m*.
prime *n* (*fig*) fleur *f*; commencement *m*:—*adj* premier; principal.
prime minister *n* premier ministre *m*.
primitive *adj* primitif.
prince *n* prince *m*.
princess *n* princesse *f*.
principal *adj* principal:—*n* principal *m*.

principle n principe m.

print vt imprimer:—n impression f; estampe f.

printer n imprimeur m; imprimante f.

prior adj antérieur, précédent.

priority n priorité f.

prison n prison f.

prisoner n prisonnier m, -ière f.

privacy n intimité f.

private adj privé; secret; particulier:— ~ly adv en privé.

privilege n privilège m.

prize n prix m:—vt apprécier, évaluer.

pro prep pour.

probability n probabilité f; vraisemblance f.

probable adj probable, vraisemblable.

probation n essai m; probation f.

probationary adj d'essai.

probe n sonde f:—vt sonder.

problem n problème m.

problematical adj problématique.

procedure n procédure f.

proceed vi procéder; provenir.

process n processus m; procédé m.

procession n procession f.

proclaim vt proclamer; promulguer.

proclamation n proclamation f; décret m.

procure vt procurer.

procurement n obtention f.

prod vt pousser.

prodigious adj prodigieux.

prodigy n prodige m.

produce vt produire; créer.

producer n producteur m, -trice f.

product n produit m; œuvre f; fruit m.

production n production f; produit m.

productive adj productif.

profess vt professer; déclarer.

profession n profession f.

professional adj professionnel.

professor n professeur m.

proficiency n capacité f.

proficient adj compétent.

profile n profil m.

profit n bénéfice, profit m:—vi profiter (de).

profitability n rentabilité f.

profitable adj profitable, avantageux.

profound adj profond.

program(me) n programme m.

programmer n programmeur m, -euse f.

progress n progrès m; cours m:—vi progresser.

progression n progression f; avance f.

progressive adj progressif.

prohibit vt prohiber; défendre.

project vt projeter:—n projet m.

projection n projection f.

prolific adj prolifique, fécond.

prolong vt prolonger.

promenade n promenade f.

prominence n proéminence f.

prominent adj proéminent.

promise n promesse f:—vt promettre.

promising adj prometteur.

promote vt promouvoir.

promoter n promoteur m.

promotion n promotion f.

prompt adj prompt:—vt suggérer.

prone adj enclin (à).

pronounce vt prononcer; déclarer.

pronounced adj marqué, prononcé.

pronouncement n déclaration f.

pronunciation n prononciation f.

proof n preuve f:—adj imperméable; résistant.

prop vt soutenir:—n appui, soutien m.

propaganda n propagande f.

propel vt propulser.

propeller n hélice f.
propensity n propension, tendance f.
proper adj propre; convenable.
property n propriété f.
prophecy n prophétie f.
prophet n prophète m.
proportion n proportion f.
proportional adj proportionnel.
proposal n proposition f; offre f.
propose vt proposer.
proposition n proposition f.
proprietor n propriétaire mf.
prosecute vt poursuivre en justice.
prosecution n poursuites fpl; accusation f.
prospect n perspective f:—vt vi prospecter.
prospective adj probable; futur.
prosper vi prospérer.
prosperity n prospérité f.
prosperous adj prospère.
prostitute n prostituée f.
protagonist n protagoniste mf.
protect vt protéger; abriter.
protection n protection f.
protective adj protecteur.
protein n protéine f.
protest vi protester:—n protestation f.
Protestant n protestant m, -e f.
protester n protestataire mf.
prototype n prototype m.
proud adj fier, orgueilleux.
prove vt prouver; justifier:—vi s'avérer; se révéler.
proverb n proverbe m.
provide vt fournir.
provided conj:—~ that pourvu que.
providence n providence f.
province n province f.
provincial adj n provincial m, -e f.
provision n provision f; disposition f.

provisional adj provisoire.
provocation n provocation f.
provocative adj provocateur.
provoke vt provoquer.
prowess n prouesse f.
prowl vi rôder.
prowler n rôdeur m, -euse f.
proximity n proximité f.
prudence n prudence f.
prudent adj prudent.
pry vi espionner.
pseudonym n pseudonyme m.
psychiatric adj psychiatrique.
psychiatrist n psychiatre mf.
psychic adj psychique.
psychoanalyst n psychanaliste mf.
psychologist n psychologue mf.
psychology n psychologie f.
puberty n puberté f.
public adj public; commun:—n public m.
publication n publication f; édition f.
publicity n publicité f.
publish vt publier.
publisher n éditeur m, -trice f.
publishing n édition f.
pudding n pudding m; dessert m.
puddle n flaque d'eau f.
puff n souple m; bouffée f:—vt souffler; dégager.
pull vt tirer; arracher:—n tirage m; secousse f.
pulley n poulie f.
pulsate vi battre.
pulse n pouls m.
pulverise vt pulvériser.
pump n pompe f:—vt pomper; puiser.
punch n coup de poing m:—vt cogner.
punctual adj ponctuel, exact.
punctuate vt ponctuer.
punctuation n ponctuation f.
punish vt punir.

punishment n châtiment m, punition f; peine f.

puny adj chétif, maigrelet.

pupil n élève mf; pupille mf.

puppet n marionnette f.

puppy n chiot m.

purchase vt acheter:—n achat m; acquisition f.

purchaser n acheteur m, -euse f.

pure adj pur.

purification n purification f.

purify vt purifier.

purity n pureté f.

purple adj n pourpre, violet m.

purpose n intention f; but, dessein m:—**on** ~ exprès, à dessein.

purse n sac à main m; porte-monnaie m invar.

pursue vi poursuivre; suivre.

pursuit n poursuite f; occupation f.

push vt pousser; presser:—n poussée f; impulsion f.

put vt mettre, poser.

putrid adj putride.

putty n mastic m.

puzzle n énigme f; casse-tête m invar.

puzzling adj curieux; inexplicable.

pyjamas npl pyjama m.

pylon n pylône m.

pyramid n pyramide f.

python n python m.

Q

quack vi cancaner:—n (sl) charlatan m.

quagmire n marécage m.

quaint adj désuet; bizarre.

quake vi trembler.

qualification n qualification f.

qualified adj qualifié.

qualify vt qualifier:—vi se qualifier.

quality n qualité f.

qualm n scrupule m.

quantity n quantité f.

quarantine n quarantaine f.

quarrel n querelle f:—vi se quereller.

quarrelsome adj querelleur.

quarry n carrière f.

quarter n quart m:—vt diviser en quatre.

quarterly adj trimestriel:—adv tous les trimestres.

quash vt écraser; annuler.

quay n quai m.

queen n reine f; femme f.

queer adj extrange:—n (sl) pédale f.

quell vt étouffer.

quench vt assouvir.

query n question f:—vt demander.

quest n recherche f.

question n question f:—vt questionner.

questionable adj discutable; douteux.

questioner n interrogateur m.

questionnaire n questionnaire m.

quibble vi chicaner.

quick adj rapide; vif.

quicken vt accélérer:—vi s'accélérer.

quiet adj calme; silencieux.

quietness *n* calme *m*, tranquillité *f*; silence *m*.

quip *n* sarcasme *m*:—*vt* railler.

quit *vt* arrêter de:—*vi* abandonner.

quite *adv* assez; complètement, absolument.

quiver *vi* trembler.

quiz *n* concours *m*; examen *m*:—*vt* interroger.

quota *n* quota *m*.

quotation *n* citation *f*.

quote *vt* citer.

R

rabbit *n* lapin *m*.

rabble *n* cohue *f*.

rabies *n* rage *f*.

race *n* course *f*; race *f*:—*vi* courir; foncer.

racial *adj* racial:—**~ist** *adj n* raciste *mf*.

rack *n* casier *m*; étagère *f*.

racket *n* vacarme *m*; raquette *f*.

radiant *adj* rayonnant, radieux.

radiate *vt vi* rayonner, irradier.

radiation *n* irradiation *f*.

radiator *n* radiateur *m*.

radical *adj* radical.

radio *n* radio *f*.

radioactive *adj* radioactif.

raft *n* radeau.

rag *n* lambeau *m*, loque *f*.

rage *n* rage *f*; fureur *f*:—*vi* faire rage.

ragged *adj* déguenillé.

raging *adj* furieux, enragé.

raid *n* raid *m*:—*vt* faire un raid sur.

rail *n* rambarde *f*; (*rail*) rail, chemin de fer *m*.

railway *n* chemin de fer *m*.

rain *n* pluie *f*:—*vi* pleuvoir.

rainbow *n* arc-en-ciel *m*.

rainy *adj* pluvieux.

raise *vt* lever, soulever.

raisin *n* raisin sec *m*.

rally *vt* (*mil*) rallier:—*vi* se rallier.

ramble *vi* errer; faire une randonnée.

ramp *n* rampe *f*.

ramshackle *adj* délabré.

rancid *adj* rance.

rancour *n* rancœur *f*.

random *adj* fortuit, fait au hasard.

range *vt* ranger:—*vi* s'étendre:—*n* rangée *f*; chaîne *f*; fourneau de cuisine *m*.

rank *n* rang *m*, classe *f*, grade *m*.

ransack *vt* saccager, piller.

ransom *n* rançon *f*.

rape *n* viol *m*:—*vt* violer.

rapid *adj* rapide.

rapidity *n* rapidité *f*.

rapist *n* violeur *m*.

rapt *adj* extasié; absorbé.

rapture *n* ravissement *m*; extase *f*.

rare *adj* rare.

rarity *n* rareté *f*.

rash *adj* imprudent:—*n* éruption (cutanée) *f*.

rashness *n* imprudence *f*.

rat *n* rat *m*.

rate *n* taux, prix *m*; vitesse *f*:—*vt* estimer, évaluer.

rather *adv* plutôt.

ratification *n* ratification *f*.

ratify *vt* ratifier.

ration *n* ration *f*.

rational *adj* rationnel.

rattle *vi* s'entrechoquer:—*n* hochet *m*; cliquetis *m*.

ravage *vt* ravager:—*n* ravage *m*.

rave *vi* délirer.

ravenous *adj* vorace.

ravine *n* ravin *m*.

raw *adj* cru; brut.

rawness *n* crudité *f*; inexpérience *f*.

ray *n* rayon *m*.

raze *vt* raser.

razor *n* rasoir *m*.

reach *vt* atteindre:—*vi* porter:—*n* portée *f*.

react *vi* réagir.

reaction *n* réaction *f*.

read *vt vi* lire.

reader *n* lecteur *m*, -trice *f*.

readily *adv* volontiers.

readiness *n* bonne volonté *f*.

reading *n* lecture *f*.

readjust *vt* réajuster.

ready *adj* prêt; enclin.

real *adj* réel, vrai.

realisation *n* réalisation *f*.

realise *vt* se rendre compte de; réaliser.

reality *n* réalité *f*.

reappear *vi* réapparaître.

rear *n* arrière *m*; derrière *m*:—*vt* élever.

reason *n* raison *f*; cause *f*:—*vt vi* raisonner.

reasonable *adj* raisonnable.

reasoning *n* raisonnement *m*.

reassure *vt* rassurer.

rebel *n* rebelle *mf*:—*vi* se rebeller.

rebellion *n* rébellion *f*.

rebound *vi* rebondir.

rebuild *vt* reconstruire.

rebuke *vt* réprimander:—*n* réprimande *f*.

recall *vt* (se) rappeler.

recapture *n* reprise *f*.

recede *vi* reculer.

receipt *n* reçu *m*; réception *f*.

receivable *adj* recevable.

receive *vt* recevoir; accueillir.

recent *adj* récent, neuf.

receptacle *n* récipient *m*.

reception *n* réception *f*.

recession *n* récession *f*.

recipe *n* recette *f*.

recipient *n* destinataire *mf*.

reciprocal *adj* ~ly *adv* réciproque(ment).

recital *n* récit *m*.

recite *vt* réciter.

reckless *adj* téméraire.

reckon *vt* compter:—*vi* calculer.

reclaim *vt* assainir; récupérer.

recline *vt* reposer:—*vi* être allongé.

recognise *vt* reconnaître.

recognition *n* reconnaissance *f*.

recoil *vi* reculer.

recollect *vt* se rappeler.

recollection *n* souvenir *m*.

recommend *vt* recommander.

recompense *n* récompense *f*:—*vt* récompenser.

reconcile *vt* réconcilier.

reconciliation *n* réconciliation *f*.

reconsider *vt* reconsidérer.

record *vt* enregistrer:—*n* rapport *m*, registre *m*; disque *m*; record *m*.

recount *vt* raconter.

recourse *n* recours *m*.

recover *vt* retrouver:—*vi* se remettre.

recovery *n* guérison *f*; reprise *f*.

recreation *n* détente *f*; récréation *f*.

recriminate *vi* récriminer.

recrimination *n* récrimination *f*.

recruit *vt* recruter:—*n* (*mil*) recrue *f*.

rectangle *n* rectangle *m*.

rectification *n* rectification *f*.

rectify *vt* rectifier.

recumbent adj couché, étendu.

recur vi se reproduire.

recurrence n répétition f.

recurrent adj répétitif.

red adj rouge:—n rouge m.

redden vt vi rougir.

redeem vt racheter, rembourser.

redemption n rachat m.

redness n rougeur, rousseur f.

redouble vt vi redoubler.

redress vt réparer; redresser.

reduce vt réduire; diminuer.

reduction n réduction f; baisse f.

redundancy n licenciement m.

redundant adj superflu.

reel n bobine f; dévidoir m:—vi chanceler.

re-enter vt rentrer.

re-establish vt rétablir; réhabiliter.

refer vt se référer à:—vi se référer.

referee n arbitre m.

reference n référence f.

refine vt raffiner, affiner.

refinement n raffinement m.

reflect vt réfléchir, refléter:—vi réfléchir.

reflection n réflexion, pensée f.

reform vt réformer:—vi se réformer.

reform n réforme f.

reformer n réformateur m, -trice f.

refrain vi:—~ from s'abstenir de.

refresh vt rafraîchir.

refrigerator n glacière f; réfrigérateur m.

refuge n refuge, asile m.

refugee n réfugié m, -e f.

refund vt rembourser:—n remboursement m.

refusal n refus m.

refuse vt refuser:—n déchets mpl.

regain vt recouvrer.

regal adj royal.

regard vt regarder:—n considération f.

regardless adv quand même.

regenerate vt régénérer.

regeneration n régénération f.

regime n régime m.

region n région f.

register n registre m:—vt enregistrer.

registration n enregistrement m.

regressive adj régressif.

regret n regret m:—vt regretter.

regular adj régulier:—n habitué m, -e f.

regularity n régularité f.

regulate vt régler.

regulation n règlement m.

rehabilitate vt réhabiliter.

rehabilitation n réhabilitation f.

reimburse vt rembourser.

reimbursement n remboursement m.

reinforce vt renforcer.

reiterate vt réitérer.

reiteration n réitération f.

reject vt rejeter.

rejection n refus m.

rejoice vt réjouir:—vi se réjouir.

relapse vi retomber:—n rechute f.

relate vt relater:—vi se rapporter.

relation n rapport m; parent m.

relationship n lien de parenté m; relation f; rapport m.

relative adj relatif:—n parent m, -e f.

relax vt relâcher:—vi se relâcher.

relaxation n relâchement m; détente f.

relay n relais m:—vt retransmettre.

release vt libérer:—n libération f.

relevant adj pertinent.

reliable adj fiable.

reliance n confiance f.

relief n soulagement m; secours m.

relieve vt soulager, alléger.

religion n religion f.

religious adj religieux.

relinquish vt abandonner.

reluctant adj peu disposé.

rely *vi* compter sur.
remain *vi* rester, demeurer.
remainder *n* reste, restant *m*.
remark *n* remarque:—*vt* (faire) remarquer.
remarkable *adj* remarquable, notable.
remedy *n* remède *m*:—*vt* remédier à.
remember *vt* se souvenir de.
remind *vt* rappeler.
reminiscence *n* réminiscence *f*.
remit *vt* remettre, pardonner.
remnant *n* reste, restant *m*.
remonstrate *vi* protester.
remote *adj* lointain, éloigné.
remoteness *n* éloignement *m*; isolement *m*.
removable *adj* amovible.
removal *n* suppression *f*.
remove *vt* enlever.
remunerate *vt* rémunérer.
render *vt* rendre, remettre.
renew *vt* renouveler.
renewal *n* renouvellement *m*.
renounce *vt* renoncer à.
renovate *vt* rénover.
renown *n* renommée *f*; célébrité *f*.
rent *n* loyer *m*:—*vt* louer.
renunciation *n* renonciation *f*.
reorganisation *n* réorganisation *f*.
reorganise *vt* réorganiser.
repair *vt* réparer:—*n* réparation *f*.
repatriate *vt* rapatrier.
repay *vt* rembourser.
repayment *n* remboursement *m*.
repeal *vt* abroger:—*n* abrogation.
repeat *vt* répéter.
repel *vt* repousser, rebuter.
repent *vi* se repentir.
repetition *n* répétition *f*.
replace *vt* replacer.
replenish *vt* remplir de nouveau.

replete *adj* rempli.
reply *n* réponse *f*:—*vi* répondre.
report *vt* rapporter:—*n* rapport *m*; compte rendu *m*.
reporter *n* journaliste *mf*.
reprehend *vt* condamner.
reprehensible *adj* répréhensible.
represent *vt* représenter.
representation *n* représentation *f*.
representative *adj* représentatif:—*n* représentant(e) *m(f)*.
repress *vt* réprimer, contenir.
repression *n* répression *f*.
reprieve *n* sursis *m*.
reprimand *vt* réprimander.
reprisal *n* représailles *fpl*.
reproach *n* reproche:—*vt* reprocher.
reproduce *vt* reproduire.
reproduction *n* reproduction *f*.
republic *n* république *f*.
republican *adj n* républicain *m*, -e *f*.
repudiate *vt* renier.
repulse *vt* repousser.
repulsion *n* répulsion *f*.
repulsive *adj* répulsif.
reputation *n* réputation *f*.
request *n* requête *f*:—*vt* demander.
require *vt* demander, nécessiter.
requirement *n* besoin *m*; exigence *f*.
requisite *adj* nécessaire, indispensable.
rescue *vt* sauver, secourir:—*n* secours *m*.
research *vt* faire de la recherche:—*n* recherche *f*.
resemblance *n* ressemblance *f*.
resemble *vt* ressembler à.
resent *vt* être contrarié.
resentment *n* ressentiment *m*.
reservation *n* réservation *f*.
reserve *vt* réserver:—*n* réserve *f*.
reside *vi* résider.
residence *n* résidence *f*.

resident n résident m, -e f.

resign vt démissionner de:—vi démissionner.

resignation n démission f.

resist vt résister, s'opposer.

resistance n résistance f.

resolute adj résolu.

resolution n résolution f.

resolve vt resoudre:—vi (se) résoudre.

resort vi recourir:—n lieu de vacances m.

resource n ressource f.

respect n respect m; égard m:—vt respecter.

respectability n respectabilité f.

respectable adj respectable.

respectful adj respectueux.

respecting prep en ce qui concerne.

respective adj respectif.

respond vi répondre.

response n réponse.

responsibility n responsabilité f.

responsible adj responsable.

rest n repos m; reste, restant m:—vi se reposer.

restitution n restitution f.

restive adj rétif, récalcitrant.

restoration n restauration f.

restore vt restaurer.

restrain vt retenir.

restrict vt restreindre.

restriction n restriction f.

restrictive adj restrictif.

result vi résulter:—n résultat m.

resume vt reprendre; résumer.

resuscitate vt réanimer.

retail vt détailler:—n vente au détail f.

retain vt retenir, conserver.

retaliate vi se venger.

reticence n réticence f.

retire vt retirer:—vi se retirer.

retired adj retraité.

retirement n isolement m.

retort vt rétorquer:—n réplique f.

retrace vt retracer.

retreat vi se retirer.

retribution n récompense f.

retrieve vt récupérer, recouvrer.

return vt rendre:—n retour m.

reunion n réunion f.

reunite vt réunir:—vi se réunir.

reveal vt révéler.

revelation n révélation f.

revenge vt venger:—n vengeance f.

revengeful adj vindicatif.

revenue n revenu m; rente f.

reverberate vt réverbérer:—vi résonner.

reverberation n réverbération f.

reversal n renversement m.

reverse vt renverser:—vi faire marche arrière:—n inverse m.

reversible adj réversible.

reversion n retour m; réversion f.

revert vi revenir; retourner.

review vt revoir:—n revue f; examen m.

revise vt réviser.

revision n révision f.

revival n reprise f; renouveau m.

revive vt ranimer.

revoke vt révoquer.

revolt vi se révolter:—n révolte f.

revolution n révolution f.

revolutionary adj n révolutionnaire mf.

revolve vt (re)tourner:—vi tourner.

revue n revue f.

reward n récompense f:—vt récompenser.

rhetorical adj rhétorique.

rheumatic adj rhumatisant.

rheumatism n rhumatisme m.

rhyme n rime f:—vi rimer.

rhythm n rythme m.

rhythmical adj rythmique.

rib *n* côte *f.*

ribbon *n* ruban *m.*

rice *n* riz *m.*

rich *adj* riche; somptueux.

richness *n* richesse *f;* abondance *f.*

rid *vt* débarrasser.

riddle *n* crible *m:—vt* cribler.

ride *vi* monter (à cheval); aller (en voiture).

ridge *n* arête, crête *f.*

ridicule *n* ridicule *m:—vt* ridiculiser.

ridiculous *adj* ~**ly** *adv* ridicule.

rifle *n* fusil *m.*

rig *vt* équiper; truquer:—*n* plate-forme de forage *f.*

right *adj* droit, bien:—~! bien!, bon!; à juste titre:—*n* droit *m;* droite *f.*

righteous *adj* droit, vertueux.

rigid *adj* rigide; sévère.

rigorous *adj* rigoureux.

rigour *n* rigueur *f;* sévérité *f.*

rim *n* bord *m,* monture *f.*

ring *n* anneau, cercle, rond *m:—vt* sonner:—*vi* sonner, retentir.

rink *n* (*also* **ice ~**) patinoire *f.*

rinse *vt* rincer.

riot *n* émeute *f.*

riotous *adj* séditieux; dissolu.

rip *vt* déchirer.

ripe *adj* mûr.

ripen *vt vi* mûrir.

ripple *n* ondulation *f,* ride *f.*

rise *vi* se lever; monter:—*n* hausse *f;* augmentation *f.*

rising *n* insurrection *f.*

risk *n* risque:—*vt* risquer.

risky *adj* risqué.

rite *n* rite *m.*

ritual *adj n* rituel *m.*

rival *adj* rival:—*n* rival *m,* -e *f:—vt* rivaliser avec.

rivalry *n* rivalité *f.*

river *n* rivière *f.*

road *n* route *f.*

roam *vt* errer dans:—*vi* errer.

roar *vi* rugir:—*n* rugissement.

roast *vt* rôtir; griller.

rob *vt* voler.

robber *n* voleur *m,* -euse *f.*

robbery *n* vol *m.*

robust *adj* robuste.

robustness *n* robustesse *f.*

rock *n* roche *f:—vt* bercer; balancer.

rocket *n* fusée *f.*

rocking chair *n* fauteuil à bascule *m.*

rocky *adj* rocheux.

rodent *n* rongeur *m.*

rogue *n* coquin, polisson *m;* gredin *m.*

roll *vt* rouler:—*vi* (se) rouler:—*n* roulement *m;* rouleau *m.*

roller *n* rouleau, cylindre *m.*

romance *n* romance *f;* roman *m.*

romantic *adj* romantique.

roof *n* toit *m;* voûte *f:—vt* couvrir.

room *n* pièce, salle *f;* espace *m.*

root *n* racine *f;* origine *f.*

rope *n* corde *f;* cordage *m.*

rose *n* rose *f.*

rosemary *n* (*bot*) romarin *m.*

rot *vi* pourrir:—*n* pourriture *f.*

rotate *vt* faire tourner:—*vi* tourner.

rotation *n* rotation *f.*

rotund *adj* rond, replet.

rouge *n* rouge (à joues) *m.*

rough *adj* accidenté, rugueux; rude.

roughness *n* rugosité *f;* rudesse *f.*

round *adj* rond, circulaire:—*n* cercle *m;* rond *m;* tour *m;* tournée *f:—adv* autour de; environ:—*vt* arrondir.

roundness *n* rondeur *f.*

rouse *vt* réveiller; exciter.

rout *n* déroute *f.*

route n itinéraire m; route f.
routine adj habituel:—n routine f.
rove vi vagabonder.
row n querelle f.
row n rangée, file f.
royal adj royal; princier.
royalty n royauté f; droits d'auteur mpl.
rub vt frotter; irriter:—n frottement m.
rubber n caoutchouc m.
rubbish n détritus mpl; ordures fpl.
rudder n gouvernail m.
ruddiness n teint vif m, rougeur f.
rude adj impoli, rude.
rudeness n impolitesse f; rudesse f.
ruffle vt ébouriffer, déranger.
rug n tapis m.
rugged adj accidenté, déchiqueté.
ruin n ruine f:—vt ruiner.
ruinous adj ruineux.

rule n règle f; règlement m:—vt gouverner, dominer.
rumble vi gronder, tonner.
ruminate vt ruminer.
rummage vi fouiller.
rumour n rumeur f.
run vt diriger:—vi courir.
rung n barreau, échelon m.
runner n coureur m.
runway n piste de décollage f.
rupture n rupture f:—vt rompre:—vi se rompre.
ruse n ruse f, stratagème m.
rush n ruée f; hâte f:—vi se précipiter.
rust n rouille f:—vi se rouiller.
rustic adj rustique:—n paysan, rustaud m.
rustle vi bruire:—vt faire bruire; froisser.
rusty adj rouillé; roux.
ruthless adj cruel, impitoyable.
rye n seigle m.

S

sabotage n sabotage m.
sachet n sachet m.
sack n sac m
sacrament n sacrement m.
sacred adj saint, sacré.
sacrifice n sacrifice m:—vt sacrifier.
sacrilege n sacrilège m.
sad adj triste, déprimé.
sadden vt attrister.
saddle n selle f; col m:—vt seller.
sadness n tristesse f.
safe adj sûr; en sécurité:—n coffre-fort m.
safeguard n sauvegarde f:—vt sauvegarder.
safety n sécurité f; sûreté f.

sage n sage m:—adj sage.
sail n voile f:—vt piloter:—vi aller à la voile.
sailing n navigation f.
sailor n marin m.
saint n saint m, -e f.
sake n bien m, égard m.
salad n salade f.
salary n salaire m.
sale n vente f; solde m.
salesman n vendeur m.
saliva n salive f.
salmon n saumon m.
saloon n bar m.
salt n sel m:—vt saler.

salt cellar *n* salière *f*.

salubrious *adj* salubre, sain.

salubrity *n* salubrité *f*.

salutary *adj* salutaire.

salute *vt* saluer:—*n* salut *m*.

salvation *n* salut *m*.

same *adj* même, identique.

sameness *n* identité *f*.

sample *n* échantillon *m*:—*vt* goûter.

sanatorium *n* sanatorium *m*.

sanctify *vt* sanctifier.

sanction *n* sanction *f*:—*vt* sanctionner.

sanctuary *n* sanctuaire *m*; asile *m*.

sand *n* sable *m*:—*vt* sabler.

sandal *n* sandale *f*.

sandwich *n* sandwich *m*.

sandy *adj* sablonneux, sableux.

sane *adj* sain.

sanguine *adj* sanguin.

sanity *n* santé mentale, raison *f*.

sapling *n* jeune arbre *m*.

sarcasm *n* sarcasme *m*.

sarcastic *adj* sarcastique.

sardine *n* sardine *f*.

satchel *n* cartable *m*.

satellite *n* satellite *m*.

sate *vt* rassasier, assouvir.

satin *n* satin *m*:—*adj* en *ou* de satin.

satire *n* satire *f*.

satirical *adj* satirique.

satisfaction *n* satisfaction *f*.

satisfactory *adj* satisfaisant.

satisfy *vt* satisfaire.

saturate *vt* saturer.

Saturday *n* samedi *m*.

sauce *n* sauce *f*; assaisonnement *m*.

saucepan *n* casserole *f*.

saucer *n* soucoupe *f*.

saunter *vi* flâner, se balader.

sausage *n* saucisse *f*.

savage *adj* sauvage:—*n* sauvage *mf*.

savagery *n* sauvagerie, barbarie *f*.

save *vt* sauver; économiser:—*adv* sauf, à l'exception de.

saving *prep* sauf, à l'exception de: —*n* sauvetage *m*.

savings bank *n* caisse d'épargne *f*.

savour *n* saveur *f*:—*vt* savourer.

saw *n* scie *f*:—*vt* scier.

say *vt* dire.

saying *n* dicton, proverbe *m*.

scaffolding *n* échafaudage *m*.

scald *vt* échauder:—*n* brûlure *f*.

scale *n* balance *f*; échelle *f*:—*vt* escalader.

scan *vt* scruter; explorer; scander.

scandal *n* scandale *m*; infamie *f*.

scandalise *vt* scandaliser.

scandalous *adj* scandaleux.

scant *adj* rare, insuffisant.

scantiness *n* insuffisance, pauvreté *f*.

scapegoat *n* bouc émissaire *m*.

scar *n* cicatrice *f*.

scarce *adj* rare.

scare *vt* effrayer:—*n* peur; panique *f*.

scarf *n* écharpe *f*.

scarlet *n* écarlate *f*:—*adj* écarlate.

scatter *vt* éparpiller; disperser.

scene *n* scène *f*; lieu *m*.

scenery *n* vue *f*; décor (de théâtre) *m*.

scenic *adj* scénique.

scent *n* parfum *m*, odeur *f*:—*vt* parfumer.

sceptic *n* sceptique *mf*.

sceptic(al) *adj* sceptique.

schedule *n* horaire *m*; programme *m*.

scheme *n* projet, plan *m*; schéma *m*: — *vt* machiner:—*vi* intriguer.

scholar *n* élève *mf*; érudit *m*, -e *f*.

school *n* école *f*:—*vt* instruire.

schoolboy *n* écolier, élève *m*.

schoolgirl *n* écolière, élève *f*.

schoolteacher *n* instituteur/trice *mf*; professeur *mf*.

science n science f.

scientific adj scientifique.

scientist n scientifique mf.

scintillate vi scintiller, étinceler.

scissors npl ciseaux mpl.

scoff vi se moquer.

scold vt réprimander:—vi grogner.

scope n portée, envergure.

scorch vt brûler:—vi se brûler.

score n score m; marque f; entaille f: —vt marquer.

scorn vt mépriser:—n mépris m.

scornful adj dédaigneux.

scoundrel n vaurien m.

scour vt récurer, frotter.

scout n (mil) éclaireur m, -euse f; guetteur m.

scowl vi se renfrogner.

scramble vi grimper; se battre, se disputer:—n bousculade f.

scrap n bout m; bagarre f; ferraille f.

scrape vt vi racler, gratter:—vt érafler.

scratch vt griffer, égratigner:—n égratignure f.

scream vi hurler:—n hurlement m.

screen n écran m; paravent m:—vt abriter; sélectionner.

screw n vis f:—vt visser.

screwdriver n tournevis m.

scribble vt gribouiller:—n gribouillage m.

script n scénario m; script m.

Scripture n Ecriture sainte f.

scrub vt récurer; annuler:—n broussailles fpl.

scruple n scrupule m.

scrupulous adj scrupuleux.

scuffle n rixe f:—vi se bagarrer.

sculptor n sculpteur m, -trice f.

sculpture n sculpture f.

scum n écume f; crasse f.

sea n mer f:—adj marin.

seafood n fruits de mer mpl.

seagull n mouette f.

seal n sceau m; phoque m:—vt sceller.

seamy adj sordide.

search vt fouiller; inspecter:—n fouille f; recherche f.

seashore n bord de mer m.

seasickness n mal de mer m.

season n saison f.

seasonable adj opportun, à propos.

seasoning n assaisonnement m.

seat n siège m; place f:—vt (faire) asseoir.

seaweed n algue f.

seclude vt éloigner, isoler.

seclusion n solitude f; isolement m.

second adj deuxième:—n second m; seconde f.

secondary adj secondaire.

secrecy n secret m; discrétion f.

secret adj n secret m.

secretary n secrétaire mf.

secretive adj secret, dissimulé.

section n section f.

sector n secteur m.

secular adj séculaire.

secure adj sûr; en sûreté:—vt assurer.

security n sécurité f; sûreté f.

sedative n sédatif m.

sediment n sédiment m; lie f.

sedition n sédition f.

seduce vt séduire.

seduction n séduction f.

seductive adj séduisant.

see vt voir, remarquer.

seed n graine f:—vi monter en graine.

seek vt chercher; demander.

seem vi paraître, sembler.

seemliness n bienséance f.

seemly adj convenable, bienséant.

seesaw n bascule f:—vi osciller.

segment n segment m.

seize *vt* saisir.

seizure *n* saisie *f*.

seldom *adv* rarement, peu souvent.

select *vt* sélectionner.

selection *n* sélection *f*.

self *n* soi-même:—**the ~** le moi:—*pref* auto-.

self-confident *adj* sûr de soi.

self-defence *n* autodéfense *f*.

self-employed *adj* indépendant.

self-interest *n* intérêt personnel *m*.

selfish *adj* égoïste.

selfishness *n* égoïsme *m*.

self-portrait *n* autoportrait *m*.

self-respect *n* respect de soi *m*.

self-service *adj* libre-service.

self-styled *adj* soi-disant.

self-sufficient *adj* autosuffisant.

self-taught *adj* autodidacte.

sell *vt* vendre:—*vi* se vendre.

seller *n* vendeur *m*, -euse *f*.

semblance *n* semblant *m*.

semicircle *n* demi-cercle *m*.

senate *n* sénat *m*.

senator *n* sénateur *m*, -trice *f*.

send *vt* envoyer.

senile *adj* sénile.

senility *n* sénilité *f*.

senior *n* aîné *m*, -e *f*:—*adj* aîné.

seniority *n* ancienneté *f*.

sensation *n* sensation *f*.

sense *n* sens *m*; sensation *f*.

senseless *adj* insensé.

sensible *adj* sensé; sensible.

sensibly *adj* raisonnablement.

sensitive *adj* sensible.

sensual *adj* sensuel.

sensuality *n* sensualité *f*.

sentence *n* phrase *f*; condamnation *f*.

sentiment *n* sentiment *m*.

sentimental *adj* sentimental.

sentinel *n* sentinelle *f*.

separable *adj* séparable.

separate *vt* séparer:—*vi* se séparer: — *adj* séparé.

separation *n* séparation *f*.

September *n* septembre *m*.

sepulchre *n* sépulcre *m*.

sequel *n* conséquence *f*; suite *f*.

sequence *n* ordre *m*, série *f*.

serenade *n* sérénade *f*:—*vt* jouer une sérénade pour.

serene *adj* serein.

serenity *n* sérénité *f*.

sergeant *n* sergent *m*.

serial *adj* de/en série:—*n* feuilleton *m*.

series *n* série *f*.

serious *adj* sérieux, grave.

sermon *n* sermon *m*.

serpent *n* serpent *m*.

servant *n* domestique *mf*.

serve *vt* servir; desservir:—*vi* servir; être utile.

service *n* service *m*; entretien *m*:—*vt* entretenir.

serviceable *adj* utilisable; pratique.

servile *adj* servile.

servitude *n* servitude *f*.

session *n* séance, session *f*.

set *vt* mettre, poser:—*n* jeu *m*; ensemble *m*:—*adj* fixe, figé.

setting *n* disposition *f*; cadre *m*; monture *f*:—**~ of the sun** coucher du soleil *m*.

settle *vt* poser, installer:—*vi* se poser; s'installer.

settlement *n* règlement *m*; établissement *m*.

seven *adj n* sept *m*.

seventeen *adj n* dix-sept *m*.

seventeenth *adj n* dix-septième *mf*.

seventh *adj n* septième *mf*.

seventieth *adj n* soixante-dixième *mf*.

seventy *adj n* soixante-dix *m*.

several *adj pn* plusieurs.

severe *adj* sévère, rigoureux.

severity *n* sévérité *f*.

sew *vt vi* coudre.

sewer *n* égout *m*.

sex *n* sexe *m*.

sexist *adj n* sexiste *mf*.

sexual *adj* sexuel.

shabby *adj* miteux.

shade *n* ombre *f*; nuance *f*:—*vt* ombrager.

shadow *n* ombre *f*.

shady *adj* ombreux, ombragé.

shaft *n* fût *m*; (*tech*) arbre *m*; rayon *m*.

shake *vt* secouer:—*vi* trembler:—*n* secousse *f*.

shallow *adj* peu profond, superficiel.

sham *vt* feindre:—*n* imposture *f*.

shame *n* honte *f*:—*vt* déshonorer.

shamefaced *adj* honteux, confus.

shameful *adj* honteux; scandaleux.

shampoo *n* shampooing *m*.

shape *vt* former; façonner:—*vi* prendre forme:—*n* forme *f*.

shapely *adj* bien proportionné.

share *n* part, portion *f*:—*vt* partager.

shark *n* requin *m*.

sharp *adj* aigu, acéré.

sharpen *vt* aiguiser, affûter.

sharpness *n* acuité *f*; aigreur *f*.

shatter *vt* fracasser.

shave *vi* se raser.

shaver *n* rasoir électrique *m*.

shaving *n* rasage *m*.

shawl *n* châle *m*.

she *pn* elle.

sheaf *n* gerbe *f*; liasse *f*.

shear *vt* tondre.

shed *n* hangar *m*; cabane *f*.

sheep *n* mouton *m*.

sheer *adj* pur; abrupt:—*adv* abruptement.

sheet *n* drap *m*; plaque *f*.

shelf *n* étagère *f*.

shell *n* coquille *f*; écorce *f*:—*vt* écosser, décortiquer; bombarder.

shelter *n* abri *m*:—*vt* abriter:—*vi* s'abriter.

shepherd *n* berger *m*.

sheriff *n* shérif *m*.

shield *n* bouclier *m*:—*vt* protéger.

shift *vi* changer; se déplacer:—*vt* changer, bouger:—*n* changement *m*.

shine *vi* briller.

shining *adj* resplendissant.

ship *n* bateau *m*; navire *m*:—*vt* embarquer.

shipment *n* cargaison *f*.

shipwreck *n* naufrage *m*.

shirt *n* chemise *f*.

shiver *vi* frissonner.

shock *n* choc *m*; coup *m*:—*vt* bouleverser; choquer.

shoe *n* chaussure *f*.

shoemaker *n* cordonnier *m*.

shoot *vt* tirer:—*vi* pousser:—*n* pousse *f*.

shooting *n* fusillade *f*; tir *m*.

shop *n* magasin *m*; atelier *m*.

shopper *n* acheteur *m*, -euse *f*.

shore *n* rivage, bord *m*.

short *adj* court, bref.

shortcoming *n* insuffisance *f*.

shorten *vt* raccourcir; abréger.

short-sighted *adj* myope.

shortwave *n* ondes courtes *fpl*.

shot *n* coup *m*; décharge *f*.

shotgun *n* fusil de chasse *m*.

shoulder *n* épaule *f*; accotement *m*.

shout *vt vi* crier:—*n* cri *m*.

shove *vt vi* pousser:—*n* poussée *f*.

shovel *n* pelle *f*:—*vt* pelleter.

show *vt* montrer:—*vi* se voir:—*n* exposition *f*.

shower n averse f; douche f.

showy adj voyant, ostentatoire.

shred n lambeau m:—vt mettre en lambeaux.

shrewd adj astucieux; perspicace.

shriek vt vi hurler:—n hurlement m.

shrill adj aigu, strident.

shrimp n crevette f.

shrink vi rétrécir.

shrivel vi se ratatiner.

shroud n voile m; linceul m.

shudder vi frissonner:—n frisson m.

shun vt fuir, éviter.

shut vt fermer; vi (se) fermer.

shutter n volet m.

shy adj timide; réservé.

shyness n timidité f.

sick adj malade; écœuré.

sicken vt rendre malade.

sickly adj maladif.

sickness n maladie f.

side n côté m; parti m:—adj latéral.

sideboard n buffet m.

sidelong adj oblique.

siege n (mil) siège m.

sieve n tamis m:—vt tamiser.

sift vt tamiser.

sigh vi soupirer:—n soupir m.

sight n vue f; spectacle m.

sightseeing n tourisme m.

sign n signe m, indication f:—vt signer.

signal n signal m.

signature n signature f.

significance n importance f.

significant adj considérable.

signify vt signifier.

silence n silence m.

silent adj silencieux.

silicon chip n puce de silicium f.

silk n soie f.

silken adj soyeux.

sill n rebord m; seuil m.

silliness n bêtise, niaiserie f.

silly adj bête, stupide.

silver n argent m:—adj en argent.

silvery adj argenté.

similar adj semblable; similaire.

similarity n ressemblance f.

simile n comparaison f.

simmer vi cuire à feux doux, mijoter.

simper vi minauder:—n sourire affecté m.

simple adj simple; naïf.

simplicity n simplicité f.

simplification n simplification f.

simplify vt simplifier.

simulate vt simuler, feindre.

simultaneous adj simultané.

sin n péché m:—vi pécher.

since adv prep depuis:—conj depuis que; puisque.

sincere adj sincère; réel, vrai:—~ly adv sincère(ment).

sincerity n sincérité f.

sinew n tendon m; nerf m.

sing vt vi chanter.

singe vt roussir.

singer n chanteur m, -euse f.

single adj seul, unique; célibataire.

singly adv séparément.

singular adj singulier.

singularity n singularité f.

sinister adj sinistre.

sink vi couler:—n évier m.

sinner n pécheur m, pécheresse f.

sinuous adj sinueux.

sir n monsieur m.

sister n sœur f.

sister-in-law n belle-sœur f.

sit vi s'asseoir.

site n emplacement m; site m.

sitting n séance, réunion f.

sitting room n salle de séjour f.

situation n situation f.

six adj n six m.

sixteen adj n seize m.

sixteenth adj n seizième mf.

sixth adj n sixième mf.

sixtieth adj n soixantième mf.

sixty adj n soixante m.

size n taille, grandeur f.

sizeable adj assez grand.

skate n patin m:—vi patiner.

skating rink n patinoire f.

skeleton n squelette m.

sketch n croquis m.

skewer n broche f; brochette f:—vt embrocher.

ski n ski m:—vi skier.

skid n dérapage m:—vi déraper.

skier n skieur m, -euse f.

skiing n ski m.

skill n habileté, adresse f.

skilful adj adroit, habile.

skim vt écrémer; effleurer.

skin n peau f:—vt écorcher.

skinny adj maigre, efflanqué.

skip vi sautiller.

skirmish n escarmouche f.

skirt n jupe f; bordure f:—vt contourner.

skulk vi rôder furtivement.

skull n crâne m.

sky n ciel m.

skylight n lucarne f.

skyscraper n gratte-ciel m invar.

slab n dalle f.

slack adj lâche, négligent.

slack(en) vt relâcher:—vi se relâcher.

slackness n ralentissement m.

slam vt claquer violemment.

slander vt calomnier:—n calomnie f.

slanderous adj calomnieux.

slang n argot m.

slant vi pencher:—n inclinaison f.

slap n gifle f:—vt gifler.

slaughter n carnage, massacre m:—vt abattre.

slave n esclave mf.

slavery n esclavage m.

slay vt tuer.

sleazy adj louche.

sledge n traîneau m.

sleep vi dormir:—n sommeil m.

sleeper n dormeur m, -euse f.

sleepiness n envie de dormir f.

sleepwalking n somnambulisme m.

sleepy adj qui a envie de dormir; endormi.

sleet n neige fondue f.

sleeve n manche f.

slender adj svelte, mince.

slenderness n sveltesse f, minceur f.

slice n tranche f; spatule f:—vt couper.

slide vi glisser:—n glissade f; diapositive f.

slight adj léger, mince:—n affront m.

slightness n fragilité f; insignifiance f.

slim adj mince:—vi maigrir.

slimming n amaigrissement m.

sling n écharpe f:—vt lancer.

slip vi (se) glisser:—vt glisser:—n glissade f; faux pas m.

slipper n pantoufle f.

slippery adj glissant.

slit vt fendre, inciser.

slogan n slogan m.

slope n inclinaison f; pente f:—vt incliner.

sloth n paresse f.

slovenliness n manque de soin m.

slovenly adj négligé, débraillé.

slow adj lent; lourd.

slowness n lenteur, lourdeur f.

sluggish adj paresseux; léthargique.

slum n taudis m.

slump n récession f.

slur *vt* dénigrer; mal articuler:—*n* calomnie *f*.

slush *n* neige fondante *f*.

sly *adj* rusé.

slyness *n* ruse, finesse *f*.

smack *n* claque *f*:—*vt* donner une claque à.

small *adj* petit, menu.

smallness *n* petitesse *f*.

smart *adj* élégant; astucieux:—*vi* brûler.

smartness *n* astuce, vivacité, finesse *f*.

smash *vt* casser, briser, se fracasser: —*n* fracas *m*.

smear *vt* enduire; salir.

smell *vt vi* sentir:—*n* odorat *m*; odeur *f*.

smelt *vt* fondre.

smile *vi* sourire:—*n* sourire *m*.

smite *vt* frapper.

smith *n* forgeron *m*.

smoke *n* fumée *f*:—*vt vi* fumer.

smoker *n* fumeur *m*, -euse *f*.

smoky *adj* enfumé; qui fume.

smooth *adj* lisse, uni:—*vt* lisser; adoucir.

smoothness *n* douceur *f*; aspect lisse *m*.

smother *vt* étouffer.

smudge *vt* salir:—*n* tache *f*.

smuggle *vt* passer en contrebande.

smuggler *n* contrebandier *m*, -ière *f*.

snack *n* collation *f*.

snail *n* escargot *m*.

snake *n* serpent *m*.

snap *vt* casser net:—claquer:—*n* claquement *m*.

snare *n* piège *m*; collet *m*.

snatch *vt* saisir.

sneer *vi* ricaner.

sneeze *vi* éternuer.

sniff *vt* renifler.

snivel *n* pleurnicherie *f*:—*vi* pleurnicher.

snob *n* snob *mf*.

snobbish *adj* snob.

snooze *n* petit somme *m*.

snore *vi* ronfler.

snow *n* neige *f*:—*vi* neiger.

snowman *n* bonhomme de neige *m*.

snowplough *n* chasse-neige *m invar*.

snowy *adj* neigeux; enneigé.

snub *vt* repousser, rejeter.

snug *adj* confortable, douillet.

so *adv* si, tellement, aussi; ainsi.

soak *vi* tremper:—*vt* faire tremper.

soap *n* savon *m*:—*vt* savonner.

soar *vi* monter en flèche.

sob *n* sanglot *m*:—*vi* sangloter.

sober *adj* sobre; sérieux.

sobriety *n* sobriété *f*.

sociability *n* sociabilité *f*.

sociable *adj* sociable.

social *adj* social, sociable.

socialist *n* socialiste *mf*.

social worker *n* assistant(e) social(e) *m(f)*.

society *n* société *f*; compagnie *f*.

sociologist *n* sociologue *mf*.

sock *n* chaussette *f*.

socket *n* prise de courant *f*.

sofa *n* sofa *m*.

soft *adj* doux, moelleux.

soften *vt* (r)amollir, adoucir.

softness *n* douceur, mollesse *f*.

software *n* logiciel *m*.

soil *vt* salir:—*n* sol *m*; terre *f*.

solace *vt* consoler:—*n* consolation *f*.

solar *adj* solaire.

solder *vt* souder:—*n* soudure *f*.

soldier *n* soldat *m*.

sole *n* plante du pied *f*:—*adj* seul, unique.

solemn *adj* solennel.

solemnity *n* solennité *f*.

solicit *vt* solliciter.

solicitor *n* notaire *m*.

solicitude *n* sollicitude *f.*
solid *adj* solide, compact:—*n* solide *m.*
solidify *vt* solidifier.
solidity *n* solidité *f.*
solitary *adj* solitaire, retiré.
solitude *n* solitude *f.*
solstice *n* solstice *m.*
soluble *adj* soluble.
solution *n* solution *f.*
solve *vt* résoudre.
solvency *n* solvabilité *f.*
solvent *adj* solvable.
some *adj* du, de la, de l', des; quelques; quelconque; certain(e)s; quelque.
somebody *pn* quelqu'un.
somehow *adv* d'une façon ou d'une autre.
something *pn* quelque chose.
sometimes *adv* quelquefois, parfois.
somewhat *adv* quelque peu.
somewhere *adv* quelque part.
somnolence *n* somnolence *f.*
somnolent *adj* somnolent.
son *n* fils *m.*
song *n* chanson *f.*
son-in-law *n* gendre *m.*
sonorous *adj* sonore.
soon *adv* bientôt.
sooner *adv* plus tôt; plutôt.
soot *n* suie *f.*
soothe *vt* calmer.
sophisticate *vt* sophistiquer.
sophisticated *adj* sophistiqué.
soporific *adj* soporifique.
sordid *adj* sordide, sale.
sore *n* plaie *f:*—*adj* douloureux, sensible.
sorrow *n* peine *f:*—*vi* se lamenter.
sorrowful *adj* triste, affligé.
sorry *adj* désolé; déplorable.
sort *n* sorte *f;* genre *m:*—*vt* classer; trier.
soul *n* âme *f.*

sound *adj* sain; valide:—*n* son *m;* bruit *m:*—*vt* sonner (de).
soundness *n* santé *f;* solidité *f.*
soup *n* soupe *f.*
sour *adj* aigre, acide.
source *n* source *f;* origine *f.*
souvenir *n* souvenir *m.*
south *n* sud *m.*
southern *adj* du sud, sud, méridional.
southward(s) *adv* vers le sud.
sovereign *adj n* souverain *m,* -e *f.*
sovereignty *n* souveraineté *f.*
sow *vt* semer.
space *n* espace *m;* intervalle *m:*—*vt* espacer.
spacious *adj* spacieux.
spade *n* bêche *f.*
span *n* envergure *f:*—*vt* enjamber.
spare *vt vi* épargner; ménager:—*adj* de trop; de réserve.
sparing *adj* limité, modéré.
spark *n* étincelle *f.*
sparkle *n* scintillement *m:*—*vi* étinceler.
sparse *adj* clairsemé.
spasm *n* spasme *m.*
spatter *vt* éclabousser.
speak *vt* parler; dire.
speaker *n* interlocuteur *m,* -trice *f;* orateur *m.*
spear *n* lance *f.*
special *adj* spécial.
speciality *n* spécialité *f.*
species *n* espèce *f.*
specific *adj* spécifique.
specification *n* spécification *f.*
specify *vt* spécifier.
specimen *n* spécimen *m.*
spectacle *n* spectacle *m.*
spectator *n* spectateur *m,* -trice *f.*
spectre *n* spectre *m.*
speculate *vi* spéculer.

speculation n spéculation f.

speculative adj spéculatif, méditatif.

speech n parole f; discours m.

speed n vitesse f; rapidité f.

speediness n promptitude, célérité f.

speed limit n limitation de vitesse f.

speedy adj rapide, prompt.

spell n charme m; période f:—vt écrire.

spelling n ortographe f.

spend vt dépenser; passer.

sphere n sphère f.

spherical adj sphérique.

spice n épice f:—vt épicer.

spicy adj épicé.

spider n araignée f.

spike n clou m:—vt clouter.

spill vt répandre:—vi se répandre.

spin vt filer:—vi tourner:—n tournoiement m.

spinal adj spinal.

spine n colonne vertébrale.

spire n flèche f; aiguille f.

spirit n esprit m; âme f; caractère m.

spirited adj vif, fougueux.

spiritless adj sans entrain, abattu.

spiritual adj spirituel.

spirituality n spiritualité f.

spit n crachat m:—vt vi cracher.

spite n dépit m:—**in ~ of** malgré.

spiteful adj rancunier.

splash vt éclabousser:—n éclaboussure f.

splendid adj splendide.

splendour n splendeur f.

splinter n éclat m:—vt (vi) (se) fendre en éclats.

split n fente f:—vt fendre.

spoil vt abîmer.

spokesman n porte-parole m invar.

sponge n éponge f.

sponsor n parrain m.

sponsorship n parrainage m.

spontaneity n spontanéité f.

spontaneous adj spontané.

spoon n cuiller f.

sporadic(al) adj sporadique.

sport n sport m; jeu m.

sportsman n sportif m.

sportswoman n sportive f.

spot n tache f; endroit m:—vt apercevoir.

spotless adj impeccable.

spouse n époux m; épouse f.

spout vi jaillir:—vt faire jaillir:—n bec m.

sprain n entorse f.

spray n spray m; pulvérisation f.

spread vt étendre:—vi s'étendre:—n diffusion f.

spring vi bondir:—n printemps m; saut m.

sprinkle vt arroser.

sprout n pousse f.

spruce adj net, impeccable.

spur n éperon m; stimulant m:—vt éperonner; stimuler.

spurn vt repousser avec mépris.

sputter vi bafouiller.

spy n espion m, -onne f:—vt espionner.

squabble vi se quereller:—n querelle f.

squad n équipe f.

squadron n escadron m.

squalid adj misérable, sordide.

squalor n saleté f; misère f.

square adj carré:—n carré m; place f.

squash vt écraser.

squat vi s'accroupir.

squeak vi grincer, crier.

squeal vi couiner.

squeeze vt presser, tordre.

squint vi loucher:—n strabisme.

squirt vt faire gicler:—n giclée f.

stab vt poignarder.

stability n stabilité.

stable n écurie f:—adj stable.

stack n pile f:—vt empiler.

staff n personnel m; bâton m.

stage n étape f; scène f.

stagger vi vaciller.

stagnation n stagnation f.

stagnate vi stagner.

stain vt tacher:—n tache f.

stair n marche f.

stairs n escalier m.

stake n pieu m:—vt marquer.

stale adj rance.

stalk n tige f.

stall n stalle f; étalage m:—vt caler.

stamina n résistance f.

stammer vi bégayer:—n bégaiement m.

stamp vt trépigner; timbrer:—n timbre m; estampille f.

stand vi être debout:—vt supporter: —n position, prise de position f; étalage m.

standard n étendard m; norme f:—adj normal.

standing n importance f; rang m.

standstill n arrêt m.

staple n agrafe f:—adj principal, de base.

star n étoile f.

starch n amidon m.

stare vi:—**to ~ at** regarder fixement.

starry adj étoilé.

start vi,vt commencer:—n début m.

starter n starter, démarreur m.

startle vt faire sursauter.

starvation n inanition, faim f.

starve vi mourir de faim.

state n état m; condition f:—vt déclarer.

stately adj majestueux, imposant.

statement n déclaration f.

statesman n homme d'Etat m.

static adj statique.

station n station f; (rail) gare f:—vt placer.

stationary adj stationnaire.

stationery n papeterie f.

statistical adj statistique.

statue n statue f.

stature n stature, taille f.

statute n statut m; loi f.

stay n séjour m:—vi rester.

steadfast adj ferme, résolu.

steadiness n fermeté f.

steady adj stable:—vt affermir.

steak n bifteck m; steak m.

steal vt vi voler.

stealthy adj furtif.

steam n vapeur f:—vt cuire à la vapeur.

steam engine n locomotive à vapeur f.

steel n acier m:—adj d'acier.

steep adj abrupt:—vt tremper.

steepness n raideur f.

steer vt diriger.

steering wheel n volant m.

stem n tige f.

stenographer n sténographe mf.

stenography n sténographie f.

step n pas m, marche f:—vi faire un pas.

stepbrother n demi-frère m.

stepsister n demi-sœur f.

stereotype vt stéréotyper.

sterile adj stérile.

sterility n stérilité f.

sterling adj de bon aloi, veritable.

stern adj sévère, rigide.

stew n ragoût m.

steward n intendant m.

stewardess n hôtesse de l'air f.

stick n bâton m:—vt coller.

sticky adj collant, poisseux.

stiff adj raide, rigide.

stiffen vt raidir:—vi se raidir.

stiffness n raideur.

stifle vt étouffer.

stifling adj suffocant.

stigmatise vt stigmatiser.

still vt calmer:—adj calme:—adv encore; toujours.

stillness n calme m.

stimulate vt stimuler.

stimulus n stimulant m.

sting vt piquer; piqûre f.

stinginess n mesquinerie f.

stingy adj mesquin.

stink vi puer:—n puanteur f.

stipulate vt stipuler.

stipulation n stipulation f.

stir vt remuer; agiter.

stitch vt coudre:—n point m.

stock n réserve f; provision f:—vt approvisionner.

stockbroker n agent de change m.

stock exchange n Bourse f.

stocking n bas m.

stoical adj stoïque.

stomach n estomac m.

stone n pierre f:—adj de pierre:—vt empierrer.

stony adj pierreux.

stool n tabouret m.

stoop vi se pencher.

stop vt arrêter:—vi s'arrêter:—n arrêt m.

stoppage n obstruction f.

storage n emmagasinage m.

store n provision f:—vt emmagasiner.

stork n cigogne f.

storm n tempête f, orage m.

stormy adj orageux.

story n histoire f; récit m.

stout adj corpulent, robuste.

stoutness n corpulence f.

stove n cuisinière f.

stow vt arrimer.

straight adj droit; direct:—adv droit; directement.

straightaway adv immédiatement.

straighten vt redresser.

strain vt tendre:—n tension f; effort m.

strait n détroit m.

strand n rive f.

strange adj inconnu; étrange.

strangeness n étrangeté f.

stranger n inconnu(e) m(f), étranger m, -ère f.

strangle vt étrangler.

strap n lanière.

stratagem n stratagème m.

strategic adj stratégique m.

strategy n stratégie f.

straw n paille f.

strawberry n fraise f.

stray vi s'égarer:—adj perdu; errant.

streak n raie f.

stream n ruisseau m:—vi ruisseler.

street n rue f.

strength n force, puissance f.

strengthen vt fortifier.

stress n pression f; stress m:—vt souligner.

stretch vt étendre:—vi s'étendre:—n extension f; étendue f.

stretcher n brancard m.

strew vt éparpiller.

strict adj strict, rigoureux.

strictness n sévérité f.

stride n grand pas m.

strife n conflit m, lutte f.

strike vt frapper:—n coup m; grève f.

striker n gréviste mf.

striking adj frappant; saisissant.

string n ficelle f, corde f.

stringent adj rigoureux.

strip vi se déshabiller:—n bande f; langue f.

stripe n raie f:—vt rayer.

strive vi s'efforcer.

stroke n coup m; caresse f:—vt caresser.

stroll vi flâner.

strong *adj* fort, vigoureux.

strongbox *n* coffre-fort *m*.

structure *n* structure *f*; construction *f*.

struggle *vi* lutter:—*n* lutte *f*.

strut *vi* se pavaner.

stubborn *adj* entêté, obstiné.

stubbornness *n* entêtement *m*.

stud *n* clou *m*; crampon *m*.

student *n*, *adj* étudiant *m*, -e *f*.

studio *n* studio, atelier *m*.

studious *adj* studieux.

study *n* étude *f*:—*vt* étudier.

stuff *n* matière *f*; étoffe *f*:—*vt* (rem)bourrer.

stuffing *n* rembourrage *m*.

stumble *vi* trébucher:—*n* trébuchement *m*.

stump *n* souche *f*; moignon *m*.

stun *vt* étourdir.

stunt *n* cascade *f*:—*vt* empêcher de croître.

stupefy *vt* stupéfier.

stupendous *adj* prodigieux.

stupid *adj* stupide.

stupidity *n* stupidité *f*.

stupor *n* stupeur *f*.

sturdiness *n* force, robustesse *f*.

sturdy *adj* robuste; hardi.

stutter *vi* bégayer.

style *n* style *m*:—*vt* appeler; dessiner.

stylish *adj* élégant.

suave *adj* suave.

subdivide *vt* subdiviser.

subdue *vt* assujettir.

subject *adj* soumis; sujet à:—*n* sujet *m*; thème *m*:—*vt* soumettre.

subjection *n* sujétion *f*.

subjugate *vt* subjuguer.

subjugation *n* subjugation *f*.

sublimate *vt* sublimer.

sublime *adj* sublime.

sublimity *n* sublimité *f*.

submarine *adj* *n* sous-marin *m*.

submerge *vt* submerger.

submersion *n* submersion *f*.

submission *n* soumission *f*.

submissive *adj* soumis.

submit *vt* soumettre:—*vi* se soumettre.

subordinate *adj* subalterne:—*vt* subordonner.

subscribe *vi* souscrire:—*vt* signer.

subscriber *n* souscripteur *m*, -trice *f*.

subscription *n* souscription *f*.

subsequent *adj* ~ly *adv* ultérieur (-ement).

subside *vi* s'affaisser.

subsidence *n* affaissement *m*.

subsidiary *adj* subsidiaire.

subsidise *vt* subventionner.

subsidy *n* subvention *f*.

subsist *vi* subsister; exister.

subsistence *n* subsistance *f*.

substance *n* substance *f*; fond *m*.

substantial *adj* substantiel.

substantiate *vt* justifier.

substitute *vt* substituer.

substitution *n* substitution *f*.

subterranean *adj* souterrain.

subtitle *n* sous-titre *m*.

subtle *adj* subtile.

subtlety *n* subtilité *f*.

subtract *vt* soustraire.

suburb *n* banlieue *f*.

suburban *adj* de banlieue.

subversive *adj* subversif.

subvert *vt* subvertir.

succeed *vi* réussir:—*vt* succéder à, suivre.

success *n* succès *m*.

successful *adj* couronné de succès.

succession *n* succession *f*.

successive *adj* successif.

successor n successeur m.

succinct adj succinct.

succumb vi succomber.

such adj tel, pareil.

suck vt vi sucer.

suckle vt allaiter.

sudden adj soudain.

suddenness n soudaineté f.

sue vt poursuivre en justice.

suffer vi souffrir.

suffering n souffrance f; douleur f.

suffice vi suffire, être suffisant.

sufficient adj suffisant.

suffocate vt vi étouffer.

suffocation n suffocation f.

sugar n sucre m:—vt sucrer.

sugary adj sucré.

suggest vt suggérer.

suggestion n suggestion f.

suicidal adj suicidaire.

suicide n suicide m; suicidé m, -e f.

suit n pétition f; costume m:—vt convenir à.

suitable adj approprié.

suitcase n valise f.

sulky adj boudeur, maussade.

sullen adj maussade; sombre.

sultry adj étouffant; chaud.

sum n somme f; total m:—to ~ up vt résumer.

summary adj n résumé m.

summer n été m.

summit n sommet m; cime f.

summon vt convoquer.

summons n convocation f.

sumptuous adj somptueux.

sun n soleil m.

sunbathe vi se faire bronzer.

sunburnt adj bronzé.

Sunday n dimanche m.

sundry adj divers, différent.

sunflower n tournesol m.

sunny adj ensoleillé.

sunrise n lever du soleil m.

sunset n coucher du soleil m.

sunshade n parasol m.

sunshine n ensoleillement m.

sunstroke n insolation f.

suntan n bronzage m.

super adj (fam) sensationnel.

superb adj superbe.

supercilious adj hautain.

superficial adj superficiel.

superfluity n superfluité f.

superfluous adj superflu.

superior adj n supérieur m, -e f.

superiority n supériorité f.

superlative adj n superlatif m.

supermarket n supermarché m.

supernatural n surnaturel.

supersede vt remplacer.

supersonic adj supersonique.

superstition n superstition f.

superstitious adj superstitieux.

supervene vi survenir.

supervise vt superviser.

supervision n surveillance f.

supervisor n surveillant m, -e f.

supper n dîner m.

supplant vt supplanter.

supple adj souple.

supplement n supplément m.

supplementary adj supplémentaire.

suppleness n souplesse f.

supplicate vt supplier.

supplication n supplication f.

supplier n fournisseur m.

supply vt fournir:—n approvisionnement m; provision f.

support vt soutenir:—n appui m.

supporter n partisan m.

suppose vt vi supposer.

supposition *n* supposition *f*.
suppress *vt* supprimer.
suppression *n* suppression *f*.
supremacy *n* suprématie *f*.
supreme *adj* suprême.
surcharge *vt* surcharger:—*n* surtaxe *f*.
sure *adj* sûr, certain:—**~ly** *adv* sûrement.
sureness *n* certitude, sûreté *f*.
surf *n* (*mar*) ressac *m*.
surface *n* surface *f*:—*vi* remonter à la surface.
surfboard *n* planche (de surf) *f*.
surge *n* vague, montée *f*.
surgeon *n* chirurgien *m*.
surgery *n* chirurgie *m*.
surgical *adj* chirurgical.
surly *adj* revêche, bourru.
surmise *vt* conjecturer:—*n* conjecture *f*.
surmount *vt* surmonter.
surname *n* nom de famille *m*.
surpass *vt* surpasser.
surplus *n* excédent *m*:—*adj* en surplus.
surprise *vt* surprendre:—*n* surprise *f*.
surrender *vi* se rendre:—*n* reddition *f*.
surreptitious *adj* subreptice.
surrogate *n* substitut *m*.
surround *vt* entourer.
survey *vt* examiner:—*n* enquête *f*.
survive *vi* survivre:—*vt* survivre à.
survivor *n* survivant *m*, -e *f*.
susceptibility *n* sensibilité *f*.
susceptible *adj* sensible.
suspect *vt* soupçonner:—*n* suspect *m*, -e *f*.
suspend *vt* suspendre.
suspense *n* incertitude *f*; suspense *m*.
suspicion *n* soupçon *m*.
suspicious *adj* soupçonneux.
sustain *vt* soutenir.
sustenance *n* (moyens de) subsistance *f*.
swagger *vi* plastronner.

swallow *vt* avaler.
swap *vt* échanger:—*n* échange *m*.
swarm *n* essaim *m*:—*vi* fourmiller.
swathe *vt* emmailloter:—*n* bande *f*.
sway *vi* se balancer, osciller:—*n* balancement *m*; emprise.
swear *vt* jurer:—*vi* jurer.
sweat *n* sueur *f*:—*vi* suer.
sweep *vt* balayer.
sweet *adj* doux, agréable; suave:—*n* bonbon *m*.
sweeten *vt* sucrer; adoucir.
sweetener *n* édulcorant *m*.
sweetness *n* goût sucré *m*, douceur *f*.
swell *vi* gonfler:—*n* houle *f*.
swelling *n* gonflement *m*.
swerve *vt* dévier.
swift *adj* rapide.
swiftness *n* rapidité, promptitude *f*.
swim *vi* nager:—*n* baignade *f*.
swimming *n* natation *f*.
swimming pool *n* piscine *f*.
swimsuit *n* maillot de bain *m*.
swindle *vt* escroquer.
swing *vi* se balancer:—*vt* balancer:—*n* balancement *m*.
swirl *n* tourbillon.
switch *n* interrupteur *m*:—*vt* changer de:—**to ~ off** éteindre:—**to ~ on** allumer.
swivel *vt* faire pivoter.
swoon *vi* s'évanouir:—*n* évanouissement *m*.
swoop *vi* fondre sur.
sword *n* épée *f*.
sycophant *n* sycophante *mf*.
syllabic *adj* syllabique.
syllable *n* syllabe *f*.
syllabus *n* programme d'un cours *m*.
symbol *n* symbole *m*.
symbolic(al) *adj* symbolique.

symbolise vt symboliser.
symmetrical adj symétrique.
symmetry n symétrie f.
sympathetic adj compatissant.
sympathise vi compatir.
sympathy n compassion f.
symphony n symphonie f.
symptom n symptôme m.
synagogue n synagogue f.

syndrome n syndrome m.
synonym n synonyme m.
synonymous adj synonyme.
synopsis n synopsis f; résumé m.
syntax n syntaxe f.
synthesis n synthèse f.
syringe n seringue f.
system n système m.
systematic adj systématique.

T

telephone number n numéro de télé-phone m.
telescope n télescope m.
telescopic adj télescopique.
televise vt téléviser.
television n télévision f.
television set n téléviseur.
tell vt dire; raconter.
temper vt tempérer:—n colère f.
temperament n tempérament m.
temperate adj tempéré.
temperature n température f.
tempest n tempête f.
temple n temple m; tempe f.
temporary adj temporaire.
tempt vt tenter.
temptation n tentation f.
ten adj n dix m.
tenacious adj tenance.
tenacity n ténacité f.
tenant n locataire mf.
tend vt garder.
tendency n tendance f.
tender adj tendre:—n offre f:—vt offrir.
tendon n tendon m.
tennis n tennis m.

tenor n (mus) ténor m; sens m.
tense adj tendu:—n (gr) temps m.
tension n tension f.
tent n tente f.
tentative adj timide, hésitant.
tenth adj n dixième mf.
tenuous adj ténu.
tepid adj tiède.
term n terme m:—vt appeler.
terminal adj terminal:—n aérogare f; terminal m.
terminate vt terminer.
termination n fin, conclusion f.
terrace n terrace f.
terrain n terrain m.
terrestrial adj terrestre.
terrible adj terrible.
terrific adj terrifiant.
terrify vt terrifier.
territorial adj territorial.
territory n territoire m.
terror n terreur f.
terrorise vt terroriser.
terrorist n terroriste mf.
terse adj concis, net.
test n essai m:—vt essayer.

table 226 telephone directory

table *n* table *f*:—*vt* mettre en forme de tableau.
tablecloth *n* nappe *f*.
tablet *n* tablette *f*; comprimé *m*.
tacit *adj* tacite.
taciturn *adj* taciturne.
tack *n* broquette *f*:—*vt* clouer.
tackle *n* attirail, équipement.
tact *n* tact *m*.
tactics *npl* tactique *f*.
tag *n* ferret *m*:—*vt* ferrer.
tail *n* queue *f*.
tailor *n* tailleur *m*.
tailoring *n* métier de tailleur *m*.
taint *vt* infecter.
tainted *adj* infecté.
take *vt* prendre.
takeoff *n* décollage *m*.
takeover *n* prise de possession *f*.
takings *npl* recette *f*.
talc *n* talc *m*.
talent *n* talent *m*.
talented *adj* talentueux.
talk *vi* parler; causer:—*n* conversation *f*.
talkative *adj* loquace.
tall *adj* grand, élevé.
tally *vi* correspondre.
tame *adj* apprivoisé:—*vt* apprivoiser.
tamper *vi* toucher à.
tan *vt vi* bronzer:—*n* bronzage *m*.
tangible *adj* tangible.
tangle *vt* enchevêtrer.
tank *n* réservoir *m*.
tanker *n* pétrolier *m*.
tantrum *n* accès de colère *m*.
tap *vt* taper doucement:—*n* petite tape *f*; robinet *m*.
tape *n* ruban *m*:—*vt* enregistrer.
tape recorder *n* magnétophone *m*.
target *n* cible *f*.
tariff *n* tarif *m*.

tarnish *vt* ternir.
tart *n* tarte, tartelette *f*.
task *n* tâche *f*.
taste *n* goût *m*; saveur *f*:—*vt* déguster.
tasteful *adj* de bon goût.
tasty *adj* savoureux.
tattoo *n* tatouage *m*:—*vt* tatouer.
taunt *vt* railler:—*n* raillerie *f*.
taut *adj* tendu.
tawdry *adj* tapageur.
tax *n* impôt *m*:—*vt* imposer.
taxable *adj* imposable.
taxation *n* imposition *f*.
taxi *n* taxi *m*.
tax payer *n* contribuable *mf*.
tea *n* thé *m*.
teach *vt* enseigner.
teacher *n* professeur *m*.
teaching *n* enseignement *m*.
team *n* équipe *f*.
teapot *n* théière *f*.
tear *vt* déchirer.
tear *n* larme *f*.
tearful *adj* larmoyant.
tease *vt* taquiner.
teaspoon *n* petite cuiller *f*.
technical *adj* technique.
technician *n* technicien *m*, -ienne *f*.
technique *n* technique *f*.
technological *adj* technologique.
technology *n* technologie *f*.
tedious *adj* ennuyeux.
tedium *n* ennui, manque d'intérêt *m*.
teenage *adj* adolescent:—**~r** *n* adolescent(e) *m(f)*.
teethe *vi* faire ses premières dents.
telegram *n* télégramme *m*.
telegraph *n* télégraphe *m*.
telepathy *n* télépathie *f*.
telephone *n* téléphone *m*.
telephone directory *n* annuaire *m*.

testify vt témoigner.

testimony n témoignage m.

test tube n éprouvette f.

tether vt attacher.

text n texte m.

textual adj textuel.

texture n texture f.

than adv que; de.

thank vt remercier.

thankful adj reconnaissant.

thanks npl remerciement(s) m(pl).

that pn cela, ça, ce; qui, que; celui-là:—conj que.

thatch n chaume m.

thaw n dégel m:—vi dégeler.

the art le, la, l', les.

theatre n théâtre m.

theatrical adj théâtral.

theft n vol m.

their poss adj leur(s).

theirs poss pn le leur; la leur; les leurs.

them pn les; leur.

theme n thème m.

themselves pn pl eux-mêmes mpl, elles-mêmes fpl; se.

then adv alors; ensuite:—conj donc; en ce cas.

theological adj théologique.

theology n théologie f.

theorem n théorème m.

theoretic(al) adj théorique.

theory n théorie f.

therapist n thérapeute mf.

therapy n thérapie f.

there adv y, là.

thereafter adv par la suite; après.

therefore adv donc, par conséquent.

thermal adj thermal.

thermometer n thermomètre m.

these pn pl ceux-ci, celles-ci.

thesis n thèse f.

they pn pl ils, elles.

thick adj épais, gros.

thicken vi (s')épaissir.

thickness n épaisseur f.

thickset adj trapu.

thief n voleur m, -euse f.

thigh n cuisse f.

thin adj mince, fin.

thing n chose f; objet m; truc m.

think vi vt penser:—~ over vt réfléchir à.

thinker n penseur m, -euse f.

thinking n pensée f; réflexion f.

third adj troisième:—n troisième mf; tiers m.

thirst n soif f.

thirsty adj assoiffé.

thirteen adj n treize m.

thirteenth adj n treizième mf.

thirtieth adj n trentième mf.

thirty adj n trente m.

this adj ce, cet, cette, ces:—pn ceci, ce.

thistle n chardon m.

thorn n épine f.

thorough adj consciencieux, approfondi:—~ly adv minutieusement, à fond.

thoroughfare n rue, artère f.

those pn pl ceux-là, celles-la:—adj ces, ces… là.

though conj bien que:—adv pourtant.

thought n pensée, réflexion f.

thoughtful adj pensif.

thoughtless adj étourdi; irréfléchi.

thousand adj n mille m.

thousandth adj n millième mf.

thrash vt battre.

thread n fil m.

threat n menace f.

threaten vt menacer.

three adj n trois m.

threshold n seuil m.

thrifty adj économe.

thrill vt faire frissonner:—n frisson m.

thrive vi prospérer.

throat n gorge f.

throb vi palpiter.

throne n trône m.

throng n foule f.

throttle n accélérateur m:—vt étrangler.

through prep à travers; pendant; par: —adj direct.

throughout prep partout dans:—adv partout.

throw vt jeter:—n jet m; lancement m.

throwaway adj à jeter.

thrust vt enfoncer:—n poussée f.

thug n voyou m.

thumb n pouce m.

thump n coup de poing m:—vt cogner à.

thunder n tonnerre m:—vi tonner.

thunderclap n coup de tonnerre m.

thunderstorm n orage m.

Thursday n jeudi m.

thus adv ainsi.

thwart vt contrecarrer.

tic n tic m.

tick n tic-tac m; instant m.

ticket n billet, ticket m.

ticket office n guichet m.

tickle vt chatouiller.

tidal wave n raz-de-marée m.

tide n marée f.

tidy adj rangé, en ordre.

tie vt attacher:—n attache f; lacet m.

tier n gradin m; étage m.

tiger n tigre m.

tight adj raide, tendu.

tighten vt (re)serrer, tendre.

tile n tuile f; carreau m.

till n caisse f:—vt labourer.

tilt vt pencher:—vi s'incliner.

timber n bois de construction m.

time n temps m; période f; heure f:—vt fixer; chronométrer.

time lag n décalage m.

timeless adj éternel.

timely adj opportun.

time zone n fuseau horaire m.

timid adj timide.

timidity n timidité f.

tin n étain m; boîte (de conserve) f.

tinge n teinte f.

tingle vi picoter.

tinkle vi tinter.

tint n teinte f:—vt teinter.

tinted adj teinté; fumé.

tiny adj minuscule.

tip n pointe f, bout m; pourboire m: —vt donner un pourboire à.

tirade n diatribe f.

tire vt fatiguer:—vi se fatiguer.

tireless adj infatigable.

tiresome adj ennuyeux, fatigant.

tissue n tissu m.

titbit n friandise f.

titillate vt titiller.

title n titre m.

titular adj titulaire.

to prep à; vers; en.

toast vt (faire) griller:—n toast m.

toaster n grille-pain m invar.

tobacco n tabac m.

toboggan n toboggan m.

today adv aujourd'hui.

toe n orteil m; pointe f.

together adv ensemble.

toil vi travailler dur:—n labeur m; peine f.

toilet n toilette f; toilettes fpl:—adj de toilette.

toilet paper n papier hygiénique m.

toiletries npl articles de toilette mpl.

token n signe m; marque f; jeton m.

tolerable adj tolérable.

tolerant *adj* tolérant.

tolerate *vt* tolérer.

toll *n* péage *m*:—*vi* sonner.

tomato *n* tomate *f*.

tomb *n* tombeau *m*; tombe *f*.

tombstone *n* pierre tombale *f*.

tomorrow *adv n* demain *m*.

ton *n* tonne *f*.

tone *n* ton *m*; tonalité *f*:—*vi* s'harmoniser.

tongs *npl* pinces *fpl*.

tongue *n* langue *f*.

tonight *adv n* ce soir (*m*).

too *adv* aussi; trop.

tool *n* outil *m*; ustensile *m*.

tooth *n* dent *f*.

toothache *n* rage de dents *f*.

toothbrush *n* brosse à dents *f*.

toothpaste *n* dentifrice *m*.

top *n* sommet *m*; haut *m*; tête *f*; dessus *m*:—*adj* du haut:—*vt* dépasser.

topic *n* sujet *m*.

topical *adj* d'actualité.

topmost *adj* le plus haut.

topographic(al) *adj* topographique.

topography *n* topographie *f*.

topple *vt* renverser:—*vi* basculer.

torch *n* torche *f*.

torment *vt* tourmenter:—*n* tourment *m*.

tornado *n* tornade *f*.

torrent *n* torrent *m*.

tortuous *adj* tortueux, sinueux.

torture *n* torture *f*:—*vt* torturer.

toss *vt* lancer, secouer.

total *adj* total, global.

totality *n* totalité *f*.

totter *vi* chanceler.

touch *vt* toucher; contact *m*; touche *f*.

touchdown *n* atterrissage *m*; but *m*.

touching *adj* touchant.

tough *adj* dur; pénible.

toughen *vt* durcir.

tour *n* voyage *m*; visite *f*.

tourism *n* tourisme *m*.

tourist *n* touriste *mf*.

tournament *n* tournoi *m*.

tow *n* remorquage *m*:—*vt* remorquer.

toward(s) *prep* vers.

towel *n* serviette *f*.

tower *n* tour *f*.

town *n* ville *f*.

town hall *n* mairie *f*.

towrope *n* câble de remorquage *m*.

toy *n* jouet *m*.

trace *n* trace, piste *f*:—*vt* tracer.

track *n* trace *f*; empreinte *f*.

tract *n* étendue; brochure *f*.

traction *n* traction *f*.

trade *n* commerce *m*; métier *m*:—*vi* commercer.

trademark *n* marque de fabrique *f*.

trader *n* négociant *m*, -e *f*.

trade(s) union *n* syndicat *m*.

trade unionist *n* syndicaliste *mf*.

trading *n* commerce *m*:—*adj* commercial.

tradition *n* tradition *f*

traditional *adj* traditionnel.

traffic *n* circulation *f*; négoce *m*.

traffic jam *n* embouteillage *m*.

tragedy *n* tragédie *f*.

tragic *adj* tragique.

trail *vt* traîner:—*n* traînée *f*.

train *vt* entraîner:—*n* train *m*.

trainer *n* entraîneur *m*.

training *n* entraînement *m*.

trait *n* trait *m*.

traitor *n* traître *m*.

tramp *n* clochard *m*, -e *f*:—*vt* piétiner.

trance *n* transe *f*; extase *f*.

tranquil *adj* tranquille.

transact *vt* traiter.

transaction n transaction f.
transcend vt transcender.
transcription n transcription f.
transfer vt transférer:—n transfert m.
transform vt transformer.
transfusion n transfusion f.
transition n transition f.
transitional adj de transition.
translate vt traduire.
translation n traduction f.
translator n traducteur m, -trice f.
transmission n transmision f.
transmit vt transmettre.
transparency n transparence f.
transparent adj transparent.
transplant vt transplanter.
transport vt transporter:—n transport m.
trap n piège m:—vt prendre au piège.
travel vi voyager:—n voyage m.
traveller n voyageur m, -euse f.
traveller's cheque n chèque de voyage m.
travesty n parodie f.
tray n plateau m.
treacherous adj traître.
treachery n traîtrise f.
tread vi marcher:—n pas m.
treason n trahison f.
treasure n trésor m.
treasurer n trésorier m, -ière f.
treat vt traiter:—n cadeau m.
treatment n traitement m.
treaty n traité m.
treble adj triple:—vt vi tripler.
tree n arbre m.
trek n randonnée f, étape f.
tremble vi trembler.
tremendous adj terrible; formidable.
trend n tendance f; mode f.
trespass vt transgresser.
trial n procès m; essai m.

triangle n triangle m.
tribal adj tribal.
tribe n tribu f.
tribunal n tribunal m.
tributary adj n tributaire m.
trick n ruse, astuce f:—vt attraper.
tricky adj délicat; difficile.
trifle n bagatelle, vétille f.
trifling adj futile, insignifiant.
trigger n détente f.
trim adj net, soigné:—vt arranger.
trip vi trébucher:—n faux pas m; voyage m.
triple adj triple:—vt vi tripler.
trite adj banal; usé.
triumph n triomphe m:—vi triompher.
triumphant adj triomphant.
trivia npl futilités fpl.
trivial adj insignifiant.
triviality n banalité f.
troop n bande f.
tropical adj tropical.
trouble vt affliger:—n problème m; ennui m.
troublesome adj pénible.
trousers npl pantalon m.
trout n truite f.
truck n camion m; wagon m.
truck driver n routier m.
truculent adj brutal, agressif.
true adj vrai, véritable.
trump n atout m.
trumpet n trompette f.
trunk n malle f.
trust n confiance f:—vt confier à.
trustworthy adj digne de confiance.
trusty adj fidèle, loyal.
truth n vérité f.
truthful adj véridique.
truthfulness n véracité f.
try vt essayer:—n tentative f; essai m.

tub n cuve f, bac m.
tube n tube m.
tuck n pli m:—vt mettre.
Tuesday n mardi m.
tug vt remorquer:—n remorqueur m.
tuition n cours, enseignement m.
tulip n tulipe f.
tumble vi tomber:—n chute f.
tumbler n verre m.
tumultuous adj tumultueux.
tune n air m; accord m.
tuneful adj mélodieux, harmonieux.
tunnel n tunnel m.
turbulence n turbulence.
turbulent adj turbulent.
turf n gazon m.
turkey n dinde f.
turmoil n agitation f; trouble m.
turn vtr (se) tourner; vt monter:—n tour m; tournure.
turning n embranchement m.
turnover n chiffre d'affaires m.
turnstile n tourniquet m.
turquoise n turquoise f.
turtle n tortue marine f.

tusk n défense f.
tutor n professeur particulier m.
tweezers npl pince à épiler f.
twelfth adj n douzième mf.
twelve adj n douze m.
twentieth adj n vingtième mf.
twenty adj n vingt m.
twice adv deux fois.
twilight n crépuscule m.
twin n jumeau m, -elle f.
twine vi s'enrouler.
twinkle vi scintiller.
twirl vi tournoyer.
twist vt tordre, tortiller.
twitch n tic m.
two adj n deux m.
twofold adj double:—adv au double.
tycoon n magnat m.
type n type m:—vi taper à la machine.
typeface n œil de caractère m.
typewriter n machine à écrire f.
typical adj typique.
tyrannical adj tyrannique.
tyrant n tyran m.
tyre n pneu m.

U

ugliness n laideur f.
ugly adj laid.
ulcer n ulcère m.
ulterior adj ultérieur.
ultimate adj final:—~ly adv finalement; à la fin.
ultimatum n ultimatum m.
umbrella n parapluie m.
umpire n arbitre m.
unable adj incapable.

unaccomplished adj inaccompli.
unaccountable adj inexplicable.
unaccustomed adj inaccoutumé.
unacknowledged adj non reconnu.
unadulterated adj pur; sans mélange.
unaltered adj inchangé.
unanimity n unanimité f.
unanimous adj unanime.
unanswerable adj incontestable.
unapproachable adj inaccessible.

unarmed *adj* désarmé.

unattached *adj* indépendant; libre.

unattainable *adj* inaccessible.

unavoidable *adj* inévitable.

unaware *adj* ignorant; inconscient.

unbalanced *adj* déséquilibré.

unbearable *adj* insupportable.

unbelievable *adj* incroyable.

unbiased *adj* impartial.

unbreakable *adj* incassable.

unbroken *adj* intact; ininterrompu.

unbutton *vt* déboutonner.

unceasing *adj* incessant.

uncertain *adj* incertain.

uncertainty *n* incertitude *f*.

unchangeable *adj* immuable.

uncharitable *adj* peu charitable.

uncivil *adj* impoli, grossier.

uncivilised *adj* non civilisé.

uncle *n* oncle *m*.

uncomfortable *adj* inconfortable.

uncommon *adj* rare, extraordinaire.

uncompromising *adj* intransigeant.

unconcerned *adj* indifférent.

unconditional *adj* inconditionnel, absolu.

unconscious *adj* inconscient.

uncork *vt* déboucher.

uncouth *adj* grossier.

uncover *vt* découvrir.

uncultivated *adj* inculte.

undecided *adj* indécis.

undeniable *adj* indéniable.

under *prep* sous; dessous:—*adv* au-dessous.

underclothing *n* sous-vêtements *mpl*.

undercover *adj* secret, clandestin.

underdeveloped *adj* sous-développé.

underestimate *vt* sous-estimer.

undergo *vt* subir.

undergraduate *n* étudiant(e) en licence *m(f)*.

undergrowth *n* broussailles *fpl*.

underhand *adj* secret, clandestin.

underline *vt* souligner.

underneath *adv* (en) dessous:—*prep* sous, au-dessous de.

underpaid *adj* sous-payé.

underprivileged *adj* défavorisé.

underside *n* dessous *m*.

understand *vt* comprendre.

understandable *adj* compréhensible.

understanding *n* compréhension:— *adj* compréhensif.

undertake *vt* entreprendre.

undertaking *n* entreprise *f*.

undervalue *vt* sous-estimer.

underwater *adj* sous-marin:—*adv* sous l'eau.

underwear *n* sous-vêtements *mpl*.

underwrite *vt* souscrire à.

undeserved *adj* immérité.

undetermined *adj* indéterminé.

undisciplined *adj* indiscipliné.

undisputed *adj* incontesté.

undivided *adj* indivisé, entier.

undo *vt* défaire; détruire.

undoing *n* ruine *f*.

undoubted *adj* ~ly *adv* indubitable(ment).

undress *vi* se déshabiller.

undue *adj* excessif.

unduly *adv* trop, excessivement.

uneasy *adj* inquiet; gêné.

uneducated *adj* sans instruction.

unemployed *adj* au chômage.

unemployment *n* chômage *m*.

unending *adj* interminable.

unequal *adj* inégal.

unequalled *adj* inégalé.

uneven *adj* inégal; impair.

unexpected *adj* inattendu.

unfailing *adj* infaillible, certain.

unfair *adj* injuste.
unfaithful *adj* infidèle.
unfashionable *adj* démodé.
unfasten *vt* détacher, défaire.
unfavourable *adj* défavorable.
unfeeling *adj* insensible.
unfinished *adj* inachevé.
unfit *adj* inapte; impropre.
unfold *vt* déplier.
unforeseen *adj* imprévu.
unforgettable *adj* inoubliable.
unfortunate *adj* malheureux.
unfounded *adj* sans fondement.
unfriendly *adj* inamical.
ungrateful *adj* ingrat.
unhappiness *n* tristesse *f*.
unhappy *adj* malheureux.
unhealthy *adj* malsain.
unheeding *adj* insouciant.
unhook *vt* décrocher.
unhurt *adj* indemne.
uniform *adj* uniforme.
uniformity *adj* uniformité *f*.
unify *vt* unifier.
unimaginable *adj* inimaginable.
uninhabitable *adj* inhabitable.
uninhabited *adj* inhabité, désert.
uninjured *adj* indemne.
unintelligible *adj* inintelligible.
unintentional *adj* involontaire.
uninterested *adj* indifférent.
uninterrupted *adj* ininterrompu.
union *n* union *f*; syndicat *m*.
unique *adj* unique, exceptionnel.
unison *n* unisson *m*.
unit *n* unité *f*.
unite *vt* unir:—*vi* s'unir.
unity *n* unité, harmonie *f*, accord *m*.
universal *adv* universel.
universe *n* univers *m*.
university *n* université *f*.

unjust *adj* injuste.
unknown *adj* inconnu.
unlawful *adj* illégal.
unlawfulness *n* illégalité *f*.
unleash *vt* lâcher.
unless *conj* à moins que/de, sauf.
unlicensed *adj* illicite.
unlikely *adj* improbable.
unlikelihood *n* improbabilité *f*.
unlimited *adj* illimité.
unload *vt* décharger.
unlucky *adj* malchanceux.
unmask *vt* démasquer.
unmerited *adj* immérité.
unmistakable *adj* indubitable
unmoved *adj* insensible, impassible.
unnecessary *adj* inutile, superflu.
unnoticed *adj* inaperçu.
unobserved *adj* inaperçu.
unoccupied *adj* inoccupé.
unoffending *adj* inoffensif.
unpack *vt* défaire.
unparalleled *adj* incomparable; sans pareil.
unpleasant *adj* désagréable.
unpopular *adj* impopulaire.
unprecedented *adj* sans précédent.
unpredictable *adj* imprévisible.
unprejudiced *adj* impartial.
unprofitable *adj* inutile; peu rentable.
unpublished *adj* inédit.
unqualified *adj* non qualifié; sans réserve.
unquestionable *adj* incontestable, indiscutable.
unreal *adj* irréel.
unreasonable *adv* déraisonnable.
unrelated *adj* sans rapport.
unrelenting *adj* implacable.
unreserved *adj* sans réserve; franc.
unrest *n* agitation *f*; troubles *mpl*.

unripe *adj* vert, pas mûr.

unroll *vt* dérouler.

unsafe *adj* dangereux, peu sûr.

unsatisfactory *adj* peu satisfaisant.

unscrew *vt* dévisser.

unseasonable *adj* hors de saison, inopportun.

unseemly *adj* inconvenant.

unsettle *vt* perturber.

unsociable *adj* insociable.

unspeakable *adj* ineffable.

unstable *adj* instable.

unsteady *adj* instable.

untamed *adj* sauvage.

untapped *adj* non exploité.

untenable *adj* insoutenable.

unthinkable *adj* inconcevable.

untidiness *n* désordre *m*.

untidy *adj* en désordre.

untie *vt* dénouer, défaire.

until *prep* jusqu'à:—*conj* jusqu'à ce que.

untimely *adj* intempestif.

untold *adj* jamais révélé; indicible.

untouched *adj* intact.

untroubled *adj* tranquille, paisible.

untrue *adj* faux.

untrustworthy *adj* indigne de confiance.

unused *adj* neuf, inutilisé.

unusual *adj* inhabituel, exceptionnel:—**~ly** *adv* exceptionnellement.

unveil *vt* dévoiler.

unwelcome *adj* importun.

unwell *adj* indisposé.

unwilling *adj* peu disposé:—**~ly** *adv* de mauvaise grâce.

unwind *vt* dérouler:—*vi* se détendre.

unwise *adj* imprudent.

unwitting *adj* involontaire.

unworkable *adj* impraticable.

unworthy *adj* indigne.

up *adv* en haut, en l'air; levé:—*prep* au haut de; vers.

upbringing *n* éducation *f*.

update *vt* mettre à jour.

upheaval *n* bouleversement *m*.

uphold *vt* soutenir.

upholstery *n* tapisserie *f*.

upkeep *n* entretien *m*.

upon *prep* sur.

upper *adj* supérieur; (plus) élevé.

uppermost *adj* le plus haut, le plus élevé:—**to be ~** prédominer.

upright *adj* droit; honnête.

uprising *n* soulèvement *m*.

uproar *n* tumulte, vacarme *m*.

uproot *vt* déraciner.

upset *vt* renverser; déranger, bouleverser:—*n* désordre *m*; bouleversement *m*:—*adj* vexé; bouleversé.

upshot *n* résultat *m*; aboutissement *m*.

upside-down *adv* sens dessus dessous.

upstairs *adv* en haut (d'un escalier).

up-to-date *adj* à jour.

upturn *n* amélioration *f*.

urban *adj* urbain.

urbane *adj* courtois.

urchin *n* oursin *m*.

urge *vt* pousser:—*n* impulsion *f*.

urgency *n* urgence *f*.

urgent *adj* urgent.

urinate *vi* uriner.

urn *n* urne *f*.

us *pn* nous.

usage *n* traitement *m*; usage *m*.

use *n* usage *m*; emploi *m*:—*vt* utiliser.

used *adj* usagé.

useful *adj* utile.

usefulness *n* utilité *f*.

useless *adj* inutile.

uselessness *n* inutilité *f*.

usher *n* huissier *m*; placeur *m*.

usual *adj* habituel, courant.
usurp *vt* usurper.
utensil *n* ustensile *m*.
uterus *n* utérus *m*.

utility *n* utilité *f*.
utmost *adj* extrême.
utter *adj* complet; total:—*vt* prononcer.
utterly *adv* complètement.

V

vacancy *n* chambre libre *f*.
vacant *adj* vacant.
vacate *vt* quitter.
vacation *n* vacances *fpl*.
vaccinate *vt* vacciner.
vacuum *n* vide *m*.
vague *adj* vague.
vain *adj* vain.
valiant *adj* courageux.
valid *adj* valide.
valley *n* vallée *f*.
valuable *adj* précieux, de valeur.
value *n* valeur *f*:—*vt* évaluer.
valve *n* soupape *f*.
van *n* camionnette *f*.
vandalise *vt* saccager.
vanish *vi* disparaître.
vanity *n* vanité *f*.
vanquish *vt* vaincre.
vantage point *n* position avantageuse *f*.
vapour *n* vapeur *f*.
variable *adj* variable; changeant.
variation *n* variation *f*.
variety *n* variété *f*.
various *adj* divers, différent.
vary *vt vi* varier:—*vi* changer.
vase *n* vase *m*.
vast *adj* vaste; immense.
vault *n* voûte *f*:—*vi* sauter.
vegetable *adj* végétal:—*n* légume *m*.

vegetarian *n* végétarien *m*, -ienne *f*.
vegetate *vi* végéter.
vegetation *n* végétation *f*.
vehemence *n* véhémence *f*.
vehement *adj* véhément.
vehicle *n* véhicule *m*.
veil *n* voile *m*.
vein *n* veine *f*; nervure *f*.
velocity *n* vitesse *f*.
velvet *n* velours *m*.
vendor *n* vendeur *m*.
venerate *vt* vénérer.
veneration *n* vénération *f*.
vengeance *n* vengeance *f*.
venom *n* venin *m*.
venomous *adj* vénéneux.
ventilate *vt* aérer.
ventilation *n* ventilation, aération *f*.
venture *n* entreprise *f*:—*vi* s'aventurer.
verb *n* (*gr*) verbe *m*.
verbal *adj* verbal, oral.
verification *n* vérification *f*.
verify *vt* vérifier.
versatile *adj* versatile.
verse *n* vers *m*.
version *n* version *f*.
versus *prep* contre.
vertical *adj* vertical.
vertigo *n* vertige *m*.
very *adv* très, fort, bien.
vessel *n* récipient *m*; navire *m*.

veteran *adj n* vétéran *m.*
veterinarian *n* vétérinaire *mf.*
veterinary *adj* vétérinaire.
veto *n* véto *m.*
vex *vt* contrarier.
vexed *adj* contrarié.
via *prep* via, par.
viaduct *n* viaduc *m.*
vibrate *vi* vibrer.
vibration *n* vibration *f.*
vice *n* vice *m*; défaut *m.*
vicinity *n* voisinage *m.*
vicious *adj* méchant.
victim *n* victime *f.*
victor *n* vainqueur *m.*
victory *n* victoire *f.*
video *n* vidéo *f*; vidéocassette *f.*
viewer *n* téléspectateur *m*, -trice *f.*
vie *vi* rivaliser.
view *n* vue *f*:—*vt* voir; examiner.
vigil *n* veille *f*; vigile *f.*
vigilance *n* vigilance *f.*
vigilant *adj* vigilant.
vigorous *adj* vigoureux.
vigour *n* vigueur *f.*
vile *adj* vil.
village *n* village *m.*
vindicate *vt* venger.
vindication *n* défense *f.*
vindictive *adj* vindicatif.
vine *n* vigne *f.*
vinegar *n* vinaigre *m.*
vineyard *n* vignoble *m.*
violate *vt* violer.
violation *n* violation *f.*
violence *n* violence *f.*
violent *adj* violent.
violin *n* (*mus*) violon *m.*
virgin *n*, *adj* vierge *f.*
virile *adj* viril.
virility *n* virilité *f.*

virtual *adj* vrai, virtuel.
virtue *n* vertu *f.*
virtuous *adj* virtueux.
virulent *adj* virulent.
visa *n* visa *m.*
vis-a-vis *prep* vis-à-vis.
visibility *n* visibilité *f.*
visible *adj* visible.
vision *n* vision *f*; vue *f.*
visit *vt* visiter:—*n* visite *f.*
visitor *n* visiteur *m*, -euse *f.*
visual *adj* visuel.
visualise *vt* s'imaginer.
vital *adj* vital; essentiel.
vitality *n* vitalité *f.*
vitamin *n* vitamine *f.*
vivacious *adj* vif.
vivid *adj* vif; vivant.
vocabulary *n* vocabulaire *m.*
vocal *adj* oral.
vocation *n* vocation *f.*
voice *n* voix *f*:—*vt* exprimer.
void *adj* vide:—*n* vide *m.*
volatile *adj* volatile.
volcano *n* volcan *m.*
volition *n* volonté *f.*
voltage *n* voltage *m.*
voluble *adj* volubile.
volume *n* volume *m.*
voluntary *adj* volontaire.
volunteer *n* volontaire *mf.*
voluptuous *adj* voluptueux.
vomit *vt vi* vomir.
voracious *adj* vorace.
vote *n* vote *m*; voix *f*:—*vt* voter.
voter *n* électeur *m*, -trice *f.*
voucher *n* bon *m.*
vow *n* vœu *m*:—*vt* jurer.
voyage *n* traversée *f.*
vulgar *adj* vulgaire; grossier.
vulnerable *adj* vulnérable.

W

wade *vi* patauger.

wafer *n* gaufrette *f*; plaque *f*.

wag *vt vi* remuer.

wage *n* salaire *m*.

wager *n* pari *m*:—*vt* parier.

wages *npl* salaire *m*.

waggon *n* chariot *m*; (*rail*) wagon *m*.

wail *n* gémissement *m*:—*vi* gémir.

waist *n* taille *f*.

wait *vi* attendre:—*n* attente *f*.

waiter *n* garçon *m*; serveur *m*.

waive *vt* renoncer à.

wake *vi* se réveiller:—*vt* réveiller.

walk *vi* marcher:—*vt* parcourir:—*n* promenade *f*.

walker *n* marcheur *m*, -euse *f*.

walking stick *n* canne *f*.

wall *n* mur *m*; paroi *f*.

wallet *n* portefeuille *m*.

wallow *vi* se vautrer.

wallpaper *n* papier peint *m*.

walnut *n* noix *f*; noyer *m*.

wander *vi* errer.

wane *vi* décroître.

want *vt* vouloir:—*vi* manquer:—*n* besoin *m*.

wanton *adj* lascif.

war *n* guerre *f*.

wardrobe *n* garde-robe *f*.

warehouse *n* entrepôt *m*.

wariness *n* circonspection *f*.

warm *adj* chaud; chaleureux:—*vt* réchauffer.

warm-hearted *adj* affectueux.

warmth *n* chaleur *f*.

warn *vt* prévenir.

warning *n* avertissement *m*.

warp *vi* se voiler:—*vt* voiler.

warrant *n* garantie *f*; mandat *m*.

warrior *n* guerrier *m*, -ière *f*.

wary *adj* prudent, circonspect.

wash *vt* laver:—*vi* se laver.

washbowl *n* lavabo *m*.

washing *n* lessive *f*.

washing machine *n* machine à laver *f*.

washing-up *n* vaisselle *f*.

wasp *n* abeille *f*.

wastage *n* gaspillage *m*.

waste *vt* gaspiller:—*n* gaspillage *m*.

wasteful *adj* gaspilleur.

watch *n* montre *f*:—*vt* regarder.

watchful *adj* vigilant.

water *n* eau *f*:—*vt* arroser.

water closet *n* W.C. *mpl*.

watercolour *n* aquarelle *f*.

waterfall *n* cascade *f*.

watering-can *n* arrosoir *m*.

watermark *n* filigrane *m*.

watershed *n* moment critique *m*.

watertight *adj* étanche.

wave *n* vague *f*:—*vi* faire signe de la main.

waver *vi* vaciller, osciller.

wavy *adj* ondulé.

wax *n* cire *f*.

way *n* chemin *m*; voie.

wayward *adj* capricieux.

we *pn* nous.

weak *adj* faible.

weaken *vt* affaiblir.

weakness *n* faiblesse *f*.

wealth *n* richesse *f*.

wealthy *adj* riche.

weapon n arme f.

wear vt porter; user:—vi s'user:—n usage m.

weariness n lassitude f.

weary adj las.

weather n temps m:—~ **forecast** n prévisions météorologiques fpl.

weave vt tisser.

web n toile f.

wed vi se marier.

wedding n mariage m; noces fpl.

wedding ring n alliance f.

wedge n cale f:—vt caler.

Wednesday n mercredi m.

weed n mauvaise herbe f:—vt désherber.

week n semaine f.

weekday n jour de semaine m.

weekend n week-end m, fin de semaine f.

weekly adj de la semaine, hebdomadaire.

weep vt vi pleurer.

weigh vt vi peser.

weight n poids m.

weighty adj lourd; important.

welcome adj opportun:—~! bienvenue !:—n accueil m:—vt accueillir.

welfare n bien-être m.

well n puits m:—adj bien, bon:—adv bien.

well-being n bien-être m.

well-bred adj bien élevé.

well-deserved adj bien mérité.

well-known adj connu, célèbre.

well-off adj aisé, dans l'aisance.

west n ouest, Occident m:—adj ouest, de/à l'ouest:—adv vers/à l'ouest.

westerly, western adj (d')ouest.

wet adj humide:—n humidité f:—vt mouiller.

whale n baleine f.

wharf n quai m.

what pn qu'est-ce qui,(qu'est-ce) que, quoi; que, qui; ce qui, ce que; quel(le), que:—adj quel(s), quelle(s):—excl quoi! comment!

whatever pn quoi que; n'importe quoi.

wheat n blé m.

wheel n roue f:—rouler.

wheelbarrow n brouette f.

wheelchair n fauteuil roulant m.

when adv conj quand.

whenever adv quand; chaque fois que.

where adv où:—conj où.

whereas conj tandis que; attendu que.

whereby pn par lequel (laquelle).

wherever adv où que.

whereupon conj sur quoi.

whether conj si.

which pn lequel; celui que, celui qui; ce qui, ce que; quoi, ce dont: —adj quel(s), quelle(s).

while n moment m:—conj pendant que; alors que; quoique.

whim n caprice m.

whimsical adj capricieux.

whip n fouet m:—vt fouetter.

whirl vi tourbillonner.

whirlpool n tourbillon m.

whirlwind n tornade f.

whisper vi chuchoter:—n chuchotement m.

whistle vi siffler:—n sifflement m.

white adj blanc:—n blanc m.

whiten vt vi blanchir.

whiteness n blancheur f.

who pn qui.

whoever pn quiconque, quel(le) que soit.

whole adj tout, entier:—n tout m; ensemble m.

wholesale n vente en gros f.

wholesome adj sain, salubre.

wholly adv complètement.

whom pn qui; que.

why n pourquoi m:—conj pourquoi.

wicked adj méchant, mauvais.

wickedness n méchanceté.

wide adj large, ample.

widen vt élargir, agrandir.

widow n veuve f.

widower n veuf m.

width n largeur f.

wield vt manier, brandir.

wife n femme f; épouse f.

wild adj sauvage, féroce.

wild life n faune f.

wilful adj délibéré.

wilfulness n obstination f.

will n volonté f; testament m.

willing adj prêt, disposé:—**~ly** adv volontiers.

willpower n volonté f.

wily adj astucieux.

win vt gagner.

wind n vent m; souffle m.

wind vt enrouler:—vi serpenter.

windmill n moulin à vent m.

window n fenêtre f.

window pane n carreau m.

windpipe n tranchée f.

windscreen n pare-brise m invar.

windy adj venteux.

wine n vin m.

wine cellar n cave (à vin) f.

wing n aile f.

wink n clin d'œil m.

winner n gagnant m, -e f.

winter n hiver m:—vi hiverner.

wintry adj d'hiver, hivernal.

wipe vt essuyer.

wire n fil m.

wisdom n sagesse, prudence f.

wise adj sage, avisé.

wish vt souhaiter, désirer:—n souhait, désir m.

wit n esprit m, intelligence f.

witch n sorcière f.

with prep avec; à; de; contre.

withdraw vt retirer:—vi se retirer.

withdrawal n retrait m.

withhold vt retenir.

within prep à l'intérieur de:—adv dedans.

without prep sans.

withstand vt résister à.

witness n témoin m:—vt attester.

wittingly adv sciemment, à dessein.

witty adj spirituel, plein d'esprit.

woe n malheur m; affliction f.

woeful adj triste, malheureux.

wolf n loup m.

woman n femme f.

womanly adj féminin, de femme.

womb n utérus m.

wonder n merveille f:—vi s'émerveiller.

wonderful adj merveilleux.

woo vt faire la cour à.

wood n bois m.

woodcut n gravure sur bois f.

wooden adj de bois, en bois.

woodwork n menuiserie f.

wool n laine f.

woollen adj de laine.

word n mot m; parole f:—vt exprimer

wording n rédaction f.

word processing n traitement de texte m.

work vi travailler:—vt faire fonctionner; façonner:—n travail m; œuvre f; emploi m.

worker n travailleur m, -euse f.

workforce n main-d'œuvre f.

workshop n atelier m.

world n monde m.

worldly adj mondain.

worldwide adj mondial.

worn-out *adj* épuisé; usé.
worry *vt* inquiéter; *n* souci *m*.
worrying *adj* inquiétant.
worse *adj adv* pire.
worship *n* culte *m*; adoration *f*:—*vt* adorer.
worst *adj* le pire:—*adv* le plus mal: — *n* le pire *m*.
worth *n* valeur *f*; mérite *m*.
worthily *adv* dignement.
worthless *adj* sans valeur.
worthy *adj* digne; louable.
wound *n* blessure *f*:—*vt* blesser.
wrap *vt* envelopper.
wreath *n* couronne, guirlande *f*.
wreck *n* naufrage *m*; ruines *fpl*:—*vt* démolir.

wrench *vt* tordre:—*n* clé *f*; torsion violente *f*.
wrestle *vi* lutter.
wretched *adj* misérable.
wrinkle *n* ride *f*:—*vt* rider:—*vi* se rider.
wrist *n* poignet *m*.
wristwatch *n* montre-bracelet *f*.
write *vt* écrire; composer.
writer *n* écrivain *m*; auteur *m*.
writing *n* écriture *f*.
wrong *n* mal *m*; tort *m*:—*adj* mauvais; injuste:—*adv* mal, inexactement:— *vt* faire du tort à, léser.
wrongful *adj* injuste.
wrongly *adv* injustement.
wry *adj* ironique.

X Y Z

xenophobe *n* xénophobe *mf*.
xenophobic *adj* xénophobique.
X-ray *n* rayon X *m*.
xylophone *n* xylophone *m*.
yacht *n* yacht *m*.
yawn *vi* bâiller:—*n* bâillement *m*.
year *n* année *f*.
yearbook *n* annuaire *m*.
yearly *adj adv* annuel(lement).
yearn *vi* languir.
yeast *n* levure *f*.
yell *vi* hurler:—*n* hurlement *m*.
yellow *adj n* jaune *m*.
yes *adv* oui.
yesterday *adv n* hier *m*.
yet *conj* pourtant:—*adv* encore.
yield *vt* produire:—*vi* se rendre:—*n* production *f*.
yog(h)urt *n* yaourt *m*.

you *pn* vous; tu; te; toi.
young *adj* jeune.
youngster *n* jeune *mf*.
your *poss adj* ton, ta, tes; votre, vos.
yours *poss pn* le tien; le vôtre.
yourself *pn* toi-même; vous-même(s).
youth *n* jeunesse *f*; jeune homme *m*.
zeal *n* zèle *m*; ardeur *f*.
zealous *adj* zélé.
zenith *n* zénith *m*.
zero *n* zéro *m*.
zest *n* enthousiasme *m*.
zigzag *n* zigzag *m*.
zip *n* fermeture éclair *f*.
zodiac *n* zodiaque *m*.
zone *n* zone *f*; secteur *m*.
zoo *n* zoo *m*.
zoologist *n* zoologiste *mf*.
zoology *n* zoologie *f*.